THE

FOUR DOCTRINES

WITH THE

NINE QUESTIONS

CONTAINING

I. The Doctrine of the New Jerusalem concerning the Lord, followed by the Nine Questions relating to the Lord, the Trinity, and the Holy Spirit.
II. The Doctrine of the New Jerusalem concerning the Holy Scripture.
III. The Doctrine of Life for the New Jerusalem from the Ten Commandments.
IV. The Doctrine of the New Jerusalem concerning Faith.

BY

EMANUEL SWEDENBORG

TRANSLATED FROM THE ORIGINAL LATIN WORKS AND EDITED
BY THE
REV. JOHN FAULKNER POTTS, B.A. Lond.

STANDARD EDITION

1949
SWEDENBORG FOUNDATION
INCORPORATED
NEW YORK

Organized in 1850 as
The American Swedenborg Printing and Publishing Society

Printed in the United States of America

PREFATORY NOTES BY THE TRANSLATOR

The *Four Doctrines* were originally published by Emanuel Swedenborg in the city of Amsterdam, in the year 1763. They were published as four separate and distinct works, in large quarto, and in the Latin language.

The *Doctrine concerning the Lord,* and the *Doctrine concerning the Holy Scripture,* were first translated into English by Mr. Peter Provo, an apothecary in London, and were published by the London Theosophical Society in the years 1784 and 1786 respectively, the printer being Mr. Robert Hindmarsh.

The *Doctrine of Life* was first translated into English by Mr. William Cookworthy, of Plymouth, England, and was published in that city in the year 1770. The second English edition, translated by the Rev. John Clowes, Rector of St. John's, Manchester, England, was published at the expense of the Manchester Printing Society, in London, in the year 1786.

The *Doctrine concerning Faith* was first translated into English by the Rev. William Cowherd, also of Manchester, England, and was published in the year 1790, by the Manchester Printing Society.

The *Four Doctrines* have since appeared in many editions, both separately and collectively, and have also been translated into French, Swedish, Danish, German, Italian, and other languages.

The Translator has been assisted in his labors by a circle of Critics, including the Rev. Samuel M. Warren, the Rev. Philip Cabell, the Rev. James Reed, and Marston Niles, Esq., who have rendered invaluable assistance, and who have contributed in a signal manner to the perfection and accuracy of the work done.

Previous translations have also been largely consulted, and many valuable things have been selected from them. Among those found especially useful may be mentioned the Rotch edition of the *Four Doctrines,* and the translation of the *Doctrine of the Sacred Scripture* of the Rev. Samuel M. Warren.

The verification of the references to Holy Scripture and to the New Church Writings themselves has been done by the Rev. Chauncey Giles Hubbell; and the same careful hand has been employed to compile and verify the Index to Passages of Scripture.

The general Index to the work has been made by the Rev. Charles H. Mann.

In the following translation no attempt has been made to furnish materials for a new translation of the English Bible or of any part of it. In such a work as this, largely expository of the internal sense of the Word, and which was originally written in the Latin language, it is manifestly of the first importance that the English reader should in so far as possible be put in possession of the very words on which the exposition is based. What we do here is to translate the *Latin of Swedenborg* into English, whether that be the Latin of passages of Holy Scripture or of anything else. The making of a new translation of the Word itself, or of any part of it, would be a perfectly distinct undertaking. Nevertheless the phraseology of the English Bible, in either of the authorized versions, has not been needlessly cast aside, but in all cases where it was found to be sufficiently close to the Latin to truly present its meaning, the familiar wording has been retained.

The word "Ultimate" used in this work as a noun, yet not recognized as such in our English dictionaries, calls for some explanation. Webster defines the adjective "ultimate" as meaning "the last in a train of progression or consequences, tended toward by all that precedes." This excellent definition affords the necessary clew. "Ultimate," used as a noun, means the same. Thus the terrestrial globe with its inhabitants is the ultimate of creation, God Himself being regarded as the first in the series or "train of progression," and the angelic heavens and world of spirits being the intermediates. In the same way speech is the ultimate of thought, and act is the ultimate of will. Being entirely new to spiritual science and Christian theology, it is not surprising that this doctrine of ultimates should demand a somewhat new terminology.

The words *instaurare* and *instauratio* we have translated "to set up anew," and "a setting up anew." These words were used by Swedenborg in connection with the renewal and erection of the church. Their dictionary meaning is to "repair," "restore," "erect," "make;" to "set on foot again" (Facciolati), to "set again in good condition" (Scheller), and so on. The translators of Swedenborg have usually rendered *instaurare* "establish;" but as the Latin word unquestionably includes the idea of renovation or renewal, of restoration, and of erection (not of original erection, but of the setting up again of something that has fallen down), it is evident that "establish" represents it very imperfectly. Moreover a church that is established, or an established church, has another meaning. For "establish" Swedenborg uses the word *stabilire*. That which is absolutely essential in making the translation in question is that the idea of *renewal* together with that of *erection* be expressed.

J. F. P.

THE DOCTRINE

OF THE

NEW JERUSALEM

CONCERNING

THE LORD

BY

EMANUEL SWEDENBORG

ORIGINALLY PUBLISHED IN AMSTERDAM IN THE YEAR 1763

TRANSLATED FROM THE ORIGINAL LATIN AND EDITED
BY THE
REV. JOHN FAULKNER POTTS, B.A. LOND.

STANDARD EDITION

SWEDENBORG FOUNDATION
INCORPORATED
NEW YORK

Organized in 1850 as
The American Swedenborg Printing and Publishing Society

AUTHOR'S PREFACE TO THE DOCTRINE OF THE LORD

Some years ago there were published the following five little works:

1. On Heaven and Hell.
2. The Doctrine of the New Jerusalem.
3. On the Last Judgment.
4. On the White Horse.
5. On the Planets and other Earths in the Universe.

In these works many things were set forth that have hitherto been unknown.

Now, by command of the Lord, who has been revealed to me, the following are to be published:

The Doctrine of the New Jerusalem concerning the Lord.

The Doctrine of the New Jerusalem concerning the Holy Scripture.

The Doctrine of Life for the New Jerusalem from the Ten Commandments.

The Doctrine of the New Jerusalem concerning Faith.

A Continuation concerning the Last Judgment.

Angelic Wisdom concerning the Divine Providence.

Angelic Wisdom concerning the Divine Omnipotence, Omnipresence, Omniscience, Infinity, and Eternity.*

Angelic Wisdom concerning the Divine Love and the Divine Wisdom.

---

*Although the treatise here named was never published as a separate work, the subjects of it are specially treated of in the first chapter of the *True Christian Religion*. See also references to the same subjects in this present work (n. 65e), in the *Doctrine of the Holy Scripture* (n. 32), and in the *Angelic Wisdom concerning the Divine Love and the Divine Wisdom* (n. 9). [TRANSLATOR.]

Angelic Wisdom concerning Life.*

It is said "the Doctrine of the New Jerusalem," and this means the Doctrine for the New Church which is at this day to be set up by the Lord; for the old church has come to its end, as is evident from what has been said in the little work on the Last Judgment (n. 33 to n. 39); and also from what is to be further said in the little works just mentioned, which are to follow. That a New Church is meant by the "New Jerusalem," foretold in the twenty-first chapter of the *Revelation* as to come after the Judgment, may be seen below, in the last chapter.

* This proposed treatise seems to have been included in the one mentioned immediately before it, which begins with an exposition of the subject of Life. The reason this treatise and the one on the *Divine Omnipotence*, etc., were not published as separate works, is explained in a letter of Swedenborg to Dr. Beyer, dated February, 1767. See *Documents concerning Swedenborg*, by R. L. Tafel, vol. ii. p. 261. [TR.]

CONTENTS*

---

* Compiled by the Translator.

THE DOCTRINE OF THE NEW JERUSALEM

CONCERNING

THE LORD

I.

UNIVERSAL HOLY SCRIPTURE TREATS OF THE LORD: THE LORD IS THE WORD.

1. We read in *John :*—

In the beginning was the Word, and the Word was with God, and God was the Word. The same was in the beginning with God. All things were made by Him, and without Him was not anything made that was made. In Him was life, and the life was the light of men. And the light shineth in the darkness, and the darkness comprehended it not (i. 1–5).

The Word was made flesh, and dwelt among us, and we beheld His glory, the glory as of the Only-begotten of the Father, full of grace and truth (verse 14).

The light is come into the world, and men loved the darkness rather than the light, because their deeds were evil (iii. 19).

While ye have the light, believe in the light, that ye may be sons of light. I am come a light into the world, that whosoever believeth in Me should not abide in the darkness (xii. 36, 46).

From these passages it is evident that the Lord is God from eternity, and that this God is the selfsame Lord who was born in the world; for it is said that the Word was with God, and God was the Word, and also that without Him was not anything made that was made; and it is added that the Word was made flesh, and they beheld Him.

It is but little understood in the church why the Lord is called the Word. It is because "the Word" signifies Divine truth or Divine wisdom, and the Lord is Divine truth itself or

1

Divine wisdom itself. And this is why He is called the Light, of which also it is said that it came into the world. As the Divine wisdom and the Divine love make a one,* and in the Lord had been a one from eternity, it is said, " In Him was life, and the life was the light of men." " Life" is Divine love; and " light" is Divine wisdom. It is this *one* that is meant by, " In the beginning the Word was with God, and God was the Word." " With God," is in God; for wisdom is in love, and love in wisdom. So in another place in *John :—*

And now, O Father, glorify Thou Me with Thine own Self, with the glory which I had with Thee before the world was (xvii. 5).

" With Thine own Self," is in Thyself, and therefore it is said, " and God was the Word;" and elsewhere, that the Lord is in the Father, and the Father in Him; and that He and the Father are one. As therefore the Word is the Divine wisdom of the Divine love, it follows that it is Jehovah Himself, thus the Lord by whom all things were made that are made; for all things have been created from Divine love by means of Divine wisdom.

2. That the Word here specifically meant is the same Word that was manifested by means of Moses, the prophets, and the evangelists, is very evident from the fact that the Word is the Divine truth itself from which angels have all their wisdom, and men all their spiritual intelligence. For this same Word that is among men in this world is also among the angels in the heavens, but in this world among men it is natural, whereas in the heavens it is spiritual. And as the Word is the Divine truth, it is also the Divine proceeding;† and this is not only from the Lord, but is also the Lord Himself; and being the Lord Himself, it follows that each and all things of the Word

---

* That is, a complex whole which constitutes a unity. [TRANSLATOR.]

† In the expression " Divine proceeding," *Divine* is not to be understood as an adjective qualifying *proceeding*, but *proceeding* is to be taken as a verb (or participle) describing the act which the Divine there performs. Thus the expression does not mean a proceeding which is Divine, but a Divine that is in the act of proceeding forth. " Divine proceeding," thus understood, exactly translates Swedenborg's *Divinum procedens*. [TR.]

have been written concerning Him alone. From *Isaiah* to *Malachi* there is nothing that is not either concerning the Lord, or, in the opposite sense, against Him. Hitherto no one has ever seen this to be so, and yet every one can see it, provided he is aware of it, and thinks of it while he is reading, especially if he knows that the Word contains not only a natural but also a spiritual sense, and that in this sense the names of persons and places signify something of the Lord, and, derivatively, something of heaven and the church from Him, or else something opposite to them. As all things of the Word both in general and in particular treat of the Lord; and as the Word, being the Divine truth, is the Lord, it is evident why it is said, " And the Word was made flesh, and dwelt among us, and we beheld His glory ;" and also why it is said, " While ye have the light, believe in the light, that ye may be sons of light: I am come a light into the world, that whosoever believeth in Me should not abide in the darkness." The "light" is the Divine truth, thus the Word. This is why, even at this day, every one who, while reading the Word, approaches the Lord alone, and prays to Him, is enlightened in the Word.

3. Briefly stated, the subjects concerning the Lord that are treated of in all the Prophets of the Old Testament, from *Isaiah* to *Malachi*, both in general and in particular, are these :—

i. The Lord came into the world in the fullness of times, which was when He was no longer known by the Jews, and when, consequently, there was nothing of the church left; and unless He had then come into the world and revealed Himself, mankind would have perished in eternal death. As He Himself says in *John :* " Except ye believe that I am, ye shall die in your sins" (viii. 24).

ii. The Lord came into the world to execute a Last Judgment, and thereby to subdue the existing dominance of the hells; which was effected by means of combats (that is, temptations) admitted into his maternal human, and the attendant continual victories ; for unless the hells had been subjugated no man could have been saved.

iii. The Lord came into the world in order to glorify His Human, that is, unite it to the Divine which was in Him from conception.

iv. The Lord came into the world in order to set up a new church which should acknowledge Him as the Redeemer and Saviour, and be redeemed and saved through love to Him and faith in Him.

v. He at the same time reduced heaven into order, so that it made a one with the church.

vi. The passion of the cross was the last combat or temptation, by means of which He completely conquered the hells and fully glorified His Human.

In the following small work on *The Holy Scripture* it will be seen that the Word treats of no other subjects than these.

4. In confirmation of this, I shall in this first chapter merely adduce passages from the Word which contain the expressions " that day," " in that day," and " in that time ;" in which, by " day," and " time," is meant the Lord's advent.   In *Isaiah:*—

It shall come to pass in the futurity of days that the mountain of the house of Jehovah shall be established in the top of the mountains.   Jehovah alone shall be exalted in that day.   The day of Jehovah of Armies shall be upon every one that is proud and lofty.   In that day a man shall cast away his idols of silver and of gold (ii. 2, 11, 12, 20).

In that day the Lord Jehovih will take away their ornament (iii. 18).

In that day shall the branch of Jehovah be beautiful and glorious (iv. 2).

In that day it shall roar against him, and he shall look unto the land, and behold darkness and distress, and the light shall be darkened in the ruins (v. 30).

It shall come to pass in that day that Jehovah shall hiss for the fly that is in the uttermost part of the rivers of Egypt.   In that day the Lord shall shave in the crossings of the river.   In that day He shall vivify.   In that day every place shall be for briers and thorns (vii. 18, 20, 21, 23).

What will ye do in the day of visitation, which shall come ?   In that day Israel shall stay upon Jehovah, the Holy One of Israel, in truth (x. 3, 20).

It shall come to pass in that day, that the Root of Jesse, which standeth for an ensign of the peoples, shall the nations seek, and His rest shall be glory.　Chiefly in that day shall the Lord seek again the remnant of His people (xi. 10, 11).

In that day thou shalt say, I will confess unto Thee, O Jehovah.　In that day shall ye say, Confess ye to Jehovah, call upon His name (xii. 1, 4).

The day of Jehovah is at hand, as a laying waste from Shaddai shall it come.　Behold, the day of Jehovah cometh, cruel, and of indignation, and of wrath, and of anger.　I will move the heaven, and the earth shall be shaken out of her place, in the day of the wrath of His anger.　His time is near, and it cometh, and the days shall not be prolonged (xiii. 6, 9, 13, 22).

It shall come to pass in that day, that the glory of Jacob shall be made thin.　In that day shall a man look unto his Maker, and his eyes to the Holy One of Israel.　In that day shall the cities of refuge be as the forsaken places of the forest (xvii. 4, 7, 9).

In that day there shall be five cities in the land of Egypt that speak with the lip of Canaan.　In that day there shall be an altar to Jehovah in the midst of Egypt.　In that day there shall be a path from Egypt to Assyria, and Israel shall be in the midst of the land (xix. 18, 19, 23, 24).

The inhabitant of the island shall say in that day, Behold our expectation (xx. 6).

A day of tumult, and of treading down, and of perplexity, from the Lord Jehovih of Armies (xxii. 5).

In that day shall Jehovah visit upon the army of the height, and upon the kings of the earth.　After a multitude of days shall they be visited ; then shall the moon blush, and the sun be ashamed (xxiv. 21, 22, 23).

It shall be said * in that day, Lo, this is our God, for whom we have waited, that He may deliver us (xxv. 9).

In that day shall this song be sung in the land of Judah, We have a strong city (xxvi. 1).

In that day Jehovah shall visit with His sword.　In that day ye shall answer to it, A vineyard of unmixed wine (xxvii. 1, 2, 12, 13).

In that day shall Jehovah of Armies be for a crown of ornament, and for a diadem (xxviii. 5).

In that day shall the deaf hear the words of the book, and the eyes of the blind shall see out of darkness (xxix. 18).

There shall be streams of waters in the day of the great slaughter, when the towers shall fall ; and the light of the moon shall be as the light of the sun, in the day that Jehovah shall bind up the hurt of His people (xxx. 25, 26).

In that day they shall cast away every man his idols of silver and of gold (xxxi. 7).

The day of Jehovah's vengeance, the year of His recompenses (xxxiv. 8).

* The Latin has " Jehovah shall say."

These two things shall come to thee in one day, the loss of children and widowhood (xlvii. 9).

My people shall know My name, and in that day that I am He that doth speak ; behold it is I (lii. 6).

Jehovah hath anointed Me to proclaim the acceptable year of Jehovah, and the day of vengeance of our God, to comfort all that mourn (lxi. 1, 2).

The day of vengeance is in My heart, and the year of My redeemed is come (lxiii. 4).

In *Jeremiah* :—

In those days ye shall say no more, The ark of the covenant of Jehovah. In that time they shall call Jerusalem the throne of Jehovah. In those days the house of Judah shall walk to the house of Israel (iii. 16–18).

In that day the heart of the king shall perish, and the heart of the princes, and the priests shall be amazed, and the prophets (iv. 9).

Behold the days come in which the land shall become a waste (vii. 32, 34).

They shall fall among them that fall, in the day of their visitation (viii. 12).

Behold the days come that I will visit all that is circumcised with what is uncircumcised (ix. 25).

In the time of their visitation they shall perish (x. 15).

There shall be no remains to them, I will bring evil upon them in the year of their visitation (xi. 23).

Behold, the days come in which it shall no more be said (xvi. 14).

I will look upon them in the nape, and not the faces, in the day of their destruction (xviii. 17).

Behold, the days come in which I will give this place for a waste (xix. 6).

Behold, the days come that I will raise unto David a righteous offshoot, who shall reign as king. In those days Judah shall be saved, and Israel shall dwell safely. Therefore, behold, the days come that they shall no more say . . . I will bring evil upon them in the year of their visitation. In the end of days ye shall understand intelligence (xxiii. 5, 6, 7, 12, 20).

Behold, the days come in which I will turn again. Alas ! for that day is great, and none shall be like it. It shall come to pass in that day that I will break the yoke, and burst the bonds (xxx. 3, 7, 8).

There shall be a day that the watchman upon Mount Ephraim shall cry, Arise ye, let us ascend Zion, unto Jehovah our God. Behold, the days come that I will make a new covenant. Behold, the days come that the city shall be built to Jehovah (xxxi. 6, 31, 38).

The days come that I will establish the good word. In those days and at that time, will I make a righteous offshoot unto David. In those days shall Judah be saved (xxxiii. 14–16).

I will bring words against this city for evil in that day. But I will deliver thee in that day (xxxix. 16, 17).

That day is to the Lord Jehovih of Armies a day of vengeance, that He will take vengeance of His enemies. The day of destruction has come upon them, the time of their visitation (xlvi. 10, 21).

Because of the day that cometh to lay waste (xlvii. 4).

I will bring upon him the year of visitation. Yet I will bring again his captivity in the end of days (xlviii. 44, 47).

I will bring destruction upon them in the time of their visitation. Her young men shall fall in the streets, and all the men of war shall be cut off in that day. In the end of days I will bring again their captivity (xlix. 8, 26, 39).

In those days, and in that time, the sons of Israel and the sons of Judah shall come together, and shall seek Jehovah their God. In those days, and in that time, the iniquity of Israel shall be sought for, and there shall be none. Woe unto them, for their day is come, the time of their visitation (l. 4, 20, 27, 31).

They are vanity, a work of errors, in the time of their visitation they shall perish (li. 18).

In *Ezekiel :—*

An end is come, the end is come, the morning cometh upon thee ; the time is come, the day of tumult is near. Behold the day, behold it cometh, the morning hath gone forth, the rod hath blossomed, violence hath budded. The day is come, the time is come upon all the multitude thereof. Their silver and gold shall not deliver them in the day of the anger of Jehovah (vii. 6, 7, 10, 12, 19).

They said of the prophet, The vision that he seeth shall come to pass after many days ; he prophesieth for times that are far off (xii. 27).

They shall not stand in the war in the day of the anger of Jehovah (xiii. 5).

Thou, O deadly wounded wicked one, the prince of Israel, whose day is done, in the time of the iniquity of the end (xxi. 25).

A city that sheddeth blood in the midst of her, that her time may come ; and thou hast caused thy days to draw near, so that thou art come to thy years (xxii. 3, 4).

Shall it not be in the day when I take from them their strength ? In that day he that escapeth shall come unto thee to the instructing of thine ears. In that day shall thy mouth be opened together with him that is escaped (xxiv. 25–27).

In that day will I cause a horn to grow unto the house of Israel (xxix. 21).

Howl ye, Woe worth the day ! for the day of Jehovah is near, the day of Jehovah is near, a day of cloud, it shall be the time of the nations. In that day shall messengers go forth from Me (xxx. 2, 3, 9).

In the day in which thou shalt go down into hell (xxxi. 15).

I will search for My flock in the day that he shall be in the midst of his flock ; and I will deliver them out of all places whither they have been scattered, in the day of cloud and of thick darkness (xxxiv. 11, 12).

In the day that I cleanse you from all your iniquities (xxxvi. 33).

Prophesy and say, In that day when My people Israel shall sit securely, shalt thou not know it ? In the futurity of days I will lead thee into My land. In that day, even the day when Gog shall come upon the land. In My zeal, in the fire of Mine indignation, if not in this day, there shall be a great earthquake upon the land of Israel (xxxviii. 14, 16, 18, 19).

Behold, it cometh, this day of which I have spoken. It shall come to pass in that day that I will give unto Gog a place for burial in the land of Israel, so that the house of Israel shall know that I am Jehovah their God, from that day and forward (xxxix. 8, 11, 22).

In *Daniel* :—

God in the heavens hath revealed secrets, what shall be in the futurity of days (ii. 28).

The time came that the saints possessed the kingdom (vii. 22).

Attend, for at the time of the end shall be the vision. And he said, Behold, I will make thee know what shall be in the last end of the anger, for at the time appointed shall the end be. The vision of the evening and the morning is truth ; shut thou up the vision, for it shall be for many days (viii. 17, 19, 26).

I am come to make thee understand what shall befall thy people in the end of days ; for the vision is yet for days (x. 14).

The intelligent shall be proved to purge and cleanse them, even to the time of the end, because it is yet for the time appointed (xi. 35).

At that time shall Michael rise up, the great prince who standeth for the sons of thy people ; and there shall be a time of trouble, such as never was since there was a nation. At that time thy people shall be delivered, every one that shall be found written in the book (xii. 1).

Thou, O Daniel, shut up the words, and seal the book, even to the time of the end. But from the time that the continual [burnt-offering] shall be taken away, and the abomination that maketh waste be set up, there shall be a thousand two hundred and ninety days. Thou shalt arise into thy lot at the end of the days (xii. 4, 11, 13).

In *Hosea :*—

I will make an end of the kingdom of the house of Israel. In that day I will break the bow of Israel. Great shall be the day of Jezreel (i. 4, 5, 11).

In that day thou shalt call Me, my Husband. In that day I will make a covenant for them. In that day I will hear (ii. 16, 18, 21).

The sons of Israel shall return, and seek Jehovah their God, and David their king, in the end of days (iii. 5).

Come, and let us return unto Jehovah ; after two days He will revive us ; in the third day He will raise us up, and we shall live before Him (vi. 1, 2).

The days of visitation are come ; the days of retribution are come (ix. 7).

In *Joel :*—

Alas for the day, for the day of Jehovah is at hand, and as a laying waste from Shaddai shall it come (i. 15).

The day of Jehovah cometh, nigh is the day of darkness and of thick darkness, a day of cloud and of obscurity. The day of Jehovah is great and very terrible ; and who can endure it ? (ii. 1, 2, 11).

Upon the servants, and upon the handmaids in those days will I pour out My spirit. The sun shall be turned into darkness, and the moon into blood, before the great and terrible day of Jehovah is come (ii. 29, 31).

Behold, in those days, and in that time, which I will bring back, I will gather all nations. The day of Jehovah is near. It shall come to pass in that day that the mountains shall drop new wine (iii. 1, 2, 14, 18).

In *Obadiah :*—

Shall I not in that day destroy the wise men out of Edom ? Neither shouldest thou have rejoiced over them in the day of their destruction, in the day of their distress. For the day of Jehovah is near upon all the nations (verses 8, 12, 15).

In *Amos :*—

He that is courageous in his heart shall flee away naked in that day (ii. 16).

In the day that I shall visit the transgressions of Israel upon him (iii. 14).

Woe unto you that desire the day of Jehovah ! What to you is the day of Jehovah ? it is one of darkness, and not of light. Shall not the day of Jehovah be darkness, and not light ? even thick darkness, and no brightness in it (v. 18, 20).

The songs of the temple shall be howlings in that day. In that day I will cause the sun to go down at noon ; and I will darken the earth in the day of light. In that day shall the beautiful virgins and the young men faint for thirst (viii. 3, 9, 13).

In that day I will raise up the tent of David that is fallen. Behold, the days come that the mountains shall drop new wine (ix. 11, 13).

In *Micah :*—

In that day shall one lament, We be utterly laid waste (ii. 4).

In the end of days the mountain of the house of Jehovah shall be established at the head of the mountains. In that day will I gather her that halteth (iv. 1, 6).

In that day I will cut off thy horses and thy chariots (v. 10).

The day of thy watchmen, and thy visitation, cometh. The day is at hand for building thy walls. In that day he shall come even to thee (vii. 4, 11, 12).

In *Habakkuk :*—

The vision is yet for an appointed time, and at the end it shall speak ; though it tarry, wait for it, because it will surely come, it will not delay (ii. 3).

O Jehovah do Thy work in the midst of the years ; in the midst of the years make known ; God cometh (iii. 2, 3).

In *Zephaniah :*—

The day of Jehovah is at hand. In the day of Jehovah's sacrifice I will visit upon the princes, and upon the king's sons. In that day there shall be the voice of a cry. At that time I will search Jerusalem with lamps. The great day of Jehovah is near. That day is a day of wrath, a day of trouble and distress, a day of wasteness and desolation, a day of darkness and thick darkness, a day of cloud and overclouding, a day of the trumpet and of sounding. In the day of Jehovah's wrath the whole land shall be devoured, and He shall make a speedy end of all them that dwell in the land (i. 7, 8, 10, 12, 14–16, 18).

Before the day of Jehovah's anger has come upon us. It may be ye shall be hid in the day of Jehovah's anger (ii. 2, 3).

Wait ye upon Me until the day that I rise up to the prey, for it is My judgment. In that day shalt thou not be ashamed for all thy works. In that day it shall be said to Jerusalem, Fear thou not. At that time I will deal with thine oppressors. At that time will I bring you in, and at that time will I gather you ; for I will make you a name, and a praise (iii. 8, 11, 16, 19, 20).

In *Zechariah :* —

Many nations shall cleave to Jehovah in that day (ii. 11).

I will remove the iniquity of that land in one day.   In that day shall
ye cry every man to his companion under the vine and under the fig-
tree (iii. 9, 10).

In those days ten men shall take hold of the skirt of a man that is a
Jew (viii. 23).

Jehovah their God shall serve them in that day, as the flock of His
people (ix. 16).

My covenant was broken in that day (xi. 11).

In that day will I make Jerusalem a stone of burden for all peoples.
In that day I will smite every horse with astonishment.   In that day
will I make the leaders of Judah like a furnace of fire among the wood.
In that day shall Jehovah defend the inhabitants of Jerusalem.   In that
day I will seek to destroy all nations.   In that day shall there be a great
mourning in Jerusalem (xii. 3, 4, 6, 8, 9, 11).

In that day there shall be a fountain opened to the house of David, and
to the inhabitants of Jerusalem.   It shall come to pass in that day I
will cut off the names of the idols in the land.   In that day the prophets
shall be ashamed (xiii. 1–4).

Behold, the day of Jehovah cometh.   His feet shall stand in that day
upon the Mount of Olives.   In that day there shall not be light and
brightness ; but it shall be one day which shall be known unto Jehovah ;
not day, nor night, at evening time there shall be light.   In that day
living waters shall go out from Jerusalem.   In that day there shall be
one Jehovah, and His name one.   In that day there shall be a great
tumult from Jehovah.   In that day shall there be upon the bells of the
horses, Holiness unto Jehovah.   In that day there shall be no more a
Canaanite in the house of Jehovah (xiv. 1, 4, 6–9, 13, 20, 21).

In *Malachi :* —

Who may abide the day of His coming, and who shall stand when He
appeareth ?   They shall be Mine in the day wherein I do make a peculiar
treasure.   Behold, the day cometh that shall burn as an oven.   Behold,
I send you Elijah the prophet before the coming of the great and terrible
day of Jehovah (iii. 2, 17 ; iv. 1, 5).

In *David :* —

In His days shall the righteous flourish, and abundance of peace, and
He shall have dominion from sea to sea, and from the river unto the
ends of the earth (*Ps.* lxxii. 7, 8).   (Besides other places.)

5. In these passages by " day" and " time" is meant the advent of the Lord.   By a " day" or " time" of darkness, of thick darkness, of gloom, of no light, of laying waste, of the end of iniquity, of destruction, is meant the advent of the Lord when He was no longer known, and when consequently there was no longer anything of the church left.   By " a day" cruel, terrible, of wrath, of anger, of tumult, of visitation, of sacrifice, of recompense, of distress, of war, of a cry, is meant the advent of the Lord to Judgment.   By " the day" in which Jehovah alone shall be exalted, in which He shall be one and His name one, in which the offshoot of Jehovah shall be for beauty and glory, in which the righteous shall flourish, in which He shall vivify, in which He shall seek His flock, in which He shall make a new covenant, in which the mountains shall drop new wine, in which living waters shall go out from Jerusalem, in which they shall look unto the God of Israel, and many similar expressions, is meant the advent of the Lord to set up again a new church which will acknowledge Him as the Redeemer and Saviour.

6. To these passages may be added some which speak of the Lord's advent more openly :—

The Lord Himself shall give you a sign : Behold a virgin shall conceive and bear a Son, and shall call His name GOD-WITH-US (*Isa.* vii. 14 ; *Matt.* i. 22, 23).

Unto us a Child is born, unto us a Son is given, and the government shall be upon His shoulder ; and His name shall be called Wonderful, Counselor, God, Hero, Father of eternity, Prince of peace.   Of the increase of His government and peace there shall be no end, upon the throne of David, and upon his kingdom, to establish it in judgment and justice, from henceforth and even to eternity (*Isa.* ix. 6, 7).

There shall come forth a Rod out of the stem of Jesse, and a Shoot shall bear fruit out of his roots : and the spirit of Jehovah shall rest upon Him, the spirit of wisdom and understanding, the spirit of counsel and might.   Righteousness shall be the girdle of His loins, and truth the girdle of His reins.   Therefore it shall come to pass in that day, that the Root of Jesse, which standeth for an ensign of the peoples, shall the nations seek, and His rest shall be glory (*Isa.* xi. 1, 2, 5, 10).

Send ye the lamb of the ruler of the land, from the rock to the wilderness, to the mountain of the daughter of Zion. By mercy has the throne been established, and one shall sit upon it in truth, in the tabernacle of David, judging and seeking judgment, and hasting righteousness (*Isa.* xvi. 1, 5).

It shall be said in that day, Lo, this is our God ; we have waited for Him that He may save us : THIS IS JEHOVAH ; we have waited for Him, we will rejoice and be glad in His salvation (*Isa.* xxv. 9).

The voice of one crying in the wilderness, Prepare ye the way of JEHOVAH, make plain in the solitude a pathway for our God. For the glory of JEHOVAH shall be revealed, and all flesh shall see it together. Behold, the LORD JEHOVIH will come in strength, and His arm shall rule for Him ; behold, His reward is with Him. He shall feed His flock like a shepherd (*Isa.* xl. 3, 5, 10, 11).

Mine elect, in whom My soul delighteth. I JEHOVAH have called Thee in righteousness, and I will give Thee for a covenant to the people, for a light to the nations, to open the blind eyes, to bring out the bound from the prison, and them that sit in darkness out of the prison house. I am JEHOVAH, this is My name, and My glory will I not give to another (*Isa.* xlii. 1, 6–8).

Who hath believed our word, and to whom is the arm of Jehovah revealed ? He hath no form ; we have seen Him, but He hath no appearance. He hath borne our diseases, and carried our griefs (*Isa.* liii. 1, 2, 4, to end).

Who is this that cometh from Edom, with sprinkled garments from Bozrah, marching in the greatness (*multitudine*) of His strength ? I that speak in righteousness, great to save : for the day of vengeance is in Mine heart, and the year of My redeemed is come. So He became their Saviour (*Isa.* lxiii. 1, 4, 8).

Behold, the days come that I will raise up to David a righteous offshoot, who shall reign a king, and shall prosper, and shall execute judgment and justice in the earth : and this is His name whereby they shall call Him, JEHOVAH OUR RIGHTEOUSNESS (*Jer.* xxiii. 5, 6 ; xxxiii. 15, 16).

Rejoice greatly, O daughter of Zion ; shout, O daughter of Jerusalem ; behold, thy King cometh unto thee, He is just and saved.* He shall speak peace to the nations ; and His dominion shall be from sea to sea, and from the river even to the ends of the earth (*Zech.* ix. 9, 10).

Rejoice and be glad, O daughter of Zion ; lo, I come, that I may dwell in the midst of thee ; and many nations shall cleave to Jehovah in that day, and shall be My people (*Zech.* ii. 10, 11).

Thou Bethlehem Ephratah, little as thou art to be among the thou-

---

* In the *Apocalypse Revealed* (n. 612), it is "a Saviour;" in the *Apocalypse Explained* (n. 31⁷), it is "just and saving;" but the Hebrew is "saved," as given here by Swedenborg. [TR.]

sands of Judah, out of thee shall one come forth unto Me that is to be Ruler in Israel, and whose goings forth are from of old, from the days of eternity. He shall stand and feed in the strength of JEHOVAH (*Micah* v. 2, 4).

Behold, I send Mine Angel, who shall prepare the way before Me, and the LORD whom ye seek shall suddenly come to His temple, even the Angel of the covenant, whom ye have desired ; behold, He cometh ; but who shall abide the day of His coming ? Behold, I send you Elijah the prophet, before the coming of the great and terrible day of Jehovah (*Mal.* iii. 1, 2 ; iv. 5).

I saw, and behold, one like the Son of man came with the clouds of heaven ; and there was given Him dominion, and glory, and a kingdom, that all peoples, nations, and languages may worship Him : His dominion is an everlasting dominion, which shall not pass away, and His kingdom that which shall not be destroyed ; and all dominions shall worship Him, and obey Him (*Dan.* vii. 13, 14, 27).

Seventy weeks are determined upon thy people, and upon thy holy city, to consummate the transgression, and to seal up the vision and the prophecy, and to anoint the holy of holies. Know, therefore, and perceive, that from the going forth of the word to restore and build Jerusalem, unto Messiah the Prince, shall be seven weeks (*Dan.* ix. 24, 25).

I will set his hand in the sea, and his right hand in the rivers : He shall cry unto Me, Thou art my Father, my God, and the rock of my salvation. I also will make him My first-born, higher than the kings of the earth. His seed also will I make to endure to eternity, and his throne as the days of the heavens (*Ps.* lxxxix. 25–27, 29).

Jehovah said unto my Lord, Sit Thou at My right hand, until I make Thine enemies Thy footstool. Jehovah shall send the scepter of Thy strength out of Zion ; rule Thou in the midst of Thine enemies. Thou art a priest to eternity after the manner of Melchizedek (*Ps.* cx. 1, 2, 4 ; *Matt.* xxii. 44 ; *Luke* xx. 42).

I have anointed My king upon Zion, the mountain of My holiness ; I will declare for a statute, Jehovah hath said unto Me, Thou art My Son, this day have I begotten Thee ; I will give the nations for Thine inheritance, and the uttermost parts of the earth for Thy possession. Kiss the Son, lest He be angry, and ye perish from the way ; blessed are all they that put their trust in Him (*Ps.* ii. 6–8, 12).

Thou hast made him a little less than the angels, but hast crowned him with glory and honor ; Thou hast made him to have dominion over the works of Thy hands ; Thou hast put all things under his feet (*Ps.* viii. 5, 6).

Jehovah, remember David, who sware unto Jehovah, and vowed to the Mighty One of Jacob, If I shall enter within the tent of my house, if I

shall go up upon my couch, if I shall give sleep to mine eyes, until I
find out a place for Jehovah, a habitation for the Mighty One of Jacob.
Lo, we heard of Him at Ephratah, we found Him in the fields of the forest.
We will enter into His tabernacles, we will bow at His footstool.   Let
Thy priests be clothed with righteousness, and let Thy saints shout for
joy (*Ps.* cxxxii. 1, 7, 9).

The passages here adduced, however, are but few.

7. That universal Holy Scripture has been written solely
about the Lord, will be more fully evident from what follows,
especially from the things to be advanced in the small work on
The Holy Scripture.   This is the one only source of the holiness of the Word, and is what is meant by the words

The testimony of Jesus is the spirit of prophecy (*Rev.* xix. 10).

II.

ITS BEING SAID THAT THE LORD FULFILLED ALL THINGS OF
THE LAW, MEANS THAT HE FULFILLED ALL THINGS OF
THE WORD.

8. At the present day many persons believe that when it is
said of the Lord that He fulfilled the law, the meaning is that
He fulfilled all the commandments of the decalogue, and thus
became righteousness, and also justified the men of this world
through this matter of faith.   This however is not the meaning.   The meaning is that the Lord fulfilled all things written
concerning Himself in the Law and the Prophets, that is, in
universal Holy Scripture, because this treats solely of Him, as
has been said in the foregoing article.   The reason why many
have believed differently, is that they have not searched the
Scriptures and seen what is there meant by "the Law."   The
Law there means, in a restricted sense, the ten commandments
of the decalogue; in a wider sense, all things written by Moses
in the five books; and in the widest sense, all things of the

Word. It is well known that *By the Law in a restricted sense
are meant the ten commandments of the decalogue.*

9. That *by the Law in a wider sense are meant all things
written by Moses in his five books,* is evident from the following
passages. In *Luke:*—

Abraham said to the rich man in hell, They have Moses and the
Prophets, let them hear them ; if they hear not Moses and the Prophets,
neither will they be persuaded though one rose from the dead (xvi. 29, 31).

In *John:*—

Philip said to Nathanael, We have found Him of whom Moses in the
Law and the Prophets did write (i. 45).

In *Matthew:*—

Think not that I am come to loosen the Law and the Prophets ; I am
not come to loosen, but to fulfill (v. 17).

All the Prophets and the Law prophesied until John (xi. 13).

In *Luke:*—

The Law and the Prophets were until John ; since then the kingdom
of God is evangelized (xvi. 16).

In *Matthew:*—

All things whatsoever that ye would that men should do to you, do ye
even so to them, for this is the Law and the Prophets (vii. 12).

Jesus said, Thou shalt love the Lord thy God with all thy heart, and
with all thy soul, and thou shalt love thy neighbor as thyself ; on these
two commandments hang all the Law and the Prophets (xxii. 37, 39, 40).

In these passages, " Moses and the Prophets," and " the Law
and the Prophets," mean all things that have been written in
the books of Moses and in the books of the prophets.

That " the Law" specifically means all things that have been
written by Moses, is further evident from the following passages. In *Luke:*—

When the days of her purification, according to the Law of Moses,
were fulfilled, they brought Jesus to Jerusalem, to present Him to the
Lord ; as it is written in the Law of the Lord : Every male that openeth
the womb shall be called holy to the Lord ; and to offer a sacrifice, according to that which is said in the Law of the Lord : A pair of turtle-

doves, or two young pigeons. And the parents brought Jesus into the temple, to do for Him after the custom of the Law. And when they had performed all things according to the Law of the Lord (ii. 22–24, 27, 39).

In *John*:—

Moses in the Law commanded us that such should be stoned (viii. 5). The Law was given by Moses (i. 17).

From these passages it appears that where such things are spoken of as are written in the books of Moses, they are sometimes called " the Law," and sometimes " Moses."

(So also in *Matt.* viii. 4; *Mark* x. 2–4; xii. 19; *Luke* xx. 28, 37; *John* iii. 14; vii. 19, 51; viii. 17; xix. 7.)

Many things that were commanded also, are called by Moses " the Law," as :

Concerning the burnt-offerings (*Lev.* vi. 9; vii. 37). Concerning the sacrifices (*Lev.* vi. 25; vii. 1–11). Concerning the meat-offering (*Lev.* vi. 14). Concerning leprosy (*Lev.* xiv. 2). Concerning jealousy (*Num.* v. 29, 30). Concerning the Naziriteship (*Num.* vi. 13, 21).

And Moses himself calls his books " the Law :"—

Moses wrote this Law, and delivered it to the priests, the sons of Levi, who bare the ark of the covenant of Jehovah; and he said to them, Take the Book of this Law, and put it at the side of the ark of the covenant of Jehovah (*Deut.* xxxi. 9, 11, 26).

It was placed at the side, because within the ark were the tables of stone, which in a restricted sense are the Law. Afterwards the books of Moses are called " The Book of the Law :"—

And Hilkiah the high priest said unto Shaphan the scribe, I have found the Book of the Law in the house of Jehovah. And when the king had heard the words of the Book of the Law, he rent his garments (2 *Kings* xxii. 8, 11; xxiii. 24).

10. That *by " the Law," in the widest sense, are meant all things of the Word,* is evident from these passages :—

Jesus said, Is it not written in your Law, I said, Ye are gods? (*John* x. 34). (This is written in *Ps.* lxxxii. 6.)

2

The multitude answered Him, We have heard out of the Law, that the Christ abideth forever (*John* xii. 34). (This is written in *Ps.* lxxxix. 29; cx. 4; and in *Dan.* vii. 11, 14.)

That the word might be fulfilled that is written in their Law, They hated Me without a cause (*John* xv. 25) (This is written in *Ps.* xxxv. 19.)

The Pharisees said, Have any of the rulers believed on Him? But this multitude that knoweth not the Law are cursed (*John* vii. 48, 49).

It is easier for heaven and earth to pass than for one tittle of the Law to fall (*Luke* xvi. 17). (Here "the Law" means all Holy Scripture.)

11. That the statement that the Lord fulfilled all things of the Law means that He fulfilled all things of the Word, is evident from passages where it is said that the Scripture was fulfilled by Him, and that all things were consummated: as from the following:—

Jesus went into the synagogue, and stood up to read, and there was delivered to Him the book of the prophet Isaiah, and He unrolled the book, and found the place where it is written, The Spirit of the Lord is upon Me, because He hath anointed Me, He hath sent Me to preach the gospel to the poor, to heal the broken-hearted, to preach deliverance to the captives, and recovering of sight to the blind, to preach the acceptable year of the Lord. And He rolled up the book and said, This day is this Scripture fulfilled in your ears (*Luke* iv. 16–21).

Search the Scriptures, for they testify of Me (*John* v. 39).

That the Scripture may be fulfilled, He that eateth bread with Me hath lifted up his heel against Me (*John* xiii. 18).

None of them is lost, but the son of perdition, that the Scripture might be fulfilled (*John* xvii. 12).

That the word might be fulfilled which He spake, Of them whom Thou gavest Me have I lost none (*John* xviii. 9).

Jesus said to Peter, Put up again thy sword into its place. How then shall the Scriptures be fulfilled, that thus it must be? But all this was done that the Scriptures of the Prophets might be fulfilled (*Matt.* xxvi. 52, 54, 56).

The Son of Man goeth as it is written of Him, that the Scriptures be fulfilled (*Mark* xiv. 21, 49).

Thus the Scripture was fulfilled which saith, He was accounted among the transgressors (*Mark* xv. 28; *Luke* xxii. 37).

That the Scripture might be fulfilled, which saith, They divided My garments among them, and upon my under-vesture did they cast a lot (*John* xix. 24).

After this, Jesus knowing that all things were now consummated, that the Scripture might be fulfilled (*John* xix. 28).

When Jesus had received the vinegar, He said, It is consummated, that is, fulfilled (*John* xix. 30).

These things were done, that the Scripture might be fulfilled, A bone of Him shall not be broken. And again another Scripture saith, They shall look on Him whom they pierced (*John* xix. 36, 37).

Besides other places, where passages are adduced from the Prophets, without its being at the same time said that the Law, or the Scripture, was fulfilled.

That all the Word has been written about the Lord, and that He came into the world to fulfill it, He also taught His disciples before His departure, in these words :—

Jesus said to His disciples, O fools, and slow of heart to believe all that the prophets have spoken ! Ought not the Christ to suffer these things, and to enter into His glory ? And beginning at Moses and all the Prophets, He expounded unto them in all the Scriptures the things concerning Himself (*Luke* xxiv. 25–27).

Jesus said to His disciples, These are the words which I spake unto you while I was yet with you, that all things must be fulfilled which were written in the Law of Moses, and in the Prophets, and in the Psalms, concerning Me (*Luke* xxiv. 44).

That in the world the Lord fulfilled all things of the Word, even to the veriest singulars * of it, is evident from these His own words :—

Verily I say unto you, Till heaven and earth pass, one jot or one tittle shall not pass from the law, till all things be accomplished (*Matt.* v. 18).

From these passages it may now be clearly seen that by its being said that the Lord fulfilled all things of the law is not meant that He fulfilled all the commandments of the decalogue, but that He fulfilled all things of the Word.

---

* The term *singular* is the correlative of *universal*, as *particular* is of *general*. The *veriest* singulars are the most absolute ones, the most singular or individually distinct of all. [TR.]

III.

THE LORD CAME INTO THE WORLD TO SUBJUGATE THE HELLS
AND TO GLORIFY HIS HUMAN; AND THE PASSION OF THE
CROSS WAS THE FINAL COMBAT, WHEREBY HE FULLY CON-
QUERED THE HELLS, AND FULLY GLORIFIED HIS HUMAN.

12. It is known in the church that the Lord conquered
death, by which is meant hell, and that He afterwards ascended
in glory into heaven; but as yet it has not been known that it
was by means of combats which are temptations that the Lord
conquered death or hell, and at the same time by means of
them glorified His Human; and that the passion of the cross
was the final combat or temptation by means of which He
effected this conquest and this glorification. Of these temptations many things are said in the Prophets and in David; but
not so many in the Evangelists. In these, the temptations
which He endured from childhood are summarily described by
His temptations in the wilderness, followed by those from the
devil; and the last of them by the things He suffered at Gethsemane and on the cross.

(Concerning His temptations in the wilderness, and by the devil, see
Matt. iv. 1–11; *Mark* i. 12, 13; and *Luke* iv. 1–13.)

By these temptations, however, are meant all His temptations
even to the last of them.   He revealed no more to His disciples
concerning them; for it is said in *Isaiah* :—

He was oppressed, yet He opened not His mouth: as a lamb that is
brought to the slaughter, and as a sheep before her shearers is dumb, so
He opened not His mouth (liii. 7).

(Concerning His temptations at Gethsemane, see *Matt.* xxvi. 36–44;
Mark xiv. 32–42; and *Luke* xxii. 39–46. And concerning the temptations on the cross, see *Matt.* xxvii. 33–50; *Mark* xv. 22–37; *Luke* xxiii.
33–49; and *John* xix. 17–34.)

Temptations are nothing else than combats against the hells.*

---

* Concerning the Lord's temptations or combats, see the small work on *The
New Jerusalem and its Heavenly Doctrine*, published in London (n. 201 and 302).
And concerning temptations in general (n. 187–200).

13. That the Lord fully conquered the hells by the passion of the cross, He Himself teaches in *John*:—

Now is the judgment of this world; now shall the prince of this world be cast out (xii. 31).

The Lord said this when the passion of the cross was at hand.

The prince of this world is judged (xvi. 11).

Be of good cheer, I have overcome the world (xvi. 33).

In *Luke*:—

Jesus said, I beheld Satan as lightning fall from heaven (x. 18).

The "world," the "prince of the world," "Satan," and "the devil," mean hell.

That by the passion of the cross the Lord also fully glorified His Human, He teaches in *John*:—

When Judas was gone out, Jesus said, Now is the Son of Man glorified, and God is glorified in Him; if God be glorified in Him, God will also glorify Him in Himself, and will straightway glorify Him (xiii. 31, 32).

Father, the hour is come, glorify Thy Son, that Thy Son also may glorify Thee (xvii. 1).

Now is My soul troubled; and He said, Father, glorify Thy name. Then came there a voice from heaven, saying, I have both glorified it, and I will glorify it again (xii. 27, 28).

In *Luke*:—

Ought not the Christ to suffer this, and to enter into His glory? (xxiv. 26).

These things are said of the Passion. Glorification is the union of the Divine and the Human; and therefore it is said, "and God will glorify Him in Himself."

14. That the Lord came into the world to reduce into order all things in heaven, and derivatively on earth; that this was effected by means of combats against the hells, which were then infesting every man that came into the world and that went out of the world; and that He thereby became Righteousness, and saved men, who otherwise could not have been saved, is foretold in many passages in the Prophets, of which only a few shall be adduced. [2] In *Isaiah* :—

Who is this that cometh from Edom, with sprinkled garments from Bozrah ; this that is glorious in His apparel, marching in the greatness of His strength ? I that speak in righteousness, mighty to save. Wherefore art Thou red in Thine apparel, and Thy garments like Him that treadeth in the wine-press ? I have trodden the wine-press alone, and of the people there was not a man with Me ; wherefore I have trodden them in Mine anger, and trampled them in My wrath ; therefore their victory is sprinkled upon My garments ; for the day of vengeance is in Mine heart, and the year of My redeemed is come. Mine own arm brought salvation unto Me ; and I brought down their victory to the earth. He said, Lo, they are My people, sons ; therefore He was their Saviour ; in His love, and in His pity, He redeemed them (lxiii. 1–9).

These things are said of the Lord's combats against the hells. The "apparel" in which He was "glorious," and which was "red," means the Word, to which violence had been done by the Jewish people. The actual combat against the hells, and the victory over them, are described by its being said that He "trod them in His anger, and trampled them in His wrath." That He fought alone, and from His own power, is described by, "of the people there was not a man with Me, Mine own arm brought salvation unto Me, I brought down their victory to the earth." That He thereby effected salvation and redemption, is described by, "therefore He was their Saviour ; in His love and in His pity He redeemed them." That this was the reason for His advent, is described by, "the day of vengeance is in Mine heart, and the year of My redeemed is come." [3] In *Isaiah* again :—

He saw that there was not any one, and He was amazed that there was none to interpose ; therefore His own arm brought salvation unto Him ; and His righteousness, it upheld Him ; therefore He put on righteousness as a coat of mail, and a helmet of salvation upon His head ; and He put on garments of vengeance, and clad Himself with zeal as a cloak : then came the Redeemer to Zion (lix. 16, 17, 20).

These words also treat of the Lord's combats against the hells while He was in the world. That He fought against them

from His own power, is meant by, " He saw that there was
not any one, therefore His own arm brought salvation unto
Him." That thereby He became righteousness, is meant by,
" His righteousness, it upheld Him, whence He put on righteousness as a coat of mail." That He thus effected redemption, is meant by, " then came the Redeemer to Zion." [4]
In *Jeremiah :*—

They are dismayed, their strong ones were beaten down, they are fled
apace, and look not back : that day is to the Lord Jehovih Zebaoth a
day of vengeance, that He may take vengeance of His enemies, and
the sword shall devour, and be sated (xlvi. 5, 10).

The Lord's combat with the hells, and His victory over them,
are described by its being said that they are dismayed, and
that their strong ones being beaten down are fled apace, and
looked not back. Their " strong ones," and " enemies," are
the hells, for all there feel hatred against the Lord. His advent into the world for this purpose is meant by, " that day is
to the Lord Jehovih Zebaoth a day of vengeance, that He may
take vengeance of His enemies." [5] In *Jeremiah :*—

Her young men shall fall in the streets, and all the men of war shall
be cut off in that day (xlix. 26).

In *Joel :*—

Jehovah hath uttered His voice before His army ; the day of Jehovah
is great and very terrible ; who therefore can endure it ? (ii. 11).

In *Zephaniah :*—

In the day of the sacrifice of Jehovah I will visit upon the princes,
upon the king's sons, upon all who are clothed with strange apparel.
That day is a day of distress, a day of the trumpet and of sounding (i.
8, 15, 16).

In *Zechariah :*—

Jehovah shall go forth, and fight against the nations, as when He
fought in the day of battle. And His feet shall stand in that day upon
the Mount of Olives, which is before the faces of Jerusalem. Then
shall ye flee into the valley of My mountains. In that day there shall

not be light and brightness. And Jehovah shall be king over all the earth ; in that day there shall be one Jehovah, and His name one (xiv. 3–6, 9).

These passages also treat of the Lord's combats. "That day" means His advent. The Mount of Olives that was before the faces of Jerusalem, was where the Lord was wont to tarry. (See *Mark* xiii. 3; xiv. 26; *Luke* xxi. 37; xxii. 39; *John* viii. 1; and elsewhere.) [6] In *David :*—

The cords of death compassed me about, the cords of hell encompassed me, the snares of death forestalled me ; therefore He sent out His arrows, and many lightnings, and discomfited them. I will pursue Mine enemies, and catch them, neither will I turn until I have consumed them. I will smite them that they shall not be able to rise. Thou hast girded me with strength unto the war, and Thou shalt put mine enemies to flight ; I will beat them small as dust before the faces of the wind, as the mire of the streets I will enfeeble them (*Ps.* xviii. 5, 14, 37–40, 42).

The "cords" and "snares of death" that encompassed and forestalled, signify temptations, which, being from hell, are called also "the cords of hell." These and all other things in this whole Psalm treat of the Lord's combats and victories; and therefore it is added, "Thou wilt make me the head of the nations; a people that have not known shall serve me" (verse 43). [7] In *David*, again :—

Gird Thy sword upon Thy thigh, O Mighty one ; Thine arrows are sharp, the people shall fall under Thee, from the heart of the king's enemies. Thy throne is for ever and to eternity : Thou hast loved righteousness, wherefore God hath anointed Thee (*Ps.* xlv. 3, 5–7).

These words also treat of combat with the hells, and of their subjugation; for this whole Psalm treats of the Lord, that is to say, of His combats, His glorification, and the salvation of the faithful by Him. In *David :*—

A fire shall go before Him, it shall burn up His enemies round about ; the earth shall see and shall fear ; the mountains shall melt like wax before the Lord of the whole earth. The heavens shall declare His righteousness, and all the people shall see His glory (*Ps.* xcvii. 3–6).

This Psalm likewise treats of the Lord, and of the like things.
[8] In *David :*—

Jehovah said unto my Lord, Sit Thou at My right hand until I make
Thine enemies Thy footstool; rule Thou in the midst of Thine enemies.
The Lord at Thy right hand hath smitten kings in the day of His anger;
He hath filled with dead bodies, He hath smitten the head over much
land (*Ps.* cx. 1, 2, 5, 6).

That these words are said of the Lord, is evident from His
own words in *Matt.* xxii. 44; *Mark* xii. 36; and *Luke* xx. 42.
To "sit at the right hand," signifies omnipotence; the "enemies" signify the hells; "kings," those there who are in falsities of evil. To "make them His footstool," "smite them in
the day of anger," and "fill with dead bodies," signifies to destroy their power; and to "smite the head over much land,"
signifies to destroy all.

[9] As the Lord alone conquered the hells, without the aid
of any angel, He is called HERO, and a MAN OF WARS (*Isa.*
xlii. 13); THE KING OF GLORY, JEHOVAH STRONG AND
MIGHTY; A HERO OF WAR (*Ps.* xxiv. 8, 10); THE MIGHTY
ONE OF JACOB (*Ps.* cxxxii. 2); and in many places, JEHOVAH
ZEBAOTH, that is, Jehovah of the Armies of War. His advent
is also called THE DAY OF JEHOVAH terrible, cruel, of indignation, of wrath, of anger, of vengeance, of destruction, of war,
of the sounding of the trumpet, of tumult, as may be seen
from the passages quoted above, in n. 4.

[10] As the Last Judgment executed by the Lord when He
was in the world was effected by means of combats with the
hells, and by their subjugation, this coming Judgment is
treated of in many passages. As in *David :*—

Jehovah cometh to judge the earth; He shall judge the world in righteousness, and the people in truth (*Ps.* xcvi. 13).

And so in many other passages. These are from the prophetical parts of the Word. [11] In its historical parts like things
are represented by the wars of the sons of Israel with various
nations; for everything that is written in the Word, whether

in prophecy or history, is written about the Lord; and this is
why the Word is Divine. Many arcana of the Lord's glorification are contained in the rituals of the Israelitish Church,
as for example in its burnt-offerings and sacrifices, in its sabbaths and feasts, and in the priesthood of Aaron and the
Levites; as they are also in all those other things in Moses
which are called laws, judgments, and statutes; and this is
what is meant by the Lord's words to His disciples :—

That He must needs fulfill all things which are written in the law of
Moses concerning Him (*Luke* xxiv. 44);

and by His saying to the Jews that Moses "wrote of Him"
(*John* v. 46).

[12] From all this it is evident that the Lord came into the
world to subjugate the hells, and to glorify His Human; and
that the passion of the cross was the final combat, by which He
fully conquered the hells, and fully glorified His Human. But
more will be seen on this subject in the following small work
on *The Holy Scripture*, where are collected together all the passages from the prophetical Word that treat of the Lord's combats with the hells and His victories over them; or, what is
the same, that treat of the Last Judgment executed by Him
when He was in the world; and also those which treat of His
passion, and of the glorification of His Human, which are so
numerous that if quoted they would fill pages.

IV.

By the Passion of the Cross the Lord did not take
away Sins, but bore them.

15. Some persons within the church believe that by the
passion of the cross the Lord took away sins, and made satisfaction to the Father, and so effected Redemption; and some,
that He transferred to Himself, bore, and cast into the depths

of the sea (that is, into hell), the sins of those who have faith
in Him.   They confirm themselves in these notions by the
words of John concerning Jesus :—

Behold the Lamb of God, that taketh away the sins of the world (*John*
i. 29) ;

and by the Lord's words in *Isaiah :*—

He hath borne our diseases, and carried our sorrows : He was
wounded for our transgressions, He was bruised for our iniquities, the
chastisement of our peace was upon Him, and by His wound has health
been given us.   Jehovah hath made to fall on Him the iniquities of
us all.   He was oppressed [*literally*, He hath endured exaction], and He
was afflicted, yet He opened not His mouth ; He is led as a lamb to the
slaughter.   He was cut off out of the land of the living for the transgression of My people, to whom the stroke was due, that He might deliver the wicked into their sepulchre, and the rich into their deaths ;
He shall see of the labor of His soul, and shall be satisfied.   By His
knowledge shall He justify many ; in that He hath borne their iniquities.   He hath poured out His soul unto death, and He was numbered with the transgressors, and He bare the sins of many, and made
intercession for the transgressors (liii. 4 to end).

Both these passages speak of the Lord's temptations and passion; and by His taking away sins and diseases, and by the
iniquities of all being made to fall on Him, is meant the like
as by His bearing sorrows and iniquities.   [2] Therefore it
shall first be stated what is meant by bearing iniquities, and
afterwards what by taking them away.   To bear iniquities
means to endure grievous temptations ; and also to suffer the
Jews to treat Him as they had treated the Word, which they
did because He was the Word.   For the church as it then existed among the Jews was utterly devastated, and it was devastated by their having perverted all things of the Word, so
that there was not any truth remaining ; and therefore they
did not acknowledge the Lord.   This was meant and signified
by all things of the Lord's passion.   The prophets were treated
in a similar way, because they represented the Lord in respect
to the Word, and derivatively in respect to the church, and

the Lord was *the* Prophet.   [3] That the Lord was *the* Prophet
is evident from the following passages :—

Jesus said, A prophet is not without honor, save in his own country,
and in his own house (*Matt.* xiii. 57 ; *Mark* vi. 4 ; *Luke* iv. 24).

Jesus said, It cannot be that a prophet perish out of Jerusalem (*Luke*
xiii. 33).

They said of Jesus, This is that prophet of Nazareth (*Matt.* xxi. 11 ;
John vii. 40).

Fear took hold on all ; and they praised God, saying that a great
prophet is risen up among us (*Luke* vii. 16).

That a prophet should be raised up out of the midst of their brethren,
whose words they shall obey (*Deut.* xviii. 15–19).

That the prophets underwent similar treatment, is evident from
the things which follow.   [4] In order that he might represent
the state of the church, the prophet Isaiah was commanded

To loose the sackcloth from off his loins, and to put off the shoe from
his foot, and to walk naked and barefoot three years, for a sign and a
wonder (*Isa.* xx. 2, 3).

In order that he might represent the state of the church, the
prophet Jeremiah was commanded

To buy for himself a girdle, and put it upon his loins, and not put it
in water, and to hide it in a hole of the rock near the river Euphrates ;
and after many days he found it rotten (*Jer.* xiii. 1–7).

The same prophet represented the state of the church by

His not taking a wife in that place, nor entering into the house of
mourning, neither going away to lament, nor entering into the house of
feasting (*Jer.* xvi. 2, 5, 8).

[5] In order that he might represent the state of the church,
the prophet Ezekiel was commanded

To cause a barber's razor to pass upon his head, and upon his beard,
and afterwards to divide it, and to burn the third part of it in the midst
of the city, to smite a third part with a sword, and to scatter a third part
in the wind ; and that he should bind a few hairs in his skirts, and at
last cast them into the midst of the fire, and burn them (*Ezek.* v. 1–4).

In order that he might represent the state of the church, the
same prophet was commanded

To make vessels of wandering, and to wander to another place in the eyes of the sons of Israel, and to bring forth the vessels by day, and go forth in the evening through a hole dug in the wall, and cover his face so that he should not see the earth ; and that so he should be for a wonder to the house of Israel, and should say, I am your sign ; like as I have done, so shall it be done unto you (*Ezek.* xii. 3–7, 11).

[6] In order that he might represent the state of the church, the prophet Hosea was commanded

To take to himself a harlot for a wife ; and he took her, and she bare him three sons, one of whom he called "Jezreel ;" the second, "That hath not obtained mercy ;" and the third, "Not my people" (*Hos.* i. 2–9).

And again he was commanded

To go and love a woman beloved of her companion, and an adulteress, whom he also bought for fifteen pieces of silver (*Hos.* iii. 1, 2).

[7] In order that he might represent the state of the church, the prophet Ezekiel was commanded

To take a tile, and engrave upon it Jerusalem, and to lay siege to it, and build a rampart and a mount against it, and to put an iron pan between himself and the city, and to lie on his left side three hundred and ninety days, and afterwards, on his right side, forty days. Also to take wheat, barley, lentils, millet, and spelt, and make bread thereof, which he should then eat by measure. And also that he should make for himself a barley cake with the dung of man ; and because he prayed that it might not be so, he was commanded to make it with cow's dung (*Ezek.* iv. 1–15).

The prophets represented other things besides ; as, for instance, Zedekiah, by

The horns of iron that he made for himself (1 *Kings* xxii. 11).

And another prophet, by being

Smitten and wounded, and by putting ashes upon his eyes (1 *Kings* xx. 35–38).

[8] In general, the prophets represented the Word in its ultimate sense, which is the sense of the letter, by a garment of hair (*Zech.* xiii. 4) ; and therefore Elijah

Was clad in such a coat, and was girt about his loins with a leathern girdle (2 *Kings* i. 8) ;

and in like manner John the Baptist,

Who had his raiment of camel's hair, and a leathern girdle about his loins, and ate locust and wild honey (*Matt.* iii. 4).

From these things it is evident that the prophets represented the state of the church, and also the Word; for he who represents the one represents the other, because the church is from the Word, and is according to the reception of it in life and faith. Therefore prophets, wherever mentioned in both Testaments, signify the doctrine of the church from the Word; and by the Lord, as the Grand Prophet, is signified the church itself, and the Word itself.

16. The state of the church from the Word thus represented in the Prophets, is what is meant by bearing the iniquities and sins of the people. That such is the case is evident from the things said of Isaiah the prophet:—

That he went naked and barefoot three years, for a sign and a wonder (*Isa.* xx. 3).

Of the prophet Ezekiel:—

That he brought forth vessels of wandering, and covered his face so that he should not see the earth, and that so he was for a portent to the house of Israel, and also said, I am your portent (*Ezek.* xii. 6, 11).

[2] That this was for them to bear iniquities, is plainly evident in *Ezekiel*, where that prophet is commanded to lie three hundred and ninety, and forty, days, upon his left side and upon his right, against Jerusalem, and to eat a barley cake made with cow's dung: As we read:—

Lie thou upon thy left side, and lay the iniquity of the house of Israel upon it, according to the number of the days that thou shalt lie upon it, thou shalt bear their iniquity. For I have laid upon thee the years of their iniquity, according to the number of the days, three hundred and ninety days, that thou bear the iniquity of the house of Israel. And when thou hast accomplished them, thou shalt lie upon thy right side, so that thou bear the iniquity of the house of Judah forty days (*Ezek.* iv. 4–6).

[3] That by his having thus borne the iniquities of the house of Israel and of the house of Judah, the prophet did not take

them away, and thus expiate them, but only represented and showed them, is evident from what there follows :—

Thus saith Jehovah, The sons of Israel shall eat their unclean bread among the nations whither I will drive them. Behold, I will break the staff of bread in Jerusalem, that they may lack bread and water, and be desolate a man and his brother, and consume away for their iniquity (verses 13, 16, 17).

[4] So when the same prophet showed himself, and said,

Behold, I am your portent, it is added, as I have done, so shall it be done unto them (*Ezek.* xii. 6, 11).

The meaning is therefore the same where it is said of the Lord :—

He hath borne our diseases, and carried our sorrows : Jehovah hath made to light on Him the iniquities of us all ; by His knowledge hath He justified many, in that He hath borne their iniquities (*Isa.* liii. 4, 6, 11) ;

where, in this whole chapter, the Lord's passion is treated of.

[5] That the Lord Himself, as the Grand Prophet, represented the state of the church in respect to the Word, is evident from all things of His passion ; as that He was betrayed by Judas ; that He was taken and condemned by the chief priests and elders ; that they buffeted Him ; that they smote Him on the head with a reed ; that they put on Him a crown of thorns ; that they divided His garments, and cast lots for His undervesture ; that they crucified Him ; that they gave Him vinegar to drink ; that they pierced His side ; that He was buried ; and that He rose again the third day. [6] That He was betrayed by Judas, signified that He was betrayed by the Jewish nation, among whom at that time was the Word, for Judas represented that nation. That He was taken and condemned by the chief priests and elders, signified that He was so treated by the whole Jewish Church. That they scourged Him, spat in His face, buffeted Him, and smote Him on the head with a reed, signified that they had done the like to the Word in respect to its Divine truths, all of which treat of the Lord. That they put on Him a crown of thorns, signified that they had

falsified and adulterated those truths. That they divided His garments, and cast lots for His under-vesture, signified that they had dispersed all the truths of the Word, but not its spiritual sense, which His under-vesture signified. That they crucified Him, signified that they had destroyed and profaned the whole Word. That they offered Him vinegar to drink, signified that everything had become falsified and false; and therefore He did not drink it, and then said, It is finished. That they pierced His side, signified that they had completely extinguished all the truth of the Word, and all its good. That He was buried, signified the rejection of the residue of the maternal human. That He rose again the third day, signified His glorification. [7] Similar things are signified by these things as foretold in the Prophets and in David. And it was for the same reason that, after He had been scourged and brought out wearing the crown of thorns and the purple robe put on Him by the soldiers, He said, Behold the Man! (*John* xix. 1, 5). This He said because by "man (*hominem*)" is signified the church; for by "Son of man" is signified the truth of the church, thus the Word. It is evident then from these things, that to bear iniquities means to represent and effigy in one's self sins against the Divine truths of the Word. That the Lord endured and suffered such things as the Son of man, and not as the Son of God, will be seen in what follows; for "the Son of man" signifies the Lord in respect to the Word.

17. Something shall now be said of what is meant by taking away sins. To take away sins means the same as to redeem man, and to save him; for the Lord came into the world to render salvation possible to man. Without His advent no mortal could have been reformed and regenerated, and so saved. But this became possible after the Lord had deprived the devil (that is, hell) of all his power; and had glorified His Human, that is, had united it to the Divine of His Father. If these things had not been done, no man would have been capable of permanently receiving any Divine truth, still less any Divine good; for the devil, whose power was previously the stronger, would have plucked it out of his heart. [**2**] From what has been said it is evident that the Lord did not take away sins by the passion of the cross; but that He takes them away, that is, removes them, in those who believe in Him by living according to His commandments; as He also teaches in *Matthew* :—

Think not that I am come to loosen the law and the prophets. Whosoever shall loosen the least of these commandments, and shall teach men so, shall be called the least in the kingdom of the heavens; but whosoever shall do and teach them shall be called great in the kingdom of the heavens (v. 17, 19).

[**3**] Who cannot see from reason alone, provided he is in some enlightenment, that sins cannot be taken away from a man except by actual repentance, which consists in his seeing his sins, imploring the Lord's help, and desisting from them? To see, believe, and teach otherwise, is not from the Word, nor from sound reason, but from cupidity and a depraved will, which are proper to man, and from this comes the debasement of his intelligence.

V.

THE IMPUTATION OF THE LORD'S MERIT IS NOTHING BUT THE REMISSION OF SINS AFTER REPENTANCE.

18. It is believed in the church that the Lord was sent by the Father to make an atonement for the human race, and that this was effected by His fulfilling the law, and by the passion of the cross; and that in this way He took away condemnation, and made satisfaction; and that without this expiation, satisfaction, and propitiation, the human race would have perished in eternal death, and this on account of justice which by some is called vengeful justice. It is true that without the Lord's advent all in the world would have perished; but how it is to be understood that the Lord fulfilled all things of the law, and why He suffered the cross, may be seen above, in chapters II.

and III., which show that it was not on account of any vengeful justice, because this is not a Divine attribute. Divine attributes are justice, love, mercy, and good; and God is justice itself, love itself, mercy itself, and good itself; and where these are, there is not anything of vengeance, and therefore no vengeful justice. [2] As the fulfilling of the law, and the passion of the cross, have hitherto been understood by many to mean that by these two things the Lord made satisfaction for mankind, and took away the condemnation that had been foreseen or appointed, there has followed from the connection, and also from the principle that man is saved by mere faith that it is so, the dogma of the imputation of the Lord's merit by our receiving, as for satisfaction, these two things that belong to His merit. But this dogma is refuted by what has been said about the fulfilling of the law by the Lord, and about His passion of the cross. At the same time we can see that the imputation of merit is a phrase destitute of meaning, unless there is meant by it the remission of sins after repentance. For nothing of the Lord can be imputed to man; but salvation can be awarded him by the Lord after he has performed repentance, that is, after he has seen and acknowledged his sins, and has then desisted from them, and this from the Lord. Then is salvation awarded him : not that he is saved by his own merit or righteousness, but by the Lord, who alone has fought and conquered the hells, and who alone still fights for man, and conquers the hells for him. [3] These things are the Lord's merit and righteousness, and they never can be imputed to man; for if they were, the Lord's merit and righteousness would be imputed to man as if they were his; and this is never done, nor can be done. If imputation were possible, an impenitent and wicked man could impute the Lord's merit to himself, and so think himself justified, and yet this would be to defile what is holy with things profane, and to profane the Lord's name; for it would be to keep the thought fixed on the Lord, and the will in hell, and yet the will is the whole man. There is a faith of God, and a faith of man; those have the faith of God who perform repentance; and those the faith of man who do not perform repentance, and yet think of imputation; and the faith of God is a living faith, and the faith of man is a dead faith. [**4**] That the Lord Himself, and His disciples, preached repentance and the remission of sins, is evident from the following passages :—

Jesus began to preach, and to say, Repent, for the kingdom of the heavens is at hand (*Matt.* iv. 17).

John said, Bring forth fruits worthy of repentance ; and now is the axe laid to the root of the trees ; every tree that bringeth not forth good fruit is hewn down, and cast into the fire (*Luke* iii. 8, 9).

Jesus said, Except ye repent, ye shall all perish (*Luke* xiii. 3, 5).

Jesus, preaching the Gospel of the kingdom of God, said, The time is fulfilled, and the kingdom of God is at hand ; repent ye, and believe the Gospel (*Mark* i. 14, 15).

Jesus sent out the disciples, who went forth and preached that men should repent (*Mark* vi. 12).

Jesus said to the apostles that they must preach in His name repentance and the remission of sins among all nations, beginning at Jerusalem (*Luke* xxiv. 47).

John preached the baptism of repentance for the remission of sins (*Luke* iii. 3 ; *Mark* i. 4).

By "baptism" is meant spiritual washing, which is a washing from sins, and is called regeneration. [**5**] Repentance and the remission of sins are thus described by the Lord in *John :*—

He came unto His own, but His own received Him not ; but to as many as received Him to them gave He power to become the sons of God, even to them that believe in His name ; who were born, not of bloods, nor of the will of the flesh, nor of the will of man, but of God (i. 11–13).

By "His own," are meant those who were then of the church, where was the Word; by "the sons of God," and "those who believe in His name," are meant those who believe in the Lord, and who believe the Word; by "bloods," are meant falsifications of the Word, and confirmations of falsity thereby ; "the will of the flesh," is man's Own pertaining to the will, which in itself is evil; "the will of man," is man's Own pertaining to the understanding, which in itself is falsity ; those "born of God," are those who have been regenerated by the Lord.   From these things it is evident that those are saved who are in the good of love and in the truths of faith from the Lord, and not those who are in what is their own.

***

VI.

THE LORD IN RESPECT TO THE DIVINE HUMAN IS CALLED THE SON OF GOD; AND IN RESPECT TO THE WORD, THE SON OF MAN.

19. In the church, the Son of God is supposed to be the second Person of the Godhead, distinct from the Person of the Father, whence comes the belief about the Son of God born from eternity.   As this belief has been universally received, and as it relates to God, no one has had any opportunity or permission to think about it from any understanding; not even as to what it is to be born from eternity; for any one who thinks about it from the understanding must needs say to himself, This transcends my understanding; but still I say it because others say it, and I believe it because others believe it. Be it known, then, that there is no Son from eternity; but that the Lord is from eternity.   When it is known what the Lord is, and what the Son, it will be possible, and not before, to think with understanding of the Triune God.

[2] That the Lord's Human, conceived of Jehovah the Father, and born of the virgin Mary, is the Son of God, is plainly evident from the following passages.   In *Luke:*—

The angel Gabriel was sent from God unto a city of Galilee named Nazareth, to a virgin betrothed to a man whose name was Joseph, of the house of David; and the virgin's name was Mary.   And the angel entered in to her, and said, Hail, thou that art highly favored, the Lord is with thee, blessed art thou among women.   And when she saw, she was troubled at his word, and cast in her mind what manner of salutation this might be.   And the angel said unto her, Fear not, Mary; for thou

hast found grace with God. And behold, thou shalt conceive and bear
a Son, and shalt call His name Jesus. He shall be great, and shall be
called THE SON OF THE MOST HIGH. But Mary said unto the angel,
How shall this be, seeing I know not a man? And the angel answered
and said unto her, The Holy Spirit shall come upon thee, and the power
of the Most High shall overshadow thee, wherefore also that HOLY THING
which shall be born of thee shall be called THE SON OF GOD (i. 26–35).

It is here said, "thou shalt conceive and bear a Son; He
shall be great, and shall be called THE SON OF THE MOST
HIGH;" and further, "that holy thing which shall be born of
thee shall be called THE SON OF GOD;" from which it is evident that the Human conceived of God, and born of the virgin
Mary, is what is called "the Son of God." [3] In *Isaiah :*—

The Lord Himself shall give you a sign; Behold, a virgin shall conceive and bear a Son, and shall call His name GOD-WITH-US (vii. 14).

That the Son born of the virgin, and conceived of God, is He
who is called "God-with-us," thus is He who is the Son of God,
is evident. That this is the case is confirmed also by *Matt.* i.
22, 23. [4] In *Isaiah :*—

Unto us a Child is born, unto us a Son is given; and the government
shall be upon His shoulder; and His name shall be called Wonderful,
Counselor, God, Hero, FATHER OF ETERNITY, Prince of peace (ix. 6).

The burden is the same here; for it is said, "Unto us a Child
is born, unto us a Son is given," who is not a Son from eternity, but a Son born in the world, as is also evident from the
words of the prophet in the next verse, which are similar to
those of the angel Gabriel to Mary in *Luke* i. 32, 33. [5] In
David :—

I will make an announcement concerning a statute, Jehovah hath said,
Thou art My Son; this day have I begotten Thee. Kiss the Son, lest He
be angry, and ye perish in the way (*Ps.* ii. 7, 12).

Neither here is there meant a Son from eternity, but a Son
born in the world; for it is a prophecy concerning the Lord
who was to come; and therefore it is called "a statute concerning which Jehovah has made an announcement" to David.

"This day," is not from eternity, but is in time. [6] In
David:—

> I will set His hand in the sea. He shall call Me, Thou art My Fa-
> ther. I will make Him My First-born (*Ps.* lxxxix. 25–27).

This whole Psalm treats of the Lord who was to come, and
therefore He is meant by Him who "shall call Jehovah His
Father," and who shall be the "First-born," thus who is the
Son of God. [7] And so in other places, where He is called

> A rod out of the stem of Jesse (*Isa.* xi. 1) ;
> An Offshoot of David (*Jer.* xxiii. 5) ;
> The seed of the woman (*Gen.* iii. 15) ;
> The Only-begotten (*John* i. 18) ;
> A Priest to eternity, and the Lord (*Ps.* cx. 4, 5).

[8] In the Jewish Church there was understood by the Son
of God the Messiah whom they had expected, and of whom
they knew that He was to be born at Bethlehem. That by
the Son of God they understood the Messiah, is evident from
the following passages. In *John*:—

> Peter said, We believe and know that Thou art THE CHRIST, THE SON
> OF THE LIVING GOD (vi. 69).

In the same Evangelist :—

> Thou art THE CHRIST THE SON OF GOD, who should come into the
> world (xi. 27).

In *Matthew*:—

> The chief priest asked Jesus whether He was THE CHRIST THE SON OF
> GOD. Jesus said, I am (xxvi. 63, 64 ; *Mark* xiv. 62).

In *John*:—

> These things are written, that ye might believe that Jesus is THE
> CHRIST THE SON OF GOD (xx. 31 ; also *Mark* i. 1).

"Christ" is a Greek word, and means "the Anointed," as also
does "Messiah" in the Hebrew language ; and therefore John
says :—

> We have found the Messiah, which is, being interpreted, THE CHRIST
> (*John* i. 41).

And in another place :—

> The woman said, I know that MESSIAS cometh, who is called CHRIST (iv. 25).

[9] It has been shown in the first chapter that the Law and the Prophets, that is, the whole Word of the Old Testament, is concerning the Lord, and therefore by the Son of God who was to come, nothing else can be meant than the Human which the Lord assumed in the world. From this it follows that the Human was what was meant, when Jesus, at His baptism, was called by Jehovah, in a voice from heaven, His Son :—

> This is MY BELOVED SON, in whom I am well pleased (*Matt.* iii. 17; *Mark* i. 11; *Luke* iii. 22).

For it was His Human that was baptized. And when He was transfigured :—

> This is MY BELOVED SON, in whom I am well pleased, hear ye Him (*Matt.* xvii. 5; *Mark* ix. 7; *Luke* ix. 35).

And in other places also, as *Matt.* viii. 29; xiv. 33; *Mark* iii. 11; xv. 39; *John* i. 34, 49; iii. 18; v. 25; x. 36; xi. 4.

20. As by "the Son of God" is meant the Lord as to the Human which He assumed in the world, which is the Divine Human, it is evident what is meant by the Lord's so frequently saying that He was sent by the Father into the world, and that He came forth from the Father. By His being sent by the Father into the world, is meant that He was conceived from Jehovah the Father. That nothing else is meant by being sent, and sent by the Father, is evident from all the passages where it is said that He did the will of the Father and His works, which were that He conquered the hells, glorified His Human, taught the Word, and set up* a new church, which could not have been done except by means of a Human conceived from Jehovah and born of a virgin, that is, unless God had been made Man. Examine the passages where " sent"

---

* Latin *instaurare*, to set up, not originally, but in restoration and repair. See Translator's Prefatory Notes, p. v. [TR.]

occurs, and you will see. As, for instance, *Matt.* x. 40; xv.
24; *Mark* ix. 37; *Luke* iv. 43; ix. 48; x. 16; *John* iii. 17,
34; iv. 34; v. 23, 24, 36–38; vi. 29, 39, 40, 44, 57; vii. 16,
18, 28, 29; viii. 16, 18, 29, 42; ix. 4; xi. 42; xii. 44, 45, 49;
xiii. 20; xiv. 24; xv. 21; xvi. 5; xvii. 3, 8, 21, 23, 25; xx. 21;
and also the passages where the Lord calls Jehovah "Father."

21. At the present day many think of the Lord no otherwise than as of a common man like themselves, because they
think solely of His Human, and not at the same time of His
Divine, when yet His Divine and His Human cannot be separated. For the Lord is God and Man, and God and Man in
the Lord are not two, but one Person, yes, altogether one, just
as soul and body are one man, according to the doctrine received in the whole Christian world which was formulated by
Councils, and is called the doctrine of the Athanasian Creed.
Therefore, lest any one should in future separate in his thought
the Divine and the Human in the Lord, I pray him to read the
passages from *Luke* quoted above, and also the following in
Matthew :—

The birth of Jesus Christ was on this wise. When His mother Mary
had been betrothed to Joseph, before they came together, she was found
with child of the Holy Spirit. And Joseph her betrothed, being a
just man, and not willing to make her a public example, was minded to
put her away privily. But while he thought on these things, behold, an
angel of the Lord appeared unto him in a dream, saying, Joseph, thou
son of David, fear not to take unto thee Mary thy betrothed, for that
which is begotten (*natus*) in her is of the Holy Spirit. And she shall
bring forth a son, and thou shalt call His name Jesus ; for He shall save
His people from their sins. And Joseph, being awaked from sleep,
did as the angel of the Lord commanded him, and took unto him his
betrothed, but knew her not till she had brought forth her first-born son ;
and he called His name Jesus (i. 18–25).

From these words, and from those written in *Luke* concerning
the Lord's nativity, and from others adduced above, it is evident that the "Son of God" is Jesus conceived of Jehovah
the Father, and born of the virgin Mary, of whom all the
Prophets and the Law prophesied until John.

22. He who knows *what* in the Lord is called "the Son of God," and what in Him is called "the Son of man," is able to see many of the secret things of the Word; for at one time the Lord calls Himself "the Son," at another "the Son of God," and at another "the Son of man," everywhere according to the subject that is being treated of. When His Divinity, His oneness with the Father, His Divine power, faith in Him, life from Him, are being treated of, He calls Himself "the Son," and "the Son of God." As, for instance, in *John* v. 17–26, and elsewhere. But where His passion, Judgment, His advent, and, in general, redemption, salvation, reformation, and regeneration, are treated of, He calls Himself "the Son of man;" the reason of which is that He is then meant in respect to the Word. In the Word of the Old Testament, the Lord is designated by various names, being there named Jehovah, Jah, Lord, God, the Lord Jehovih, Jehovah Zebaoth, the God of Israel, the Holy One of Israel, the Mighty One of Jacob, Shaddai, the Rock, and also Creator, Former, Saviour, Redeemer, everywhere according to the subject that is being treated of. And the same in the Word of the New Testament, where He is named Jesus, Christ, the Lord, God, the Son of God, the Son of man, the Prophet, the Lamb, with other names, also everywhere according to the subject there treated of.

23. Having stated on what grounds the Lord is called "the Son of God," we will now state those on which He is called "the Son of man." The Lord is called "the Son of man" where the subject treated of is His passion, Judgment, His advent, and, in general, redemption, salvation, reformation, and regeneration. The reason is that "the Son of man" is the Lord in respect to the Word; and as the Word He suffered, judges, came into the world, redeems, saves, reforms, and regenerates. That such is the case is evident from what now follows.

24. *That the Lord is called "the Son of man" when His passion is treated of,* is evident from these passages:—

Jesus said to His disciples, Behold, we go up to Jerusalem, and the Son of man shall be delivered unto the chief priests and scribes, and they shall condemn Him to death, and shall deliver Him to the nations, and they shall scourge Him, and spit on Him, and shall kill Him; but on the third day He shall rise again (*Mark* x. 33, 34). (And so in other places where He foretells His passion, as in *Matt.* xx. 18, 19; *Mark* viii. 31; *Luke* ix. 22.)

Jesus said to His disciples, Behold, the hour is at hand, and the Son of man is betrayed into the hands of sinners (*Matt.* xxvi. 45).

The angel said to the women that came to the sepulchre, Remember how He spake unto you, that the Son of man must be delivered into the hands of sinful men, and be crucified, and the third day rise again (*Luke* xxiv. 6, 7).

The reason the Lord then called Himself " the Son of man," is that He suffered Himself to be treated in the same way as they had treated the Word, as has been shown above very fully.

25. *That the Lord is called " the Son of man" when the Judgment is treated of,* is evident from these passages :—

When the Son of man shall come in His glory, then shall He sit upon the throne of His glory, and He shall set the sheep on His right hand, and the goats on the left (*Matt.* xxv. 31, 33).

When the Son of man shall sit on the throne of His glory, He shall judge the twelve tribes of Israel (*Matt.* xix. 28).

The Son of man shall come in the glory of His Father, and shall render to every one according to his deeds (*Matt.* xvi. 27).

Watch ye at every season, that ye may be accounted worthy to stand before the Son of man (*Luke* xxi. 36).

In such an hour as ye think not, the Son of man cometh (*Matt.* xxiv. 44; *Luke* xii. 40).

The Father judgeth no one, but hath given all judgment to the Son, because He is the Son of man (*John* v. 22, 27).

The reason why the Lord calls Himself " the Son of man" when the Judgment is treated of, is that all judgment is effected according to the Divine truth which is in the Word. That this judges every one, is said by the Lord Himself in *John* :—

If any one hear My words, and believe not, I judge him not, for I came not to judge the world. The Word that I have spoken, the same shall judge him in the last day (xii. 47, 48).

The Son of man has not come to judge the world, but that through Him it might be saved ; he that believeth in Him is not judged ; but he that believeth not is judged already, because he hath not believed in the name of the Only-begotten Son of God (iii. 17, 18).

(That the Lord judges no one to hell, and casts no one into hell, but that an evil spirit casts himself in, may be seen in the work on *Heaven and Hell*, n. 545–550, 574.)   By "the name" of Jehovah, of the Lord, of the Son of God, is meant the Divine truth, and therefore also the Word, which is from Him, and about Him, and therefore is Himself.

26. *That the Lord is called "the Son of man" when His advent is treated of*, is evident from these passages :—

The disciples said to Jesus, What shall be the sign of Thy coming, and of the consummation of the age ?   And then the Lord foretold the successive states of the church down to its end ; and of its end He said, Then shall appear the sign of the Son of man, and they shall see the Son of man coming in the clouds of heaven with power and glory (*Matt.* xxiv. 3, 30 ; *Mark* xiii. 26 ; *Luke* xxi. 27).

"The consummation of the age," means the last time of the church ; His "coming in the clouds of heaven with glory," means the opening of the Word, and the making manifest that the Word has been written about Him alone.   In *Daniel :*—

I saw and behold one like the Son of man came with clouds of the heavens (vii. 13).

In the *Revelation :*—

Behold, He cometh with clouds, and every eye shall see Him (i. 7).

This also is said of the Son of man, as is evident from verse 13.

I saw and behold a white cloud, and upon the cloud one sat like unto the Son of man (xiv. 14).

[**2**] That by "the Son of God" the Lord meant one thing in Himself, and by "the Son of man" another, is evident from His reply to the chief priest :—

The high priest said unto Jesus, I adjure Thee by the living God that Thou tell us whether Thou be the Christ, the Son of God.   Jesus said unto him, Thou hast said : nevertheless, I say unto you, Hereafter shall ye see the Son of man sitting at the right hand of power, and coming in the clouds of heaven (*Matt.* xxvi. 63, 64).

Here He first confessed that He was the Son of God, and afterwards said that they should see the Son of man sitting at the right hand of power, and coming in the clouds of heaven, by which is meant that after the passion of the cross He would possess the Divine power of opening the Word and setting up the church anew,* which could not be effected before, because He had not then conquered hell and glorified His Human. (What is signified by sitting upon the clouds of heaven, and coming in glory, has been set forth in the work on *Heaven and Hell*, n. 1.)

27. *That the Lord is called "the Son of man" when Redemption, Salvation, Reformation, and Regeneration are treated of,* is evident from these passages :—

The Son of man came to give His life a redemption for many (*Matt.* xx. 28; *Mark* x. 45).

The Son of man is come to save, and not to destroy (*Matt.* xviii. 11; *Luke* ix. 56).

The Son of man is come to seek and save that which was lost (*Luke* xix. 10).

The Son of man is come that the world through Him may be saved (*John* iii. 17).

He that soweth the good seed is the Son of man (*Matt.* xiii. 37).

Redemption and salvation are here treated of, and as the Lord effects these by means of the Word, He here calls Himself "the Son of man." The Lord says,

That the Son of man has power (*potestas*)† to forgive sins (*Mark* ii. 10; *Luke* v. 24) (that is, to save). And also,

That He is the Lord of the Sabbath, because He is the Son of man (*Matt.* xii. 8; *Mark* ii. 28; *Luke* vi. 5) (*i.e.* because He is the Word, which He is Himself then teaching).

He says, further, in *John :*—

Labor not for the meat which perisheth, but for that meat which endureth unto everlasting life, which the Son of man shall give unto you (vi. 27).

By "meat" is meant all truth and good of doctrine from the Word, thus from the Lord; and this is also meant there by

* See the foot-note on p. 39.

† *Potestas*, Greek ἐξουσια, is the authority, command, and power that is exercised by a ruler. [Tr.]

the manna, and by the bread which came down from heaven; and also by the following in the same chapter:—

Except ye shall eat the flesh of the Son of man, and drink His blood, ye have no life in you (verse 53).

"Flesh," or "bread," is the good of love from the Word; "blood," or "wine," is the good of faith from the Word, both from the Lord.

[2] The like is signified by "the Son of man" in other passages where He is mentioned, as in the following:—

The foxes have holes, and the birds nests, but the Son of man hath not where to lay His head (*Matt.* viii. 20; *Luke* ix. 58).

By this is meant that the Word would have no place among the Jews, as also the Lord said in *John* viii. 37; and also that they had it not abiding in them, because they had not acknowledged Him (*John* v. 38). In the *Revelation* also "the Son of man" means the Lord in respect to the Word:—

In the midst of the seven lampstands I saw one like unto the Son of man, clothed with a garment down to the foot, and girt about the paps with a golden girdle (i. 13, etc.).

Here, in various ways, the Lord is represented as the Word, and He is therefore called "the Son of man." In *David:*—

Let Thy hand be upon the man of Thy right hand, upon the Son of man whom Thou hast made strong for Thyself: so will not we go back from Thee; quicken us (*Ps.* lxxx. 17, 18).

"The man of Thy right hand," also means the Lord in respect to the Word; and so does "the Son of man." He is called "the man of the right hand," because the Lord has power from the Divine truth, which also the Word is, and He had Divine power when He had fulfilled the whole Word: and therefore He had said

That they should see the Son of man sitting at the right hand of the Father, with power (*Mark* xiv. 62).

28. *That "the Son of man" signifies the Lord in respect to the Word, was the reason why the prophets also were called sons of*

man. The reason why the prophets were called sons of man, was that they represented the Lord in respect to the Word, and consequently signified the doctrine of the church from the Word. In heaven nothing else is understood by "prophets" as mentioned in the Word; for the spiritual signification of "prophet," as well as of "son of man," is *the doctrine of the church from the Word;* and, when predicated of the Lord, "prophet" means *the Word* itself.

That the prophet Daniel is called "son of man" may be seen in *Dan.* viii. 17.

That the prophet Ezekiel is called "son of man" may be seen in *Ezek.* ii. 1, 3, 6, 8; iii. 1, 3, 4, 10, 17, 25; iv. 1, 16; v. 1; vi. 2; vii. 2; viii. 5, 6, 8, 12, 15; xi. 2, 4, 15; xii. 2, 3, 9, 18, 22, 27; xiii. 2, 17; xiv. 3, 13; xv. 2; xvi. 2; xvii. 2; xx. 3, 4, 27, 46; xxi. 2, 6, 9, 12, 14, 19, 28; xxii. 18, 24; xxiii. 2, 36; xxiv. 2, 16, 25; xxv. 2; xxvi. 2; xxvii. 2; xxviii. 2, 12, 21; xxix. 2, 18; xxx. 2, 21; xxxi. 2; xxxii. 2, 18; xxxiii. 2, 7, 10, 12, 24, 30; xxxiv. 2; xxxv. 2; xxxvi. 1, 17; xxxvii. 3, 9, 11, 16; xxxviii. 2, 14; xxxix. 1, 17; xl. 4; xliii. 7, 10, 18; xliv. 5. From what has been said it is now evident that the Lord in respect to the Divine Human is called "the Son of God," and in respect to the Word, "the Son of man."

VII.

The Lord made Divine His Human from the Divine that was in Himself, and thus became one with the Father.

29. The *Doctrine of the Church* that is received in the whole Christian world is that

Our Lord Jesus Christ, the Son of God, is God and Man, who, although He is God and Man, yet He is not two, but one Christ; one, by the taking of the manhood into God; one altogether, by unity of person; for as the reasonable soul and flesh is one man, so God and man is one Christ.

These words are taken from the doctrine of the Athanasian Creed, which has been received in the whole Christian world; and they are what is essential in it concerning the unition of the Divine and the Human in the Lord. What is said further in that Creed about the Lord will be explained in its own chapter. From these words it is quite evident that it is in accordance with *the faith of the Christian Church* that the Divine and the Human in the Lord are not two, but one, as the soul and body are one man, and that the Divine in Him assumed the Human. [**2**] From this it follows that the Divine cannot be separated from the Human, nor the Human from the Divine, for this would be like separating the soul from the body. That this is so must be admitted by every one who reads what is cited above (n. 9, 21) from two of the evangelists (namely, *Luke* i. 26–35, and *Matt.* i. 18–25) concerning the Lord's birth; from which it is manifest that Jesus was conceived of Jehovah God, and born of the virgin Mary; so that the Divine was in Him, and was His soul. As therefore His soul was the very Divine of the Father, it follows that His body, or Human, must also have become Divine; for where the one is Divine, the other must be so too. In this way and in no other are the Father and the Son one, and the Father in the Son and the Son in the Father, and all things of the Son the Father's, and all things of the Father the Son's, as the Lord Himself teaches in His Word. [**3**] But how this unition was effected, shall be shown in the following order:—

i. The Lord from eternity is Jehovah.

ii. The Lord from eternity, or Jehovah, assumed the Human to save men.

iii. He made Divine the Human from the Divine in Himself.

iv. He made Divine the Human by means of temptations admitted into Himself.

v. The full unition of the Divine and the Human in Him was effected by means of the passion of the cross, which was the last temptation.

vi. By successive steps He put off the human taken from

the mother, and put on a Human from the Divine within Him, which is the Divine Human, and is the Son of God.

vii. That thus God became Man, as in first principles, so also in ultimates.

30. i. *That the Lord from eternity is Jehovah,* is known from the Word; for the Lord said to the Jews,

Verily I say unto you, before Abraham was, I am (*John* viii. 58).

And He says in another place,

Glorify Thou Me, O Father, with the glory which I had with Thee before the world was (*John* xvii. 5).

By this is meant the Lord from eternity, and not a Son from eternity; for "the Son" is His Human that was conceived of Jehovah the Father, and born of the virgin Mary, in time, as has been shown above. [2] That the Lord from eternity is Jehovah Himself, is evident from many passages in the Word, of which at present there shall be adduced only these few :—

It shall be said in that day, THIS IS OUR GOD ; we have waited for Him that He may deliver us ; THIS IS JEHOVAH, we have waited for Him ; we will rejoice and be glad in His salvation (*Isa.* xxv. 9).

From these words it is evident that Jehovah God Himself was awaited.

The voice of one crying in the wilderness, Prepare ye the way of JEHOVAH, make plain in the solitude a path for OUR GOD. The glory of JEHOVAH shall be revealed, and all flesh shall see it together. Behold, THE LORD JEHOVIH shall come in strength (*Isa.* xl. 3, 5, 10 ; *Matt.* iii. 3 ; *Mark* i. 3 ; *Luke* iii. 4).

Here, too, the Lord is called Jehovah, who should come.   [3]

I Jehovah will give thee for a covenant to the people, for a light of the nations. I Jehovah, this is My name ; and My glory will I not give to another (*Isa.* xlii. 6–8).

"A covenant to the people," and "a light of the nations," is the Lord as to the Human ; and as this is from Jehovah, and has become one with Jehovah, it is said, *I Jehovah, this is My name, and My glory will I not give to another,* that is, not to

another than Himself. To give glory, means to glorify, or to
unite to Himself.   [**4**]

THE LORD whom ye seek, shall suddenly come to His temple (*Mal.*
iii. 1).

By the "temple" is meant the temple of His body (*John* ii.
19, 21).

THE DAY-SPRING FROM ON HIGH hath visited us (*Luke* i. 78).

"The day-spring from on high" also is Jehovah, or the Lord
from eternity.

From what has been said it is evident that by the Lord from
eternity is meant His Divine *a Quo,** which in the Word is
"Jehovah."   But from the passages to be quoted below, it will
be evident that by Lord, and also by Jehovah, after His
Human was glorified, is meant the Divine and the Human together, as a one; and that by the Son, alone, is meant the
Divine Human.

31. ii. *That the Lord from eternity, or Jehovah, assumed the
Human to save men,* has been confirmed from the Word in
preceding chapters; and that man could not have been saved
in any other way, will be shown elsewhere.   That He assumed
a Human, is evident from the passages in the Word where it
is said that He went forth from the Father, descended from
heaven, and was sent into the world.   As from these:—

I went out from the Father, and am come into the world (*John* xvi. 28).

I went out and am come from God ; neither came I of Myself, but He
sent Me (*John* viii. 42).

The Father loveth you, because ye have believed that I came out
from God (*John* xvi. 27).

No one hath ascended into heaven, but He that came down from
heaven (*John* iii. 13).

The bread of God is He that cometh down from heaven, and giveth
life unto the world (*John* vi. 33, 35, 41, 50, 51).

He that cometh from above is above all ; He that cometh from heaven
is above all (*John* iii. 31).

I know the Father because I am from Him, and He hath sent Me
(*John* vii. 29).

* *Literally,* the Divine from which ; that is, the Divine which is the source. [TR.]

4

(That to be "sent by the Father into the world" means to assume a Human, may be seen above, at n. 20.)

32. iii. *That the Lord made His Human Divine from the Divine in Himself,* is evident from many passages of the Word, of which those shall be here adduced which confirm :—

1. *That this was done by successive steps :—*

Jesus grew and waxed strong in spirit and in wisdom, and the grace of God was upon Him (*Luke* ii. 40).

Jesus increased in wisdom, in age, and in grace with God and men (verse 52).

[**2**] 2. *That the Divine operated through the Human, as the soul does through the body :—*

The Son can do nothing from Himself, but what He seeth the Father doing (*John* v. 19).

I do nothing of Myself, but as My Father hath taught Me, I speak these things ; and He that hath sent Me is with Me ; He hath not left Me alone (*John* viii. 28, 29 ; v. 30).

I have not spoken of Myself, but the Father who sent Me, He hath given Me a commandment, what I should say, and what I should speak (*John* xii. 49).

The words that I speak unto you I speak not of Myself, but the Father that dwelleth in Me, He doeth the works (*John* xiv. 10).

I am not alone, because the Father is with Me (*John* xvi. 32).

[**3**] 3. *That the Divine and Human operated unanimously :—*

What things soever the Father doeth, these also doeth the Son likewise (*John* v. 19).

As the Father raiseth up the dead and quickeneth them, even so the Son quickeneth whom He will (*John* v. 21).

As the Father hath life in Himself so hath He given to the Son to have life in Himself (*John* v. 26).

Now they have known that all things which Thou hast given Me, are of Thee (*John* xvii. 7).

[**4**] 4. *That the Divine was united to the Human, and the Human to the Divine :—*

If ye had known Me ye would have known My Father also ; and ye have seen Him. He said to Philip, who desired to see the Father, Have I been so long time with you, and yet hast thou not known Me, Philip ?

He that hath seen Me, hath seen the Father.   Believest thou not that I am in the Father, and the Father in Me ?   Believe Me, that I am in the Father, and the Father in Me (*John* xiv. 7–11).

If I do not the works of My Father, believe Me not; but if I do, believe the works ; that ye may know and believe that the Father is in Me, and I in the Father (*John* x. 37, 38).

That they all may be one, as Thou, Father, art in Me, and I in Thee (*John* xvii. 21).

At that day ye shall know that I am in My Father (*John* xiv. 20).

No one is able to pluck the sheep out of My Father's hand ; I and the Father are one (*John* x. 29, 30).

The Father loveth the Son, and hath given all things into His hand (*John* iii. 35).

All things that the Father hath are Mine (*John* xvi. 15).

All Mine are Thine, and Thine are Mine (*John* xvii. 10).

Thou hast given the Son power (*potestas*) over all flesh (*John* xvii. 2).

All power (*potestas*) is given unto Me in heaven and on earth (*Matt.* xxviii. 18).

[5] 5. *That the Divine Human is to be approached,* is evident from these passages :—

That all may honor the Son, even as they honor the Father (*John* v. 23).

If ye had known Me, ye would have known My Father also (*John* viii. 19).

He that seeth Me, seeth Him that sent Me (*John* xii. 45).

If ye had known Me, ye would have known My Father also ; and from henceforth ye know Him, and have seen Him (*John* xiv. 7).

He that receiveth Me, receiveth Him that sent Me (*John* xiii. 20).

The reason of this is that no one can see the Divine Itself which is called " the Father ;" but the Divine Human can be seen ; for the Lord says,

No one hath seen God at any time ; the Only-begotten Son who is in the bosom of the Father, He hath set Him forth (*John* i. 18).

Not that any one hath seen the Father, save He that is with the Father ; He hath seen the Father (*John* vi. 46).

Ye have not heard the Father's voice at any time, nor seen His shape (*John* v. 37).

[6] 6. *As the Lord made His Human Divine from the Divine in Himself, and as the Human is to be approached, and*

is the Son of God, we must put our faith in the Lord, who is both Father and Son.   This is evident from these passages :—

Jesus said, As many as received Him, to them gave He power (*potestas*) to be the sons of God, even to them that believe in His name (*John* i. 12).

That whosoever believeth in Him should not perish, but have eternal life (*John* iii. 15).

God so loved the world that He gave His Only-begotten Son, that whosoever believeth in Him should have eternal life (*John* iii. 16).

He that believeth in the Son is not judged ; but he that believeth not hath been judged already, because he hath not believed in the name of the Only-begotten Son of God (*John* iii. 18).

He that believeth in the Son hath eternal life ; but he that believeth not the Son, shall not see life, but the wrath of God abideth on him (*John* iii. 36).

The bread of God is He that cometh down from heaven, and giveth life unto the world.   He that cometh to Me shall never hunger, and he that believeth in Me shall never thirst (*John* vi. 33, 35).

This is the will of Him that sent Me, that every one who seeth the Son, and believeth in Him, may have eternal life, and I will raise him up at the last day (*John* vi. 40).

They said to Jesus, What shall we do that we may work the works of God ?   Jesus answered, This is the work of God, that ye believe in Him whom He hath sent (*John* vi. 28, 29).

Verily I say unto you, He that believeth in Me hath eternal life (*John* vi. 47).

Jesus cried, saying, If any one thirst let him come unto Me and drink; he that believeth in Me, as the Scripture hath said, out of his belly shall flow rivers of living water (*John* vii. 37, 38).

Unless ye believe that I am, ye shall die in your sins (*John* viii. 24).

Jesus said, I am the resurrection and the life ; he that believeth in Me, though he were dead, shall live ; and whosoever liveth and believeth in Me shall never die (*John* xi. 25, 26).

Jesus said, I am come a light into the world, that whosoever believeth in Me should not abide in darkness (*John* xii. 46 ; viii. 12).

While ye have the light, believe in the light, that ye may become sons of light (*John* xii. 36).

Verily I say unto you, that the dead shall hear the voice of the Son of God, and they that hear shall live (*John* v. 25).

Abide in Me, and I in you.   I am the vine, ye are the branches ; he that abideth in Me, and I in him, the same bringeth forth much fruit; for without Me ye can do nothing (*John* xv. 4, 5).

That they should abide in the Lord, and the Lord in them (*John* xiv. 20; xvii. 23).

I am the way, the truth, and the life; no one cometh unto the Father but by Me (*John* xiv. 6).

[7] In these and all other passages where "the Father" is mentioned, there is meant the Divine which was in the Lord from conception, and which, according to the Doctrine of Faith of the Christian world, was circumstanced as is the soul in the body with man. The Human itself from this Divine is the Son of God. Now as this Human was made Divine, therefore, in order to prevent man from approaching the Father only, and thereby in thought, faith, and thence in worship, separating the Father from the Lord in whom the Father is, after the Lord had taught that He and the Father are one; that the Father is in Him, and He in the Father; that all should abide in Him; and that no one cometh to the Father but by Him, He taught also that we must believe in Him, and that man is saved by a faith directed to Him. [8] Many in Christendom can form no idea of the fact that the Human in the Lord was made Divine, the chief reason of which is that they think of a man from his material body, and not from his spiritual body. And yet the truth is that all the angels (who are spiritual) are also men in a complete form; and, what is more, the whole Divine which proceeds from Jehovah God, from its first principles in heaven, down to its ultimate in this world, has a tendency to the human form.*

33. iv. *That the Lord made His Human Divine by means of temptations admitted into Himself, and by means of continual victories in them,* has been treated of above, n. 12–14; to which shall be·added only this: Temptations are nothing but combats against evils and falsities; and as evils and falsities are from hell, temptations are combats against hell. More-

---

* That angels are human forms, and that everything Divine has a tendency to the human form, may be seen in the work on *Heaven and Hell* (n. 73–77, 453–460), and more fully in the works which follow this present one, which will be from Angelic Wisdom concerning the Lord.

over with the men who are undergoing spiritual temptations, there are present evil spirits from hell, who induce them. The man is unaware that evil spirits induce the temptations; yet that they do so has been granted me to know from much experience. [2] This is the reason why man is drawn out of hell and elevated into heaven when from the Lord he conquers in temptations; and this again is why man becomes spiritual, and therefore an angel, by means of temptations, or combats against evils. The Lord, however, fought from His own power against all the hells, and completely mastered and subjugated them; and as He at the same time glorified His Human, He holds them so to eternity. [3] For before the Lord's advent the hells had grown up to such a height that they were beginning to infest the very angels of heaven, and also every man that came into the world and went out of it. The cause of so high a growth of the hells was the complete devastation of the church, and the consequent prevalence of idolatries which caused the men of this world to be in mere falsities and evils; and the hells are from men. Hence it was that no man could have been saved unless the Lord had come into the world. [4] Of these combats of the Lord the Psalms and Prophets treat much, but the Evangelists little. It is these combats which are meant by the temptations that the Lord endured, the last of which was the passion of the cross. And it is on account of them that the Lord is called Saviour and Redeemer. This is so far known in the church as to lead them to say that the Lord conquered death or the devil (that is, hell), and that He rose again victorious; and also that without the Lord there is no salvation. That the Lord also glorified His Human, and thereby became the Saviour, Redeemer, Reformer, and Regenerator to eternity, will be seen in what follows. [5] That by means of these combats or temptations the Lord has become our Saviour, is evident from the passages quoted above in n. 12–14; and also from this one in *Isaiah* :—

The day of vengeance is in Mine heart, and the year of My redeemed is come; I have trampled them in Mine anger, I have brought down their victory to the earth; so He became their Saviour (lxiii. 4, 6, 8). This chapter treats of the Lord's combats.

Also from this passage in *David*:—

Lift up your heads, ye gates; and be ye lifted up, ye doors of the world, that the King of glory may come in. Who is this King of glory? Jehovah mighty and a Hero, Jehovah a Hero of war (*Ps.* xxiv. 7, 8).

These words also treat of the Lord.

34. v. *That the full unition of the Divine and the Human in the Lord was effected by means of the passion of the cross, which was the last temptation,* has been established above in its proper chapter, where it has been shown that the Lord came into the world in order to subjugate the hells and glorify His Human, and that the passion of the cross was the last combat, by means of which He fully conquered the hells, and fully glorified His Human. Now as by the passion of the cross the Lord fully glorified His Human (that is, united it to His Divine, and thus made His Human also Divine), it follows that He is Jehovah and God as to both the Divine and the Human. And therefore in many passages in the Word He is called Jehovah, God, and the Holy One of Israel the Redeemer, Saviour, and Former. [2] As in the following:—

Mary said, My soul doth magnify THE LORD, and my spirit hath exulted in GOD MY SAVIOUR (*Luke* i. 46, 47).

The angel said to the shepherds, Behold, I bring you good tidings of great joy, which shall be to all people; that there is born this day, in the city of David, a Saviour, who is Christ the Lord (*Luke* ii. 10, 11).

They said, This is indeed the Christ, the Saviour of the world (*John* iv. 42).

I Jehovah God will help thee, and thy Redeemer is the Holy One of Israel (*Isa.* xli. 14).

Thus saith Jehovah thy Creator, O Jacob; and thy Former, O Israel; for I have redeemed thee. I am Jehovah thy God, the Holy One of Israel, thy Saviour (*Isa.* xliii. 1, 3).

Thus saith Jehovah your Redeemer, the Holy One of Israel: I am Jehovah your Holy One, the Creator of Israel, your King (*Isa.* xliii. 14, 15).

Thus saith Jehovah, the Holy One of Israel, and his Former (*Isa.* xlv. 11).

Thus saith Jehovah thy Redeemer, the Holy One of Israel (*Isa.* xlviii. 17).

That all flesh may know that I Jehovah am thy Saviour and thy Redeemer, the Mighty One of Jacob (*Isa.* xlix. 26).

Then shall the Redeemer come to Zion (*Isa.* lix. 20).

That thou mayest know that I Jehovah am thy Saviour and thy Redeemer, the Mighty One of Jacob (*Isa.* lx. 16).

Jehovah thy Former from the womb (*Isa.* xlix. 5).

Jehovah my Rock, and my Redeemer (*Ps.* xix. 14).

They remembered that God was their Rock, and the High God their Redeemer (*Ps.* lxxviii. 35).

Thus saith Jehovah thy Redeemer, and thy Former from the womb (*Isa.* xliv. 24).

As for our Redeemer, Jehovah of Armies is His name, the Holy One of Israel (*Isa.* xlvii. 4).

With mercy of eternity will I have mercy on thee, saith Jehovah thy Redeemer (*Isa.* liv. 8).

Their Redeemer is strong, Jehovah of Armies is His name (*Jer.* l. 34).

Let Israel hope in Jehovah, for with Jehovah there is mercy, and with Him is plenteous redemption; and He shall redeem Israel from all his iniquities (*Ps.* cxxx. 7, 8).

Jehovah is my Rock and my fortress; the horn of my salvation, my Saviour (2 *Sam.* xxii. 2, 3).

Thus saith Jehovah, the Redeemer of Israel, His Holy One, Kings shall see and stand, because of Jehovah who is faithful, the Holy One of Israel, who hath chosen thee (*Isa.* xlix. 7).

Surely God is in thee, and there is none else, there is no God. Verily Thou art a God that hidest Thyself, O God of Israel, the Saviour (*Isa.* xlv. 14, 15).

Thus saith Jehovah, the King of Israel, and his Redeemer Jehovah of Armies, Besides Me there is no God (*Isa.* xliv. 6).

I am Jehovah, and besides Me there is no Saviour (*Isa.* xliii. 11).

Am not I Jehovah? and there is no God else besides Me; and a Saviour, there is none besides Me (*Isa.* xlv. 21).

I am Jehovah thy God, and thou shalt know no God but Me, and besides Me there is no Saviour (*Hos.* xiii. 4).

Am not I Jehovah, and there is no other God besides Me; a just God and a Saviour, there is none besides Me: look unto Me and be ye saved, all the ends of the earth; for I am God, and there is none else (*Isa.* xlv. 21, 22).

Jehovah of Armies is His name, and thy Redeemer the Holy One of Israel, the God of the whole earth shall He be called (*Isa.* liv. 5).

[3] From these passages it may be seen that the Lord's Divine called "the Father" (and here "Jehovah" and "God"), and the Divine Human called "the Son" (and here "the Redeemer" and "Saviour," and also "the Former," which means the Reformer and Regenerator), are not two, but one. For not only is mention made of Jehovah, God, and the Holy One of Israel the Redeemer and Saviour, but the expression "Jehovah the Redeemer and Saviour" is used, and even "I am Jehovah the Saviour, and there is none besides Me." From this it is very evident that the Divine and the Human in the Lord are one Person; and that the Human also is Divine. For the Redeemer and Saviour of the world is no other than the Lord in respect to the Divine Human, and this is what is called the Son. Moreover redemption and salvation are an attribute proper to His Human, which is called merit and righteousness; for it was His Human that endured temptations and the passion of the cross; and therefore it was by means of His Human that He effected redemption and salvation. [4] As, therefore, after the unition of the Human with the Divine in Him, which was like that of the soul and body in man, they were no longer two but one Person (according to the Doctrine of the Christian world), it follows that the Lord is Jehovah and God as to both the Divine and the Human. And this therefore is why it is said on the one hand that Jehovah and the Holy One of Israel are the Redeemer and Saviour, and on the other that the Redeemer and Saviour are Jehovah, as may be seen from the passages that have been quoted. Thus it is said,

Christ the Saviour (*Luke* ii. 11 ; *John* iv. 42).

God and the God of Israel the Saviour and Redeemer (*Luke* i. 47 ; *Isa.* xlv. 15 ; liv. 5 ; *Ps.* lxxviii. 35).

Jehovah the Holy One of Israel the Saviour and Redeemer (*Isa.* xli. 14 ; xliii. 3, 11, 14, 15 ; xlviii. 17 ; xlix. 7 ; liv. 5).

Jehovah the Saviour, Redeemer, and Former (*Isa.* xliv. 6 ; xlvii. 4 ; xlix. 26 ; liv. 8 ; lxiii. 16 ; l. 34 ; *Ps.* xix. 14 ; cxxx. 7, 8 ; 2 *Sam.* xxii. 2, 3).

Jehovah God the Redeemer and Saviour, and besides Me there is none else (*Isa.* xliii. 11 ; xliv. 6 ; xlv. 14, 15, 21, 22 ; *Hos.* xiii. 4).

35. vi. *By successive steps the Lord put off the human taken from the mother, and put on a Human from the Divine within Him, which is the Divine Human, and is the Son of God.* That in the Lord were the Divine and the human, the Divine from Jehovah the Father, and the human from the virgin Mary, is known. Hence He was God and Man, having a Divine essence and a human nature; a Divine essence from the Father, and a human nature from the mother; and therefore was equal to the Father as to the Divine, and less than the Father as to the human. It is also known that this human nature from the mother was not transmuted into the Divine essence, nor commingled with it, for this is taught in the Doctrine of Faith which is called the Athanasian Creed. For a human nature cannot be transmuted into the Divine essence, nor can it be commingled therewith. [**2**] In accordance with the same creed is also our doctrine, that the Divine assumed the Human, that is, united itself to it, as a soul to its body, so that they were not two, but one Person. From this it follows that the Lord put off the human from the mother, which in itself was like that of another man, and thus material, and put on a Human from the Father, which in itself was like His Divine, and thus substantial, so that the Human too became Divine. This is why in the Word of the Prophets the Lord even as to the Human is called Jehovah, and God; and in the Word of the Evangelists, Lord, God, Messiah or Christ, and the Son of God in whom we must believe, and by whom we are to be saved. [**3**] As from His birth the Lord had a human from the mother, and as He by successive steps put it off, it follows that while He was in the world He had two states, the one called the state of humiliation or emptying out (*exinanitio*), and the other the state of glorification or unition with the Divine called the Father. He was in the state of humiliation at the time and in the degree that He was in the human from the mother; and in that of glorification at the time and in the degree that He was in the Human from the Father. In the state of humiliation He prayed to the Father as to one who was other than

Himself; but in the state of glorification He spoke with the Father as with Himself. In this latter state He said that the Father was in Him and He in the Father, and that the Father and He were one. But in the state of humiliation He underwent temptations, and suffered the cross, and prayed to the Father not to forsake Him. For the Divine could not be tempted, much less could it suffer the cross. From what has been said it is now evident that by means of temptations and continual victories in them, and by the passion of the cross which was the last of the temptations, the Lord completely conquered the hells, and fully glorified His Human, as has been shown above. [4] That the Lord put off the human taken from the mother, and put on a Human from the Divine in Himself called the Father, is evident also from the fact that whenever He addressed His mother directly, He did not call her Mother, but Woman. Only three times in the Evangelists do we read that He thus addressed or spoke of her, twice calling her Woman, and once not recognizing her as His mother. Of the two occasions when He called her Woman we read in *John*:—

The mother of Jesus said unto Him, They have no wine. Jesus saith unto her, Woman, what [belongs] to Me, and to thee? Mine hour is not yet come (ii. 3, 4).

When from the cross, Jesus sees His mother, and the disciple standing by whom He loved, He saith to His mother, Woman, behold thy son; and then He saith to the disciple, Behold thy mother (xix. 26, 27).

And of the one occasion when He did not recognize her, in *Luke*:—

It was told Jesus by certain who said, Thy mother and Thy brethren stand without, desiring to see Thee. Jesus answering said unto them, My mother and My brethren are these, who hear the Word of God, and do it (viii. 20, 21; *Matt.* xii. 46–49; *Mark* iii. 31–35).

In other places Mary is called His "mother," but not from His own mouth. [5] The same inference is confirmed by the fact that the Lord did not admit that He was the son of David. For we read in the Evangelists :—

Jesus asked the Pharisees, saying, What think ye of Christ? whose son is He? They say unto Him, The Son of David. He saith unto them, How then doth David in spirit call Him Lord, saying, The Lord said unto my Lord, Sit Thou on My right hand till I make Thine enemies Thy footstool? If then David calls Him Lord, how is He his son? And no one was able to answer Him a word (*Matt.* xxii. 41–46; *Mark* xii. 35–37; *Luke* xx. 41–44; *Ps.* cx. 1).

From what has been said it is evident that in respect to the glorified Human the Lord was the son neither of Mary nor of David. [6] Of what quality was His glorified Human, He showed to Peter, James, and John when transfigured before them :—

That His face shone as the sun, and His raiment was like the light; and then a voice out of the cloud said, This is My beloved Son, in whom I am well pleased, hear ye Him (*Matt.* xvii. 1–8; *Mark* ix. 2–8; *Luke* ix. 28–36).

The Lord was also seen by John as the sun shining in his strength (*Rev.* i. 16).

[7] That the Lord's Human was glorified, is evident from what is said about His glorification in the Evangelists :—

The hour is come that the Son of man should be glorified. Jesus said, Father, glorify Thy name : then came there a voice from heaven, saying, I both have glorified it and will glorify it again (*John* xii. 23, 28).

As the Lord was glorified by successive steps, it is said " I both have glorified it, and will glorify it again." Again in the same Evangelist :—

After Judas had gone out, Jesus said, Now is the Son of man glorified, and God is glorified in Him : God shall also glorify Him in Himself, and shall straightway glorify Him (*John* xiii. 31, 32).

Jesus said, Father, the hour is come ; glorify Thy Son, that Thy Son may also glorify Thee (*John* xvii. 1, 5).

And in *Luke :—*

Behooved it not the Christ to suffer this, and to enter into His glory ? (*Luke* xxiv. 26).

These things are said concerning His Human. [8] The reason the Lord said " God is glorified in Him," and " God shall glorify

Him in Himself," and also " Glorify Thy Son that Thy Son may also glorify Thee," is that the unition was reciprocal, being that of the Divine with the Human and of the Human with the Divine.   On this account He said also, " I am in the Father, and the Father in Me" (*John* xiv. 10, 11) ; and " All Mine are Thine, and Thine are Mine" (*John* xvii. 10) ; so that the unition was plenary.   It is the same with all unition—unless it is reciprocal, it is not. full.   Such therefore must also be the uniting of the Lord with man, and of man with the Lord.   As He teaches :—

In that day ye shall know that ye are in Me, and I in you (*John* xiv. 20).

Abide in Me, and I in you ; he that abideth in Me, and I in him, the same bringeth forth much fruit (*John* xv. 4, 5).

[9] As the Lord's Human was glorified, that is, made Divine, He rose again after death on the third day with His whole body, which does not take place with any man ; for a man rises again solely as to the spirit, and not as to the body.   In order that men may know, and no one doubt, that the Lord rose again with His whole body, He not only said so through the angels in the sepulchre, but also showed Himself to His disciples in His human body, saying to them when they believed that they saw a spirit :—

See My hands and My feet, that it is I Myself ; handle Me and see ; for a spirit hath not flesh and bones as ye see Me have ; and when He had thus spoken, He showed them His hands and His feet (*Luke* xxiv. 39, 40 ; *John* xx. 20).

And He said to Thomas, Reach hither thy finger, and behold My hands ; and reach hither thy hand, and thrust it into My side ; and be not faithless but believing ; then said Thomas, My Lord and my God (*John* xx. 27, 28).

[10] In order to evince still further that He was not a spirit but a Man, the Lord said to His disciples,

Have ye here any meat ?   And they gave Him a piece of a broiled fish, and of a honey-comb ; and He took it and did eat before them (*Luke* xxiv. 41–43).

As His body was no longer material, but Divine substantial, He came in to His disciples when the doors were shut (*John* xx. 19, 26) ; and after He had been seen He became invisible (*Luke* xxiv. 31). Being such, the Lord was then taken up, and sat at the right hand of God ; as we read :—

It came to pass that while Jesus blessed His disciples, He was parted from them, and carried up into heaven (*Luke* xxiv. 51).

After He had spoken unto them, He was carried up into heaven, and sat at the right hand of God (*Mark* xvi. 19).

To " sit at the right hand of God," signifies Divine omnipotence.

[**11**] As the Lord ascended into heaven, and sat at the right hand of God (by which is signified Divine omnipotence) with the Divine and the Human united into a one, it follows that His human substance or essence is just as is His Divine substance or essence. To think otherwise would be like thinking that His Divine was taken up into heaven and sat at the right hand of God, but not His Human together with it, which is contrary to Scripture, and also to the Christian Doctrine, which is that in Christ God and Man are like soul and body, and to separate these is contrary to sound reason. This unition of the Father with the Son, or of the Divine with the Human, is meant also in the following :—

I came forth from the Father, and am come into the world ; again I leave the world, and go to the Father (*John* xvi. 28).

I go away, and come to Him that sent Me (*John* vii. 33 ; xvi. 5, 16 ; xvii. 11, 13 ; xx. 17).

If then ye shall see the Son of man ascending where He was before (*John* vi. 62).

No one hath ascended into heaven but He that came down from heaven (*John* iii. 13).

Every man who is saved ascends into heaven, but not of himself. He ascends by the Lord's aid. The Lord alone ascended of Himself.

36. vii. *Thus God became Man, as in first principles so also in ultimates.* That God is a Man, and that every angel and every spirit is a man from God, has been partially shown in

the work on *Heaven and Hell,* and will be further shown in the
works entitled *Angelic Wisdom.* From the beginning, however,
God was a Man in first principles and not in ultimates; but
after He had assumed the Human in the world, He became a
Man in ultimates also. This follows from what has been already established—that the Lord united His Human to His
Divine, and thus made His Human Divine. It is from this
that the Lord is called the beginning and the end, the first and
the last, the Alpha and the Omega:—

I am the Alpha and the Omega, the beginning and the end, saith the
Lord, who is, and who was, and who is to come, the Almighty (*Rev.* i. 8,
11).

When John saw the Son of man in the midst of the seven lampstands,
he fell at His feet as dead; but He laid His right hand upon him, saying,
I am the first and the last (*Rev.* i. 13, 17; ii. 8; xxi. 6).

Behold, I come quickly, to give every one according to his work: I
am the Alpha and the Omega, the beginning and the end, the first and
the last (xxii. 12, 13).

Thus saith Jehovah the King of Israel, and his Redeemer Jehovah of
Armies, I am the first and the last (*Isa.* xliv. 6; xlviii. 12).

VIII.

The Lord is God Himself, from Whom and concerning Whom is the Word.

37. In chapter I. we undertook to show that universal Holy
Scripture treats of the Lord, and that the Lord is the Word.
This shall now be further shown from passages of the Word
in which the Lord is called "Jehovah," the "God of Israel
and of Jacob," the "Holy One of Israel," the "Lord," and
"God;" and also "King," "Jehovah's Anointed," and "David."
I may first mention that I have been permitted to run through
all the Prophets and the Psalms of David, and to examine
each verse and see what it treats of, and I have seen that the
only subjects treated of are: the church set up anew and to

be set up anew by the Lord; the advent, combats, glorification, redemption, and salvation, of the Lord; heaven from Him; and, with these, their opposites. As all these are works of the Lord, it became evident that universal Holy Scripture is concerning Him, and therefore that the Lord is the Word. [2] But this can be seen only by those who are in enlightenment from the Lord, and who also know the spiritual sense of the Word. All the angels of heaven are in this sense, and therefore when the Word is being read by a man, they so comprehend it. For spirits and angels are constantly with man, and as they are spiritual they understand spiritually all that a man understands naturally. That all Holy Scripture is concerning the Lord, may be obscurely seen, and as through a glass, darkly, from the passages of the Word already cited in chapter I. (n. 1–6), as also from those concerning the Lord now to be quoted, to show how frequently He is called the Lord [that is, Jehovah] and God; and from which it is apparent that it is He who spoke through the prophets, by whom it is everywhere said, " Jehovah spake," " Thus saith Jehovah," " The saying of Jehovah."

[3] That the Lord existed before His advent into the world, is evident from the following passages :—

John the Baptist said concerning the Lord, He it is who coming after me was before me, whose shoe's latchet I am not worthy to unloose. This is He of whom I said, After me cometh a man who was before me, for He was before me (*John* i. 27, 30).

They fell down before the throne (on which was the Lord) saying, We give Thee thanks, Lord God Almighty, who art, and who wast, and who art to come (*Rev.* xi. 16, 17).

Thou Bethlehem Ephratah, though thou be little among the thousands of Judah, out of thee shall He go forth unto Me that shall be Ruler in Israel, whose goings forth have been from of old, from the days of eternity (*Micah* v. 2).

The same is evident from the Lord's words in the Evangelists : that He " was before Abraham," that He had glory with the Father " before the foundation of the world," that He " had gone forth from the Father," and that " the Word was from the beginning with God," that "God was the Word," and that this "was made flesh."

That the Lord is called "Jehovah," the "God of Israel and of Jacob," the "Holy One of Israel," "God," and "Lord," and also "King," "Jehovah's Anointed," and "David," is evident from what now follows.

38. *That the Lord is called "Jehovah,"* is evident from these passages :—

Thus saith Jehovah thy Creator, O Jacob, and thy Former, O Israel, Fear not, for I have redeemed thee. I am Jehovah thy God, the Holy One of Israel, thy Saviour (*Isa.* xliii. 1, 3).

I am Jehovah your Holy One, the Creator of Israel, your King (verse 15).

The Holy One of Israel, and his Former, O God of Israel, the Saviour (*Isa.* xlv. 11, 15).

That all flesh may know that I Jehovah am thy Saviour and thy Redeemer, the Mighty One of Jacob (*Isa.* xlix. 26).

That thou mayest know that I Jehovah am thy Saviour and thy Redeemer, the Mighty One of Jacob (*Isa.* lx. 16).

Jehovah thy Former from the womb (*Isa.* xlix. 5).

Jehovah my Rock, and my Redeemer (*Ps.* xix. 14).

Thus saith Jehovah thy Maker and Former from the womb. Thus saith Jehovah the King of Israel, and his Redeemer, Jehovah of Armies (*Isa.* xliv. 2, 6).

As for our Redeemer, Jehovah of Armies is His name, the Holy One of Israel (*Isa.* xlvii. 4).

With the mercy of eternity will I have mercy on thee, saith Jehovah thy Redeemer (*Isa.* liv. 8).

Their Redeemer is strong, Jehovah of Armies is His name (*Jer.* i. 34).

Jehovah God, my Rock, my fortress, the horn of my salvation, my Saviour (2 *Sam.* xxii. 2, 3).

Thus saith Jehovah your Redeemer, the Holy One of Israel (*Isa.* xliii. 14; xlviii. 17).

Thus saith Jehovah the Redeemer of Israel, his Holy One, Kings shall see (*Isa.* xlix. 7).

I am Jehovah, and besides Me there is no Saviour (*Isa.* xliii. 11).

Am not I Jehovah, and there is none besides Me, and there is no Saviour besides Me. Look unto Me and be ye saved all the ends of the earth (*Isa.* xlv. 21, 22).

I am Jehovah thy God, and there is no Saviour besides Me (*Hos.* xiii. 4).

Thou hast redeemed me, O Jehovah God of truth (*Ps.* xxxi. 5).

Let Israel hope in Jehovah, for with Jehovah there is mercy, and with Him is plenteous redemption, and He shall redeem Israel from all his iniquities (*Ps.* cxxx. 7, 8).

Jehovah of Armies is His name, and thy Redeemer the Holy One of Israel, the God of the whole earth shall He be called (*Isa.* liv. 5).

In these passages Jehovah is called the "Redeemer and Saviour;" and as the Lord alone is the Redeemer and Saviour, it is He who is meant by "Jehovah." That the Lord is Jehovah, that is, that Jehovah is the Lord, is evident also from the following passages :—

There shall come forth a rod out of the stem of Jesse, and a shoot out of his roots shall bear fruit, and the Spirit of Jehovah shall rest upon Him (*Isa.* xi. 1, 2).

It shall be said in that day, Lo, this is our God ; we have waited for Him, and He will save us ; this is Jehovah, we have waited for Him ; we will rejoice and be glad in His salvation (*Isa.* xxv. 9).

The voice of him that crieth in the wilderness, Prepare ye the way of Jehovah, make plain in the solitude a pathway for our God. For the glory of Jehovah shall be revealed, and all flesh shall see it. Behold the Lord Jehovih shall come in strength, and His arm shall rule for Him (*Isa.* xl. 3, 5, 10).

I Jehovah will give thee for a covenant to the people, for a light of the nations. I am Jehovah, that is My name, and My glory will I not give to another (*Isa.* xlii. 6, 8).

Behold the days come that I will raise unto David a righteous offshoot, who shall reign a King, and shall prosper, and shall execute judgment and justice in the earth ; and this is His name whereby He shall be called, Jehovah our righteousness (*Jer.* xxiii. 5, 6 ; xxxiii. 15, 16).

Thou Bethlehem Ephratah, out of thee shall He go forth unto Me that shall be a Ruler in Israel ; He shall stand and feed [His flock] in the strength of Jehovah (*Micah* v. 2, 4).

Unto us a child is born, unto us a son is given, and the government shall be upon His shoulder, and His name shall be called God, Hero, the Father of eternity, upon the throne of David to establish and to found it in judgment and in justice, from henceforth and even to eternity (*Isa.* ix. 6, 7).

Jehovah shall go forth and fight against the nations ; and His feet shall stand upon the Mount of Olives before the faces of Jerusalem (*Zech.* xiv. 3, 4).

Lift up your heads, O ye gates; and be ye lifted up, ye doors of the world, that the King of glory may come in.   Who is this King of glory ? Jehovah strong and a Hero, Jehovah a Hero of war (*Ps.* xxiv. 7–10).

In that day shall Jehovah of Armies be for a crown of ornament, and for a diadem of beauty, unto the residue of His people (*Isa.* xxviii. 5).

I will send you Elijah the prophet, before the coming of the great day of Jehovah (*Mal.* iv. 5).

Not to mention other passages where mention is made of the great and near day of Jehovah; as *Ezek.* xxx. 3; *Joel* ii. 11; *Amos* v. 18, 20; *Zeph.* i. 14, 15, 18.

39. ii. *That the Lord is called "the God of Israel," and "the God of Jacob,"* is evident from the following passages :—

Moses took the blood and sprinkled it upon the people, and said, Behold the blood of the covenant which Jehovah hath made with you. And they saw the God of Israel, under whose feet was as it were a work of sapphire stone, and as it were the substance of heaven (*Exod.* xxiv. 8, 10).

The multitude wondered when they saw the dumb speaking, the lame walking, and the blind seeing; and they glorified the God of Israel (*Matt.* xv. 31).

Blessed be the Lord God of Israel, for He hath visited and wrought deliverance for His people Israel, when He raised up a horn of salvation for us in the house of David (*Luke* i. 68, 69).

I will give thee the treasures of darkness, and hidden riches of secret places, that thou mayest know that I Jehovah, who have called thee by thy name, am the God of Israel (*Isa.* xlv. 3).

O house of Jacob, who swear in the name of Jehovah, and of the God of Israel; for they are called of the city of holiness, and stay themselves upon the God of Israel, Jehovah of Armies is His name (*Isa.* xlviii. 1, 2).

Jacob shall see his children in the midst of him, they shall sanctify My name, and they shall sanctify the Holy One of Jacob, they shall fear the God of Israel (*Isa.* xxix. 23).

In the end of the days many people shall go and say, Come ye and let us go up to the mountain of Jehovah, to the house of the God of Jacob, who shall teach us of His ways, that we may walk in His paths (*Isa.* ii. 2, 3; *Micah* iv. 1, 2).

That all flesh may know that I Jehovah am thy Saviour and thy Redeemer, the Mighty One of Jacob (*Isa.* xlix. 26).

I Jehovah am thy Saviour and thy Redeemer, the Mighty One of Jacob (*Isa.* lx. 16).

Thou art in pain, O earth, before the Lord, before the God of Jacob (*Ps.* cxiv. 7).

David sware to Jehovah, he vowed to the Mighty One of Jacob, Surely I will not come into the tent of my house, until I find out a place for Jehovah, a habitation for the Mighty One of Jacob; we have heard of Him at Ephratah (Bethlehem) (*Ps.* cxxxii. 2, 3, 5, 6).

Blessed be the God of Israel; the whole earth shall be filled with His glory (*Ps.* lxxii. 18, 19).

Not to quote those passages in which the Lord is called the God of Israel the Redeemer and Saviour; as *Luke* i. 47; *Isa.* xlv. 15; liv. 5; *Ps.* lxxviii. 35.

Besides many other passages, in which He is called the God of Israel only; as *Isa.* xvii. 6; xxi. 10, 17; xxiv. 15; xxix. 23; *Jer.* vii. 3; ix. 15; xi. 3; xiii. 12; xvi. 9; xix. 3, 15; xxiii. 2; xxiv. 5; xxv. 15, 27; xxix. 4, 8, 21, 25; xxx. 2; xxxi. 23; xxxii. 14, 15, 36; xxxiii. 4; xxxiv. 2, 13; xxxv. 13, 17, 18, 19; xxxvii. 7; xxxviii. 17; xxxix. 16; xlii. 9, 15, 18; xliii. 10; xliv. 2, 7, 11, 25; xlviii. 1; l. 18; li. 33; *Ezek.* viii. 4; ix. 3; x. 19, 20; xi. 22; xliii. 2; xliv. 2; *Zeph.* ii. 9; *Ps.* xli. 13; lix. 5; lxviii. 8.

40. iii. *That the Lord is called " the Holy One of Israel,"* is evident from these passages :—

The angel said to Mary, That Holy thing which shall be born of thee shall be called the Son of God (*Luke* i. 35).

I saw in the visions, and behold, a Watcher and a Holy One came down from heaven (*Dan.* iv. 13, 23).

God came from Teman, and the Holy One from Mount Paran (*Hab.* iii. 3).

I am Jehovah your Holy One, the Creator of Israel, your King (*Isa.* xliii. 15).

The Holy One of Israel, and his Former (*Isa.* xlv. 11).

Thus saith Jehovah, the Redeemer of Israel, His Holy One (*Isa.* xlix. 7).

I am Jehovah thy God, the Holy One of Israel thy Saviour (*Isa.* xliii. 3).

As for our Redeemer, Jehovah of Armies is His name, the Holy One of Israel (*Isa.* xlvii. 4).

Thus saith Jehovah your Redeemer, the Holy One of Israel (*Isa.* xliii. 14; xlviii. 17).

Jehovah of Armies is His name, and thy Redeemer the Holy One of Israel (*Isa.* liv. 5).

They tempted God, and the Holy One of Israel (*Ps.* lxxviii. 41).

They have forsaken Jehovah, and have provoked the Holy One of Israel (*Isa.* i. 4).

They have said, Cause the Holy One of Israel to cease from our faces; wherefore thus saith the Holy One of Israel (*Isa.* xxx. 11, 12).

Who say, Let Him hasten His work that we may see, and let the counsel of the Holy One of Israel draw nigh and come (*Isa.* v. 19).

In that day they shall stay upon Jehovah, the Holy One of Israel, in truth (*Isa.* x. 20).

Cry out and shout, O daughter of Zion, for great is the Holy One of Israel in the midst of thee (*Isa.* xii. 6).

The saying of the God of Israel, In that day shall a man look to his Maker, and his eyes shall have respect to the Holy One of Israel (*Isa.* xvii. 6, 7).

The meek shall increase their joy in Jehovah, and the needy among men shall rejoice in the Holy One of Israel (*Isa.* xxix. 19 ; xli. 16).

Nations shall run unto thee because of Jehovah thy God, and because of the Holy One of Israel (*Isa.* lv. 5).

The isles shall confide in Me, to bring thy sons from far, unto the name of Jehovah of Armies, and to the Holy One of Israel (*Isa.* lx. 9).

The land is full of guilt against the Holy One of Israel (*Jer.* li. 5).

Babylon hath been proud against Jehovah, against the Holy One of Israel (*Jer.* i. 29).

(Besides many other passages.)

By "the Holy One of Israel" is meant the Lord as to the Divine Human ; for the angel Gabriel said to Mary, "That Holy thing which shall be born of thee shall be called the Son of God" (*Luke* i. 35). That Jehovah and the Holy One of Israel, although distinctively mentioned, are one and the same, is evident from the passages here quoted, in which it is said that Jehovah is that Holy One of Israel.

41. iv. *That the Lord is called "Lord" and "God,"* is evident from so many passages that if quoted they would fill pages. Let these few suffice :—

When by the Lord's command Thomas had seen His hands and touched His side, he said, My Lord and my God (*John* xx. 27, 28).

They remembered that God was their Rock, and the High God their Redeemer (*Ps.* lxxviii. 35).

Jehovah of Armies is His name, and thy Redeemer the Holy One of Israel, the God of the whole earth shall He be called (*Isa.* liv. 5).

The same is evident from the fact that they adored Him, and fell upon their faces before Him (*Matt.* ix. 18 ; xiv. 33 ; xv. 25 ; xxviii. 9 ; *Mark* i. 40 ; v. 22 ; vii. 25 ; x. 17 ; *Luke* xvii. 15, 16 ; *John* ix. 38).

So in *David* :—

We heard of Him at Ephratah ; we will enter into His dwelling places, and will bow ourselves at His footstool (*Ps.* cxxxii. 6, 7).

And it is the same in heaven :—

I was in the spirit, and behold a throne was set in heaven, and one sat on the throne like a jasper and sardine stone, and there was a rainbow round about the throne, in sight like unto an emerald. And the four and twenty elders fell down before Him that sat on the throne, and adored Him that liveth for ever and ever, and cast their crowns before the throne (*Rev.* iv. 2, 3, 10).

I saw in the right hand of Him that sat upon the throne a book sealed within and on the back side, sealed with seven seals, and no one was able to open the book. Then one of the elders said, Behold the Lion of the tribe of Judah, the root of David, hath prevailed to open the book, and to loose the seven seals thereof ; and I beheld in the midst of the throne a Lamb standing, and He came and took the book, and they fell down before the Lamb, and worshiped Him that liveth for ever and ever (v. 1, 3, 5–8, 14).

42. v. *The reason why the Lord is called " King" and " the Anointed,"* is that He was the Messiah, or Christ ; and " Messiah" or " Christ" means the king and the anointed. This is why, in the Word, the Lord is meant by " king," and also by " David," who was king over Judah and Israel. That the Lord is called " king" and " Jehovah's anointed," is evident from many passages in the Word :—

The Lamb shall overcome them ; for He is Lord of lords and King of kings (*Rev.* xvii. 14).

He that sat upon the white horse had on His vesture a name written, King of kings and Lord of lords (xix. 16).

It is from the Lord's being called a " king," that heaven and the church are called His " kingdom," and that His advent into the world is called " the Gospel of the kingdom." That heaven and the church are called His kingdom, may be seen in *Matt.* xii. 28 ; xvi. 28 ; *Mark* i. 14, 15 ; ix. 1 ; xv. 43 ; *Luke* i. 33 ; iv. 43 ; viii. 1, 10 ; ix. 2, 11, 60 ; x. 11 ; xvi. 16 ; xix. 11 ; xxi. 31 ; xxii. 18 ; xxiii. 51. And in *Daniel :—*

God shall set up a kingdom which shall never be destroyed ; it shall break in pieces and consume all these kingdoms, and it shall stand for ever (ii. 44).

I saw in the night visions, and behold one like the Son of man came with the clouds of the heavens. And there was given Him dominion, and glory, and a kingdom, that all peoples, nations, and languages should worship Him; His dominion is an everlasting dominion, and His kingdom that which shall not be destroyed (vii. 13, 14, 27).

That His advent is called "the Gospel of the kingdom," may be seen in *Matt.* iv. 23; ix. 35; xxiv. 14.

43. vi. *That the Lord is called "David,"* is evident from these passages :—

In that day they shall serve Jehovah their God, and David their king, whom I will raise up to them (*Jer.* xxx. 8, 9).

Afterwards the sons of Israel shall return, and shall seek Jehovah their God, and David their king, and shall come with fear to Jehovah, and to His goodness in the end of days (*Hos.* iii. 5).

I will raise up one shepherd over them, who shall feed them ; My servant David, he shall feed them, and he shall be their shepherd : and I Jehovah will be their God, and My servant David a prince in the midst of them (*Ezek.* xxxiv. 23, 24).

That they may be My people, and that I may be their God ; and David My servant shall be king over them, that they may all have one shepherd ; then shall they dwell upon the land, they and their sons and their sons' sons, even to eternity ; and David shall be their prince to eternity ; and I will make a covenant of peace, and it shall be a covenant of eternity with them (*Ezek.* xxxvii. 23–26).

I will make a covenant of eternity with you, the sure mercies of David : behold, I have given him for a witness to the people, a prince and a lawgiver to the nations (*Isa.* lv. 3, 4).

In that day I will raise up the tent of David that is fallen, and close up the breaches thereof ; I will restore his ruins, and will build it as in the days of eternity (*Amos* ix. 11).

The house of David shall be as God, as the angel of Jehovah before them (*Zech.* xii. 8).

In that day there shall be a fountain open to the house of David (*Zech.* xiii. 1).

44. He who knows that the Lord is meant by David, may know why David so frequently wrote of the Lord in his Psalms while writing about himself ; as in these words :—

I have made a covenant with My chosen, I have sworn unto David My servant ; thy seed will I establish to eternity, and will build up thy

throne to generation and generation ; and the heavens shall confess thy
wonder, thy truth also in the congregation of the saints. Thou spakest
in vision to Thine holy one and saidst, I have laid help upon one that is
mighty, I have exalted one chosen out of the people, I have found David
My servant, with My holy oil have I anointed him, with whom My hand
shall be established, Mine arm also shall strengthen him, My truth and
My mercy shall be with him, and in My name shall his horn be exalted,
I will set his hand in the sea, and his right hand in the rivers. He shall
cry unto Me, Thou art my Father, my God, and the rock of my salvation.
I will also make him My first-born, higher than the kings of the earth ;
My covenant shall stand fast with him ; his seed will I make to endure
to eternity, and his throne as the days of the heavens. Once have I
sworn by My holiness that I will not lie unto David ; his seed shall endure to eternity, and his throne as the sun before Me ; it shall be established to eternity as the moon, and a faithful witness in the clouds (*Ps.*
lxxxix. 3–5, 19–21, 24–29, 35–37).

And so in other Psalms, as *Ps.* xlv. 1–17 ; cxxii. 4, 5 ; cxxxii. 8–18.

IX.

GOD IS ONE, AND THE LORD IS THAT GOD.

45. From the numerous passages quoted from the Word in
the preceding chapter, it is evident that the Lord is called
Jehovah, the God of Israel and of Jacob, the Holy One of Israel, Lord, and God, and also King, the Anointed, and David,
from which it may be seen, as yet however as through a glass,
darkly, that the Lord is God Himself, from and about whom
is the Word. Now it is known in the whole world that God
is one, and no man possessed of sound reason denies it. It
remains therefore to confirm this from the Word ; and, in ad-
dition, that the Lord is that God.

i. *That God is one,* is confirmed by these passages of the
Word :—

Jesus said, The first of all the commandments is, Hear, O Israel, The
Lord our God is one Lord ; therefore thou shalt love the Lord thy God
with all thy heart, and with all thy soul (*Mark* xii. 29, 30).

Hear, O Israel, Jehovah our God is one Jehovah ; and thou shalt love Jehovah thy God with all thy heart, and with all thy soul (*Deut.* vi. 4, 5).

One came unto Jesus and said, Good Master, what good thing shall I do that I may have eternal life ?   Jesus said unto him, Why callest thou Me good ?   There is none good but the one God (*Matt.* xix. 16, 17).

That all the kingdoms of the earth may know that Thou alone art Jehovah (*Isa.* xxxvii. 20).

I am Jehovah and there is none else ; there is no God besides Me : that they may know from the rising of the sun, and from the west, that there is no God besides Me : I am Jehovah and there is none else (*Isa.* xlv. 5, 6).

O Jehovah of Armies, God of Israel, that dwellest on the cherubim, Thou art the God, even Thou alone, over all the kingdoms of the earth (*Isa.* xxxvii. 16).

Is there a God besides Me ? and a Rock ? I know not any (*Isa.* xliv. 8).

Who is God save Jehovah ? and who is a Rock save our God ? (*Ps.* xviii. 31).

ii. *That the Lord is that God,* is confirmed by these passages of the Word :—

Surely God is in thee, and there is none else, there is no God.   Verily Thou art a God that hidest Thyself, O God of Israel, the Saviour (*Isa.* xlv. 14, 15).

Have not I Jehovah ? and there is no God else besides Me, a just God and a Saviour, there is none besides Me.   Look unto Me that ye may be saved, all the ends of the earth ; for I am God, and there is none else (*Isa.* xlv. 21, 22).

I am Jehovah, and besides Me there is no Saviour (*Isa.* xliii. 11).

I am Jehovah thy God, and thou shalt acknowledge no God but Me ; for there is no Saviour besides Me (*Hos.* xiii. 4).

Thus saith Jehovah the King of Israel, and his Redeemer Jehovah of Armies, I am the First and I am the Last, and besides Me there is no God (*Isa.* xliv. 6).

Jehovah of Armies is His name, and thy Redeemer the Holy One of Israel ; the God of the whole earth shall He be called (*Isa.* liv. 5).

In that day Jehovah shall be king over all the earth ; in that day there shall be one Jehovah, and His name one (*Zech.* xiv. 9).

As the Lord alone is the Saviour and the Redeemer, and as it is said that Jehovah is that Saviour and Redeemer, and that there is none besides Him, it follows that the one God is no other than the Lord.

X.

THE HOLY SPIRIT IS THE DIVINE PROCEEDING FROM THE
LORD, AND THIS IS THE LORD HIMSELF.

46. Jesus has said in *Matthew* :—

All power (*potestas*) is given unto Me in heaven and on earth ; go ye
therefore and make disciples of all nations, baptizing them into the name
of the Father, and of the Son, and of the Holy Spirit ; teaching them to
observe all things whatsoever I have commanded you ; and lo I am with
you all the days even to the consummation of the age (xxviii. 18–20).

It has already been shown that the Divine called "the Father," and the Divine called "the Son," are a one in the Lord ;
and it shall now be shown that "the Holy Spirit" is the same
as the Lord. [**2**] The reason why the Lord said that they
were to baptize into the name of the Father and of the Son
and of the Holy Spirit, is that there is in the Lord a trine or
trinity ; for there is the Divine called the Father, the Divine
Human called the Son, and the proceeding Divine called the
Holy Spirit. The Divine called the Father, and the Divine
called the Son, are the Divine *ex Quo ;** and the proceeding
Divine is the Divine *per Quod.†*   That the Divine which proceeds from the Lord is no other than the Divine which is
Himself, will be seen in the treatises on the *Divine Providence,
Omnipotence, Omnipresence,* and *Omniscience ;‡* for it is a matter of deep investigation. [**3**] That there is a trine in the
Lord may be illustrated by comparison with an angel, who
has a soul and a body, and also a proceeding. That which
proceeds from him is himself outside of him. I have been
permitted to learn many things about this proceeding, but this
is not the place to present them. [**4**] After death the first
thing the angels teach every man who looks to God is that the

---

* *Literally*, the Divine from which ; that is, the Divine which is the source. [TR.]

† *Literally*, the Divine by means of which ; that is, the Divine which is the in-
strument or executive agency. [TR.]

‡ See foot-note to Author's preface. [TR.]

Holy Spirit is not any other than the Lord; and that "to go forth" and "to proceed" is nothing else than to enlighten and teach by the presence, which is according to the reception, of the Lord.   The result is that after death very many people put away the idea they had formed in this world about the Holy Spirit, and receive the idea that it is the Lord's presence with man through angels and spirits, by and according to which the man is enlightened and taught.   [5] Moreover, it is usual in the Word to name two Divines, and sometimes three, which yet are one; as Jehovah and God, Jehovah and the Holy One of Israel, Jehovah and the Mighty One of Jacob, and also God and the Lamb.   And as these are one, it is said in other places, Jehovah alone is God, Jehovah alone is holy, and He is the Holy One of Israel, and there is none besides Him; and also instead of God it is sometimes said the Lamb, and instead of the Lamb, God; this is done in the *Revelation ;* the other expressions occur in the Prophets.   [6] That it is the Lord only who is meant by the Father, Son, and Holy Spirit in *Matt.* xxviii. 19, is evident from what there precedes and what follows.   In the preceding verse the Lord says, "All power is given unto Me in heaven and on earth," and in the following verse He says, "Lo, I am with you all the days, even to the consummation of the age;" thus He speaks of Himself only, so that He spoke in that manner [about the Father, Son, and Holy Spirit] to make His disciples aware that there is a trinity in Him.   [7] In order that it may be known that the Holy Spirit is not a Divine other than the Lord Himself, it shall be shown what is meant by "spirit" in the Word.   By "spirit" is meant, i. Man's life in general.   ii. As man's life varies according to his state, by "spirit" is meant the varying affection of life in man.   iii. Also the life of one who is regenerate, which is called spiritual life.   iv. But where "spirit" is said of the Lord, His Divine life is meant, thus the Lord Himself. v. Specifically, the life of His wisdom, which is called the Divine truth.   vi. Jehovah Himself, that is, the Lord, spoke the Word through the prophets.

47. i. *That by " spirit" is meant man's life,* is evident from ordinary discourse, in which it is said that a man, when he dies, yields up his spirit, so that by "spirit" in this sense is meant the life of the respiration, and in fact the term "spirit" is derived from the respiration, and this is why, in the Hebrew language, there is one word for both "spirit" and "wind." There are in man two fountains of life, one is the motion of the heart, and the other is the respiration of the lungs. The life from the respiration of the lungs is what is properly meant by "spirit" and also by "soul." That this acts as one with the man's thought from the understanding, and that the life from the heart's motion acts as one with his will's love, will be seen in its own place. That man's life is meant in the Word by "spirit," is evident from these passages :—

Thou gatherest in their breath (*spiritum*), they expire, and return into dust (*Ps.* civ. 29).

He remembered that they were flesh, a wind (*spiritus*) that passeth away, and cometh not again (*Ps.* lxxviii. 39).

When his breath has gone forth, he will return into earth (*Ps.* cxlvi. 4).

Hezekiah lamented that the life of his spirit should go forth (*Isa.* xxxviii. 16).

The spirit of Jacob revived (*Gen.* xlv. 27).

A molten image is falsehood, and there is no breath in it (*Jer.* li. 17).

The Lord Jehovih said to the dry bones, I will cause breath to enter into you, that ye may live. Come from the four winds O breath, and breathe upon these slain, and they shall live ; and the breath came into them, and they revived (*Ezek.* xxxvii. 5, 6, 9, 10).

Jesus took the daughter [of Jairus] by the hand, and her spirit returned, and she rose up immediately (*Luke* viii. 54, 55).

48. ii. *As man's life varies according to his state, by "spirit" is meant the varying affection of life in man.* As, 1 : *The life of wisdom :—*

Bezaleel was filled with the spirit of wisdom, intelligence, and knowledge (*Exod.* xxxi. 3).

Thou shalt speak unto all that are wise-hearted, whom I have filled with the spirit of wisdom (*Exod.* xxviii. 3).

Joshua was filled with the spirit of wisdom (*Deut.* xxxiv. 9).

Nebuchadnezzar said of Daniel [in whom is the spirit of the holy gods. The queen said] that an excellent spirit of knowledge, intelligence, and wisdom was in him (*Dan.* iv. 8 ; v. 12).

They that erred in spirit shall know intelligence (*Isa.* xxix. 24).

2. *The excitation of life :—*

Jehovah hath stirred up the spirit of the kings of Media (*Jer.* li. 11).

Jehovah hath stirred up the spirit of Zerubbabel, and the spirit of all the remnant of the people (*Haggai* i. 14).

I will put a spirit in the king of Assyria, that he may hear a rumor, and shall return into his own land (*Isa.* xxxvii. 7).

Jehovah hardened the spirit of Sihon the king (*Deut.* ii. 30).

That which cometh up upon your spirit shall not be at all (*Ezek.* xx. 32).

3. *Freedom of life :—*

[It is said of] the four living creatures (which were cherubs) seen by the prophet, Whithersoever the spirit was to go, they went (*Ezek.* i. 12, 20).

4. *Life in fear, pain or grief, and anger :—*

That every heart may melt, and all hands be let down, and every spirit be faint (*Ezek.* xxi. 7).

My spirit hath failed upon me ; my heart is amazed in the midst of me (*Ps.* cxlii. 3 ; cxliii. 4).

My spirit is consumed (*Ps.* cxliii. 7).

As for me Daniel, my spirit was grieved (*Dan.* vii. 15).

The spirit of Pharaoh was troubled (*Gen.* xli. 8).

Nebuchadnezzar said, My spirit was troubled (*Dan.* ii. 3).

I went in sadness in the heat of my spirit (*Ezek.* iii. 14).

5. *A life of various evil affections :—*

Provided that in his spirit there is no guile (*Ps.* xxxii. 2).

Jehovah hath mingled a spirit of perversities in the midst thereof (*Isa.* xix. 14).

He said to the foolish prophets that go away after their own spirit (*Ezek.* xiii. 3).

The prophet is a fool, the man [that hath a] spirit is mad (*Hos.* ix. 7).

Take ye heed to your spirit, and deal not treacherously (*Mal.* ii. 16).

The spirit of whoredoms hath led them astray (*Hos.* iv. 12).

The spirit of whoredoms is in the midst of them (*Hos.* v. 4).

When the spirit of jealousy hath passed upon him (*Num.* v. 14).

A man who wandereth in spirit and chattereth a lie (*Micah* ii. 11).

A generation whose spirit was not steadfast with God (*Ps.* lxxviii. 8).

Jehovah hath poured out upon you the spirit of deep sleep (*Isa.* xxix. 10).

Ye shall conceive chaff, ye shall bring forth stubble ; as for your spirit, fire shall devour you (*Isa.* xxxiii. 11).

6. *Infernal life :—*

I will cause the unclean spirit to pass out of the land (*Zech.* xiii. 2).

When the unclean spirit is gone out of a man, he walketh through dry places, and he afterwards joineth to himself seven spirits worse than himself, and they enter in and dwell there (*Matt.* xii. 43–45).

Babylon is become the hold of every foul spirit (*Rev.* xviii. 2).

7. *Besides the infernal spirits themselves by whom men are troubled :—*

Matt. viii. 16 ; x. 1 ; xii. 43–45 ; *Mark* i. 23–27 ; ix. 17–29 ; *Luke* iv. 33, 36 ; vi. 17, 18 ; vii. 21 ; viii. 2, 29 ; ix. 39, 42, 55 ; xi. 24–26 ; xiii. 11 ; *Rev.* xiii. 15 ; xvi. 13, 14.

49. iii. *That by "spirit" is meant the life of one who is regenerate, which is called spiritual life :—*

Jesus said, Except a man be born of water and of the spirit, he cannot enter into the kingdom of God (*John* iii. 5).

I will give you a new heart, and a new spirit. I will put My spirit within you, and cause you to walk in My statutes (*Ezek.* xxxvi. 26, 27).

To give a new heart and a new spirit (*Ezek.* xi. 19).

Create in me a clean heart, O God, and renew a steadfast spirit within me. Restore unto me the joy of Thy salvation, and let a willing spirit uphold me (*Ps.* li. 10, 12).

Make you a new heart, and a new spirit ; for why will ye die, O house of Israel (*Ezek.* xviii. 31).

Thou sendest forth Thy spirit, they are created, and Thou renewest the faces of the earth (*Ps.* civ. 30).

The hour cometh, and now is, when the true worshipers shall worship the Father in spirit and in truth (*John* iv. 23).

Jehovah God giveth breath (*animam*) to the people, and spirit to them that walk therein (*Isa.* xlii. 5).

Jehovah formeth the spirit of man in the midst of him (*Zech.* xii. 1).

With my soul have I awaited Thee in the night ; with my spirit in the midst of me have I awaited Thee in the morning (*Isa.* xxvi. 9).

In that day shall Jehovah be for a spirit of judgment to him that sitteth in judgment (*Isa.* xxviii. 5, 6).

My spirit hath rejoiced in God my Saviour (*Luke* i. 47).

They have quieted my spirit in the land of the north (*Zech.* vi. 8).

Into Thy hand I commend my spirit ; Thou hast redeemed me (*Ps.* xxxi. 5).

Did not He make one, and the rest in whom was spirit ? (*Mal.* ii. 15).

After three days and a half the spirit of life from God entered into the two witnesses that had been killed by the beast (*Rev.* xi. 11).

I Jehovah the former of the mountains, and the creator of the wind (*spiritus*) (*Amos* iv. 13).

O God, the God of the spirits as to all flesh (*Num.* xvi. 22 ; xxvii. 18).

I will pour upon the house of David, and upon the inhabitant of Jerusalem, the spirit from on high (*Zech.* xii. 10).

Until He hath poured upon us the spirit from on high (*Isa.* xxxii. 15).

I will pour waters upon him that is thirsty, and brooks upon the dry [ground], I will pour My spirit upon thy seed (*Isa.* xliv. 3).

I will pour My spirit upon all flesh, also upon the servants and the handmaids ; in those days will I pour out My spirit (*Joel* ii. 28, 29). (To pour out the spirit means to regenerate ; as does also to give a new heart and a new spirit.)

[**2**] *That by " spirit" is meant spiritual life in those who are in humiliation :—*

I dwell in a contrite and humble spirit, and to revive the spirit of the humble, and to revive the heart of the contrite ones (*Isa.* lvii. 15).

The sacrifices of God are a broken spirit, a broken and contrite heart, O God, Thou wilt not despise (*Ps.* li. 17).

He will give the oil of joy for mourning, and the garment of praise for the spirit of heaviness (*Isa.* lxi. 3).

A woman forsaken and grieved in spirit (*Isa.* liv. 6).

Blessed are the poor in spirit, for theirs is the kingdom of the heavens. (*Matt.* v. 3).

50. iv. *That where " spirit" is said of the Lord, there is meant His Divine life, thus the Lord Himself,* is evident from these passages :—

He whom the Father hath sent speaketh the words of God, for God hath not given the spirit by measure unto Him ; the Father loveth the Son, and hath given all things into His hand (*John* iii. 34, 35).

There shall go forth a rod out of the stem of Jesse, and the spirit of Jehovah shall rest upon Him, the spirit of wisdom and intelligence, the spirit of counsel and might (*Isa.* xi. 1, 2).

I have put My spirit upon Him, He shall bring forth judgment to the nations (*Isa.* xlii. 1).

When the enemy shall come as a pent-up stream, the spirit of Jehovah shall lift up a standard against him ; then shall the Redeemer come to Zion (*Isa.* lix. 19, 20).

The spirit of the Lord Jehovih is upon Me ; Jehovah hath anointed Me to preach good tidings to the poor (*Isa.* lxi. 1 ; *Luke* iv. 18).

Jesus knowing in His spirit that they so reasoned within themselves (*Mark* ii. 8).

Jesus exulted in spirit, and said (*Luke* x. 21).

Jesus was troubled in His spirit (*John* xiii. 21).

Jesus sighed in His spirit (*Mark* viii. 12).

[2] *"Spirit"* as used for Jehovah Himself, that is, the Lord :—

God is a Spirit (*John* iv. 24).

Who hath directed the Spirit of Jehovah, or who is a man of His counsel ? (*Isa.* xl. 13).

The Spirit of Jehovah led them by the hand of Moses (*Isa.* lxiii. 12, (4).

Whither shall I go from Thy Spirit, and whither shall I flee ? (*Ps.* xxxix. 7).

Jehovah said, Not by might, but by My Spirit shall he do it (*Zech.* iv. 6).

They provoked the Spirit of His holiness, therefore He was turned to be their enemy (*Isa.* lxiii. 10 ; *Ps.* cvi. 33, 40).

My Spirit shall not strive with man for ever, for he is flesh (*Gen.* vi. 3).

I will not contend to eternity, for the Spirit should fail before Me (*Isa.* lvii. 16).

The blasphemy against the Holy Spirit shall not be forgiven ; but he who shall speak a word against the Son of man, it shall be forgiven (*Matt.* xii. 31, 32 ; *Mark* iii. 28–30 ; *Luke* xii. 10).

"Blasphemy against the Holy Spirit," is blasphemy against the Lord's Divine ; "a word against the Son of man," is something said against the Word by wrongly interpreting its meaning ; for "the Son of man" is the Lord in respect to the Word, as has been shown above.

51. v. *That by " spirit," when said of the Lord, is specifically meant the life of His wisdom, which is Divine Truth :—*

I tell you the truth, it is expedient for you that I go away, for if I go not away the Comforter will not come unto you, but if I go away I will send Him unto you (*John* xvi. 7).

When He, the Spirit of Truth, is come, He will lead you into all truth. He shall not speak from Himself ; but whatsoever He shall hear, that shall He speak (*John* xvi. 13).

He shall glorify Me, for He shall receive of Mine, and shall declare it unto you : all things that the Father hath are Mine ; therefore said I that He shall receive of Mine and shall declare it unto you (*John* xvi. 14, 15).

I will ask the Father, that He may give you another Comforter, the Spirit of Truth, whom the world cannot receive, because it seeth Him not, neither knoweth Him ; but ye know Him, for He abideth with you, and shall be in you : I will not leave you orphans, I come to you, and ye shall see Me (*John* xiv. 16–19).

When the Comforter is come, whom I will send unto you from the Father, even the Spirit of Truth, He shall testify of Me (*John* xv. 26).

Jesus cried, saying, If any one thirst let him come unto Me and drink ; he that believeth in Me, as the Scripture hath said, out of his belly shall flow streams of living water. This He said of the spirit which they that believe in Him should receive. For the Holy Spirit was not yet, because Jesus was not yet glorified (*John* vii. 37–39).

Jesus breathed on His disciples, and said, Receive ye the Holy Spirit (*John* xx. 22).

[2] That by the " Comforter," the " Spirit of Truth," and the " Holy Spirit," the Lord meant Himself, is evident from His words—that " the world did not as yet know Him," for they did not as yet know the Lord. And when He said that He " would send it," He added, " I will not leave you orphans, I come to you, and ye shall see Me" (*John* xiv. 16–19, 26, 28) ; and in another place, " Lo I am with you all the days, even to the consummation of the age" (*Matt.* xxviii. 20) ; and when Thomas said, " We know not whither Thou goest," Jesus said, " I am the way and the truth" (*John* xiv. 5, 6).

[3] As the " Spirit of Truth" or " Holy Spirit" is the same as the Lord, who is the Truth itself, it is said, " the Holy Spirit was not yet, because Jesus was not yet glorified" (*John* vii. 39) ; for after His glorification or complete unition with the Father, which was effected by the passion of the cross, the Lord was Divine wisdom and Divine truth itself, thus the Holy Spirit. The reason why the Lord breathed on the disciples and said, " Receive ye the Holy Spirit," was that all the breathing of heaven is from the Lord. For angels as well as men have

breathing and beating of the heart; their breathing being according to their reception of wisdom from the Lord, and their
beating of the heart or pulse being according to their reception
of Divine love from the Lord. That this is so will be seen in
its own place.

[4] That "the Holy Spirit" is Divine Truth from the Lord,
is further evident from these passages :—

When they bring you to the synagogues, be not anxious as to what ye
shall say ; for the Holy Spirit shall teach you in the same hour what ye
ought to say (*Luke* xii. 11, 12 ; xxi. 14 ; *Mark* xiii. 11).

Jehovah said, My spirit that is upon thee, and My words which I have
put in thy mouth, shall not depart out of thy mouth (*Isa.* lix. 21).

There shall go forth a Rod out of the stem of Jesse, and He shall
smite the earth with the rod of His mouth, and with the breath (*spiritu*)
of His lips shall He slay the wicked, and truth shall be the girdle of His
thighs (*Isa.* xi. 1, 4, 5).

Now with the mouth He hath commanded, and His spirit hath gathered
them (*Isa.* xxxiv. 16).

They who worship God must worship in spirit and in truth (*John* iv. 24).

It is the spirit that quickeneth, the flesh profiteth nothing ; the words
that I speak unto you, they are spirit and they are life (*John* vi. 63).

John said, I baptize you with water unto repentance ; but He that
cometh after me shall baptize you with the Holy Spirit and with fire
(*Matt.* iii. 11 ; *Mark* i. 8 ; *Luke* iii. 16).

To "baptize with the Holy Spirit and with fire," is to regenerate by means of the Divine truth which is of faith and the
Divine good which is of love.

When Jesus was baptized, the heavens were opened, and He saw the
Holy Spirit descending like a dove (*Matt.* iii. 16 ; *Mark* i. 10 ; *Luke* iii.
21, 22 ; *John* i. 32, 33).

A dove is a representative of purification and regeneration by
means of Divine truth.

[5] As by "the Holy Spirit," where the Lord is treated of,
is meant His Divine life, thus Himself, and, specifically, the
life of His wisdom which is called Divine truth, by the
"spirit" mentioned in the writings of the prophets which is
called also the "Holy Spirit," is meant Divine truth from the
Lord. Thus in the following passages :—

The Spirit said unto the churches (*Rev.* ii. 7, 11, 29 ; iii. 1, 6, 13, 22).

The seven lamps of fire burning before the throne are the seven spirits of God (*Rev.* iv. 5).

In the midst of the elders a Lamb standing, having seven eyes, which are the seven spirits of God sent forth into all the earth (*Rev.* v. 6).

" Lamps of fire," and the Lord's " eyes," signify Divine truths, and " seven" signifies what is holy.

The Spirit said, that they may rest from their labors (*Rev.* xiv. 13).

The Spirit and the bride say, Come (*Rev.* xxii. 17).

They made their heart adamant, that they should not hear the law or the words which Jehovah hath sent in His Spirit by the hand of the prophets (*Zech.* vii. 12).

The spirit of Elijah came upon Elisha (2 *Kings* ii. 15).

John went before in the spirit and power of Elijah (*Luke* i. 17).

Elizabeth was filled with the Holy Spirit and prophesied (*Luke* i. 41).

Zacharias, filled with the Holy Spirit, prophesied (*Luke* i. 67).

David said in the Holy Spirit, The Lord said to my Lord, Sit at **My** right hand (*Mark* xii. 36).

The testimony of Jesus is the spirit of prophecy (*Rev.* xix. 10).

As, therefore, by the " Holy Spirit" there is meant, specifically, the Lord as to Divine wisdom, and derivatively as to Divine truth, it is evident why it is said of the Holy Spirit that it enlightens, teaches, inspires.

52. vi. *Jehovah Himself (that is, the Lord) spoke the Word through the prophets.* We read of the prophets that they were in vision, and that Jehovah spoke to them. When they were in vision they were not in the body, but in their spirit, in which state they saw things such as are in heaven. But when Jehovah spoke to them, they were in the body, and heard Him speaking. These two states of the prophets should be carefully distinguished. In their state of vision, the eyes of their spirit were opened, and those of their body shut, and they then seemed to themselves to be carried from place to place, the body remaining in its own place. In this state, at times, were Ezekiel, Zechariah, Daniel, and John when he wrote the *Revelation ;* and it is then said that they were " in vision," or " in the spirit." Thus *Ezekiel* says :—

The spirit lifted me up, and brought me into Chaldea to the captivity, in the vision of God, in the Spirit of God; thus went up above me the vision which I saw (xi. 1, 24).

He says too,

That the spirit took him up, and he heard behind him an earthquake, and other things (iii. 12, 14).

Also that the spirit lifted him up between the earth and the heaven, and brought him in the visions of God to Jerusalem, and he saw abominations (viii. 3, etc.).

In like manner in the vision of God, or in the spirit, he saw

The four living creatures, which were cherubs (i. and x.).

And also the new earth and the new temple, and an angel measuring them (xl. to xlviii.).

That he was then in the visions of God, he says in xl. 2; and that the spirit took him up, in xliii. 5.   The case was the same with Zechariah, in whom at the time there was an angel,

When he saw a man riding among the myrtle-trees (*Zech.* i. 8, etc.).

When he saw four horns, and afterwards a man who had a measuring line in his hand (i. 18; ii. 1).

When he saw Joshua the high priest (iii. 1, etc.).

When he saw a lampstand, and two olive-trees (iv. 2, 3).

When he saw a flying roll, and an ephah (v. 1, 6).

And when he saw four chariots going out between two mountains, and horses (vi. 1, etc.).

In a similar state was Daniel,

When he saw four beasts coming up out of the sea (*Dan.* vii. 3).

And when he saw the combats of the ram and the he-goat (viii. 1, etc).

That he saw these things in visions, is stated in vii. 1, 2, 7, 13; viii. 2; x. 1, 7, 8.   That the angel Gabriel was seen by him in vision, and spoke with him, is stated in ix. 21, 22.   The case was the same with John when he wrote the *Revelation*, who says,

That he was in the spirit on the Lord's day (*Rev.* i. 10).

That he was carried away in the spirit into the wilderness (xvii. 3).

Into a high mountain in the spirit (xxi. 10).

That he saw horses in vision (ix. 17).

And elsewhere that he saw the things which he described, thus in spirit, or in vision (i. 12 ; iv. 1 ; v. 1 ; vi. 1 ; and in every other chapter).

53. As to the Word itself, however, it is not said in the Prophets that they spoke it from the Holy Spirit, but that they spoke it from Jehovah, from Jehovah of Armies, from the Lord Jehovih ; for we read " the Word of Jehovah came unto me," " Jehovah said unto me," and very frequently " Jehovah said," and " the word (*dictum*) of Jehovah." And, as the Lord is Jehovah, as has been shown above, it follows that all the Word has been spoken by Him. That no one may doubt this to be the case, I will give the references, in *Jeremiah* only, to the places where these four expressions occur :—*Jer.* i. 4, 7, 11–14, 19 ; ii. 1–5, 9, 19, 22, 29, 31 ; iii. 1, 6, 10, 12, 14, 16 ; iv. 1, 3, 9, 17, 27 ; v. 11, 14, 18, 22, 29 ; vi. 6, 9, 12, 15, 16, 21, 22 ; vii. 1, 3, 11, 13, 19–21 ; viii. 1, 3, 12, 13 ; ix. 3, 7, 9, 13, 15, 17, 22, 24, 25 ; x. 1, 2, 18 ; xi. 1, 6, 9, 11, 17, 21, 22 ; xii. 14, 17 ; xiii. 1, 6, 9, 11–15, 25 ; xiv. 1, 10, 14, 15 ; xv. 1–3, 6, 11, 19, 20 ; xvi. 1, 3, 5, 9, 14, 16 ; xvii. 5, 19, 20, 21, 24 ; xviii. 1, 5, 6, 11, 13 ; xix. 1, 3, 6, 12, 15 ; xx. 4 ; xxi. 1, 4, 7, 8, 11, 12 ; xxii. 2, 5, 6, 11, 16, 18, 24, 29, 30 ; xxiii. 2, 5, 7, 12, 15, 24, 29, 31, 38 ; xxiv. 3, 5, 8 ; xxv. 1, 3, 7–9, 15, 27–29, 32 ; xxvi. 1, 2, 18 ; xxvii. 1, 2, 4, 8, 11, 16, 19, 21, 22 ; xxviii. 2, 12, 14, 16 ; xxix. 4, 8, 9, 16, 19–21, 25, 30–32 ; xxx. 1–5, 8, 10–12, 17, 18 ; xxxi. 1, 2, 7, 10, 15–17, 23, 27, 28, 31–38 ; xxxii. 1, 6, 14, 15, 25, 26, 28, 30, 36, 42 ; xxxiii. 1, 2, 4, 10–13, 17, 19, 20, 23, 25 ; xxxiv. 1, 2, 4, 8, 12, 13, 17, 22 ; xxxv. 1, 13, 17–19 ; xxxvi. 1, 6, 27, 29, 30 ; xxxvii. 6, 7, 9 ; xxxviii. 2, 3, 17 ; xxxix. 15–18 ; xl. 1 ; xlii. 7, 9, 15, 18, 19 ; xliii. 8, 10 ; xliv. 1, 2, 7, 11, 24–26, 30 ; xlv. 1, 2, 5 ; xlvi. 1, 23, 25, 28 ; xlvii. 1 ; xlviii. 1, 8, 12, 30, 35, 38, 40, 43, 44, 47 ; xlix. 2, 5–7, 12, 13, 16, 18, 26, 28, 30, 32, 35, 37–39 ; l. 1, 4, 10, 18, 20, 21, 30, 31, 33, 35, 40 ; li. 25, 33, 36, 39, 52, 58. These from *Jeremiah* only. All the other prophets speak in the same way, and none say that the Holy Spirit has spoken, or that Jehovah has spoken to them by means of the Holy Spirit.

54. From all this then it is evident that JEHOVAH (who is THE LORD FROM ETERNITY) spoke through the prophets; and that where the HOLY SPIRIT is mentioned, it is the Lord Himself. It follows that GOD IS ONE IN BOTH PERSON AND ESSENCE, AND THAT THIS GOD IS THE LORD.

XI.

THE DOCTRINE OF THE ATHANASIAN CREED AGREES WITH THE TRUTH, PROVIDED THAT BY A TRINITY OF PERSONS IS UNDERSTOOD A TRINITY OF PERSON, AND THAT THIS TRINITY IS IN THE LORD.

55. The recognition by Christians of three Divine Persons, and thus as it were of three Gods, has arisen from there being in the Lord a Trine, one of which is called the Father, the second the Son, and the third the Holy Spirit. This Trine is also referred to in the Word under distinct names; just as we refer by distinct names to soul, to body, and to that which proceeds from them, which, however, taken together, form a one. In the sense of the letter the Word is of such a nature that things which form a one it distinguishes from each other as if they did not form a one. This is why Jehovah (who is the Lord from eternity) is sometimes called " Jehovah," sometimes " Jehovah of Armies," sometimes " God," sometimes " the Lord ;" and at the same time He is called " Creator," " Saviour," " Redeemer," and " Former," and even " Shaddai ;" and His Human which He assumed in this world, " Jesus," " Christ," " Messiah," " Son of God," " Son of man ;" and, in the Word of the Old Testament, " God," " Holy One of Israel," " Jehovah's Anointed," " King," " Prince," " Counselor," " Angel," " David." [2] In consequence of this feature of the Word in the sense of the letter (that it speaks of as many those who really form a one) Christians, who at first were simple folk, and understood everything in accordance with the literal import of the words, dis·

criminated the Divinity into three Persons. On account of their
simplicity this was permitted, but in such a manner that they
should believe the Son to be Infinite, Uncreate, Almighty, God,
and Lord, altogether equal to the Father; and that they should
also believe that these are not two, or three; but one in essence,
majesty, and glory, and therefore in Divinity.   [3] They who
believe this in simplicity in accordance with doctrine, and do
not confirm themselves in the idea of three Gods, but of the
three make a one, after death are taught by the Lord by means
of angels that He Himself is that one God, and that Trine.
And this teaching is received by all who come into heaven; for
no one can be admitted into heaven who thinks of three Gods,
however much he may say One; for the life of the whole
heaven, and the wisdom of all the angels, are founded upon the
acknowledgment and consequent confession of one God, and
upon the faith that this one God is also Man, and that He is the
Lord, who is at once both God and Man.   [4] From all this it
is evident that it was of Divine permission that Christians at
first received the doctrine of three Persons, provided that they
at the same time received the idea that the Lord is God, Infinite,
Almighty, and Jehovah.   For unless they had received this too,
it would have been all over with the church, because the
church is the church from the Lord; and the eternal life of all
is from the Lord, and from no other.   [5] That the church is
the church from the Lord is evident from this alone, that the
whole Word from beginning to end treats solely of the Lord, as
was shown above; and that we must believe in Him, and that
they who do not believe in Him have not eternal life, but that
the anger of God abideth on them (*John* iii. 36).   [6] Now as
every one sees in himself that if God is one, He is one in both
Person and Essence (for no one thinks differently, or can think
differently, while thinking that God is one), I will here cite the
whole of the Creed which takes its name from Athanasius, and
will afterwards show that all things said therein are true, provided that instead of a trinity of Persons there is understood
a trinity of Person.

56. The *Creed* is as follows :—

Whosoever will be saved, before all things it is necessary that he hold the Catholic (*other authorities say*, Christian) Faith ; which faith, except every one do keep whole and undefiled, without doubt he shall perish everlastingly. And the Catholic (*others say*, Christian) Faith is this : That we worship one God in Trinity, and the Trinity in Unity, neither confounding the persons, nor dividing the substance (*others say*, essence). For there is one person of the Father, another of the Son, and another of the Holy Spirit ; but the Godhead of the Father, of the Son, and of the Holy Spirit, is all one, the glory equal, the majesty coeternal. Such as the Father is, such is the Son, and such is the Holy Spirit. The Father uncreate, the Son uncreate, and the Holy Spirit uncreate. The Father incomprehensible (*infinitus*), the Son incomprehensible (*infinitus*), and the Holy Spirit incomprehensible (*infinitus*). The Father eternal, the Son eternal, and the Holy Spirit eternal : and yet there are not three eternals, but One Eternal : as also there are not three incomprehensibles (*infiniti*), nor three uncreates ; but one uncreate, and one incomprehensible (*infinitus*). So likewise the Father is almighty, the Son almighty, and the Holy Spirit almighty ; and yet there are not three Almighties, but One Almighty. So the Father is God, the Son is God, and the Holy Spirit is God : and yet there are not three gods, but One God. So likewise the Father is Lord, the Son Lord, and the Holy Spirit Lord ; and yet not three lords, but One Lord. For like as we are compelled by the Christian verity to acknowledge every person by himself to be God and Lord, so are we forbidden by the Catholic Religion to say there be three gods or three lords (*others say*, still we cannot, according to the Christian faith, mention three gods or three lords). The Father is made of none, neither created, nor begotten (*natus*) : the Son is of the Father alone, not made, nor created, but begotten (*natus*) : the Holy Spirit is of the Father and of the Son, neither made, nor created, nor begotten (*natus*), but proceeding. So there is one Father, not three Fathers ; one Son, not three Sons ; one Holy Spirit, not three Holy Spirits. And in this Trinity none is afore or after another ; none is greater or less than another ; but the whole three persons are coeternal together, and coequal. So that in all things, as is aforesaid, the Unity in Trinity and the Trinity in Unity is to be worshiped (*others say*, three persons in one Godhead, and one God in three persons, is to be worshiped). He therefore that will be saved, must thus think of the Trinity.

Furthermore, it is necessary to everlasting salvation that he also believe rightly the incarnation of our Lord Jesus Christ (*others say*, that he firmly believes that our Lord is very Man). For the right faith is that we believe and confess that our Lord Jesus Christ, the Son of God, is

God and Man; God of the substance (*or* essence; *others*, nature) of the Father, begotten before the worlds; and Man of the substance (*others say*, nature) of his mother, born in the world; perfect God, and perfect Man, of a reasonable soul and human flesh (*corpore*) subsisting; equal to the Father as touching his Godhead, and inferior to the Father as touching his manhood.   Who although he be God and Man, yet he is not two, but one Christ; one, not by conversion of the Godhead into flesh (*corpus*); but by taking of the manhood into God (*others say*, He is one, yet not that the Godhead was transmuted into manhood, but the Godhead took up the Manhood to itself); one altogether, not by confusion (*others say*, commingling) of substance, but by unity of person (*others say*, He is altogether One, not that the two natures are commixed, but he is one person).   For as the reasonable soul and flesh (*corpus*) is one man, so God and man is one Christ, Who suffered for our salvation, descended into hell, rose again the third day from the dead.   He ascended into heaven, He sitteth on the right hand of the Father, God Almighty, from whence He shall come to judge the quick and the dead.   At whose coming all men shall rise again with their bodies, and shall give account for their own works.   And they that have done good shall go into life everlasting, and they that have done evil into everlasting fire.

57. That all things of the Creed are true in so far as its verbal expressions are concerned, provided that instead of a Trinity of Persons there is understood a Trinity of Person, will be seen if we transcribe it again, with this latter trinity substituted in it. A Trinity of Person is this : THAT THE LORD'S DIVINE IS THE FATHER, THE DIVINE HUMAN THE SON, AND THE PROCEEDING DIVINE THE HOLY SPIRIT. When this trinity is understood, the man can both think of and say One God; but who fails to see that otherwise he cannot but think of three Gods?   Athanasius himself saw this, and this is why there were inserted these words :— ·

As we are compelled by the Christian verity to acknowledge every person by himself to be God and Lord ; so are we forbidden by the Catholic religion (or, by the Christian faith) to say (or name) three gods or three lords.

This amounts to saying, Although it is allowable, by the Christian verity, to acknowledge, or think of, three Gods and Lords, yet it is not allowable, by the Christian faith, to say or name more than one God and one Lord. And yet it is acknowledgment and thought which conjoin man with the Lord and heaven, and not mere speech. Besides, no one can comprehend how the Divine, which is one, can be divided into three Persons, each of whom is God, for the Divine is not divisible. And to make the three one through the essence or substance does not take away the idea of three Gods, but merely conveys an idea of their unanimity.

58. That in so far as its verbal expressions are concerned, all things of this Creed are true, provided that instead of a Trinity of Persons there is understood a Trinity of Person, is evident from the same when rewritten in this form :—

Whosoever will be saved, it is necessary that he hold this Christian Faith ; and the Christian Faith is, that we worship one God in Trinity, and Trinity in Unity, not confounding the Trine of Person, nor dividing the Essence. The Trine of one Person is what is called the Father, Son, and Holy Spirit. The Divinity of the Father, Son, and Holy Spirit is one and the same, the glory and majesty equal. Such as the Father is, such is the Son, and such is the Holy Spirit. The Father is uncreate, the Son uncreate, and the Holy Spirit uncreate. The Father is infinite, the Son infinite, and the Holy Spirit infinite. And yet there are not three infinites, nor three uncreates, but one Uncreate, and one Infinite. So likewise the Father is Almighty, the Son Almighty, and the Holy Spirit Almighty ; and yet there are not three almighties, but one Almighty. So the Father is God, the Son is God, and the Holy Spirit is God ; and yet there are not three gods, but one God. So likewise the Father is Lord, the Son is Lord, and the Holy Spirit is Lord ; and yet there are not three lords, but one Lord. For as by the Christian verity we acknowledge a trine in one Person, who is God and Lord, so by the Christian faith we can say one God and one Lord. The Father is made of none, neither created, nor born ; the Son is of the Father alone, not made, nor created, but born ; the Holy Spirit is of the Father and of the Son, not made, nor created, nor born, but proceeding. So there is one Father, not three Fathers ; one Son, not three Sons ; one Holy Spirit, not three Holy Spirits. And in this Trinity none is greatest or least, but they are altogether equal. So that in all things, as is aforesaid, the Unity in Trinity, and Trinity in Unity, is to be worshiped.

59. So far in the Creed as to the Trinity and Unity of God. The Creed then treats of the Lord's assumption of the Human in the world, called the Incarnation. Everything said in the Creed on this point also is true, provided we make a clear distinction between the human from the mother in which the Lord was when in a state of humiliation or emptying out (*exinanitio*) [see *Isa.* liii. 12], as when He suffered temptations and the cross; and the Human from the Father, in which He was when in a state of glorification or unition. For in the world the Lord assumed a Human conceived of Jehovah (who is the Lord from eternity), and born of the virgin Mary; so that He had both a Divine and a human, a Divine from His Divine from eternity, and a human from the mother Mary in time; but this latter human He put off, and put on a Human that was Divine. This Human is what is called the Divine Human, and is meant in the Word by the " Son of God." When therefore the things first said in the Creed about the Incarnation are understood of the maternal human (in which the Lord was when in a state of humiliation), and the things that follow, of the Divine Human (in which He was when in a state of glorification), all things there are in agreement. With the maternal human (in which the Lord was when in a state of humiliation) agree the following statements, that come first in the Creed :—

That Jesus Christ was God and Man, God of the Substance of the Father, and Man of the substance of the mother, born in the world; perfect God and perfect Man, of a rational soul and human body consisting; equal to the Father as touching the Godhead, but inferior to the Father as touching the manhood.

That this manhood was not converted into the Godhead, nor commixed therewith; it being put off, and the Divine Human assumed in its place.

With the Divine Human (in which He was when in a state of glorification, and is now to eternity) agree the following words in the Creed :—

Although our Lord Jesus Christ, the Son of God, be God and Man, yet he is not two, but one Christ; yea, he is altogether one, for he is one person; for as the reasonable soul and body are one man, so God and Man are one Christ.

60. That in the Lord, God and Man (as is said in the Creed) are not two, but one Person, yea, altogether one, as soul and body are one, is clear from many things said by the Lord Himself, as that the Father and He are one; that all things of the Father are His, and all His the Father's; that He is in the Father, and the Father in Him; that all things are given into His hand; that He has all power; that He is the God of heaven and earth; that whosoever believes in Him has eternal life; and further from its being said of Him that He was taken up into heaven as to both the Divine and the Human, and that, with respect to both, He sits on the right hand of God, which means that He is Almighty: not to repeat many passages of the Word treating of His Divine Human which are copiously quoted above, and all of which bear witness that GOD IS ONE IN BOTH PERSON AND ESSENCE; THAT THE TRINITY IS IN HIM; AND THAT THIS GOD IS THE LORD.

61. The reason why these truths relative to the Lord are now for the first time made publicly known, is that it has been foretold in the *Revelation* (chapters xxi. and xxii.) that a New Church, in which this doctrine will hold the chief place, is to be instituted by the Lord at the end of the former church. It is this Church which is meant by the "New Jerusalem," and no one can come into it who does not acknowledge the Lord as the God of heaven and earth. This I can declare—that the universal heaven acknowledges the Lord alone; and that no one who does not acknowledge Him is admitted into heaven; for heaven is heaven from the Lord. It is precisely this acknowledgment from love and faith which causes all there to be in the Lord and the Lord in them, as the Lord Himself teaches in *John:*—

In that day ye shall know that I am in My Father, and ye in Me, and I in you (xiv. 20).

Abide in Me, and I in you. I am the vine, ye are the branches; he that abideth in Me and I in him, the same bringeth forth much fruit, for without Me ye can do nothing; if any one abide not in Me, he is cast forth (xv. 4–6; xvii. 22, 23).

The reason why this has not been previously seen from the Word, is that if it had been previously seen it would not have been received, because the Last Judgment had not been effected. Before that event the power of hell prevailed over the power of heaven, and as man is in the midst between the two, it is evident that the devil (which is hell) would have plucked it out of men's hearts, and would also have profaned it. But this state of power on the part of hell was completely broken by the Last Judgment, which has now been executed. Since that Judgment—thus now—every man who craves to be enlightened and wise can be so. (On this subject see the work on *Heaven and Hell*, n. 589–596, 597–603; and also that on the *Last Judgment*, n. 65–72, 73, 74.)

XII.

BY THE "NEW JERUSALEM" (SPOKEN OF IN THE *REVELATION*) IS MEANT A NEW CHURCH.

62. In the *Revelation*, after a description of the state of the Christian Church as it would be at its end, and as it now is,* and after those of that church who are signified by the false prophet, the dragon, the harlot, and the beasts, are said to have been cast into hell, it is added :—

I saw a new heaven and a new earth, for the former heaven and the former earth were passed away. And I John saw the Holy City New Jerusalem coming down from God out of heaven. And I heard a great voice out of heaven, saying, Behold, the tabernacle of God is with men, and He will dwell with them, and they shall be His people, and God Himself shall be with them, their God. And He that sat upon the throne said, Behold, I make all things new. And He said unto me, Write, for these words are true and faithful (*Rev.* xxi. 1–3, 5).

By the "new heaven," and by the "new earth," which John saw, after the former heaven and the former earth had passed

* That is, in 1763. [TR.]

away, is not meant a new starry and atmospheric heaven such as appears before the eyes of men, nor a new earth such as that on which men dwell; but there is meant a newness of the church in the spiritual world, and a newness of the church in the natural world. As a newness of the church in both worlds, spiritual and natural, was effected by the Lord when He was in this world, a like prediction had been made in the Prophets, namely, that a new heaven and a new earth would then come into existence (as in *Isa.* lxv. 17; lxvi. 22, and else-where), which cannot possibly mean a heaven visible to the eyes, and an earth habitable by men. By the term *spiritual world* is meant the world where angels and spirits dwell, and by the term *natural world* is meant the world where men dwell. That a newness of the church in the spiritual world has been recently effected, and that a newness of the church in the natural world will be effected, has been partly shown in the little work on the *Last Judgment*, and will be shown more fully in the *Continuation* of that work.

63. By the "Holy City Jerusalem" is meant this New Church as to doctrine, and therefore it was seen coming down from God out of heaven, for the doctrine of genuine truth comes to us from the Lord through heaven, and from no other source. As the Church in respect to doctrine is meant by the City New Jerusalem, it is said:—

Prepared as a bride adorned for her Husband (verse 2);

and afterwards,

There came unto me one of the seven angels, and talked with me, saying, Come hither, I will show thee the bride, the Lamb's wife; and he carried me away in the spirit to a great and high mountain, and showed me that great city, the Holy Jerusalem, descending out of heaven from God (verses 9, 10).

That by "bride" and "wife" is meant the church, when the Lord is meant by "bridegroom" and "husband," is well known. The church is a "bride" when she is desirous to re-ceive the Lord; and a "wife," when she does receive Him.

That the Lord is meant by "her Husband" is evident; for it is said, "the bride the Lamb's wife."

64. The reason why "Jerusalem" means the church as to doctrine, is that there and at no other place in the land of Canaan were the temple and altar, the offering of sacrifices, and therefore the Divine worship; and for this reason the three yearly feasts were celebrated there, to which every male in the whole country was commanded to go. This is why "Jerusalem" signifies the church in respect to worship, and therefore as to doctrine—for worship is prescribed in doctrine, and is performed according to it. An additional reason is that the Lord was present in Jerusalem, and taught in its temple, and afterwards glorified His Human there. Besides, "city" in the spiritual sense of the Word signifies doctrine, and therefore "holy city" signifies the doctrine of Divine truth from the Lord.* **[2]** That by "Jerusalem" is meant the church as to doctrine, is further evident from other passages in the Word, as from these :—

> For Zion's sake I will not hold my peace, and for Jerusalem's sake I will not rest, until the righteousness thereof go forth as brightness, and the salvation thereof as a lamp that burneth. Then shall the nations see thy righteousness, and all kings thy glory; and thou shalt be called by a new name, which the mouth of Jehovah shall name; and thou shalt be a crown of ornament in the hand of Jehovah, and a kingdom's diadem in the hand of thy God; for Jehovah shall delight in thee, and thy land shall be married. Behold, thy salvation cometh; behold, His reward is with Him; and they shall call them the holy people, the redeemed of Jehovah; and thou shalt be called, A city sought out, not forsaken (*Isa.* lxii. 1–4, 11, 12).

This whole chapter treats of the Lord's advent, and of a New Church to be set up by Him. This New Church is here meant by "Jerusalem called by a new name which the mouth of

---

* That by "city" in the Word is signified the doctrine of the church and of religion, may be seen in the *Arcana Cœlestia* (n. 402, 2449, 2943, 3216, 4492, 4493). That by the gate of a city is signified the doctrine by means of which there is entrance into the church (n. 2943, 4477, 4478). That on this account the elders sat in the gate of the city, and judged, *ibid*. That "to go out of the gate" is to fall back from doctrine (n. 4492, 4493). That in heaven cities and palaces are presented representatively when angels and spirits are conversing about doctrinal matters (n. 3216).

Jehovah shall name," and which shall be " a crown of ornament in the hand of Jehovah, and a kingdom's diadem in the
hand of God," and in which Jehovah shall " delight," and
which shall be called " a city sought out, not forsaken."   These
words cannot possibly mean the Jerusalem in which were the
Jews at the time of the Lord's coming into the world, for that
city was of a wholly contrary character, and might rather be
called Sodom, as indeed it is called in *Rev.* xi. 8; *Isa.* iii. 9;
Jer. xxiii. 14; *Ezek.* xvi. 46, 48.   [**3**] Again in *Isaiah :*—

> Behold, I create a new heaven and a new earth, and the former shall
> not be remembered : be ye glad and rejoice to eternities in that which I
> create ; for behold I create Jerusalem a rejoicing, and her people a glad-
> ness, that I may rejoice over Jerusalem, and be glad over My people.
> Then shall the wolf and the lamb feed together ; they shall not do
> harm in all the mountain of My holiness (lxv. 17–19, 25).

This chapter also treats of the Lord's advent, and of a church
to be set up anew by Him.   This church was not set up anew
among those who were in Jerusalem, but among those outside
of it, so that it is this church which is meant by the Jerusalem
that should be to the Lord a rejoicing, and whose people should
be to Him a gladness, and where also the wolf and the lamb
should feed together, and where they should do no harm.
Here, too, it is said, just as in the *Revelation,* that the Lord
will " create a new heaven and a new earth," the meaning being similar ; and it is added that He will " create Jerusalem."
[**4**] In another place in *Isaiah :*—

> Awake ! awake ! put on thy strength, O Zion ; put on thy beautiful
> garments, O Jerusalem, the holy city, for henceforth there shall no
> more come into thee the uncircumcised and the unclean.   Shake thyself
> from the dust, arise, and sit down, O Jerusalem.   My people shall know
> (*cognoscet*) My name in that day, for I am He that doth speak, behold it
> is I.   Jehovah hath comforted His people ; He hath redeemed Jerusa-
> lem (lii. 1, 2, 6, 9).

This chapter also treats of the Lord's advent, and of the church
to be set up anew by Him ; so that by the Jerusalem into
which the uncircumcised and the unclean should no more come,

and which the Lord should redeem, is meant the church; and by "Jerusalem the holy city," the church as to doctrine from the Lord. [5] In *Zephaniah :—*

Shout, O daughter of Zion ; be glad with all the heart, O daughter of Jerusalem ; the King of Israel is in the midst of thee ; fear evil no longer : He will be glad over thee with joy, He will rest in thy love, He will exult over thee with a shout : I will make you a name and a praise to all the people of the earth (iii. 14–17, 20).

Here in like manner it treats of the Lord and of a church from Him, over which "the King of Israel" (who is the Lord) will be glad with joy, will exult with a shout, and in whose love He will rest, and whose members He will make a name and a praise to all people of the earth. [6] In *Isaiah :—*

Thus saith Jehovah thy Redeemer, and thy Former, saying to Jerusalem, Thou shalt be inhabited ; and to the cities of Judah, Ye shall be built (xliv. 24, 26).

In *Daniel :—*

Know (*Scito*) and perceive that from the going forth of the word even to the restoring and the building up of Jerusalem, even to Messiah the Prince, shall be seven weeks (ix. 25).

It is evident that here also "Jerusalem" means the church, because this was indeed restored and built by the Lord, but not the Jerusalem that was the residence of the Jews.

[7] "Jerusalem" means a church from the Lord in the following passages also. In *Zechariah :—*

Thus saith Jehovah, I will return to Zion, and I will dwell in the midst of Jerusalem ; whence Jerusalem shall be called the city of truth ; and the mountain of Jehovah Zebaoth, the mountain of holiness (viii. 3, 20–23).

In *Joel :—*

Then shall ye know that I am Jehovah your God, dwelling in Zion, the mountain of holiness ; and Jerusalem shall be holiness : and it shall come to pass in that day that the mountains shall drop new wine, and the hills shall flow with milk, and Jerusalem shall abide from generation to generation (iii. 17–20).

7

In *Isaiah :*—

In that day shall the shoot of Jehovah be for ornament and glory ; and it shall come to pass that he that is left in Zion, and he that remaineth in Jerusalem shall be called holy ; even every one that is written for life in Jerusalem (iv. 2, 3).

In *Micah :*—

In the latter days it shall come to pass that the mountain of the house of Jehovah shall be established in the head of the mountains ; for doctrine shall go forth out of Zion, and the word of Jehovah from Jerusalem : unto thee shall come the former kingdom, the kingdom of the daughter of Jerusalem (iv. 1, 2, 8).

In *Jeremiah :*—

At that time they shall call Jerusalem the throne of Jehovah ; and all nations shall be gathered to the name of Jehovah to Jerusalem ; neither shall they walk any more after the confirmation of their evil heart (iii. 17).

In *Isaiah :*—

Look upon Zion the city of our set feast ; thine eyes shall see Jerusalem a quiet habitation, a tabernacle that shall not be scattered ; not one of the stakes thereof shall ever be removed, neither shall any of the cords thereof be plucked away (xxxiii. 20).

Besides other passages, as *Isa.* xxiv. 23 ; xxxvii. 32 ; lxvi. 10–14 ; *Zech.* xii. 3, 6, 8, 9, 10 ; xiv. 8, 11, 12, 21 ; *Mal.* iii. 1, 4 ; *Ps.* cxxii. 1–7 ; cxxxvii. 5, 6.

[8] That in these passages " Jerusalem" means the church which was to be set up anew by the Lord, and which actually was set up anew by Him, and not the Jerusalem in the land of Canaan that was inhabited by the Jews, is evident from those passages in the Word where it is said of the latter Jerusalem that it should utterly perish and be destroyed ; as *Jer.* v. 1 ; vi. 6, 7 ; vii. 17, 20, etc. ; viii. 5–7, etc. ; ix. 10, 11, 13, etc. ; xiii. 9, 10, 14 ; xiv. 16 ; *Lam.* i. 8, 9, 15, 17 ; *Ezek.* iv. 1 to end ; v. 9 to end ; xii. 18, 19 ; xv. 6–8 ; xvi. 1 to end ; xxiii. 1–49 ; *Matt.* xxiii. 33, 37, 39 ; *Luke* xix. 41–44 ; xxi. 20–22 ; xxiii. 28–30 ; and in many other places.

65. In the *Revelation* occur the words, A New Heaven and a New Earth; and afterwards, Behold I make all Things New, which mean nothing else than that in the church now to be set up anew by the Lord The Doctrine will be New. This doctrine did not exist in the former church, the reason of which is that if it had, it would not have been received, because the Last Judgment had not then been executed, and previous to that Judgment the power of hell prevailed over the power of heaven, so that if the doctrine had been given before, even from the Lord's mouth, it would not have remained with men; nor does it at this day remain except with those who approach the Lord alone, and acknowledge Him as the God of heaven and earth. (See above, at n. 61.) This same doctrine had indeed been given in the Word; but as not long after its setting up anew the church was turned into Babylon, and afterwards, with others, into Philistia, that doctrine could not be seen from the Word, for the church sees the Word from the principles of its religion and from its doctrine, and in no other way.

The new things contained in the present little work are, in general, as follows :—

i. God is one in Person and Essence, and this God is the Lord.

ii. All Holy Scripture treats of Him alone.

iii. He came into the world to subdue the hells, and to glorify His Human; and He accomplished both by admitting temptations into Himself, and did so fully by the last of them which was the passion of the cross. Thereby He became the Redeemer and Saviour; and thereby merit and righteousness are His alone.

iv. The statement that He "fulfilled all things of the law" means that He fulfilled all things of the Word.

v. By the passion of the cross He did not take away sins, but bore them as the Prophet, that is to say, He suffered that there should be represented, in Himself, the church in respect to its maltreatment of the Word.

vi. The imputation of His merit is not anything at all unless thereby is meant the forgiveness of sins after repentance.

These things are contained in this little work. In those which follow it, which are to be *Concerning the Holy Scripture, Concerning the Doctrine of Life, Concerning Faith,* and *Concerning the Divine Love and the Divine Wisdom,* still other new things will be seen.

NINE QUESTIONS

CHIEFLY RELATING TO

THE LORD, THE TRINITY,

AND THE

HOLY SPIRIT

PROPOSED BY THE

REV. THOMAS HARTLEY, M.A.

FORMERLY RECTOR OF WINWICK, NORTHAMPTONSHIRE, ENGLAND

TO

EMANUEL SWEDENBORG

WITH HIS ANSWERS

TRANSLATED FROM THE ORIGINAL LATIN EDITION OF HINDMARSH
(PUBLISHED IN LONDON IN 1785)
BY THE
REV. JOHN FAULKNER POTTS, B.A. LOND.

STANDARD EDITION

SWEDENBORG FOUNDATION
INCORPORATED
NEW YORK

Organized in 1850 as
The American Swedenborg Printing and Publishing Society

PREFATORY NOTE BY THE TRANSLATOR.—This little tract, which in accordance with an old and well-established custom, and for self-evident reasons, is placed immediately after the *Doctrine of the Lord*, was first printed and published in the original Latin in London, in the year 1785, by Robert Hindmarsh, from a manuscript copy in the handwriting of Mr. Hartley, and received from him by Mr. Hindmarsh in that year.

The date at which the Answers to the *Nine Questions* were written by Swedenborg is very closely indicated in the reply to Question vii., where by referring to the work entitled *The True Christian Religion*, Swedenborg shows that his answers were written after the publication of that work. They therefore contain his latest utterances on the subject of the doctrine of the Lord and of the Divine Trinity.

The following translation has been made from a copy of the very handsome Latin quarto of Hindmarsh which is preserved in the Library of the Academy of the New Church, at Bryn Athyn, Pennsylvania.

NINE QUESTIONS,

CHIEFLY RELATING TO

THE LORD, THE TRINITY, AND THE HOLY SPIRIT,

WITH THE ANSWERS

QUESTION I.

In what sense did the Lord call Himself the SON OF MAN, if He took only flesh from the mother, and not a rational soul? Has the human sonship regard solely to the human flesh?

ANSWER.

The Lord called Himself the Son of man because He was the Word or Divine truth even as to the Human; for in the spiritual sense "Son of man" signifies the truth of the church from the Word. The same was signified by "prophet," because the prophets taught truths from the Word; and therefore the Lord, who was a Prophet in a pre-eminent degree, and also the Word, and therefore the Divine truth, called Himself, as to the Human, the Son of man. This is why, in the Prophets and Psalms *passim* where the vastation of truth in the church is treated of, it is said that the Son of man abides not there; and this also is why the prophets themselves were called sons of man, as Ezekiel in *Ezek.* ii. 1, 3, 6, 8; iii. 1, 3, 4, 10, 17, 25; and very frequently in the succeeding chapters; and also Daniel. That such is the case has been shown from many passages quoted in the *Angelic Wisdom concerning the Lord,** which consult if at hand.

---

* This is the work published by Swedenborg under the (translated) title, *The Doctrine of the New Jerusalem concerning the Lord.* [TR.]

1

QUESTION II.

Had the Lord a rational soul from Jehovah the Father, to which was united the Divine *Esse*, whence He became very God and very Man?

ANSWER.

The Lord from eternity (that is, Jehovah) was Divine love and Divine wisdom, and He then had a Divine Celestial and a Divine Spiritual; but not, before He assumed the Human, a Divine Natural. And as the Rational is predicated solely of the celestial and spiritual Natural, it follows that by the assumption of the Human, Jehovah the Lord did also put on the Divine Rational. He had a Divine Rational before the assumption of the Human, but by means of influx into the angelic heaven; and when He had manifested Himself in this world, He did so by means of an angel whom He filled with His Divinity. For the purely Divine Essence (which as just said was purely Divine celestial and Divine spiritual) transcends both the angelic and the human Rational. But that Divine Rational existed by means of influx. Its nature may be inferred from what is said below on the sixth point. Luther and Melanchthon teach that in Christ Man is God and God is Man, which also is according to Holy Scripture, as may be seen in the *True Christian Religion*, n. 137. But Calvin denied it, and merely affirmed that Christ is God and Man.

QUESTION III.

Was there not always a Trinity in the Divine nature, to be understood in this way : the Divine Love, the Divine Wisdom, and the quickening Spirit, or Holy proceeding?

ANSWER.

The Divine Trinity in one Person is to be understood as soul, body, and proceeding operation, which together constitute one essence, for the one is from the other, and therefore the one belongs to the other. In the same way there is a trinity in each man, which taken together constitutes one person, to wit, the soul, the body, and the operation that goes forth. But in man this trinity is finite, because man is only an organ of life; whereas in the Lord the Trinity is infinite and thus Divine, because the Lord is life itself even in respect to the Human, as He Himself teaches in *John* v. 26; xiv. 6; and also elsewhere.

QUESTION IV.

Does not the Son, by whom Jehovah is said to have created the worlds (*Heb.* i. 2; xi. 3), signify the same as the Divine wisdom in *Jer.* x. 12; li. 15; so that the essential Wisdom or *Logos* of God in first principles, is now become the Truth or *Logos* of God in ultimates?

ANSWER.

That the Lord (that is, the Word or Divine truth through which all things were made that were made, and through which the world was created, *John* i. 3, 10) was the Divine wisdom which together with the Divine love constitutes one Divine Essence, and thus one and the same God, follows of course; for the Divine wisdom is also the Divine truth, because all things of wisdom are truths, and wisdom produces nothing but truths, for it is their containant, exactly in accordance with *Jer.* x. 12; li. 15. The same is understood also by the statement that is made in *Ps.* xxxiii. 6. The "spirit (or "breath") of Jehovah's mouth" also is wisdom; and the "word" there mentioned is the Divine love and the Divine wisdom together, for it is said, "And God was the Word" (*John* i. 1).

QUESTION V.

Is not the "Holy Spirit" in the New Testament the same as the "Spirit of God" in the Old Testament, with the sole difference that before the Lord's incarnation it proceeded either immediately from the Divine *Esse* or Jehovah, or mediately through angels, and after the incarnation through the Son or Divine Human ?

Is not the Holy Spirit the same as the sphere of God ?

ANSWER.

The Spirit of God and the Holy Spirit are two distinct things. The Spirit of God neither did nor could operate on man except imperceptibly; whereas the Holy Spirit, which proceeds solely from the Lord, operates on man perceptibly, and enables him to comprehend spiritual truths in a natural way; for the Lord has united the Divine Natural to the Divine Celestial and the Divine Spiritual, and He operates from these two through that. Besides, "Holy" in the Word is predicated solely of Divine truth, thus of the Lord, who is Divine truth not only in the celestial and spiritual but also in the natural sense; and therefore it is said in the *Revelation* that the Lord alone is Holy (xv. 3, 4). (See also the *Apocalypse Revealed*, n. 173.) It is also said in *John :* "The Holy Spirit was not yet, because Jesus was not yet glorified" (vii. 39).

The Holy Spirit is the same as the Divine sphere if by this is meant the Divine love and Divine wisdom, which two proceed from Jehovah the Lord from the sun of the angelic heaven, as do heat and light from the sun of the natural world and constitute its sphere. For in its essence the heat of the sun of the angelic heaven is love, and the light wisdom. And to these two the heat and light of the sun of this world correspond.

QUESTION VI.

Was the Divine Human of Jehovah, before the incarnation, a Person subsisting *per se*, as the Manifestation (*existere*),

Form, or Body of God? Or was it an angelic form assumed on occasion for the sake of manifestation?

Does it not follow that the Divine Human before the incarnation was different from the Divine Human which now is since the incarnation, seeing that the Divine Trinity is in the Lord's Person?

ANSWER.

Before the incarnation there was not any Divine Human except a representative one by means of some angel whom Jehovah the Lord filled with His Spirit, as has been said above. And as that was representative, all things of the church at that time were representative, and like shadows; but after the incarnation the representatives ceased, like the shades of evening or night at the rising of the sun. That representative Human in which Jehovah then presented Himself in this world before His actual advent, was not of such efficacy as to be able spiritually to enlighten men, and therefore enlightenment was then effected solely by means of types and figures.

QUESTION VII.

May not the Most Holy Trinity be properly said to be one and the same Lord in three characters, distinctions of offices, or relations toward men, as Creator, Redeemer, and Sanctifier; Father, Son, and Holy Spirit; Divine *Esse*, Divine Human, and Holy proceeding: not as three Persons, out of which there would necessarily be made three Gods?

ANSWER.

The Most Holy Trinity in one Person is to be apprehended as the Divine *Esse*, the Divine Human, and the Divine proceeding; thus as soul, body, and derivative power (*virtus*) and operation, precisely as given in the Memorable Relation inserted in the work entitled *The True Christian Religion*, n. **188.** As productions from these there follow in order creation, redemption, and regeneration; for creation is an attribute of the Divine *Esse*, redemption of the Divine Human from the Divine *Esse*, and regeneration of the Holy Spirit, which is the primary power (*virtus*), or operation, by the Divine Human from the Divine *Esse*, according to what has been advanced in the *True Christian Religion*, n. 153–155.

QUESTION VIII.

It is said in 1 *Cor.* xv. 45, " The first man Adam was made a living soul;" and in the genealogy in *Luke* iii. he is placed as the first after God, and it is said, "who was the son of God." Does not the regarding of Adam as a church contradict this ?

ANSWER.

In the genealogy in *Luke* it is said that Adam was "of God," that is, created by God, and not the son of God.

QUESTION IX.

If there was no individual called Noah, how comes it to be said in *Ezek.* xiv. 14: "Though these three men, Noah, Daniel, and Job," etc. ?

I lay no great stress on these matters [says Mr. Hartley], but I had a mind to propose them.

ANSWER.

The reason Noah is mentioned in *Ezek.* xiv. 14 is that he had been mentioned in *Genesis*, and consequently the same is signified in the Prophet as in Moses, namely, that the man with his three sons was significative of a subsequent church, on which subject see what has been delivered in the *Arcana Cœlestia.*

THE DOCTRINE

OF THE

NEW JERUSALEM

CONCERNING THE

HOLY SCRIPTURE

BY

EMANUEL SWEDENBORG

ORIGINALLY PUBLISHED IN AMSTERDAM IN THE YEAR 1763

TRANSLATED FROM THE ORIGINAL LATIN AND EDITED
BY THE
REV. JOHN FAULKNER POTTS, B.A. LOND.

STANDARD EDITION

SWEDENBORG FOUNDATION
INCORPORATED
NEW YORK

Organized in 1850 as
The American Swedenborg Printing and Publishing Society

CONTENTS*

*Compiled by the Translator.

THE DOCTRINE OF THE NEW JERUSALEM

CONCERNING THE

HOLY SCRIPTURE

I.

The Holy Scripture or Word is Divine Truth itself.

1. It is in everybody's mouth that the Word is from God, is Divinely inspired, and is therefore holy; and yet hitherto no one has known wherein it is Divine. For in the letter the Word appears like a common writing, in a style that is strange, and neither so sublime nor so brilliant as apparently are the writings of the day. For this reason a man who worships nature as God, or in preference to God, and who consequently thinks from himself and what is proper to himself, and not from heaven from the Lord, may easily fall into error in respect to the Word, and into contempt for it, and while reading it may say to himself, What is this? what is that? can this be Divine? could God, whose wisdom is infinite, speak in this manner? wherein consists its holiness, and whence comes its holiness, except from religious feeling and its consequent persuasion?

2. But he who thinks in this way does not consider that Jehovah Himself, the God of heaven and earth, spoke the Word through Moses and the prophets, and that it must therefore be Divine truth itself, for what Jehovah Himself speaks can be nothing else. Nor does he consider that the Lord, who is the same as Jehovah, spoke the Word that is in the Gospels, much of it with His own mouth, and the rest from the spirit of His mouth, which is the Holy Spirit.   This is why, as He Himself says, there is Life in His words, that He is the Light which enlightens, and that He is the Truth.*   [2] That the words which the Lord Himself spoke in the Gospels are Life, is declared in *John :*—

The words that I speak unto you, they are spirit, and they are life (vi. 63).

Jesus said to the woman at Jacob's well, If thou knewest the gift of God, and who it is that saith to thee, Give Me to drink, thou wouldest have asked of Him, and He would have given thee living water.   Whosoever drinketh of the water that I shall give him shall never thirst ; but the water that I shall give him shall be in him a well of water springing up into eternal life (iv. 6, 10, 14).

"Jacob's well" signifies the Word, as also in *Deut.* xxxiii. 28, for which reason the Lord sat there and conversed with the woman.   And "water" signifies the truth that is in the Word. [3] Again in *John :*—

If any man thirst, let him come unto Me, and drink.   He that believeth in Me, as the Scripture hath said, out of his belly shall flow rivers of living water (vii. 37, 38).

Peter said unto Jesus, Thou hast the words of eternal life (vi. 68).

And therefore the Lord says in *Mark :*—

Heaven and earth shall pass away ; but My words shall not pass away (xiii. 31).

The reason the Lord's words are "Life," is that He Himself is the "Life" and the "Truth," as He teaches in *John :*—

I am the way, the truth, and the life (xiv. 6).

In the beginning was the Word, and the Word was with God, and God was the Word ; in Him was life ; and the life was the light of men (i. 1, 4.)

"The Word" here means the Lord as to Divine truth, in which alone there is life and there is light.   [4] It is on this account that the Word, which is from the Lord and which is the Lord, is called

---

* That Jehovah Himself spoke the Word through the prophets, has been shown in *The Doctrine of the New Jerusalem concerning the Lord* (n. 52, 53).

A fountain of living waters (*Jer.* ii. 13 ; xvii. 13 ; xxxi. 9) :
A fountain of salvation (*Isa.* xii. 3) :
A fountain (*Zech.* xiii. 1) :
A river of the water of life (*Rev.* xxii. 1).

And it is said that

The Lamb that is in the midst of the throne shall feed them, and shall lead them unto living fountains of waters (*Rev.* vii. 17).

Besides other passages where the Word is called the "Sanctuary" and the "Tabernacle" in which the Lord dwells with man.

3. But the natural man cannot be persuaded by these considerations to believe that the Word is Divine truth itself wherein are Divine wisdom and Divine life; for he judges it by its style, and in this they do not appear. Yet the style of the Word is the Divine style itself, with which no other style, however sublime and excellent it may seem, is at all to be compared; for every other style is as darkness is to light. The style of the Word is such that there is holiness in every sentence, and in every word, and in some places in even the very letters. This is why the Word conjoins man with the Lord, and opens heaven. From the Lord proceed two things: Divine love, and Divine wisdom (or, what is the same, Divine good, and Divine truth, for Divine good is of His Divine love, and Divine truth is of His Divine wisdom), and in its essence the Word is both of these; and as it conjoins man with the Lord, and opens heaven, it follows that the man who reads it from the Lord, and not from himself alone, is filled by it with the good of love and the truths of wisdom; his will with the good of love, and his understanding with the truths of wisdom. In this way man has life by means of the Word.

4. Therefore in order to remove all doubt as to such being the character of the Word, the Lord has revealed to me the Word's internal sense. In its essence this sense is spiritual, and in relation to the external sense, which is natural, is as soul is to body. This sense is the spirit which gives life to the letter;

it can therefore bear witness to the Divinity and Holiness of the Word, and convince even the natural man, if he is willing to be convinced.

II.

In the Word there is a Spiritual Sense, hitherto
unknown.

This subject shall be considered in the following order:

i. What the spiritual sense is.

ii. This sense is in all things of the Word and in every single particular of it.

iii. From this sense it is that the Word is divinely inspired, and is holy in every word.

iv. Hitherto this sense has been unknown.

v. Henceforth it will be imparted solely to him who from the Lord is in genuine truths.

5. i. *What the spiritual sense is.* The spiritual sense of the Word is not that sense which shines forth from the sense of the letter while one is studying and unfolding the meaning of the Word with intent to confirm some tenet of the church. This is the literal sense of the Word. The spiritual sense does not appear in the sense of the letter, being within it as the soul in the body, as thought in the eyes, and as affection in the face, which act as a one, like cause and effect. It is this sense chiefly which renders the Word spiritual, not for men only, but for angels also; and therefore by means of this sense the Word gives communication with the heavens.

6. From the Lord proceed the Celestial, the Spiritual, and the Natural, one after another. That is called the Celestial which proceeds from His Divine love, and is Divine good; that is called the Spiritual which proceeds from His Divine wisdom, and is Divine truth; the Natural is from both, being their complex in the ultimate. The angels of the

Lord's celestial kingdom, of whom is composed the third or highest heaven, are in that Divine which proceeds from the Lord that is called the Celestial, for they are in the good of love from the Lord. The angels of the Lord's spiritual kingdom, of whom is composed the second or middle heaven, are in that Divine which proceeds from the Lord that is called the Spiritual, for they are in truths of wisdom from the Lord.* But the men of the church on earth are in the Divine Natural, which also proceeds from the Lord. From this it follows that the Divine in proceeding from the Lord to its ultimates descends through three degrees, and is named the Celestial, the Spiritual, and the Natural. The Divine which comes down from the Lord to men descends through these three degrees; and when it has come down, it holds these three degrees contained within it. Such is everything Divine, so that when it is in its ultimate degree it is in its fullness. Such is the Word: in its ultimate sense it is natural, in its interior sense it is spiritual, and in its inmost sense it is celestial; and in each sense it is Divine. That such is the nature of the Word does not appear in the sense of the letter, which sense is natural, for the reason that hitherto the man of this world has known nothing about the heavens; and consequently has not known what the Spiritual is, nor what the Celestial is, nor therefore the distinction between them and the Natural.

7. The distinction between these degrees cannot be known unless correspondence is known. For these three degrees are altogether distinct from each other, like end, cause, and effect, or like prior, posterior, and postreme; yet they make one by correspondences, for the Natural corresponds to the Spiritual, and also to the Celestial. What correspondence is may be seen in the work on *Heaven and Hell*, where the subject of the correspondence of all things of heaven with all things of man has been treated of (n. 87–102); and also the correspond-

---

* That there are two kingdoms of which the heavens consist, one of which is called the celestial kingdom, and the other the spiritual kingdom, may be seen in the work on *Heaven and Hell* (n. 20-28).

ence of heaven with all things of the earth (n. 103–115). The same will further appear below, from examples adduced from the Word.

8. As therefore the Word interiorly is spiritual and celestial, it is written exclusively by correspondences. And what is thus written is in its ultimate sense written in a style such as is that of the Prophets and Evangelists, which, although it may appear common, yet conceals within it Divine and all angelic wisdom.

9. ii. *The spiritual sense is in all things of the Word, and in every single particular of it.* This cannot be better seen than by examples, such as the following. John says in the *Revelation* :—

> I saw heaven opened, and behold a white horse, and He that sat upon him was called Faithful and True, and in righteousness He doth judge and make war. His eyes were as a flame of fire, and on His head were many crowns, and He had a name written that no man knew but He Himself, and He was clothed with a vesture dipped in blood, and His name is called THE WORD OF GOD. And His armies in heaven followed Him upon white horses, clothed in fine linen, white and clean. And He hath on His vesture and on His thigh a name written, KING OF KINGS AND LORD OF LORDS. And I saw an angel standing in the sun, and he cried with a loud voice, Come and gather yourselves together to the great supper, that ye may eat the flesh of kings, and the flesh of captains, and the flesh of mighty men, and the flesh of horses, and of them that sit on them, and the flesh of all men, both free and bond, and small and great (xix. 11–18).

What these things signify cannot be known except from the spiritual sense of the Word, and no one can know the spiritual sense except from a knowledge of correspondences, for all the above words are correspondences, and not one word there is without meaning. The knowledge of correspondences teaches what is signified by the white horse, what by Him who sat thereon, what by His eyes that were as a flame of fire, what by the crowns that were upon His head, what by His vesture dipped in blood, what by the white linen in which they were clothed who were of His army in heaven, what by the angel standing in the sun, what by the great supper to which they should come and gather themselves, and what by the flesh of kings, and captains, and others, which they should eat. The signification of each of these things in the spiritual sense may be seen in the little work on *The White Horse*, where they are explained, so that it is unnecessary to explain them further here. In that little work it has been shown that the Lord in respect to the Word is here described; and that by His eyes which were as a flame of fire, and by the crowns that were upon His head, and by the name that no one knew but He Himself, is meant the spiritual sense of the Word, and that no one can know it but the Lord Himself and he to whom He wills to reveal it; and also that by His vesture dipped in blood is meant the natural sense of the Word, which is the sense of its letter, to which violence has been done. That it is the Word which is thus described is very evident, for it is said "His name is called THE WORD OF GOD;" and that it is the Lord who is meant is equally clear, for it is said that the name of Him who sat on the white horse was written, KING OF KINGS AND LORD OF LORDS. That at the end of the church the spiritual sense of the Word is to be opened, is signified not only by what is said of the white horse and of Him who sat thereon, but also by the great supper to which the angel standing in the sun invited all to come, and to eat the flesh of kings and of captains, of mighty men, of horses, and of them that sat on them, and of all both free and bond. All these expressions would be empty words and devoid of spirit and life, unless there were what is spiritual within them, like soul in body.

10. In the *Revelation*, chapter xxi., the Holy Jerusalem is thus described :—

That there was a light in her like unto a stone most precious, as it were a jasper stone, clear as crystal ; that she had a wall great and high, having twelve gates, and over the gates twelve angels, and the names written thereon of the twelve tribes of the sons of Israel ; that the wall was a hundred and forty-four cubits, which is the measure of a man, that is, of an angel; and that the structure of the wall was of jasper, and its foundations of every precious stone, of jasper, sapphire, chalcedony, emerald, sardonyx, sardius, chrysolite, beryl, topaz, chrysoprase, jacinth, and amethyst; that the twelve gates were twelve pearls; that the city itself was pure gold, like unto pure glass; and that it was four-square; and that the length, the breadth, and the height thereof were equal, twelve thousand furlongs; with many other particulars.

That all these things are to be understood spiritually, is evident from the fact that by the Holy Jerusalem is meant a New Church which is to be set up by the Lord, as has been shown in *The Doctrine concerning the Lord* (n. 62–65). And as the church is here signified by Jerusalem, it follows that all the things said of it as a city—concerning its gates, its wall, the foundations of its wall, and their measures—contain a spiritual sense; for the things that are of the church are spiritual. But what the several things signify has been explained in the work *On the New Jerusalem*, published in London in the year 1758 (n. 1). I therefore refrain from a further explanation of them here. It is sufficient that it be known from that source that there is a spiritual sense in each several particular of the description, like a soul in its body; and that without this sense nothing of the church would be understood in the things there written; such as that the city was of pure gold; that its gates were of pearls; its wall of jasper; the foundations of its wall of precious stones; that its wall was of a hundred and forty-four cubits, which is the measure of a man, that is, of an angel; and that the city itself was twelve thousand furlongs in length, breadth, and height; and so on. But whoever, from a knowledge of correspondences, has come to know the spiritual sense, will understand these particulars; as that the wall and its foundations signify doctrine from the literal sense of the Word; and that the numbers twelve, one hundred and forty-four, and twelve thousand, signify like things, namely, all the truths and goods of the church in one complex.

11. In the *Revelation*, chapter vii., it is said:—

That there were sealed one hundred and forty-four thousand—twelve thousand of each tribe of Israel—of the tribe of Judah, of the tribe of

Reuben, of Gad, of Asher, of Naphtali, of Manasseh, of Simeon, of Levi, of Issachar, of Zebulon, of Joseph, and of Benjamin.

The spiritual sense of these words is that all are saved in whom is the church from the Lord; for, in the spiritual sense, to be sealed on the forehead, or to be sealed, signifies to be acknowledged by the Lord and saved. The twelve tribes of Israel signify all of that church; twelve, twelve thousand, and a hundred and forty-four thousand, signify all; Israel signifies the church; and each tribe some specific thing of the church. He who does not know this spiritual signification of these words may imagine that only this precise number are to be saved, and they solely from the Israelitish and Jewish nation.

12. In the *Revelation*, chapter vi., it is said :—

That when the Lamb opened the first seal of the book, there went forth a white horse, and that he who sat thereon had a bow, and to him was given a crown ; that when He opened the second seal there went forth a red horse, and that to him who sat thereon was given a great sword ; that when He opened the third seal there went forth a black horse, and that he who sat thereon had a pair of balances in his hand ; and that when He opened the fourth seal there went forth a pale horse, and that the name of him who sat thereon was Death.

What these things signify can be unfolded solely by means of the spiritual sense; and it is completely unfolded when it is known what is signified by the opening of the seals, by a horse, and by the other things mentioned. By them are described the successive states of the church, from its beginning to its end, in respect to its understanding of the Word. The "opening of the seals of the book by the Lamb" signifies the manifestation by the Lord of those states of the church. A "horse" signifies the understanding of the Word; the "white horse," the understanding of truth from the Word in the first state of the church; the "bow" of him who sat upon that horse, the doctrine of charity and faith fighting against falsities; the "crown," eternal life the prize of victory. The "red horse" signifies the understanding of the Word destroyed in respect to good, in the second state of the church; the "great sword," falsity fighting against truth. The "black horse" signifies the understanding of the Word destroyed in respect to truth, in the third state of the church; the "pair of balances," the estimation of truth so small that there was scarcely any. The "pale horse" signifies the understanding of the Word annihilated by evils of life and the derivative falsities, in the fourth or last state of the church; and "Death" signifies eternal condemnation. It is not apparent in the sense of the letter or natural sense that such is the signification of these things in the spiritual sense, so that unless the spiritual sense were at some time opened, the Word as to this and all other things in the *Revelation* would be so completely closed that at last no one would know wherein its Divine holiness lies. It is equally so in respect to what is signified by the "four horses" and the "four chariots" that came forth from between two mountains of brass (*Zech.* vi. 1–8).

13. In the *Revelation*, chapter ix., we read :—

The fifth angel sounded, and I saw a star fall from heaven unto the earth, and to him was given the key of the bottomless pit ; and he opened the bottomless pit, and there went up a smoke out of the pit as the smoke of a great furnace ; and the sun and the air were darkened by reason of the smoke of the pit ; and there came out of the smoke locusts upon the earth, and unto them was given power as the scorpions of the earth have power. The shapes of the locusts were like unto horses prepared for war, and on their heads were as it were crowns like gold ; and their faces were as the faces of men ; and they had hair as the hair of women ; and their teeth were as the teeth of lions ; and they had breastplates as of iron ; and the sound of their wings was as the sound of chariots, of many horses running to war ; and they had tails like scorpions ; and there were stings in their tails ; and their power was to hurt men five months. And they had a king over them, the angel of the bottomless pit, whose name in the Hebrew is Abaddon, but in the Greek he hath the name Apollyon (verses 1–3, 7–11).

Neither could these things be understood by any one unless the spiritual sense were revealed to him; for nothing here is said emptily, but every single thing has its signification. The subject here treated of is the state of the church when all knowledges of truth from the Word have been destroyed, and consequently man, having become sensuous, persuades himself that

falsities are truths. [2] The "star fallen from heaven," signifies the knowledges of truth destroyed; the "sun and air
darkened," signifies the light of truth become thick darkness;
the "locusts that came out of the smoke of the pit," signify
falsities in the outermost things such as exist with those who
have become sensuous, and who see and judge all things from
fallacies; a "scorpion" signifies their persuasiveness.   That the
locusts appeared "like horses prepared for war," signifies their
reasonings as it were from the understanding of truth; that the
locusts had "crowns like gold upon their heads, and faces as
the faces of men," signifies that they appeared to themselves
as conquerors, and as wise; their having "hair as the hair of
women," signifies that they appeared to themselves as if they
were in the affection of truth; their having "teeth as the teeth
of lions," signifies that sensuous things, which are ultimate
things of the natural man, appeared to them as having power
over all things. [3] Their having "breastplates as breastplates
of iron," signifies augmentations from fallacies by which they
fight and prevail; that "the sound of their wings was as the
sound of chariots running to war," signifies reasonings as if
from the truths of doctrine from the Word for which they
were to fight; their having "tails like scorpions," signifies per-
suasions; their having "stings in their tails," signifies their
cunning arts of deceiving thereby; their having "power to
hurt men five months," signifies that they induce a kind of
stupor on those who are in the understanding of truth and
perception of good; their having "a king over them, the angel
of the bottomless pit, whose name is Abaddon or Apollyon,"
signifies that their falsities were from hell, where dwell those
who are merely natural and in self-intelligence. [4] This is
the spiritual sense of these words, of which nothing appears
in the sense of the letter. Everywhere in the *Revelation* it is
the same. Be it known that in the spiritual sense all things
hang together in a continuous connection, which is fitted together in such a manner by the force and meaning of all the
words in the literal or natural sense, that if even a little word

were taken out of it, the connection would be broken and the coherence would perish. In order to prevent this, it is added at the end of this prophetical book,

That not a word shall be taken away (*Rev.* xxii. 19).

It is the same with the books of the prophets of the Old Testament: in order to prevent anything from being taken away from them, it came to pass of the Lord's Divine Providence that everything therein down to the very letters was counted. This was done by the Masorites.

14. In speaking to His disciples about the consummation of the age (which is the last time of the church), at the end of His predictions concerning the successive changes of state in the church, the Lord says,

Immediately after the affliction of those days shall the sun be darkened, and the moon shall not give her light, and the stars shall fall from heaven, and the powers of the heavens shall be shaken. And then shall appear the sign of the Son of man in heaven, and then shall all the tribes of the earth wail, and they shall see the Son of man coming in the clouds of heaven with power and much glory. And He shall send His angels with a trumpet and a great voice, and they shall gather together His elect from the four winds, from the end of the heavens even to the end of them (*Matt.* xxiv. 29–31).

[2] By these words, in the spiritual sense, is not meant that the sun and moon would be darkened, that the stars would fall from heaven, that the Lord's sign would appear in heaven, and that He would be seen in the clouds together with angels with trumpets, but by every word is meant some spiritual thing that is of the church, concerning the state of which at its end these things were spoken. For, in the spiritual sense, the "sun, which shall be darkened," means the Lord as to love; the "moon, which shall not give her light," means the Lord as to faith; the "stars, which shall fall from heaven," mean the knowledges of what is good and true that would perish; the "sign of the Son of man in heaven," means the appearing of Divine truth; the "tribes of the earth, which shall wail," means the lack of all truth that is of faith, and of all good

that is of love; the "coming of the Son of man in the clouds of heaven with power and glory," means the Lord's presence in the Word, and revelation; "clouds" signify the sense of the letter of the Word, and "glory," the spiritual sense of the Word; the "angels with a trumpet and a great voice," signifies heaven whence comes Divine truth; to "gather together the elect from the four winds, from the end of the heavens even to the end of them," signifies a newness of the church in respect to love and faith.   [**3**] That there is not meant a darkening of the sun and moon, nor a falling of the stars to the earth, is very evident from the Prophets, in which like things are said about the state of the church when the Lord should come into the world.   As in *Isaiah :*—

Behold the day of Jehovah cometh, cruel, and of wrath of anger ; the stars of the heavens, and the constellations thereof, shall not give their light, the sun shall be darkened in his rising, and the moon shall not cause her light to shine : I will visit upon the world its wickedness (xiii. 9–11 ; xxiv. 21, 23).

In *Joel :*—

The day of Jehovah cometh, a day of darkness and of thick darkness ; the sun and the moon shall be blackened, and the stars shall withdraw their shining (ii. 1, 2, 10 ; iii. 15).

In *Ezekiel :*—

I will cover the heavens, and blacken the stars ; I will cover the sun with a cloud, and the moon shall not cause her light to shine ; all the luminaries of light I will make dark, and will set darkness upon thy land (xxxii. 7, 8).

"The day of Jehovah" means the Lord's advent, which took place when there was no longer anything good and true left in the church, and not any knowledge of the Lord.

15. In order that it may be seen that without the spiritual sense the prophetical parts of the Word of the Old Testament are in many passages not intelligible, I will adduce a few, such as the following in *Isaiah :*—

Then shall Jehovah stir up a scourge against Asshur, according to the smiting of Midian at the rock of Oreb, and his rod shall be upon the sea, which he shall lift up in the way of Egypt. And it shall come to pass in that day that his burden shall be taken away from off thy shoulder, and his yoke from off thy neck. He shall come against Aiath ; he shall pass to Migron ; against Michmash he shall command his arms ; they shall pass over Mebara ; Gebah shall be a lodging to us ; Ramah shall tremble ; Gibeah of Saul shall flee. Wail with thy voice O daughter of Gallim ; hearken O Laish, O wretched Anathoth. Madmenah shall be a wanderer ; the inhabitants of Gebim shall gather themselves together. Is there as yet a day to stand in Nob ? the mountain of the daughter of Zion, the hill of Jerusalem, shall shake her hand. Jehovah shall cut' off the thickets of the forest with iron, and Lebanon shall fall by a magnificent one (x. 26–32, 34).

Here we meet with mere names, from which nothing can be drawn except by the aid of the spiritual sense, in which all the names in the Word signify things of heaven and the church. From this sense it is gathered that these words signify that the whole church has been devastated by memory-knowledges (*scientifica*)* perverting all truth, and confirming falsity. [2] In another place in the same Prophet :—

In that day the envy of Ephraim shall depart, and the enemies of Judah shall be cut off ; Ephraim shall not envy Judah, and Judah shall not straiten Ephraim ; but they shall fly upon the shoulder of the Philistines toward the sea, together shall they spoil the sons of the east, Edom and Moab shall be the putting forth of their hand. Jehovah shall utter a curse against the tongue of the Egyptian sea, and with the vehemence of His spirit He shall shake His hand over the river, and shall smite it into seven streams, so that He shall make a way [to pass over it] with shoes. Then shall there be a path for the remnant of His people, which remnant shall be from Asshur (xi. 13–16).

Here also no one would see anything Divine except one who knows what is signified by the several names ; and yet the subject treated of is the Lord's advent, and what shall then come to pass, as is plainly evident from verses 1 to 10. Who, therefore, without the aid of the spiritual sense, would see that by these things in their order is signified that they who are in falsities from ignorance, yet have not suffered themselves to be led astray by evils, will come to the Lord, and that the

* See foot-note on p. 21.

church will then understand the Word; and that falsities will then no longer harm them. [3] The case is the same where there are not names, as in *Ezekiel:*—

Thus saith the Lord Jehovih, Son of man, say unto the bird of every wing, and to every wild beast of the field, Assemble yourselves and come, gather yourselves from round about to My sacrifice which I sacrifice for you, a great sacrifice upon the mountains of Israel, that ye may eat flesh and drink blood; ye shall eat the flesh of the mighty, and drink the blood of the princes of the earth; ye shall eat fat to satiety, and drink blood to drunkenness, of My sacrifice which I have sacrificed for you. Ye shall be sated at My table with the horse and the chariot, with the mighty man, and with every man of war. Thus will I set My glory among the nations (xxxix. 17–21).

One who does not know from the spiritual sense what is signified by a sacrifice, by flesh and blood, by a horse, a chariot, a mighty man, and a man of war, would suppose that such things were to be eaten and drunk. But the spiritual sense teaches that to "eat the flesh and drink the blood of the sacrifice which the Lord Jehovih will offer upon the mountains of Israel," signifies to appropriate to one's self Divine good and Divine truth from the Word; for the subject treated of is the calling together of all to the Lord's kingdom, and, specifically, the setting up anew of the church by the Lord among the nations. Who cannot see that by "flesh" is not here meant flesh, nor blood by "blood"? As that people should drink blood to drunkenness, and that they should be sated with horse, chariot, mighty man, and every man of war. So in a thousand other passages in the Prophets.

16. Without the spiritual sense no one would know why the prophet Jeremiah was commanded

To buy himself a girdle, and put it on his loins; and not to draw it through the waters, but to hide it in a hole of the rock by Euphrates (*Jer.* xiii. 1–7).

Or why the prophet Isaiah was commanded

To loose the sackcloth from off his loins, and put the shoe from off his foot, and go naked and barefoot three years (*Isa.* xx. 2, 3).

Or why the prophet Ezekiel was commanded

To pass a razor upon his head and upon his beard, and afterwards to divide the hairs, and burn a third part in the midst of the city, smite a third part with the sword, scatter a third part in the wind, and bind a few of them in his skirts, and at last throw them into the midst of the fire (*Ezek.* v. 1–4).

Or why the same prophet was commanded

To lie upon his left side three hundred and ninety days, and upon his right side forty days, and to make himself a cake of wheat, and barley, and millet, and spelt, with the dung of an ox, and eat it ; and in the meantime to raise a rampart and a mound against Jerusalem, and besiege it (*Ezek.* iv. 1–15).

Or why the prophet Hosea was twice commanded

To take to himself a harlot to wife (*Hos.* i. 2–9 ; iii. 2, 3).

And many like things.   Moreover, without the spiritual sense who would know what is signified by all the things pertaining to the tabernacle, such as the ark, the mercy-seat, cherubim, lampstand, altar of incense, the bread of faces on the table, and its veils and curtains ?   Who without the spiritual sense would know what is signified by Aaron's garments of holiness, by his coat, cloak, ephod, urim and thummim, mitre, and other things ?   Who without the spiritual sense would know what is signified by all the things enjoined concerning the burnt-offerings, sacrifices, meat-offerings, and drink-offerings ? and also concerning the sabbaths and feasts ?   The truth is that not the least thing was commanded concerning them that did not signify something of the Lord, heaven, and the church. From these few examples it may be clearly seen that there is a spiritual sense in all things of the Word and in every particular of it.

17. That the Lord when in the world spoke by correspondences, thus that He spoke spiritually while He spoke naturally, is evident from His parables, in each and every word of which there is a spiritual sense.   Take for example the parable of the ten virgins :—

The kingdom of the heavens is like unto ten virgins, who took their lamps and went forth to meet the bridegroom : five of them were wise, and five were foolish ; they that were foolish took their lamps, and took no oil, but the wise took oil in their lamps. While the bridegroom tarried they all slumbered and slept ; and at midnight there was a cry made, Behold, the bridegroom cometh, go ye out to meet him. Then all those virgins awaked, and trimmed their lamps ; and the foolish said unto the wise, Give us of your oil, for our lamps are gone out ; but the wise answered, saying, Not so, lest there be not enough for us and you ; but go ye rather to them that sell, and buy for yourselves. And while they went away to buy, the bridegroom came, and they that were ready went in with him to the wedding, and the door was shut. Afterwards came also the other virgins, saying, Lord, lord, open to us ; but he answered and said, Verily I say unto you, I know you not (*Matt.* xxv. 1–12).

[2] That there is a spiritual sense in each and every one of these things, and a consequent Divine holiness, can be seen by him only who knows that a spiritual sense exists, and what is its nature. In the spiritual sense, the "kingdom of God" means heaven and the church; the "bridegroom," the Lord ; the "wedding," the marriage of the Lord with heaven and the church by means of the good of love and of faith. "Virgins" signify those who are of the church ; "ten," all ; "five," some ; "lamps," the truths of faith; "oil," the good of love ; to "sleep," and to "awake," the life of man in this world which is natural life, and his life after death which is spiritual; to "buy," to procure for themselves; to "go to them that sell and buy oil," to procure for themselves the good of love from others after death ; and as this can then be no longer procured, although they came with their lamps and the oil they had bought to the door where the wedding was, yet the bridegroom said to them "I know you not." The reason is that after his life in this world a man remains such as he had lived in this world. [3] From all this it is evident that the Lord spoke exclusively by correspondences, and this because He spoke from the Divine that was in Him, and was His. That the "bridegroom" signifies the Lord ; the "kingdom of the heavens," the church ; a "wedding," the marriage of the Lord

9

with the church by means of the good of love and of faith; "ten," all; "five," some; to "sleep," a natural state; to "buy," to procure for one's self; a "door," entrance into heaven; and "not to know them," when spoken by the Lord, not to be in His love, is evident from many passages in the prophetic Word where these expressions have a like signification. It is because "virgins" signify those who are of the church that the virgin and daughter of Zion, of Jerusalem, of Judah, and of Israel, are so often mentioned in the prophetic Word. And it is because "oil" signifies the good of love that all the holy things of the Israelitish Church were anointed with oil. It is the same with all the other parables, and with all the words the Lord spoke, and that were written in the Gospels. This is why the Lord says that

His words are spirit and are life (*John* vi. 63).

[4] It is the same with all the Lord's miracles, which were Divine because they signified the various states of those with whom the church was to be set up anew by the Lord. Thus when the blind received sight, it signified that they who had been in ignorance of truth should receive intelligence; when the deaf received hearing, it signified that they who had previously heard nothing about the Lord and the Word should hearken and obey; when the dead were raised, it signified that they who otherwise would spiritually perish would become living; and so on. This is meant by the Lord's reply to the disciples of John, who sent them to ask whether He was the One that should come :—

Tell John the things which ye do hear and see : the blind receive their sight, and the lame walk, the lepers are cleansed, and the deaf hear, the dead rise again, and the poor hear the Gospel (*Matt.* xi. 3–5).

Moreover, all the miracles related in the Word contain in them such things as belong to the Lord, to heaven, and to the church. This makes these miracles Divine, and distinguishes them from those which are not Divine. These few examples are given in order to illustrate what the spiritual sense is, and to show that it is in all things of the Word and in every particular of it.

18. iii. *From the spiritual sense it is that the Word is divinely inspired, and is holy in every word.* It is said in the church that the Word is holy, and this because Jehovah God spoke it; but as its holiness is not apparent from the letter alone, he who on this account once doubts its holiness, afterwards confirms his doubt when reading the Word by many things in it, for he then thinks, Can this be holy ? can this be Divine ? Therefore lest such a thought should flow in with many, and should afterwards prevail, and thereby the conjunction of the Lord with the church, in which is the Word, should perish, it has now pleased the Lord to reveal the spiritual sense, in order that it may be known where in the Word this holiness lies hid.   [2] This again may be illustrated by examples. The Word treats sometimes of Egypt, sometimes of Asshur, sometimes of Edom, of Moab, of the sons of Ammon, of Tyre and Sidon, of Gog; and one who does not know that these names signify things of heaven and the church may be led into the error that the Word treats much of nations and peoples, and but little of heaven and the church; thus much of earthly, and little of heavenly things. But when he knows what is signified by them, or by their names, he can come out of error into truth.   [3] And so when he sees in the Word such frequent mention of gardens, groves, and forests, and also of the trees in them, as the olive, vine, cedar, poplar, oak; and also such frequent mention of the lamb, sheep, goat, calf, ox ; and likewise of mountains, hills, valleys, and the fountains, rivers, and waters in them, and many like things, one who knows nothing about the spiritual sense of the Word must believe that these things only are meant. For he is not aware that a garden, grove, and forest, mean wisdom, intelligence, and knowledge ; that an olive, vine, cedar, poplar, and oak, mean the celestial, spiritual, rational, natural, and sensuous good and truth of the church; that a lamb, sheep, goat, calf, and ox, mean innocence, charity, and natural affection; that mountains, hills, and valleys, mean higher, lower, and lowest things of the church; that Egypt signifies memory-knowledge,* Asshur reason, Edom

* See foot-note on p. 21.

the Natural, Moab the adulteration of good, the sons of Ammon the adulteration of truth, Tyre and Sidon the knowledges of truth and good, and Gog external worship without internal. But when a man knows these things he is able to consider that the Word treats solely of heavenly things, and that these earthly things are merely the subjects (*subjecta*) in which the heavenly things are. [4] But let this also be illustrated by an example from the Word. We read in *David*:—

> The voice of Jehovah is upon the waters; the God of glory maketh it to thunder; Jehovah is upon the great waters. The voice of Jehovah breaketh the cedars; yea, Jehovah breaketh in pieces the cedars of Lebanon. He maketh them also to skip like a calf, Lebanon and Sirion like a son of unicorns. The voice of Jehovah cutteth out as a flame of fire. The voice of Jehovah maketh the wilderness to tremble; it maketh the wilderness of Kadesh to tremble. The voice of Jehovah maketh the hinds to be in travail, and layeth bare the forests; but in His temple every one saith, Glory (*Ps.* xxix. 3–9).

He who is not aware that everything here, even as to every single word, is divinely holy, may, if a merely natural man, say to himself, What is this—that Jehovah sitteth upon the waters, that by His voice He breaketh the cedars, maketh them skip like a calf, and Lebanon like a son of unicorns, and maketh the hinds to be in travail, and so on? For he knows not that in the spiritual sense the power of Divine truth, or of the Word, is described by these things. [5] In this sense, the "voice of Jehovah," here called "thunder," means the Divine truth or Word in its power. The "great waters," upon which Jehovah sits, mean the truths of the Word. The "cedars," and "Lebanon," which He "breaks," and "breaks in pieces," mean the false things of the rational man. The "calf," and a "son of unicorns," mean the false things of the natural and of the sensuous man. The "flame of fire," means the affection of what is false. The "wilderness," and the "wilderness of Kadesh," mean the church in which there is not anything true and good. The "hinds" which the voice of Jehovah causes to be in travail, mean the nations who are in natural good.

And the "forests" which He lays bare, mean the knowledges (*scientiae et cognitiones*)* which the Word opens to them. Therefore these words follow: "In His temple every one saith, Glory," which mean that there are Divine truths in each and every thing of the Word. For the "temple" signifies the Lord, and therefore the Word, and also heaven and the church; and "glory" signifies Divine truth. From all this it is evident that there is not a word in this passage that is not descriptive of the Divine power of the Word against falsities of every kind in natural men, and of the Divine power in reforming the nations.

19. There is a still more interior sense in the Word which is called CELESTIAL, and of which something has been said above (n. 6); but this sense can with difficulty be made plain, because it does not fall so much into the thought of the understanding as into the affection of the will. The reason there is in the Word this still more interior sense called celestial, is that there proceeds from the Lord Divine good and Divine truth, Divine good from His Divine love, and Divine truth from His Divine wisdom; and both are in the Word, for the Word is the Divine proceeding;† and it is for this reason that the Word gives life to those who devoutly read it. But this subject will be spoken of in the chapter in which it will be shown that there is a marriage of the Lord and the church, and a derivative marriage of good and truth, in each and every thing of the Word.

20. iv. *Hitherto the spiritual sense of the Word has been unknown.* It has been shown in the work on *Heaven and Hell* (n. 87–105) that all things of nature, and likewise of the human

---

* Note the careful distinction made by Swedenborg between those knowledges that are merely in the external memory, and those which a man has some real knowledge of by experience or in some other way, and which are therefore not mere matters of memory. The former he calls "memory-knowledges (*scientiae* or *scientifica*);" the latter simply "knowledges (*cognitiones*)." This distinction runs all through these works, and must not be lost sight of, the recognition of it being vital to the understanding of important doctrines. [TR.]

† That is, the Divine in the act of proceeding. See foot-note to *Doctrine of the Lord* (n. 2, page 2). [TR.]

body, and also every single particular in them, correspond to spiritual things. Hitherto, however, it has not been known what correspondence is, although in the most ancient times this was very well known; for the science of correspondences was then the science of sciences, and was so universal that all the writings and books were written by means of correspondences. [2] The book of *Job*, which is an ancient book, is full of correspondences. The hieroglyphics of the Egyptians, and also the fabulous stories of highest antiquity, were nothing but correspondences. All the ancient churches were churches representative of heavenly things; their rites, and also the ordinances according to which their worship was instituted, consisted exclusively of correspondences. So did all things of the church among the sons of Jacob; their burnt-offerings and sacrifices, with each and every thing thereto pertaining, were correspondences; so was the tabernacle with all its contents; so were their feasts, the feast of unleavened things, the feast of tabernacles, and the feast of first-fruits; so was the priesthood of Aaron and the Levites, and also the holy garments of Aaron and his sons; besides all the ordinances and judgments that concerned their worship and their life. [3] And as Divine things present themselves in the world by correspondences, the Word has been written exclusively by means of them. And therefore the Lord spoke by correspondences, because He spoke from His Divine, for that which is from the Divine, descending into nature, is turned into such things as correspond to Divine things, and which then store up and conceal in their bosom the Divine things that are called celestial and spiritual.

21. I have been instructed that the men of the Most Ancient Church (the church before the flood) were of a genius so heavenly that they spoke with angels of heaven, and that they were able to speak with them by means of correspondences. From this the state of their wisdom was rendered such that whatever they saw in this world they thought about not only in a natural way, but spiritually also at the same time, so that they thought unitedly with angels. I have been instructed besides that Enoch (of whom mention is made in *Genesis* v. 21–24) together with his associates, collected correspondences from the lips of those men of the Most Ancient Church, and transmitted the knowledge of them to posterity, and that in consequence of this the science of correspondences was not only known but was also much cultivated in many kingdoms of Asia, especially in the land of Canaan, in Egypt, Assyria, Chaldea, Syria, Arabia, and also in Tyre, Sidon, and Nineveh; and that it was carried over from places on the sea-coast there into Greece; but there it was turned into fabulous stories, as is evident from the earliest writers of that country.

22. But when in process of time the representative things of the church, which were correspondences, were converted into things idolatrous and also into magic, then of the Lord's Divine Providence the knowledge of correspondences was gradually blotted out of remembrance, and among the Israelitish and Jewish people was altogether lost and annihilated. The worship of that nation did indeed consist exclusively of correspondences, and was consequently representative of heavenly things; but still they did not know what anything of it signified, for they were utterly natural men, and therefore were neither willing nor able to know anything about spiritual things, nor consequently about correspondences.

23. The reason why, in ancient times, the idolatries of the nations originated from the knowledge of correspondences, was that all things visible on the earth have a correspondence; not only trees, but also beasts and birds of every kind, and likewise fishes, and all other things. The ancients, possessing a knowledge of correspondences, made for themselves images that corresponded to heavenly things, and delighted in them because they signified things such as belong to heaven, and therefore to the church. They therefore set them not only in their temples, but also in their houses, not to be worshiped, but to call to remembrance the heavenly things they signified. Consequently in Egypt and elsewhere there were images of calves,

oxen, serpents, also of children, old men, maidens; because
calves and oxen signified affections and powers of the natural
man; serpents, the sagacity of the sensuous man; children, innocence and charity; old men, wisdom; and maidens, affections
of truth; and so on.   When the knowledge of correspondences
had been blotted out of remembrance, their descendants began
to worship as holy, and at last as deities, the images and em-
blems set up by the ancients, because they stood in and about
their temples.   [2] So with other nations; as, with the Philistines at Ashdod, Dagon (concerning whom see 1 *Sam.* v. 1 to
end), whose upper part was like a man, and his lower like a fish.
This image was so devised because a man signifies intelligence,
and a fish knowledge, which make a one.   It was also because
they possessed a knowledge of correspondences that the ancients worshiped in gardens and groves, in accordance with
the kinds of trees in them; and also upon mountains and hills.
For gardens and groves signified wisdom and intelligence, and
each particular tree something relating thereto; as the olive, the
good of love; the vine, truth from that good; the cedar, rational
good and truth.   A mountain signified the highest heaven;
and a hill, the heaven under it.   [3] The knowledge of correspondences survived among a number of the orientals, even
until the Lord's advent, as is evident from the wise men of the
east who came to the Lord at His birth; and this was why a
star went before them, and why they brought with them as gifts,
gold, frankincense, and myrrh (*Matt.* ii. 1, 2, 9–11).   For the
"star that went before them" signified knowledge (*cognitio*)
from heaven; "gold," celestial good; "frankincense," spiritual good; and "myrrh," natural good; from which three is all
worship.   [4] Nevertheless there was no knowledge of correspondences whatever among the Israelitish and Jewish nation,
although everything in their worship, and all the judgments
and ordinances delivered them through Moses, and all things
of the Word, were nothing but correspondences.   The reason
was that at heart they were idolaters, and of such a character
that they were not even willing to know that anything of their

worship signified what is celestial and spiritual; for they desired that all those things should be holy in themselves and in
connection with *them ;* so that if celestial and spiritual things
had been disclosed to them, they would not only have rejected
but would have profaned them.   Therefore heaven was so
closed toward them that they scarcely knew that there is a life
eternal.   That this was the case is clearly evident from the fact
that they did not acknowledge the Lord, although universal holy
Scripture prophesied concerning Him, and foretold His advent;
and they rejected Him for this sole reason—that He taught of
a heavenly and not an earthly kingdom; for they wanted a
Messiah who would exalt them above every other nation in the
world, and not a Messiah who cared for their eternal salvation.
For the rest, they affirm that the Word contains within it many
arcana that are called mystical; but are unwilling to learn
that these refer to the Lord; they however are quite willing to
learn when it is said that the reference is to gold.

24. The reason why the knowledge of correspondences,
which gives the spiritual sense of the Word, was not disclosed
in times after those, is that the Christians of the primitive
church were so very simple that it could not be disclosed to
them; for it would have been of no use to them, nor would it
have been understood.   After their day, in consequence of the
papal dominion, darkness came over all the Christian world;
and they who are of that dominion, and have confirmed themselves in its falsities, neither can nor will apprehend anything
spiritual, nor consequently what is the correspondence in the
Word of natural things with spiritual.   For thereby they would
be convinced that by "Peter" is not meant Peter, but the Lord
as a Rock; and they would also be convinced that the Word
is Divine even to its inmosts, and that a decree of the Pope is
relatively of no account.   On the other hand, after the Reformation, as men began to effect a separation between faith
and charity, and to worship God in three Persons—thus three
gods, whom they conceived to be one—heavenly truths were
hidden from them; and if they had been disclosed they would

have falsified them and applied them to faith alone, and not one of them to charity and love. And thus they would have closed heaven against themselves.

25. The reason why the spiritual sense of the Word has been at this day disclosed by the Lord is that the doctrine of genuine truth has now been revealed; and this doctrine, and no other, is in accord with the spiritual sense of the Word. This sense, moreover, is signified by the appearing of the Lord in the clouds of heaven with glory and power (*Matt.* xxiv. 30, 31); which chapter treats of the consummation of the age, by which is meant the last time of the church. The opening of the Word as to its spiritual sense was also promised in the *Revelation.* It is there meant by the "white horse," and by the "great supper" to which all are invited (xix. 11–18). That for a long time the spiritual sense will not be recognized, and that this is entirely owing to those who are in falsities of doctrine, especially concerning the Lord, and who therefore do not admit truths, is meant in the *Revelation* by the "beast," and by the "kings of the earth," who should make war with him that sat upon the white horse (xix. 19). By the "beast" are meant the Papists, as in chapter xvii. 3; and by the "kings of the earth" are meant the Reformed who are in false things of doctrine.

26. v. *Henceforth the spiritual sense of the Word will be imparted solely to him who from the Lord is in genuine truths.* The reason of this is that no one can see the spiritual sense except from the Lord alone, nor unless from Him he is in genuine truths. For the spiritual sense of the Word treats solely of the Lord and His kingdom; and this is the sense in which are His angels in heaven, for it is His Divine truth there. To this sense a man can do violence if he has a knowledge of correspondences, and wishes by means of it and from self-intelligence to investigate the spiritual sense of the Word. For through some correspondences with which he is acquainted he may pervert the meaning of it, and may even force it to confirm what is false, and this would be doing violence to Divine

truth, and also to heaven.   And therefore if any one purposes
to open that sense from himself and not from the Lord, heaven
is closed ; and then the man either sees nothing, or else becomes
spiritually insane.   [2] Another reason is that the Lord teaches
every one by means of the Word, and He teaches from those
truths which the man already has, and not without a medium
does He pour new truths in, so that unless man is in Divine
truths, or if he is only in a few truths and at the same time in
falsities, he may from these falsify the truths, as it is well
known is done by every heretic in regard to the Word's sense
of the letter.   Therefore in order to prevent anybody from entering into the spiritual sense of the Word, or from perverting
the genuine truth that belongs to that sense, guards have been
set by the Lord, which in the Word are meant by the cherubim.
[3] That guards have been set has been represented to me in
the following manner :—

It was granted me to see great purses, having the appearance of sacks,
in which silver was stored up in great abundance.   As the purses were
open, it seemed as if any one might take out, and even pillage, the silver
therein deposited ; but near those purses sat two angels as guards.   The
place where the purses were laid appeared like a manger in a stable.   In
an adjoining apartment were seen modest maidens together with a chaste
wife, and near that apartment stood two little children, and it was said
that they were to be sported with, not in childish fashion, but wisely.
After this there appeared a harlot, and also a horse lying dead.
   [4] On seeing these things I was instructed that by them was represented the sense of the letter of the Word, in which is the spiritual
sense.   The large purses full of silver, signified knowledges of truth in
great abundance.   Their being open and yet guarded by angels, signified
that every one may get knowledges of truth from the Word, but that
care is taken lest any one should falsify the spiritual sense, in which are
pure truths.   The manger in a stable in which the purses lay, signified
spiritual instruction for the understanding—a manger signifies this
because the horse that feeds from it signifies the understanding.   [5]
The modest maidens seen in the adjoining apartment, signified affections
of truth ; and the chaste wife, the conjunction of good and truth.   The
little children signified the innocence of wisdom therein : they were
angels from the third heaven, who all appear like little children.   The
harlot, together with the dead horse, signified the falsification of the

Word by many of this day, whereby all understanding of truth perishes. The harlot signified falsification; and the dead horse, no understanding of truth.*

III.

THE SENSE OF THE LETTER OF THE WORD IS THE BASIS, THE CONTAINANT, AND THE SUPPORT OF ITS SPIRITUAL AND CELESTIAL SENSES.

27. In every Divine work there is a first, a middle, and a last (or ultimate); and the first passes through the middle to the last (or ultimate), and so comes into manifest being and subsists. Hence the last or ultimate is the *Basis*. But the first is in the middle, and through the middle in the ultimate; so that the ultimate is the *Containant*. And as the ultimate is the containant and the basis, it is also the *Support*.

28. The learned reader will comprehend that these three may be called end, cause, and effect; also *esse*, *fieri*, and *existere*;† and that the end is the *esse*, the cause the *fieri*, and the effect the *existere*; consequently, that in every complete thing there is a trine, which is called first, middle, and ultimate; also end, cause, and effect; and also *esse*, *fieri*, and *existere*. When these things are comprehended, it is also comprehended that every Divine work is complete and perfect in its ultimate; and likewise that the whole is in the ultimate, which is a trine, because the prior things are *together*, or simultaneously, in it.‡

---

* Quoted from the *Spiritual Diary* (n. 3605a), and the *De Verbo* (n. 1); and repeated in the *Apocalypse Revealed* (n. 255), and in the *True Christian Religion* (n. 277). [TR.]

† That is, *being, becoming*, and *coming forth*. The *Being* of a thing is what we call its existence; and therefore it was said by the ancients that "in God we live, and move, and have our being" (*Acts* xvii. 28). Here our being means the inmost of our life (*Arcana Coelestia*, 5605e). The *becoming* of a thing is its being taking form. And the *coming forth* of a thing is the presentation or manifestation of that thing as an actual reality. Thus the Latin word *existere* has a very different meaning from the English *exist*, and cannot be translated by it without causing a complete misconception in the mind of the English reader. [TR.]

‡ That is, the two prior degrees are in the ultimate degree in simultaneous order; for a full explanation of which see below at n. 38, and also the *Angelic Wisdom concerning the Divine Love and the Divine Wisdom* (n. 205–207). [TR.]

29. It is from this that by "three," in the Word, in the spiritual sense, is meant what is complete and perfect; and also the whole simultaneously. And as this is the signification of the number three, it is employed in the Word whenever any such thing is marked out for notice. As in the following passages :—

Isaiah went naked and barefoot three years (*Isa.* xx. 3).

Jehovah called Samuel three times, and Samuel ran three times to Eli, and Eli understood him the third time (1 *Sam.* iii. 1–8).

David said to Jonathan that he would hide himself in the field three days ; and Jonathan afterwards shot three arrows at the side of the stone ; and after that, David bowed himself down three times before Jonathan (1 *Sam.* xx. 5, 12–41).

Elijah stretched himself three times over the widow's son (1 *Kings* xvii. 21).

Elijah commanded that they should pour water on the burnt-offering three times (1 *Kings* xviii. 34).

Jesus said, The kingdom of the heavens is like unto leaven, which a woman took and hid in three measures of meal, till the whole was leavened (*Matt.* xiii. 33).

Jesus said unto Peter that he should deny Him thrice (*Matt.* xxvi. 34).

The Lord said three times unto Peter, Lovest thou Me ? (*John* xxi. 15–17).

Jonah was in the whale's belly three days and three nights (*Jonah* i. 17).

Jesus said, Destroy this temple, and in three days I will raise it up (*John* ii. 19 ; *Matt.* xxvi. 61).

Jesus prayed three times in Gethsemane (*Matt.* xxvi. 39–44).

Jesus rose again on the third day (*Matt.* xxviii. 1).

Besides many other passages where the number "three" is mentioned ; and it is mentioned wherever a finished and perfect work is treated of, because this is signified by that number.

30. These things are premised with a view to those which follow, in order that they may be comprehended with understanding ; and for the present purpose that it may be comprehended that the natural sense of the Word which is the sense of the letter, is the basis, the containant, and the support of its spiritual sense and of its celestial sense.

31. It has been said above (n. 6, 19) that there are three senses in the Word; and also that the celestial sense is its first, the spiritual sense its middle, and the natural sense its ultimate sense. From this the rational man may infer that the first of the Word, which is celestial, passes through its middle, which is spiritual, to its ultimate, which is natural; and thus that its ultimate is the *Basis*. Furthermore that the first of the Word which is celestial, is in its middle which is spiritual, and through this is in its ultimate which is natural, and that consequently its ultimate which is natural and is the sense of the letter, is the *Containant*. And as the sense of the letter is the Basis and the Containant, it is also the *Support*.

32. But how these things come to pass cannot be told in a few words. Indeed they are arcana in which are the angels of heaven, and which will be unfolded, so far as can possibly be done, in the treatises mentioned in the Preface to the *Doctrine of the Lord*—and which will be from Angelic Wisdom—On the *Divine Providence, Omnipotence, Omnipresence, Omniscience,* On the *Divine Love and the Divine Wisdom,* and On *Life.** For the present it is sufficient to conclude from what has been said above, that the Word—which is in an especial sense a Divine work for the salvation of mankind—in respect to its ultimate sense which is natural and is called the sense of the letter, is the Basis, the Containant, and the Support of the two interior senses.

33. From all this it follows that without the sense of the letter, the Word would be like a palace without a foundation, and thus like a palace in the air and not on the earth, which would be but the shadow of a palace, that would vanish away. Furthermore, that without the sense of the letter the Word would be like a temple containing many holy things, and in its midst a sanctuary, but without roof and walls, which are its containants, and in the absence or loss of which its holy things would be plundered by thieves, or invaded by beasts of earth and birds of heaven, and thus be dispersed. Or it would be like the tabernacle (in the inmost of which was the ark of the

* See translator's foot-notes to Author's Preface to the *Doctrine of the Lord.*

covenant, and in its middle the golden lampstand, the golden altar for incense, and the table on which were the loaves of faces, which were its holy things) without its ultimates, which were the curtains and veils.   Nay, without the sense of the letter, the Word would be like a human body without its coverings which are called skins, and without its supports which are called bones ; lacking which supports and coverings all the interior things of the body would fall asunder.   And it would be like the heart and lungs in the chest without their covering which is called the pleura, and their supports which are called the ribs.   Or like the brain without its covering which is called the dura mater, and without its general covering, containant, and support, which is called the skull.   Thus would it be with the Word without the sense of the letter ; and therefore it is said in *Isaiah :—*

Jehovah createth upon all the glory a covering (iv. 5).

34. So would it be with the heavens where angels are, without the world where men are.   The human race is the basis, containant, and support of the heavens ; and the Word is among men and in them.   For all the heavens have been discriminated into two kingdoms, called the celestial kingdom and the spiritual kingdom ; these two kingdoms are founded upon a natural kingdom, in which are men.   And so therefore is it with the Word which is among men and in men.   (That the angelic heavens have been discriminated into two kingdoms, the celestial, and the spiritual, may be seen in the work on *Heaven and Hell,* n. 20–28.)

35. It has been shown in the *Doctrine of the Lord* (n. 28), that the prophets of the Old Testament represented the Lord in respect to the Word, and thereby signified the doctrine of the church from the Word, and that for this reason they were called " sons of man."   From this it follows that by means of the various things they suffered and endured, they represented the violence done by the Jews to the sense of the letter of the Word.   Thus :—

The prophet Isaiah was commanded to put off the sackcloth from off nis loins, and to put off his shoe from off his foot, and to go naked and barefoot three years (*Isa.* xx. 2, 3).

And so

The prophet Ezekiel was commanded to pass a barber's razor upon his head and upon his beard, and to burn a third part in the midst of the city, to smite a third part with the sword, and to scatter a third part in the wind, and to wrap a few of the hairs in his skirts, and at last to cast them into the midst of the fire and burn them (*Ezek.* v. 1-4).

[2] As the "prophets" represented the Word, and consequently signified the doctrine of the church from the Word, as said above, and as the "head" signifies wisdom from the Word, therefore the "hair" and "beard" signify the ultimate of truth. By reason of this signification, it was a mark of deep mourning, and also a great disgrace, for any one to make himself bald, or to be seen bald. For this and no other reason it was that the prophet shaved off the hair of his head and his beard, that so he might represent the state of the Jewish Church in respect to the Word. For this and no other reason was it that

The forty-two children who called Elisha bald were torn to pieces by two she-bears (2 *Kings* ii. 23, 24).

For as before said a "prophet" represented the Word, and "baldness" signified the Word without its ultimate sense. [3] It will be seen in the next chapter (n. 49) that the "Nazirites" represented the Lord in respect to the Word in its ultimates; and therefore it was an ordinance for them that they should let their hair grow, and shave off none of it. Moreover the term "Nazirite" in the Hebrew tongue means the hair of the head.

It was also an ordinance for the high priest that he should not shave his head (*Lev.* xxi. 10).

Likewise for the head of a household (*Lev.* xxi. 5).

[4] This was why baldness was to them a great disgrace, as is evident from the following passages :—

On all heads baldness, and every beard shaven (*Isa.* xv. 2 ; *Jer.* xlviii. 37).

Shame upon all faces, and baldness upon all heads (*Ezek.* vii. 18).

Every head made bald, and every shoulder plucked (*Ezek.* xxix. 18).

I will cause sackcloth to come up upon all loins, and baldness upon every head (*Amos* viii. 10).

Put on baldness, and shave thee on account of the sons of thy delights, and enlarge thy baldness, for they are gone into exile from thee (*Micah* i. 16).

To "put on baldness" and to "enlarge" it, here signifies to falsify the truths of the Word in its ultimates, for when these are falsified (as was done by the Jews) the whole Word is destroyed; for the ultimates of the Word are its props and supports; indeed, each word is a prop and a support to its celestial and spiritual truths. As the "hair" signifies truth in the ultimates, in the spiritual world all who despise the Word, and falsify its sense of the letter, appear bald; whereas they who honor and love it appear with becoming hair. On this subject see also below (n. 49).

36. The Word in its ultimate or natural sense, which is the sense of the letter, is signified also by the wall of the holy Jerusalem, the structure of which was of jasper; and by the foundations of the wall, which were precious stones; and likewise by the gates, which were pearls (*Rev.* xxi. 18–21); for Jerusalem signifies the church as to doctrine. But of these things more in the following chapter. From what has been adduced it is now evident that the sense of the letter of the Word, which is the natural sense, is the Basis, Containant, and Support of its interior senses, which are the spiritual and the celestial.

_____

IV.

DIVINE TRUTH IN THE SENSE OF THE LETTER OF THE WORD IS IN ITS FULLNESS, IN ITS HOLINESS, AND IN ITS POWER.

37. The reason why the Word in the sense of the letter is in its fullness, in its holiness, and in its power, is that the two prior or interior senses, which are called the spiritual and the celestial, are together or simultaneous (*sunt simul*) in the natural sense, which is the sense of the letter, as was said above (n. 28). But how they are simultaneous in that sense shall now be told in a few words.

38. There are in heaven and in this world a successive order and a simultaneous order. In successive order one thing succeeds and follows another from highest to lowest; but in simultaneous order one thing is next another from inmost to outmost. Successive order is like a column with successive parts from the top to the bottom; but simultaneous order is like a connected structure with successive circumferences from center to surface. It shall now be told how successive order becomes simultaneous order in the ultimate. It is in this way: The highest things of successive order become the inmost ones of simultaneous order, and the lowest things of successive order become the outermost ones of simultaneous order. Comparatively speaking it is as if the column of successive parts were to sink down and become a connected body in a plane. [2] Thus is the simultaneous formed from the successive, and this in all things both in general and in particular of the natural world, and also of the spiritual world; for everywhere there is a first, a middle, and an ultimate, and the first aims at and goes through the middle to its ultimate. Apply this to the Word. The Celestial, the Spiritual, and the Natural proceed from the Lord in successive order, and in the ultimate are in simultaneous order; and it is in this way that the celestial and spiritual senses of the Word are simultaneous in its natural sense. When this is comprehended, it may be seen how the natural sense of the Word, which is the sense of the letter, is the basis, containant, and support of its spiritual and celestial senses; and how in the sense of the letter of the Word Divine good and Divine truth are in their fullness, in their holiness, and in their power.

39. From all this it is evident that in the sense of the letter the Word is the very Word itself, for within this sense there are spirit and life, the spiritual sense being its spirit, and the celestial sense its life. This is what the Lord says:—

The words that I speak unto you are spirit and are life (*John* vi. 63).

The Lord spoke His words before the world, and in the natural sense. The spiritual sense and the celestial sense without the natural sense which is the sense of the letter, are not the Word; for without it they are like spirit and life without a body; and are (as before said, n. 33) like a palace without a foundation.

40. The truths of the sense of the letter of the Word are in part not naked truths, but appearances of truth, and are as it were likenesses and comparisons taken from things such as exist in nature, and thus accommodated and adapted to the apprehension of the simple and of little children. But being correspondences they are receptacles and abodes of genuine truth; and are like enclosing and containing vessels, as a crystal cup encloses noble wine, and as a silver plate holds palatable food. They are also like garments which clothe, as swathings do an infant, and a pretty dress a maiden. They are also like the memory-knowledges (*scientifica*) of the natural man which contain within them perceptions and affections of truth of the spiritual man. The naked truths themselves which are enclosed, held, clothed, and contained, are in the spiritual sense of the Word; and the naked goods are in its celestial sense. [2] But let this be illustrated from the Word. Jesus said:—

Woe unto you, Scribes and Pharisees, because ye cleanse the outside of the cup and of the platter, but within they are full of extortion and excess. Thou blind Pharisee, cleanse first the inside of the cup and of the platter, that the outside thereof may be clean also (*Matt.* xxiii. 25, 26).

The Lord here spoke by means of ultimate things which are containants, and said "cup and platter;" and "cup" means wine, and "wine" the truth of the Word; and "platter" means food, and "food" the good of the Word. To "cleanse the inside of the cup and platter," means to purify by means of the Word the interior things which belong to will and thought and thus to love and faith. "That the outside may be clean also," means that in this way, exterior things, which are the actions and the conversation, will have been made pure, for these derive their essence from the interior things. [3] Again, Jesus said :—

> There was a certain rich man, who was clothed in crimson and fine linen, and living in mirth and splendor every day ; and there was a certain poor man, named Lazarus, who was laid at his porch, full of sores (*Luke* xvi. 19, 20).

Here also the Lord spoke by means of natural things that were correspondences, and contained spiritual things. The "rich man" means the Jewish nation, which is called "rich" because it possessed the Word, in which are spiritual riches. The "crimson and fine linen" with which he was clothed, signify the good and truth of the Word; "crimson" its good, and "fine linen" its truth. To "live in mirth and splendor every day," signifies the delight they had in possessing and reading the Word. The "poor man Lazarus," means the Gentiles who had not the Word; and that these were despised and scorned by the Jews, is meant by Lazarus lying at the rich man's porch full of sores. [4] The reason the Gentiles are meant by "Lazarus" is that the Gentiles were beloved by the Lord, as

> Lazarus, who was raised from the dead was beloved by the Lord (*John* xi. 3, 5, 36), and is called His friend (xi. 11), and reclined with the Lord at table (xii. 2).

From the two foregoing passages it is evident that the truths and goods of the sense of the letter of the Word are as vessels and as garments for the naked truth and good that lie hidden in its spiritual and celestial senses.

41. Such being the Word in the sense of the letter, it follows that they who are in Divine truths, and in the faith that the Word within, in its bosom, is Divine holiness—and much more they who are in the faith that it is from its spiritual and celestial senses that the Word is Divine holiness—see Divine truths in natural light while reading the Word in enlightenment from the Lord. For the light of heaven (in which is the spiritual sense of the Word) flows into the natural light in which is its sense of the letter, and illumines man's intellectual called the rational, and causes him to see and recognize Divine truths, both where they stand in plain view, and where they lie concealed. With some these Divine truths flow in along with the light of heaven; sometimes even when they are not aware of it.

42. As, in its inmost bosom, from its celestial sense, our Word is like a flame that enkindles; and as, in its middle bosom, from its spiritual sense, it is like a light that enlightens; it follows that in its ultimate bosom, from its natural sense which has within it the two more interior senses, the Word is like a ruby and a diamond; like a ruby from its celestial flame, and like a diamond from its spiritual light. And as from its transparency the Word is like this in the sense of the letter, the Word in this sense of the letter is meant by the foundations of the wall of the New Jerusalem; by the Urim and Thummim in Aaron's ephod; by the garden of Eden in which had been the king of Tyre; by the curtains and veils of the Tabernacle; and by the externals of the Temple at Jerusalem. But in its very glory the Word was represented by the Lord when He was transfigured.

43. That *the truths of the Word's sense of the letter are meant by the foundations of the wall of the New Jerusalem* (*Rev.* xxi.), follows from the fact that the "New Jerusalem" means the New Church as to doctrine (as has been shown in the *Doctrine of the Lord*, n. 62, 63); so that its "wall," and the "foundations of the wall," can mean nothing but the external of the Word which is the sense of the letter, for this is the source of doctrine, and through doctrine of the church, and this sense is like a wall with its foundations that encloses and protects a city. Concerning the wall of the New Jerusalem and its foundations we read in the *Revelation:*—

The angel measured the wall thereof, a hundred and forty and four cubits, which was the measure of a man, that is, of an angel. And the wall had twelve foundations, adorned with every precious stone. The first foundation was jasper; the second, sapphire; the third, chalcedony; the fourth, emerald; the fifth, sardonyx; the sixth, sardius; the seventh, chrysolite; the eighth, beryl; the ninth, topaz; the tenth, chrysoprase; the eleventh, jacinth · the twelfth, amethyst (xxi. 17–20).

The number " 144" signifies all the truths and goods of the church derived from doctrine that is drawn from the sense of the letter of the Word. The like is signified by " 12." A " man" signifies intelligence; an " angel," Divine truth the source of intelligence; " measure," the quality of these; the " wall" and its " foundations," the sense of the letter of the Word; and the " precious stones," the truths and goods of the Word in their order, which are the source of doctrine, and through doctrine of the church.

44. *The truths and goods of the sense of the letter of the Word are meant by the Urim and Thummim.* The Urim and Thummim were on the ephod of Aaron, whose priesthood represented the Lord as to Divine good and as to the work of salvation. The garments of the priesthood or of holiness represented Divine truth from Divine good. The ephod represented Divine truth in its ultimate, thus the Word in the sense of the letter, for this, as before said, is Divine truth in its ultimate. Consequently the twelve precious stones bearing the names of the twelve tribes of Israel (which were the Urim and Thummim) represented Divine truths from Divine good in their whole complex. [2] Concerning these we read in Moses :—

They shall make the ephod of [gold,] hyacinthine blue, and bright-crimson, of scarlet double-dyed, and fine linen intertwined. And thou shalt make a breast-plate of judgment according to the work of the ephod ; and thou shalt set it with settings of stones, four rows of stones : a ruby, a topaz, and an emerald, the first row ; a chrysoprase, a sapphire, and a diamond, the second row ; a cyanus, an agate, and an amethyst, the third row ; a thalassius, a sardius, and a jasper, the fourth row. These stones shall be according to the names of the sons of Israel ; the engravings of a signet according to his name shall be for the twelve tribes. And Aaron shall carry upon the breast-plate of judgment the Urim and Thummim ; and let them be upon the heart of Aaron when he goeth in before Jehovah (*Exod.* xxviii. 6, 15–21, 29, 30).

[3] What was represented by Aaron's garments—his ephod, robe, vest, mitre, belt—has been unfolded in the *Arcana Coelestia* on this chapter, where it is shown that the ephod represented Divine truth in its ultimate ; the precious stones in it,

truths pellucid from good; the twelve precious stones, all ultimate truths pellucid from the good of love in their order; the
twelve tribes of Israel, all things of the church; the breast-
plate, Divine truth from Divine good; the Urim and Thummim, the shining forth in ultimates of Divine truth from Divine good (for Urim means a shining fire; and Thummim, in
the angelic language, means a shining forth, and in the Hebrew,
entirety).   Besides many other things, it is there shown also
that answers were given by variegations of light and a simultaneous tacit perception, or by a living voice.   From all this
it is evident that these precious stones signified truths from
good in the ultimate sense of the Word; nor are answers from
heaven given by other means, for in this sense the Divine proceeding is in its fullness.   [4] That precious stones and diadems signify Divine truths in their ultimates, such as are the
truths of the sense of the letter of the Word, has been made
very evident to me from precious stones and diadems in the
spiritual world, among the angels and spirits there whom I
have seen wearing them—I have seen them in their caskets also
—and it has been given me to know that they correspond to
truths in ultimates, and, what is more, that from these truths
they exist and come into view.   As these truths are signified
by diadems and precious stones, John saw diadems

Upon the head of the dragon (*Rev.* xii. 3):
Upon the horns of the beast (*Rev.* xiii. 1):
And precious stones upon the harlot that sat on the scarlet beast
(*Rev.* xvii. 4).

Diadems and precious stones were seen upon the dragon, the
beast, and the harlot, because these signify the people in the
Christian world who are in possession of the Word.

45. *The truths of the sense of the letter of the Word are
meant by the precious stones in the garden of Eden, in which, in
Ezekiel, the king of Tyre is said to have been.*   We read in
Ezekiel:—

King of Tyre, thou sealest up thy sum, full of wisdom, and perfect in
beauty.   Thou hast been in Eden the garden of God; every precious

stone was thy covering, the ruby, the topaz, and the diamond, the beryl, the sardonyx, and the jasper, the sapphire, the chrysoprase, and the emerald, and gold (xxviii. 12, 13).

"Tyre," in the Word, signifies the knowledges of truth and good; a "king," the truth of the church; the "garden of Eden," wisdom and intelligence from the Word; "precious stones," truths pellucid from good such as are in the sense of the letter of the Word. As the stones signify these truths, they are called his "covering." That the sense of the letter covers up the interiors of the Word, may be seen in a preceding chapter.

46. *The sense of the letter of the Word is signified by the curtains and veils of the Tabernacle.* The Tabernacle represented heaven and the church, and therefore the form of it was shown by Jehovah upon Mount Sinai. Consequently all things in the Tabernacle—the lampstand, the golden altar for incense, and the table whereon were the loaves of faces—represented and consequently signified holy things of heaven and the church. The Holy of holies wherein was the ark of the covenant represented and consequently signified what is inmost of heaven and the church; and the Law itself written on the two tables of stone and enclosed in the ark signified the Lord as to the Word. Now as external things derive their essence from internal things, and both of these from the inmost, which in this case was the Law, it follows that holy things of the Word were represented and signified by all things of the Tabernacle. Therefore the ultimate things of the Tabernacle which were the curtains and veils (and thus its coverings and containants), signified the ultimate things of the Word, which are the truths and goods of the sense of the letter. And because these ultimates of the Word were signified,

All the curtains and veils were made of fine linen intertwined, of hyacinthine blue and bright-crimson, and of scarlet double-dyed, with cherabim (*Exod.* xxvi. 1, 31, 36).

What the Tabernacle and all things in it represented and sigfied generally and specifically, has been unfolded in the *Arcana*

Coelestia on this chapter of *Exodus*. It is there shown that the "curtains" and "veils" represented external things of heaven and the church, and therefore of the Word; and that "fine linen" signified truth from a spiritual origin; "hyacinthine blue," truth from a celestial origin; "bright-crimson," celestial good; "scarlet double-dyed," spiritual good; and "cherubim," guards of the interior things of the Word.

47. *The external things of the Temple at Jerusalem represented external things of the Word, which belong to the sense of its letter.* This is because the Temple represented the same as did the Tabernacle, namely, heaven and the church, and consequently the Word. That the Temple at Jerusalem represented the Lord's Divine Human, He Himself teaches in *John*:—

Destroy this Temple, and in three days I will raise it up; He spake of the Temple of His Body (ii. 19, 21).

Where the Lord is meant, there also is meant the Word, for the Lord is the Word. Now as the interior things of the Temple represented interior things of heaven and the church (and therefore of the Word), its exterior things represented and signified exterior things of heaven and the church, and therefore exterior things of the Word, which belong to the sense of its letter. Concerning the exterior things of the Temple we read:—

That they were built of whole stone, not hewn, and within of cedar; and that all its walls within were carved with cherubim, palm-trees, and openings of flowers; and that the floor was overlaid with gold (1 *Kings* vi. 7, 29, 30);

all of which things also signify external things of the Word, which are holy things of the sense of the letter.

48. *The Word in its glory was represented by the Lord when He was transfigured.* Concerning the Lord as transfigured before Peter, James, and John, we read:—

That His face did shine as the sun, and His garments became white as the light. That Moses and Elias appeared talking with Him. That a bright cloud overshadowed the disciples; and that a voice was heard out of the cloud, saying, This is My beloved Son, hear ye Him (*Matt.* xvii. 1–5).

I have been instructed that the Lord then represented the Word; "His face that did shine as the sun," His Divine good; "His garments that became as the light," His Divine truth; "Moses and Elias," the historical and the prophetical Word; "Moses," the Word that was written by him and the historical Word in general, and "Elias," the prophetical Word; and the "bright cloud that overshadowed the disciples," the Word in the sense of the letter; and therefore a voice was heard from this cloud which said, "This is My beloved Son, hear ye Him." For all utterances and answers from heaven are made exclusively by means of ultimate things such as are in the sense of the letter of the Word. For they are made in fullness, from the Lord.

49. So far we have shown that the Word in the natural sense which is the sense of the letter, is in its holiness and its fullness. Something shall now be said to show that in this sense the Word is also in its power. How great and of what nature is the power of Divine truth in the heavens and also on earth, is evident from what has been said in the work on *Heaven and Hell* concerning the power of the angels of heaven (n. 228–233). The power of Divine truth is directed especially against falsities and evils, thus against the hells. The fight against these must be waged by means of truths from the sense of the letter of the Word. Moreover it is by means of the truths in a man that the Lord has the power to save him; for man is reformed and regenerated and is at the same time taken out of hell and introduced into heaven, by means of truths from the sense of the letter of the Word. This power the Lord took upon Himself, even as to His Divine Human, after He had fulfilled all things of the Word down to its ultimates. [2] Therefore when by the passion of the cross He was about to fulfill those which remained, He said to the chief priest,

Hereafter ye shall see the Son of man sitting at the right hand of power, and coming in the clouds of heaven (*Matt.* xxvi. 64 ; *Mark* xiv. 62).

The "Son of man," is the Lord as to the Word; the "clouds of heaven," are the Word in the sense of the letter; to "sit at the right hand of God," is omnipotence by means of the Word. (As also in *Mark* xvi. 19.)   The Lord's power from the ultimate things of truth was represented by the Nazirites in the Jewish Church; and by Samson, of whom it is said that he was a Nazirite from his mother's womb, and that his power lay in his hair.   Nazirite and Naziriteship also mean the hair. [3] That Samson's power lay in his hair, he himself made plain, saying,

There hath not come a razor upon my head, because I have been a Nazirite from my mother's womb ; if I be shaven, then my strength will go from me, and I shall become weak, and be like any other man (*Judges* xvi. 17).

No one can know why the Naziriteship (by which is meant the hair) was instituted, or whence it came that Samson's strength was from the hair, unless he knows what is signified in the Word by the "head."   The "head" signifies the heavenly wisdom which angels and men have from the Lord by means of Divine truth; consequently the "hair of the head" signifies heavenly wisdom in ultimate things, and also Divine truth in ultimate things.   [4] As, from correspondence with the heavens, this is the signification of the "hair," it was a statute for the Nazirites that :—

They should not shave the hair of their heads, because this is the Naziriteship of God upon their heads (*Num.* vi. 1–21).

And for the same reason it was ordained that :—

The high priest and his sons should not shave their heads, lest they should die, and wrath should come upon the whole house of Israel (*Lev.* x. 6.)

[5] As, on account of this signification, which is from correspondence, the hair was so holy, the Son of man, who is the Lord as to the Word, is described even as to His hairs :—

That they were white like wool, as white as snow (*Rev.* i. 14) :
In like manner the Ancient of days (*Dan.* vii. 9).

(On this subject see also above, n. 35.)   In short, the reason why the power of Divine truth or of the Word is in the sense of the letter, is that there the Word is in its fullness; and it is also because in that sense are, at the same time and together (*simul*), the angels of both the Lord's kingdoms and men on earth.

V.

The Doctrine of the Church is to be drawn from the Sense of the Letter of the Word, and is to be confirmed thereby.

50. It has been shown in the preceding chapter that the Word in the sense of the letter is in its fullness, in its holiness, and in its power; and as the Lord is the Word (for He is the all of the Word), it follows that He is most of all present in the sense of the letter, and that from it He teaches and enlightens man.   But these things shall be set forth in the following order:—

i. The Word cannot be understood without doctrine.

ii. Doctrine must be drawn from the sense of the letter of the Word.

iii. But the Divine truth which must be of doctrine appears to none but those who are in enlightenment from the Lord.

51. i. *The Word cannot be understood without doctrine.* This is because the Word in the sense of the letter consists exclusively of correspondences, to the end that things spiritual and celestial may be simultaneous or together therein, and that every word may be their containant and support.   For this reason, in some places in the sense of the letter the truths are not naked, but clothed, and are then called appearances of truth.   Many truths also are accommodated to the capacity of simple folk, who do not uplift their thoughts above such things as they see before their eyes.   There are also some things that appear like contradictions, although the Word when viewed in its own light contains no contradiction.   And again in certain passages in the Prophets, names of persons and places are gathered together from which, in the letter, no sense can be elicited, as in those passages adduced above (n. 15).   Such being the Word in the sense of the letter, it is evident that it cannot be understood without doctrine.   [2] But to illustrate this by examples.   It is said,

That Jehovah repents (*Exod.* xxxii. 12, 14 ; *Jonah* iii. 9 ; iv. 2) ;

And also

That Jehovah does not repent (*Num.* xxiii. 19 ; 1 *Sam.* xv. 29).

Without doctrine these passages cannot be reconciled.   It is said

That Jehovah visits the iniquity of the fathers upon the sons to the third and fourth generation (*Num.* xiv. 18) ;

And it is also said that

The father shall not die for the son, nor the son for the father, but every one for his own sin (*Deut.* xxiv. 16).

Interpreted by doctrine these passages are not discordant, but are in agreement.   [3] Jesus says,

Ask, and it shall be given you ; seek, and ye shall find ; knock, and it shall be opened unto you ; for every one that asketh shall receive ; and he that seeketh shall find ; and to him that knocketh it shall be opened (*Matt.* vii. 7, 8 ; xxi. 21, 22).

Without doctrine it might be believed that every one will receive what he asks for ; but from doctrine it is believed that whatever a man asks not from himself but from the Lord is given ; for this also is what the Lord says,

If ye abide in Me, and My words abide in you, ye shall ask what ye will, and it shall be done unto you (*John* xv. 7).

[4] The Lord says,

Blessed are the poor, for theirs is the kingdom of God (*Luke* vi. 20).

Without doctrine it may be thought that heaven is for the poor and not for the rich, but doctrine teaches that the poor in spirit are meant, for the Lord says,

Blessed are the poor in spirit; for theirs is the kingdom of heaven (*Matt.* v. 3).

[5] The Lord says,

Judge not, that ye be not judged; for with what judgment ye judge ye shall be judged (*Matt.* vii. 1, 2; *Luke* vi. 37).

Without doctrine this might be cited to confirm the notion that it is not to be said of what is evil that it is evil, thus that an evil person is not to be judged to be evil; yet according to doctrine it is lawful to judge, but justly; for the Lord says,

Judge righteous judgment (*John* vii. 24).

[6] Jesus says,

Be not ye called Teacher, for One is your Teacher, even the Christ. And call no man your father on the earth; for One is your Father in the heavens. Neither be ye called masters; for One is your Master, the Christ (*Matt.* xxiii. 8–10).

Without doctrine it would seem that it is not lawful to call any person teacher, father, or master; but from doctrine it is known that in the natural sense it is lawful to do this, but not in the spiritual sense.   [7] Jesus said to His disciples,

When the Son of man shall sit upon the throne of His glory, ye also shall sit upon twelve thrones, judging the twelve tribes of Israel (*Matt.* xix. 28).

From these words it may be inferred that the Lord's disciples will sit in judgment, when yet they can judge no one.   Doctrine therefore must reveal this secret by explaining that the Lord alone, who is omniscient and knows the hearts of all, will sit in judgment, and is able to judge; and that His twelve disciples mean the church as to all the truths and goods it possesses from the Lord through the Word; from which doctrine concludes that these truths will judge every one, according to the Lord's words in *John* iii. 17, 18; xii. 47, 48.   [8] He who reads the Word without doctrine does not see the consistency of what is said in the Prophets about the Jewish nation and Jerusalem—that the church with that nation, and its seat in that city, will remain to eternity; as in the following passages:—

Jehovah will visit His flock the house of Judah, and will make them as a horse of glory in war ; from him shall come forth the corner stone, from him the nail, and from him the bow of war (*Zech.* x. 3, 4, 6, 7).

Behold I come, that I may dwell in the midst of thee.   And Jehovah shall make Judah an inheritance, and shall again choose Jerusalem (*Zech.* ii. 10, 12).

It shall come to pass in that day that the mountains shall drop new wine, and the hills shall flow with milk, and Judah shall be to eternity, and Jerusalem from generation to generation (*Joel* iii. 18–20).

Behold, the days come in which I will sow the house of Israel and the house of Judah with the seed of man, and in which I will make a new covenant with the house of Israel, and with the house of Judah ; and this shall be the covenant, I will put My law in their inward parts, and will write it upon their heart ; and I will be their God, and they shall be My people (*Jer.* xxxi. 27, 31, 33).

In that day ten men shall take hold, out of all the languages of the nations, of the skirt of a man that is a Jew, saying, We will go with you, for we have heard that God is with you (*Zech.* viii. 23).

So in other places, as *Isa.* xliv. 21, 24, 26 ; xlix. 22, 23 ; lxv. 9 ; lxvi. 20, 22 ; *Jer.* iii. 18 ; xxiii. 5 ; l. 19, 20 ; *Nahum* i. 15 ; *Mal.* iii. 4.

In these passages the Lord's advent is treated of, and that this [establishment of the Jews] will then come to pass.   [9] But the contrary is declared in many other places, of which this passage only shall be adduced :—

I will hide My face from them, I will see what their latter end shall be, for they are a generation of perversions, sons in whom is no faithfulness.   I said, I will cast them into outermost corners, I will make the remembrance of them to cease from man, for they are a nation void of counsel, neither is there understanding in them ; their vine is of the vine of Sodom, and of the fields of Gomorrah ; their grapes are grapes of gall ; their clusters are of bitternesses ; their wine is the poison of dragons, and the cruel venom of asps.   Is not this hidden with Me, sealed up among My treasures ?   To Me belongeth vengeance and retribution (*Deut.* xxxii. 20–35).

It is of that same nation that these things are said.   And things of the same purport are said elsewhere,

As in *Isa.* iii. 1, 2, 8 ; v. 3, 6 ; *Deut.* ix. 5, 6 ; *Matt.* xii. 39 ; xxiii. 27, 28 ; *John* viii. 44 ; and in *Jeremiah* and *Ezekiel* throughout.

These passages which seem contradictory will however from doctrine be seen to accord, for this teaches that in the Word

"Israel" and "Judah" do not mean Israel and Judah, but the church in both senses, in one that it is devastated, in the other that it is to be set up anew by the Lord.

Other things like these exist in the Word, from which it plainly appears that the Word cannot be understood without doctrine.

52. From all this it is evident that they who read the Word without doctrine, or who do not acquire for themselves doctrine from the Word, are in obscurity as to every truth, and that their minds are wavering and uncertain, prone to errors, and pliant to heresies, which they also embrace wherever inclination or authority favors, and their reputation is not endangered. For the Word is to them like a lampstand without a lamp, and in their gloom they seem to see many things, and yet see scarcely anything, for doctrine alone is a lamp. I have seen such persons examined by angels, and found to be able to confirm from the Word whatever they please, and it was also found that they confirm what is of their own love and of the love of those whom they favor. And I have seen them stripped of their garments, a sign that they were devoid of truths; for in the spiritual world garments are truths.

53. ii. *Doctrine must be drawn from the sense of the letter of the Word, and be confirmed thereby.* The reason of this is that there and not elsewhere is the Lord present with man, and enlightens him and teaches him the truths of the church. Moreover the Lord never operates anything except in what is full, and the Word is in its fullness in the sense of the letter, as has been shown above. This is why doctrine must be drawn from the sense of the letter.

54. That by means of doctrine the Word not only becomes intelligible, but also as it were shines with light, is because without doctrine it is not understood, and is like a lampstand without a lamp, as has been shown above. By means of doctrine therefore the Word is understood, and is like a lampstand with a lighted lamp. The man then sees more things than he had seen before, and also understands those things which before he had not understood. Dark and contradictory things he either does not see and passes over, or sees and interprets them so that they agree with the doctrine. The experience of the Christian world attests that the Word is seen from doctrine, and is also interpreted according to it. All the Reformed see and interpret the Word from and according to their own doctrine; so do the Papists from and according to theirs, and even the Jews do so from and according to theirs; thus from a false doctrine all see falsities, and from a true doctrine truths. It is evident therefore that true doctrine is like a lamp in the dark, and a guide-post on the way. But doctrine is not only to be drawn from the sense of the letter of the Word, but must also be confirmed thereby; for if not so confirmed the truth of doctrine appears as if only man's intelligence were in it, and not the Lord's Divine wisdom; and so the doctrine would be like a house in the air, and not on the earth, and would lack a foundation.

55. The doctrine of genuine truth can also be drawn in full from the sense of the letter of the Word, because in this sense the Word is like a man clothed whose face and hands are bare. All things that concern man's life, and consequently his salvation, are bare; but the rest are clothed. In many places also where they are clothed they shine through their clothing, like a face through a thin veil of silk. The truths of the Word also appear and shine through their clothing more and more clearly in proportion as they are multiplied by a love for them, and are ranged in order by this love. But this also is by means of doctrine.

56. It might be believed that the doctrine of genuine truth could be procured by means of the spiritual sense of the Word which is furnished through a knowledge of correspondences. But doctrine is not procured by means of that sense, but is only lighted up and corroborated. For as said before (n. 26), no one comes into the spiritual sense of the Word by means of correspondences unless he is first in genuine truths from doctrine. If a man is not first in genuine truths he may falsify the Word by

11

means of some correspondences with which he is acquainted, by connecting them together and interpreting them so as to confirm that which cleaves to his mind from some principle previously received. Moreover the spiritual sense of the Word is not given any one except by the Lord alone, and it is guarded by Him as heaven is guarded, for heaven is in it. It is better therefore for man to study the Word in the sense of the letter; from this alone is doctrine furnished.

57. iii. *The genuine truth which must be of doctrine appears in the sense of the letter to none but those who are in enlightenment from the Lord.* Enlightenment is from the Lord alone, and exists with those who love truths because they are truths and make them of use for life. With others there is no enlightenment in the Word. The reason why enlightenment is from the Lord alone is that the Lord is in all things of the Word. The reason why enlightenment exists with those who love truths because they are truths and make them of use for life, is that such are in the Lord and the Lord in them. For the Lord is His own Divine truth, and when this is loved because it is Divine truth (and it is loved when it is made of use), the Lord is in it with the man. This the Lord teaches in *John :*—

In that day ye shall know that ye are in Me and I in you. He that hath My commandments, and doeth them, he loveth Me, and I will love him, and will manifest Myself to him ; and I will come unto him, and make My abode with him (xiv. 20, 21, 23).

And in *Matthew :*—

Blessed are the pure in heart, for they shall see God (v. 8).

These are they who are in enlightenment when they are reading the Word, and to whom the Word shines and is translucent.

58. The reason why the Word shines and is translucent with such, is that there is a spiritual and celestial sense in every particular of the Word, and these senses are in the light of heaven, so that through these senses and by their light the Lord flows into the natural sense, and into the light of it with a man. This causes the man to acknowledge the truth from an interior perception, and afterwards to see it in his own thought,

and this as often as he is in the affection of truth for the sake
of truth.   For perception comes from affection, and thought
from perception, and thus is produced the acknowledgment
which is called faith.   But of these things more will be said
in the following chapter concerning the conjunction of the
Lord with man by means of the Word.

59. With such men the first thing is to get for themselves
doctrine from the sense of the letter of the Word, and thus
light a lamp for their further advance.   Then after doctrine
has been procured, and a lamp thus lighted, they see the Word
by its means.   Those however who do not procure doctrine
for themselves, first make investigation as to whether the doctrine delivered by others and received by the general body
accords with the Word, and they assent to what accords, and
from what does not accord they dissent.   In this way it becomes
to them their own doctrine, and through doctrine their faith.
But this takes place only with those who not being taken up
with worldly affairs are able to exercise discernment.   If these
persons love truths because they are truths, and make them of
use for life, they are in enlightenment from the Lord.   All
others who are in some life according to truths can learn from
them.

60. The contrary takes place with those who read the Word
from the doctrine of a false religion, and still more with those
who confirm that doctrine from the Word, having in view
their own glory or this world's riches.   With them the truth of
the Word is as it were in the shade of night, and what is false
is as in the light of day.   They read what is true, but do not
see it; and if they see the shadow of it they falsify it.   These
are they of whom the Lord says that

They have eyes, but see not ; and ears, but do not understand (*Matt.*
xiii. 13).

For nothing else blinds a man except his Own* and the confirmation of what is false.   Man's Own is the love of self and

* The Latin word *proprium* is the term used in the original text that in this and
other places has been rendered by the expression "Own."   The dictionary meaning

the derivative conceit of self-intelligence ; and the confirmation of what is false is thick darkness counterfeiting the light. The light of such men is merely natural, and their sight is like that of one who sees phantoms in the gloom.

61. I have been permitted to converse with many after death who had believed that they would shine in heaven like the stars, because, as they said, they had regarded the Word as holy, had often read it through, had collected from it many things by which they had confirmed the tenets of their faith, and had thereby been celebrated in the world as learned men. On this account they believed they would be Michaels and Raphaels. [2] Many of them however have been examined in respect to what was the love from which they had studied the Word, and some of them were found to have done so from the love of self, that they might appear great in the world, and be revered as dignitaries of the church; and others of them had done so from the love of the world, that they might get rich. When examined as to what they knew from the Word, it was found that they knew nothing of genuine truth from it, but only such as is called truth falsified, which in itself is falsity. And they were told that this was because their ends (or what is the same their loves) had been themselves and the world, and not the Lord and heaven. When men read the Word while themselves and the world are the ends in view, their minds cleave to themselves and the world, and this causes them to be constantly thinking from their Own, which is in thick darkness in respect to all things of heaven, in which state the man cannot be withdrawn by the Lord from his Own, and thus be raised into the light of heaven, and consequently cannot receive through heaven any influx from the Lord. [3] I

---

of *proprius*, as an adjective, is "one's own," "proper," "belonging to one's self alone," "special," "particular," "peculiar." The neuter of this which is the word *proprium*, when used as a noun means "possession," "property ;" also "a peculiarity," "characteristic mark," "distinguishing sign," "characteristic." The English adjective "own" is defined by Webster to mean "belonging to," "belonging exclusively or especially to," "peculiar ;" so that our word "own" is a very exact equivalent of *proprius*, and if we make it a noun by writing it "Own," in order to answer to the Latin *proprium*, we effect a very close translation. [TR.]

have even seen them admitted into heaven, but when they were found to be devoid of truths, they were cast down; yet the conceit remained that they deserved heaven. Very different has it been with those who had studied the Word from the affection of knowing truth because it is truth, and because it is of service to the uses of life, not only to their own uses but also to those of the neighbor. I have seen these raised up into heaven, and thus into the light in which is Divine truth there, and at the same time exalted into angelic wisdom and its happiness, which is eternal life.

VI.

By means of the Sense of the Letter of the Word there is conjunction with the Lord and association with the Angels.

62. The reason why there is conjunction with the Lord by means of the Word is that the Word treats solely of Him, and the Lord is consequently its all in all and is called the Word, as has been shown in the *Doctrine of the Lord*. The reason why the conjunction is in the sense of the letter, is that in this sense the Word is in its fullness, its holiness, and its power, as has been shown above in its proper chapter. The conjunction is not apparent to the man, but is in the affection of truth, and in his perception of it, thus is in the man's love for and faith in Divine truth.

63. The reason why there is association with the angels of heaven by means of the sense of the letter, is that the spiritual sense and celestial sense are in it, and the angels are in these senses, the angels of the spiritual kingdom being in the Word's spiritual sense, and those of the celestial kingdom in its celestial sense. These senses are evolved from the Word's natural sense which is the sense of the letter while a true man is in it.

The evolution is instantaneous; consequently so is the association.

64. It has been made plain to me by much experience that the spiritual angels are in the spiritual sense of the Word, and the celestial angels in its celestial sense. While reading the Word in its sense of the letter it has been given me to perceive that communication was effected with the heavens, now with this society of them, now with that, and that what I understood according to the natural sense, the spiritual angels understood according to the spiritual sense, and the celestial angels according to the celestial sense, and this in an instant. As I have perceived this communication many thousands of times, there remains with me no doubt about it. Moreover there are spirits beneath the heavens who abuse this communication: they recite some sayings from the sense of the letter, and immediately observe and take note of the society with which communication is effected. This I have frequently seen and heard. From these things it has been given me to know by actual experience that the Word in respect to its sense of the letter is the Divine medium of conjunction with the Lord and with heaven. (Concerning this conjunction by the Word see also what is said in the work on *Heaven and Hell*, n. 303–310.)

65. The way in which the evolution of these senses is effected shall also be told in a few words. But for the understanding of this it will be necessary to recall what has been said above about successive order and simultaneous order, namely, that in successive order what is celestial, what is spiritual, and what is natural follow one after another, from highest things in heaven down to ultimate things in the world, and that the same things are in the ultimate (which is natural) in simultaneous order, one next another from the inmost things to the outermost ones, and that in like manner there are successive senses of the Word, celestial and spiritual, simultaneously in the natural sense. When these things are comprehended, the way in which the two senses, celestial and spiritual, are evolved from the natural sense while a man is reading the Word may in some measure be unfolded before the understanding; for a spiritual angel then calls forth what is spiritual, and a celestial angel what is celestial, nor can they do otherwise, because such things are homogeneous and in accordance with their nature and essence.

66. But this may be illustrated in the first place by comparisons drawn from the three kingdoms of nature: animal, vegetable, and mineral. *From the animal kingdom:* When the food becomes chyle, the blood vessels extract and call forth from it their blood, the nervous fibres their fluid, and the substances that are the origins of the fibres their animal spirit. *From the vegetable kingdom:* The tree, with its trunk, branches, leaves, and fruit, stands upon its root, and by means of its root it extracts and calls forth from the ground a grosser sap for the trunk, branches, and leaves, a purer for the pulp of the fruit, and the purest for the seeds within the fruit. *From the mineral kingdom:* In some places in the bowels of the earth there are minerals impregnated with gold, silver, and iron, and each of these metals draws its own element from the exhalations stored up in the earth.

67. We may now illustrate by an example how from the natural sense in which is the Word with men, the spiritual angels draw forth their own sense, and the celestial angels theirs. Take as an example five commandments of the decalogue:—

Honor thy father and thy mother. By "father and mother" a man understands his father and mother on earth, and all who stand in their place, and by to "honor" he understands to hold in honor and obey them. But a spiritual angel understands the Lord by "father," and the church by "mother," and by to "honor" he understands to love. And a celestial angel understands the Lord's Divine love by "father," and His Divine wisdom by "mother," and by to "honor" to do what is good from Him.

[2] *Thou shalt not steal.* By to "steal" a man understands to steal, defraud, or under any pretext take from his neighbor his goods. A spiritual angel understands to deprive others of

their truths of faith and goods of charity by means of falsities and evils. And a celestial angel understands to attribute to himself what is the Lord's, and to claim for himself His righteousness and merit.

[3] *Thou shalt not commit adultery.* By "committing adultery" a man understands to commit adultery and fornication, to do obscene things, speak lascivious words, and harbor filthy thoughts. A spiritual angel understands to adulterate the goods of the Word, and falsify its truths. And a celestial angel understands to deny the Lord's Divinity and to profane the Word.

[4] *Thou shalt not kill.* By "killing," a man understands also bearing hatred, and desiring revenge even to the death. A spiritual angel understands to act as a devil and destroy men's souls. And a celestial angel understands to bear hatred against the Lord, and against what is His.

[5] *Thou shalt not bear false witness.* By "bearing false witness" a man understands also to lie and defame. A spiritual angel understands to say and persuade that what is false is true and what is evil good, and the reverse. And a celestial angel understands to blaspheme the Lord and the Word.

[6] From these examples it may be seen how the Spiritual and Celestial of the Word are evolved and drawn out from the natural sense in which they are. Wonderful to say, the angels draw out their senses without knowing what the man is thinking about, and yet the thoughts of the angels and of the men make a one by means of correspondences, like end, cause, and effect. Moreover ends actually are in the celestial kingdom, causes in the spiritual kingdom, and effects in the natural kingdom. This conjunction by means of correspondences is such from creation. This then is the source of man's association with angels by means of the Word.

68. Another reason why association of man with angels exists by means of the natural or literal sense of the Word, is that in every man from creation there are three degrees of life, celestial, spiritual, and natural, but so long as he is in this world he is in the Natural, and is at the same time in the Spiritual in so far as he is in genuine truths, and in the Celestial in so far as he is in a life according to them; but still he does not come into the Spiritual or Celestial itself until after death. But of this more elsewhere.

69. From all this it is evident that in the Word alone (through the fact that it is conjunction with the Lord and association with the angels) there is spirit and life, as the Lord teaches:—

The words that I speak unto you, they are spirit and they are life (*John* vi. 63).

The water that I shall give you shall be in you a fountain of water springing up into eternal life (*John* iv. 14).

Man doth not live by bread alone, but by every word that proceedeth out of the mouth of God (*Matt.* iv. 4).

Labor for the meat that endureth unto eternal life, which the Son of man shall give unto you (*John* vi. 27).

VII.

The Word is in all the Heavens, and is the Source of Angelic Wisdom.

70. Hitherto it has not been known that the Word is in the heavens, nor could it be made known so long as the church was ignorant that angels and spirits are men like the men in this world, and that they possess in every respect like things to those possessed by men, with the sole difference that they themselves are spiritual, and that all things they possess are from a spiritual origin; while men in this world are natural, and all things they possess are from a natural origin. So long as this fact was hidden it could not be known that the Word exists in the heavens also, and is read by angels there, and also by spirits who are beneath the heavens. But that this might not be forever hidden, it has been granted me to be in company with angels and spirits, to converse with them, see what exists with them, and afterwards relate many things that I have heard and seen. This has been done in a work on *Heaven and Hell*, published in London in 1758; in which work it may be seen that angels and spirits are men, and that they possess in abundance all things that men possess in this world. That angels and spirits are men, may be seen in that work (n. 73–77, and 453–456). That they possess like things to those possessed by men in this world (n. 170–190): Also that they have Divine worship, and preachings in places of worship (n. 221–227): That they have writings and also books (n. 258–264): And that they have the Word (n. 259).

71. As regards the Word in heaven, it is written in a spiritual style, which differs entirely from a natural style. The spiritual style consists solely of letters, each of which contains a meaning, and there are points above the letters which exalt the meaning. With the angels of the spiritual kingdom the letters resemble printed letters in our world; and with the angels of the celestial kingdom the letters (each of which also contains a complete meaning) resemble the ancient Hebrew letters, curved in various ways, and with marks above and within. Such being the style of their writing, there are no names of persons and places in their Word such as there are in ours, but instead of the names there are the things which they signify. Thus instead of Moses there is the historical Word, instead of Elijah, the prophetical Word; instead of Abraham, Isaac, and Jacob, the Lord as to His Divinity and Divine Human; instead of Aaron, the priestly office; instead of David, the kingly office, each of the Lord; instead of the names of the twelve sons of Jacob, or of the tribes of Israel, various things of heaven and the church; and like things instead of the names of the Lord's twelve disciples; instead of Zion and Jerusalem, the church in respect to the Word and doctrine from the Word; instead of the land of Canaan, the church itself; instead of the cities therein on this side and beyond Jordan, various things of the church and of its doctrine; and so with all the other names

It is the same with the numbers : neither do these appear in the Word that is in heaven, but instead of them the things to which the numbers that are in our Word correspond. It is evident from these examples that the Word in heaven is a Word that corresponds to our Word, and thus that the two are a one, for correspondences make a one.

72. It is a wonderful thing that the Word in the heavens is so written that the simple understand it in simplicity, and the wise in wisdom, for there are many points and marks over the letters, which as has been said exalt the meaning, and to these the simple do not attend, nor are they even aware of them ; whereas the wise pay attention to them, each one according to his wisdom, even to the highest wisdom. In every larger society of heaven, a copy of the Word, written by angels inspired by the Lord, is kept in its sanctuary, lest being elsewhere it should be altered in some point. In respect to the fact that the simple understand it in simplicity and the wise in wisdom, our Word is indeed like that in heaven, but this is effected in a different way.

73. The angels acknowledge that all their wisdom comes through the Word, for they are in light in proportion to their understanding of the Word. The light of heaven is Divine wisdom, which to their eyes is light. In the sanctuary where the copy of the Word is kept, there is a flaming and bright light that surpasses every degree of light in heaven that is outside of it. The cause is the same as above mentioned ; it is that the Lord is in the Word.

74. The wisdom of the celestial angels surpasses that of the spiritual angels almost as much as this surpasses the wisdom of men, and the reason is that the celestial angels are in the good of love from the Lord, while the spiritual angels are in truths of wisdom from Him, and wherever there is the good of love there resides at the same time wisdom ; but where there are truths there resides no more of wisdom than there is good of love together with it. This is the reason why the Word in the celestial kingdom is written differently from that in the spiritual kingdom; for goods of love are expressed in the Word of the celestial kingdom, and the marks denote affections, whereas truths of wisdom are expressed in the Word of the spiritual kingdom, and the marks denote perceptions.

75. From what has been said may be inferred the nature of the wisdom that lies hidden in the Word that is in this world. In fact all angelic wisdom, which is unutterable, lies hidden in it, for it is the containant of the same, and after death a man who is being made an angel by the Lord by means of the Word comes into that wisdom.

VIII.

The Church is from the Word, and is such as is its Understanding of the Word.

76. That the church is from the Word does not admit of doubt, for the Word is Divine truth itself (n. 1–4); the doctrine of the church is from the Word (n. 50–61); and through the Word there is conjunction with the Lord (n. 62–69). But doubt may arise as to whether the understanding of the Word is what makes the church, for there are those who believe that they are of the church because they have the Word, read it or hear it from a preacher, and know something of its sense of the letter, yet how this or that in the Word is to be understood they do not know, and some of them little care. It shall therefore be proved that it is not the Word that makes the church, but the understanding of it, and that such as is the understanding of the Word among those who are in the church, such is the church itself. The proof of this is as follows.

77. The Word is the Word according to the understanding of it in a man, that is, as it is understood. If it is not understood, the Word is indeed called the Word, but it is not the Word with the man. The Word is the truth according to the

understanding of it, for it may not be the truth, because it may
be falsified.   The Word is spirit and life according to the understanding of it, for its letter if not understood is dead. And
as a man has truth and life according to his understanding of
the Word, so has he faith and love according thereto, for truth
is of faith, and love is of life.   Now as the church exists by
means of faith and love, and according to them, it follows that
the church is the church through the understanding of the
Word and according thereto; a noble church if in genuine
truths, an ignoble church if not in genuine truths, and a destroyed church if in falsified truths.

78. Further: it is through the Word that the Lord is present with a man and is conjoined with him, for the Lord is the
Word, and as it were speaks with the man in it.   The Lord is
also Divine truth itself, as likewise is the Word.   From this
it is evident that the Lord is present with a man and is at the
same time conjoined with him, according to his understanding
of the Word, for according to this the man has truth and the
derivative faith, and also love and the derivative life.   The
Lord is indeed present with a man through the reading of the
Word, but He is conjoined with him through the understanding of truth from the Word, and according thereto; and in proportion as the Lord has been conjoined with a man, in the
same proportion the church is in him.   The church is within
man; the church that is outside of him is the church with a
number of men who have the church within them.   This is
meant by the Lord's words to the Pharisees who asked when
the kingdom of God would come :—

The kingdom of God is within you (*Luke* xvii. 21).

Here the "kingdom of God" means the Lord, and from Him,
the church.

79. In many places in the Prophets where the church is
treated of, the understanding of the Word is treated of, and it is
taught that there is no church except where the Word is rightly
understood, and that such as is the understanding of the Word

with those in the church, such is the church.   In many places also in the Prophets the church with the Israelitish and Jewish nation is described as being totally destroyed and annihilated through their falsification of the meaning or understanding of the Word, for naught but this destroys the church.   [2] The understanding of the Word, both true and false, is described in the Prophets by " Ephraim," especially in *Hosea*, for in the Word " Ephraim" signifies the understanding of the Word in the church.   And as the understanding of the Word makes the church, Ephraim is called,

A dear son, and a child of delights (*Jer.* xxxi. 20) ;
The first-born (ver. 9) ;
The strength of Jehovah's head (*Ps.* lx. 7 ; cviii. 8) ;
Mighty (*Zech.* x. 7) ;
Filled with the bow (ix. 13) ;

and the sons of Ephraim are called,

Armed, and shooters with the bow (*Ps.* lxxviii. 9).

The " bow" signifies doctrine from the Word fighting against falsities.   Therefore also,

Ephraim was passed over to Israel's right hand, and was blessed ; and was also accepted instead of Reuben (*Gen.* xlviii. 5, 11–15).

And therefore,

Ephraim, together with his brother Manasseh (under the name of Joseph their father), was exalted above all by Moses when he blessed the sons of Israel (*Deut.* xxxiii. 13–17).

[3] The quality of the church when the understanding of the Word has been destroyed, is also described in the Prophets by " Ephraim," especially in *Hosea*, as is evident from the following passages :—

Israel and Ephraim shall stagger ; Ephraim shall be in the solitude ; Ephraim is oppressed and shattered in judgment.   I will be unto Ephraim as a lion ; I will tear and go away ; I will carry off, and there shall be none to deliver (*Hos.* v. 5, 9, 11–14).

O Ephraim, what shall I do unto thee ? for thy holiness is as a cloud of the dawn, and like the dew that falleth in the morning, it goeth away (vi. 4).

They shall not dwell in the land of Jehovah ; but Ephraim shall return to Egypt, and shall eat in Assyria that which is unclean (ix. 3).

[4] The "land of Jehovah" is the church ; "Egypt" is the memory-knowledge (*scientificum*) of the natural man ; "Assyria" is the derivative reasoning : by these two the Word is falsified in respect to the understanding of it, and therefore it is said that "Ephraim shall return to Egypt, and shall eat in Assyria that which is unclean." [5] Again :—

Ephraim feedeth on wind, and followeth after the east wind ; every day he multiplieth lying and wasteness ; he maketh a covenant with Assyria, and oil is carried down into Egypt (xii. 1).

To "feed on wind," to "follow after the east wind," and to "multiply lying and wasteness," is to falsify truths, and thus destroy the church. [6] The like is signified also by the "whoredom" of Ephraim (for "whoredom" signifies the falsification of the understanding of the Word, that is, of its genuine truth) in the following passages :—

I know Ephraim, that he hath altogether committed whoredom, and Israel is defiled (*Hos.* v. 3).

In the house of Israel I have seen a foul thing ; there Ephraim hath committed whoredom, and Israel hath been defiled (vi. 10).

"Israel" is the church itself, and "Ephraim" is the understanding of the Word, from and according to which is the church, and therefore it is said "Ephraim hath committed whoredom, and Israel hath been defiled." [7] As the church among the Jews had been utterly destroyed through falsifications of the Word, it is said of Ephraim,

I will give thee up, Ephraim, I will deliver thee over, Israel, as Admah, and I will set thee as Zeboim (*Hos.* xi. 8).

Now as the Prophet *Hosea*, from the first chapter to the last, treats of the falsification of the Word, and of the destruction of the church thereby ; and as the falsification of truth is there signified by "whoredom," therefore in order that he might represent this state of the church, that prophet was commanded to take unto himself a harlot for a woman, and of her to beget sons (chap. i.) ; and, a second time, to take a woman who was an adulteress (chap. iii.). [8] These passages have been adduced in order that it may be known and confirmed from the Word that such as is the understanding of the Word in the church, such is the church : excellent and precious if this understanding is from genuine truths of the Word, but ruined and even foul if it is from truths falsified. In confirmation of the truth that Ephraim signifies the understanding of the Word, and in the opposite sense the same falsified, and that the destruction of the church comes from this, the other passages in which Ephraim is treated of may be consulted,

As *Hos.* iv. 17, 18 ; vii. 1, 11 ; viii. 9, 11 ; ix. 11–13, 16 ; x. 11 ; xi. 3 ; xii. 1, 8, 14 ; xiii. 1, 12 ; *Isa.* xvii. 3 ; xxviii. 1 ; *Jer.* iv. 15 ; xxxi. 6, 18 ; l. 19 ; *Ezek.* xxxvii. 16 ; xlviii. 5 ; *Obad.* 19 ; *Zech.* ix. 10.

IX.

There is a Marriage of the Lord and the Church and a derivative Marriage of Good and Truth in each and every thing of the Word.

80. Hitherto this has not been seen, nor could it be seen, because the spiritual sense of the Word has not until now been disclosed, and it cannot be seen except by means of this sense. For in the Word two senses, the spiritual and the celestial, lie hidden within the sense of the letter. In the spiritual sense the things in the Word refer especially to the church, and in the celestial sense, especially to the Lord. In the spiritual sense they also refer to Divine truth, and in the celestial to Divine good. From this comes the marriage in question in the sense of the letter of the Word. But this appears to those only who know from the Word's spiritual and celestial sense the significations of the words and names, for some of these are predicated of good, and some of truth, and some include both, so that without this knowledge the marriage that exists in each and every thing of the Word could not be seen.   This is the reason why this secret has not been disclosed before.

81. As there is such a marriage in each and every thing of the Word, there frequently occur in it two expressions that appear like repetitions of the same thing.   They however are not repetitions, for one of them has reference to good and the other to truth, and both taken together effect a conjunction of good and truth, and thus form one thing.   From this too comes the Divinity of the Word and its holiness, for in every Divine work good is conjoined with truth and truth with good.

82. It is said that in each and every thing of the Word there is a marriage of the Lord and the church and a derivative marriage of good and truth, because wherever there is a marriage of the Lord and the church there is also a marriage of good and truth, for the latter is from the former.   For when the church or man of the church is in truths, the Lord inflows into his truths with good, and vivifies them.   Or what is the same, when through truths the church or man of the church is in intelligence, the Lord inflows into his intelligence through the good of love and of charity, and thus pours life into it.

83. With every man there are two faculties of life, called Understanding and Will.   The understanding is the receptacle of truth and the derivative wisdom, and the will is the receptacle of good and the derivative love.   For a man to be a man of the church these two must make a one, and this they do when the man forms his understanding from genuine truths, which to all appearance is done as by himself ; and when his will is infilled with the good of love, which is done by the Lord. From this the man has a life of truth and a life of good, a life of truth in the understanding from the will, and a life of good in the will through the understanding.   This is the marriage of truth and good in a man, and also the marriage of the Lord and the church in him.   But concerning this reciprocal conjunction called a marriage, more will be seen in *The Angelic Wisdom concerning the Divine Providence, Concerning the Divine Love and Divine Wisdom*, and *Concerning Life*.

12

84. Readers of the Word who pay attention to the matter can see that there are pairs of expressions in it that appear like repetitions of the same thing, such as " brother " [and " companion," " poor "] and " needy," " waste " and " solitude," " vacuity " and " emptiness," " foe " and " enemy," " sin " and " iniquity," " anger " and " wrath," " nation " and " people," " joy " and " gladness," " mourning " and " weeping," " righteousness " and " judgment," etc.   These expressions appear synonymous but are not so, for " brother," " poor," " waste," [" vacuity,"] " foe," " sin," " anger," " nation," " joy," " mourning," and " righteousness," are predicated of good, and in the opposite sense of evil; whereas " companion," " needy," " solitude," " emptiness," " enemy," " iniquity," " wrath," " people," " gladness," " weeping," and " judgment," are predicated of truth, and in the opposite sense of falsity.   And yet it seems to a reader who is not acquainted with this secret, that " poor " and " needy," " waste " and " solitude," " vacuity " and " emptiness," " foe " and " enemy," are one and the same thing; and in like manner " sin " and " iniquity," " anger " and " wrath," " nation " and " people," " joy " and " gladness," " mourning " and " weeping," " righteousness " and " judgment;" and yet they are not one thing, but become one thing by conjunction.   Many things are also joined together in the Word, such as " fire " and " flame," " gold " and " silver," " brass " and " iron," " wood " and " stone," " bread " and " water," " bread " and " wine," " bright-crimson " and " fine-linen," etc., which is done because " fire," " gold," " brass," " wood," " bread," and " bright-crimson," signify good; and " flame," " silver," " iron," " stone," " water," " wine," and " fine-linen," signify truth.   And in the same way it is said that men are to " love God with all the heart and with all the soul;" and that God will " create in a man a new heart and a new spirit;" for " heart " is predicated of the good of love, and " soul " of the truth from that good.   There are also words that are used alone, or without a mate, because they partake of both good and truth.   But these and many other things are not apparent except to the angels, and to those also who while in the natural sense are also in the spiritual sense.

85. That such pairs of expressions which appear like repetitions of the same thing, run through the Word, would be too prolix a matter to show from the Word, for whole sheets could be filled with it; but to remove all doubt about it I will quote passages in which occur the expressions "righteousness" (or "justice") and "judgment," "nation" and "people," and "joy" and "gladness." First, "righteousness" and "judgment:"—

The city was full of judgment, righteousness lodged in her (*Isa.* i. 21).

Zion shall be redeemed in judgment, and they that return of her in righteousness (verse 27).

Jehovah Zebaoth shall be exalted in judgment, and God the Holy One shall be sanctified in righteousness (v. 16).

He shall sit upon the throne of David, and upon his kingdom, to establish it in judgment and in righteousness (ix. 7).

Jehovah shall be exalted, for He dwelleth on high; He hath filled Zion with judgment and righteousness (xxxiii. 5).

Thus saith Jehovah, Keep ye judgment, and do righteousness; for My salvation is near, that My righteousness may be revealed (lvi. 1).

As a nation that did righteousness, and forsook not the judgment of their God; they ask of Me the judgments of righteousness (lviii. 2).

Swear by the living Jehovah in judgment and in righteousness (*Jer.* iv. 2).

Let him that glorieth glory in this, that Jehovah doeth judgment and righteousness in the earth (ix. 24).

Do ye judgment and righteousness; Woe unto him that buildeth his house without righteousness, and his chambers without judgment; Did not thy father do judgment and righteousness? and then it was well with him (xxii. 3, 13, 15).

I will raise unto David a righteous offshoot, and He shall reign as king, and shall do judgment and justice in the land (xxiii. 5; xxxiii. 15).

If a man be just, and do judgment and righteousness (*Ezek.* xviii. 5).

If the wicked turn from his sin, and do judgment and righteousness, it shall not be mentioned against him: he hath done judgment and righteousness; he shall surely live (xxxiii. 14, 16, 19).

I will betroth thee unto Me to eternity; in righteousness and in judgment; and in mercy and in compassions (*Hos.* ii. 19).

Let judgment flow as water, and righteousness as a mighty torrent (*Amos* v. 24).

Ye have turned judgment into gall, and the fruit of righteousness into wormwood (vi. 12).

Jehovah will plead my cause, and execute judgment for me : He will bring me forth into the light, and I shall behold His righteousness (*Micah* vii. 9).

O Jehovah, Thy righteousness is like the mountains of God ; Thy judgments are a great abyss (*Ps.* xxxvi. 6).

Jehovah will bring forth thy righteousness as the light, and thy judgment as the noonday (xxxvii. 6).

Jehovah shall judge thy people in righteousness, and thy miserable in judgment (lxxii. 2).

Righteousness and judgment are the support of Thy throne (lxxxix. 14).

When I shall have learned the judgments of Thy righteousness. Seven times a day do I praise Thee, because of the judgments of Thy righteousness (cxix. 7, 164).

God executeth the justice of Jehovah, and His judgment with Israel (*Deut.* xxxiii. 21.)

The Spirit of Truth shall convict the world in respect of righteousness, and of judgment (*John* xvi. 8, 9, 10).   (And in other places.)

The reason "judgment" and "righteousness" are mentioned so frequently is that "judgment" is predicated of truths, and "righteousness" of good, and therefore to "do judgment and righteousness" means to act from truth and from good.   The reason "judgment" is predicated of truth, and "righteousness" of good, is that the Lord's government in the spiritual kingdom is called "judgment," and in the celestial kingdom "righteousness" (on which subject see the work on *Heaven and Hell,* n. 214, 215).   As "judgment" is predicated of truth, in some passages we read

Truth and righteousness (as in *Isa.* xi. 5 ; *Ps.* lxxxv. 11 ; and elsewhere).

86. That repetitions of the same thing occur in the Word on account of the marriage of good and truth, may be seen quite clearly from passages where "nations" and "peoples" are mentioned :—

Woe to the sinful nation, to a people laden with iniquity (*Isa.* i. 4).

The peoples that walk in darkness have seen a great light : Thou hast multiplied the nation (ix. 2, 3).

Asshur, the rod of Mine anger, I will send him against a hypocritical nation, and against the people of My wrath will I give him a charge (x. 5, 6).

It shall come to pass in that day, that the root of Jesse, which standeth for an ensign of the peoples, shall the nations seek (xi. 10).

Jehovah that smiteth the peoples with an incurable stroke, that ruleth the nations with anger (xiv. 6).

In that day shall a present be brought unto Jehovah of Armies of a people scattered and peeled, and a nation meted out and trodden down (xviii. 7).

The mighty people shall honor Thee, the city of the powerful nations shall fear Thee (xxv. 3).

Jehovah will swallow up the covering over all peoples, and the veil over all nations (verse 7).

Come near ye nations, and hearken ye peoples (xxxiv. 1).

I have called thee for a covenant for the people, for a light of the nations (xlii. 6).

Let all the nations be gathered together, and let the peoples assemble (xliii. 9).

Behold, I will lift up My hand toward the nations, and My standard toward the peoples (xlix. 22).

I have given Him for a witness to the peoples, a prince and a lawgiver to the nations (lv. 4, 5).

Behold, a people cometh from the land of the north ; and a great nation from the sides of the earth (*Jer.* vi. 22).

I will not make thee hear the calumny of the nations any more, neither shalt thou bear the reproach of the peoples any more (*Ezek.* xxxvi. 15).

All peoples and nations shall worship Him (*Dan.* vii. 14).

Let not the nations make a byword of them, and say among the peoples, Where is their God ? (*Joel* ii. 17).

The remnant of My people shall spoil them, and the residue of My nation shall inherit them (*Zeph.* ii. 9).

Many peoples and numerous nations shall come to seek Jehovah Zebaoth in Jerusalem (*Zech.* viii. 22).

Mine eyes have seen Thy salvation, which Thou hast prepared before the face of all peoples, a light for revelation to the nations (*Luke* ii. 30–32).

Thou hast redeemed us by Thy blood out of every people and nation (*Rev.* v. 9).

Thou must prophesy again concerning peoples and nations (*Rev.* x. 11).

Thou shalt set me for a head of the nations : a people whom I have not known shall serve me (*Ps.* xviii. 43).

Jehovah bringeth the counsel of the nations to nought, He overturneth the thoughts of the peoples (xxxiii. 10).

Thou makest us a byword among the nations, a shaking of the head among the peoples (xliv. 14).

Jehovah shall subdue the peoples under us, and the nations under our feet. Jehovah hath reigned over the nations ; the willing ones of the peoples are gathered together (xlvii. 3, 8, 9).

Let the people confess unto Thee ; let the nations be glad and shout for joy ; for Thou shalt judge the peoples with equity, and lead the nations upon earth (lxvii. 3, 4).

Remember me, O Jehovah, in the good pleasure of Thy people ; that I may rejoice in the joy of Thy nations (cvi. 4, 5).

The reason "nations" and "peoples" are mentioned together is that "nations" mean those in good, and in the opposite sense in evil ; and "peoples" those in truths, and in the opposite sense in falsities. For this reason those of the Lord's spiritual kingdom are called "peoples," and those of His celestial kingdom "nations ;" for in the spiritual kingdom all are in truths and consequently in wisdom, and in the celestial kingdom all are in good and consequently in love.

87. The same rule holds good for other words ; for example, where "joy" is mentioned, so is "gladness :"—

Behold joy and gladness, slaying the ox (*Isa.* xxii. 13).

They shall obtain joy and gladness, and sorrow and sighing shall flee away (xxxv. 10 ; li. 11).

Gladness and joy are cut off from the house of our God (*Joel* i. 16).

There shall be taken away the voice of joy, and the voice of gladness (*Jer.* vii. 34 ; xxv. 10).

The fast of the tenth [month] shall be to the house of Judah for joy and gladness (*Zech.* viii. 19).

That we may rejoice all our days, make Thou us glad (*Ps.* xc. 14, 15).

Be ye glad in Jerusalem, and rejoice in her (*Isa.* lxvi. 10).

Rejoice and be glad, O daughter of Edom (*Lam.* iv. 21).

The heavens shall be glad, and the earth shall rejoice (*Ps.* xcvi. 11).

Make me to hear joy and gladness (li. 8).

Joy and gladness shall be found in Zion, confession and the voice of singing (*Isa.* li. 3).

There shall be gladness, and many shall rejoice at his birth (*Luke* i.14).

I will cause to cease the voice of joy and the voice of gladness, the voice of the bridegroom and the voice of the bride (*Jer.* vii. 34 ; xvi. 9 ; xxv. 10).

There shall be heard in this place the voice of joy and the voice of gladness, the voice of the bridegroom and the voice of the bride (xxxiii. 10, 11).

The reason why both "joy" and "gladness" are mentioned is that "joy" is of good and "gladness" of truth, or "joy" is of love and "gladness" of wisdom. For joy is of the heart and gladness of the soul, or joy is of the will and gladness of the understanding. That there is a marriage of the Lord and the church in these expressions also, is evident from its being said,

The voice of joy and the voice of gladness, the voice of the bridegroom and the voice of the bride (*Jer.* vii. 34 ; xvi. 9 ; xxv. 10 ; xxxiii. 10, 11).

The Lord is the "bridegroom," and the church is the "bride."

That the Lord is the bridegroom, see *Matt.* ix. 15; *Mark* ii. 19, 20; *Luke* v. 34, 35 ;
And that the church is the bride, *Rev.* xxi. 2, 9 ; xxii. 17.

And therefore John the Baptist said of Jesus :—

He that hath the bride is the bridegroom (*John* iii. 29).

88. On account of the marriage of the Lord with the church, or what is the same, on account of the marriage of Divine good and Divine truth in each and every thing of the Word, "Jehovah" and "God," and also "Jehovah" and the "Holy One of Israel," are mentioned in very many places as if they were two although they are one, for by "Jehovah" is meant the Lord as to Divine good, and by "God" and the "Holy One of Israel" the Lord as to Divine truth. That "Jehovah" and "God," and also "Jehovah" and the "Holy One of Israel," are mentioned in very many places in the Word although One is meant who is the Lord, may be seen in the *Doctrine concerning the Lord* (n. 34, 38, and 46).

89. As there is the marriage of the Lord and the church in all things of the Word and in every single particular of it, it is evident that all things of the Word and also every particular of it treat of the Lord, as we set out to show in the *Doctrine concerning the Lord* (n. 1–7). The church (which likewise is treated of) is also the Lord; for the Lord teaches that the man of the church is in Him, and He in the man (*John* vi. 56; xiv. 20, 21; xv. 5, 7).

90. As the subject here treated of is the Divinity and holiness of the Word, to what has already been said we may add something worthy of mention. A small piece of paper marked with Hebrew letters, but written as the ancients wrote them, was once sent me from heaven. In those times some of the letters that now are partly formed with straight lines were curved, and had little horns that turned upward. The angels who were then with me said that they themselves discerned complete meanings from the very letters, and that they knew them especially from the curvings of the lines and of the points of each letter. And they explained what the letters meant when taken each by itself and what when taken together; and said that the H that was added to the names of Abram and Sarai means what is infinite and eternal. They also explained in my presence from the letters or syllables alone the meaning of the Word in *Psalm* xxxii. 2, showing that the sum of their meaning is, *That the Lord is merciful even to those who do evil.* [2] They informed me that the writing in the third heaven consists of curved letters that are bent in various ways, and that each letter possesses a complete meaning; that the vowels there indicate a sound that corresponds to the affection, and that in that heaven they cannot utter the vowels *i* and *e*, but instead of them *y* and *eu*, but that they do use the vowels *a*, *o*, and *u*, because they give a full sound.* Further: that they do not pronounce any consonants as hard, but soft, and that it is from

---

* These letters are to be pronounced as follows :—

> i as in mach*i*ne.
> e like the *a* in b*a*by.
> y like the German *ü*, or the French *u*.
> eu as in French, or like the German *ö*.
> a as in f*a*ther.

In Swedish, *o* and *oo* are sounded as follows :—

> o either as *oo* in b*oo*th, or as *o* in note.
> u somewhat like the *ew* in h*ew*.

But the natural scale as set forth by Helmholtz and Donders would assign to *o* the sound of *o* in note, and to *u* the sound of *oo* in booth. [TR.]

this that certain Hebrew letters have a dot in the center as a sign that they are to be pronounced as [hard, and are without this dot when] soft; and they said that hardness in pronouncing the letters is in use in the spiritual heaven because there they are in truths, and truth admits of what is hard, but not good, in which are the angels of the celestial kingdom or third heaven.   They also said that these angels possess the Word written with curved letters that have significant points and little horns.   This shows what is meant by the words of the Lord:—

One jot or one tittle shall in no wise pass from the law till all be fulfilled (*Matt.* v. 18);

It is easier for heaven and earth to pass away than for one tittle of the law to fail (*Luke* xvi. 17).

X.

IT IS POSSIBLE FOR HERESIES TO BE DRAWN FROM THE SENSE OF THE LETTER OF THE WORD, BUT IT IS HURTFUL TO CONFIRM THEM.

91. It has been shown above that the Word cannot be understood without doctrine, and that doctrine is like a lamp that enables genuine truths to be seen, the reason of which is that the Word has been written entirely by correspondences, and consequently many things in it are appearances of truth and not naked truths; and many things also have been written in adaptation to the apprehension of the natural and even of the sensuous man, yet so that the simple may understand it in simplicity, the intelligent in intelligence, and the wise in wisdom.   The result is that the appearances of truth in the Word, which are truths clothed, may be caught at as naked truths, and when they are confirmed they become falsities.   But this is done by those who believe themselves wise above others, although they are not wise, for being wise consists in seeing whether a thing is true before it is confirmed, and not in confirming whatever one pleases. This last is done by those who excel in a genius for confirming and are in the conceit of self-intelligence, but the former is done by those who love truths and are affected by them because they are truths, and who make them uses of the life, for these persons are enlightened by the Lord, and see truths by the light of the truths; whereas the others are enlightened by themselves and see falsities by the light of the falsities.

92. That appearances of truth, which are truths clothed, may be caught at out of the Word as naked truths, and that when confirmed they become falsities, is evident from the many heresies there have been and still are in Christendom. The heresies themselves do not condemn men, but an evil life does, as also do the confirmations from the Word, and from reasonings from the natural man, of the falsities that are in the heresy. For every one is born into the religion of his parents, is initiated into it from his infancy, and afterwards holds to it, being unable to withdraw himself from its falsities through being engaged with his business in the world. But to live in evil, and to confirm falsities even to the destruction of genuine truth, is what condemns. For he who remains in his own religion, and believes in God, or if in Christendom, in the Lord, regarding the Word as holy, and from a religious principle living according to the ten commandments, does not swear allegiance to falsities, and therefore as soon as he hears truths, and perceives them in his own way, he can embrace them and so be led away from falsities; but not so the man who has confirmed the falsities of his religion, for confirmed falsity remains and cannot be rooted out. For after confirmation a falsity becomes as if the man had sworn to the truth of it, especially if it chimes in with his own self-love (*amor proprii*), and the derivative conceit of his own wisdom.

93. I have conversed with some in the spiritual world who had lived many ages ago, and had confirmed themselves in the falsities of their religion, and I found that they still remained

steadfast in the same.   I have also conversed there with some
who had been of the same religion as they, and had thought as
they did, but had not confirmed themselves in its falsities, and
I found that after being instructed by angels these had rejected
the falsities and had imbibed truths, and that these were saved,
but not the others.   After death every man is instructed by
angels, and those who see truths, and from truths falsities, are
received.   For the power to see truths spiritually is then given
every one, and those see them who have not confirmed themselves in falsities, but those who have confirmed themselves do
not want to see truths, and if they do see them they turn their
backs on them, and then either ridicule or falsify them.

94. Let us illustrate this by an example.   In many places
in the Word, anger, wrath, and vengeance are attributed to the
Lord, and it is also said that He punishes, that He casts into
hell, that He tempts, and many other such things.   He who
believes all this in simplicity, and on that account fears God
and takes care not to sin against Him, is not condemned for
that simple belief.   But the man who confirms himself in these
ideas to such a degree as to believe that anger, wrath, revenge,
thus things that are of evil, exist in the Lord, and that from
anger, wrath, and revenge He punishes a man and casts him
into hell, is condemned, because he has destroyed the genuine
truth that the Lord is love itself, mercy itself, and good itself,
and that one who is these cannot be angry, wrathful, and revengeful.   These things are attributed to the Lord because
such is the appearance.   So with many other things.

95. That many things in the sense of the letter are apparent
truths, having genuine truths hidden within them, and that it
is not hurtful to think and speak in accordance with such
truths, but that it is hurtful to confirm them to such a degree
as to destroy the genuine truth hidden within, may be illustrated
by an example in nature, which is presented because what is
natural teaches and convinces more clearly than what is spiritual.   [2] To the eye the sun appears to revolve round the earth
daily, and also annually, and therefore in the Word the sun is

said to rise and set, thus making morning, noon, evening, and night, and also making the seasons of spring, summer, autumn, and winter, and thus days and years; when yet the sun stands motionless, for it is an ocean of fire, and it is the earth that revolves daily, and is carried round the sun annually. The man who in simplicity and ignorance supposes that the sun is carried round the earth, does not destroy the natural truth that the earth daily rotates on its axis, and is annually carried along the ecliptic. But the man who by the Word and by reasonings from the natural man confirms as real the apparent motion and course of the sun, does invalidate the truth and does destroy it. [3] That the sun moves is an apparent truth; that it does not move is a genuine truth. Every one may speak in accordance with the apparent truth, and does so speak, but to think in accordance with it from confirmation blunts and darkens the rational understanding. It is the same with respect to the stars in the sidereal heavens. The apparent truth is that they too, like the sun, are carried round the earth once a day, and it is therefore said of the stars also that they rise and set. But the genuine truth is that the stars are fixed, and that their heavens stand motionless. Still, every one may speak in accordance with the appearance.

96. The reason why it is hurtful to confirm the apparent truth of the Word to the point of destroying the genuine truth that lies hidden within, is that each and all things of the sense of the letter of the Word communicate with heaven, and open it, as before shown (n. 62–69). So that when a man applies this sense to confirm loves of the world that are contrary to loves of heaven, the internal of the Word is made false, and the result is that when its external of the sense of the letter, and which now has a false internal, communicates with heaven, heaven is closed, for the angels, who are in the internal of the Word, reject that external of it. Thus it is evident that a false internal, or truth falsified, takes away communication with heaven and closes heaven. This is why it is hurtful to confirm any heretical falsity.

96a. The Word is like a garden, a heavenly paradise, that contains delicacies and delights of every kind, delicacies in its fruits and delights in its flowers; and in the midst of the garden trees of life with fountains of living water near them, while forest trees surround it. The man who from doctrine is in Divine truths is at its center where the trees of life are, and is in the actual enjoyment of its delicacies and delights; whereas the man who is in truths not from doctrine, but from the sense of the letter only, is at the outskirts, and sees nothing but the forest vegetation. And one who is in the doctrine of a false religion, and who has confirmed himself in its falsity, is not even in the forest, but is out beyond it in a sandy plain where there is not even grass. That such are their several states after death will be shown in its proper place.

97. Be it known moreover that the literal sense of the Word is a guard to the genuine truths that lie hidden within. It is a guard in this respect, that it can be turned this way or that, and explained according to the way it is taken, yet without injury or violence to its internal. It does no harm for the sense of the letter to be understood in one way by one person and in a different way by another; but it does harm for the Divine truths that lie hidden within to be perverted, because this inflicts violence on the Word. The sense of the letter is a guard against this, and the guard is effectual in the case of those who are in falsities from their religion, but do not confirm those falsities, for these persons do the Word no violence. [2] This guard is signified by cherubs, and in the Word is described by them. This is signified by the cherubs that were stationed at the entrance of the garden of Eden after Adam and his wife had been cast out, of which we read as follows :—

When Jehovah God had driven out the man, He made to dwell at the east of the garden of Eden the cherubim, and the flame of a sword which turned every way, to keep the way of the tree of life (*Gen.* iii. 24).

The "cherubim" signify a guard; the "way of the tree of life," signifies the access to the Lord which men have by means of

the Word; the "flame of a sword that turned every way," signifies Divine truth in ultimates, this being like the Word in the
sense of the letter, which can be so turned.   [3] The same is
meant by

The cherubs of gold that were placed upon the two ends of the mercy-
seat that was upon the ark in the tabernacle (*Exod.* xxv. 18–21).

As this was signified by cherubs,

The Lord spoke with Moses from between them (*Exod.* xxv. 22 ; xxxvii.
9 ; *Num.* vii. 89).

That the Lord does not speak to man except in what is full,
and that the Word in the sense of the letter is Divine truth in
fullness, may be seen above (n. 37–49).   So therefore did the
Lord speak to Moses from between the cherubs.   In no wise
different was the signification of

The cherubs on the curtains of the tabernacle, and on the veil (*Exod.*
xxvi. 1, 31),

for the curtains and veils of the tabernacle represented the ultimate things of heaven and the church, and therefore of the
Word, as may be seen above (n. 46).   Nor in any wise different
was the signification of

The cherubs in the midst of the temple in Jerusalem (1 *Kings* vi. 23–
28).
The cherubs carved on the walls and doors of the temple (verses 29, 32,
35).
Or the cherubs in the new temple (*Ezek.* xli. 18–20) ;

as also may be seen above (n. 47).   [4] As cherubs signified
a guard that the Lord, heaven, and Divine truth such as is
within the Word, be not approached immediately, but mediately through ultimate things, it is said of the king of Tyre,

Thou sealest up the measure, full of wisdom and perfect in beauty ;
thou hast been in Eden the garden of God ; every precious stone was thy
covering ; thou, O cherub, art the outspreading of that which covereth ;
I have destroyed thee, O covering cherub, in the midst of the stones of
fire (*Ezek.* xxviii. 12–14, 16).

"Tyre" signifies the church in respect to the knowledges of truth and good, and therefore its "king" signifies the Word, in which and from which are these knowledges. It is evident that the Word in its ultimate, which is the sense of the letter, is here signified by that king, and also that a guard is signified by a "cherub," for it is said, "thou sealest up the measure; every precious stone was thy covering;" and "thou, O cherub, art the outspreading of that which covereth;" and also "O covering cherub." That the "precious stones" mentioned in this passage mean truths of the literal sense of the Word, may be seen above (n. 45). As "cherubs" signify what is ultimate of Divine truth as a guard, it is said in David:—

Jehovah bowed the heavens also and came down ; and He rode upon a cherub (*Ps.* xviii. 9, 10).

O Shepherd of Israel, Thou that sittest upon the cherubim, shine forth (*Ps.* lxxx. 1).

Jehovah sitteth upon the cherubim (*Ps.* xcix. 1.)

To "ride upon cherubs," and to "sit upon them," means upon the ultimate sense of the Word. [5] Divine truth in the Word, and the quality of it, are described by the cherubs in the first, ninth, and tenth chapters of *Ezekiel ;* but as no one can know what is signified by the several particulars of the description of them, except one to whom the spiritual sense has been opened, it has been disclosed to me what in brief is signified by all the things said about the cherubs in the first chapter of *Ezekiel,* which are as follows :—

The external Divine sphere of the Word is described (verse 4) ;

It is represented as a man (verse 5) ;

And conjoined with spiritual and celestial things (verse 6) ;

The Natural of the Word, its quality (verse 7) ;

The Spiritual and the Celestial of the Word conjoined with its Natural, their quality (verses 8, 9) ;

The Divine love of the good and truth celestial, spiritual, and natural therein, severally and also together (verses 10, 11) ;

They all look to the one thing (verse 12) ;

The sphere of the Word from the Lord's Divine good and Divine truth, from which the Word is alive (verses 13, 14) ;

The doctrine of good and truth in the Word and from the Word (verses 15–21) ;

The Divine of the Lord above the Word and in it (verses 22, 23) ;

And from it (verses 24, 25) ;

The Lord is above the heavens (verse 26) ;

And Divine love and Divine wisdom are His (verses 27, 28). These summaries have been compared with the Word in heaven, and are in conformity with it.

XI.

THE LORD CAME INTO THE WORLD TO FULFILL ALL THINGS OF THE WORD, AND THEREBY TO BECOME DIVINE TRUTH OR THE WORD EVEN IN ULTIMATES.

98. That the Lord came into the world to fulfill all things of the Word, may be seen in the *Doctrine concerning the Lord* (n. 8–11). And that He thereby became Divine truth or the Word even in ultimates, is meant by these words in *John :*—

The Word became flesh, and dwelt among us, and we beheld His glory, the glory as of the Only-begotten of the Father, full of grace and truth (i. 14).

To "become flesh" is to become the Word in ultimates. What the Lord was as the Word in ultimates He showed His disciples when He was transfigured,

(*Matt.* xvii. 2, etc. ; *Mark* ix. 2, etc. ; *Luke* ix. 28, etc.) ;

and it is there said that Moses and Elias were seen in glory. By "Moses and Elias" is meant the Word, as may be seen above (n. 48). The Lord, as the Word in ultimates, is also described by John in *Rev.* i 13–16, where all things in the description of

Him signify ultimate things of Divine truth or of the Word.
The Lord had indeed been the Word before, but only in first
principles, for it is said:—

In the beginning was the Word, and the Word was with God, and God
was the Word ; the same was in the beginning with God (*John* i. 1, 2) ;

but when the Word became flesh, then the Lord became the
Word in ultimates also.   It is from this that He is called,

The First and the Last (*Rev.* i. 8, 11, 17 ; ii. 8 ; xxi. 6 ; xxii. 13).

99. The state of the church was completely changed by the
Lord's becoming the Word in ultimates.   All the churches that
had existed before His advent were representative churches,
and could see Divine truth in the shade only ; but after the
Lord's coming into the world a church was instituted by Him
that saw Divine truth in the light.   The difference is like that
between evening and morning, and the state of the church before His advent is also called " the evening," and that of the
church after it " the morning."   Before His coming into the
world the Lord was indeed present with the men of the church,
but mediately through heaven, whereas since His coming into
the world He is present with them immediately, for in the world
He put on the Divine Natural, in which He is present with
men.   The glorification of the Lord is the glorification of His
Human that He assumed in the world, and the Lord's glorified
Human is the Divine Natural.

100. Few understand how the Lord is the Word, for they
think that the Lord may indeed enlighten and teach men by
means of the Word without His being on that account called
the Word.   Be it known however that every man is his own
love, and consequently his own good and his own truth.   It is
solely from this that a man is a man, and there is nothing else
in him that is man.   It is from the fact that a man is his own
good and his own truth that angels and spirits are men, for all
the good and truth that proceeds from the Lord is in its form
a man.   And as the Lord is Divine good and Divine truth itself, He is *the* Man, from whom every man is a man.   That

13

all Divine good and Divine truth is in its form a man, may be seen in the work on *Heaven and Hell* (n. 460), and more clearly in treatises that are to follow, on the subject of *Angelic Wisdom.*

XII.

BEFORE THE WORD THAT IS NOW IN THE WORLD THERE WAS A WORD WHICH IS LOST.

101. From what is related in the books of Moses it is evident that worship by means of sacrifices was known, and that men prophesied from the mouth of Jehovah, before the Word was given to the Israelitish nation through Moses and the prophets. That worship by means of sacrifices was known, is evident from these facts :—

The sons of Israel were commanded to overturn the altars of the nations, break in pieces their images, and cut down their groves (*Exod.* xxxiv. 13 ; *Deut.* vii. 5 ; xii. 3).

In Shittim Israel began to commit whoredom with the daughters of Moab ; they called the people to the sacrifices of their gods, and the people did eat, and bowed down to their gods ; and Israel joined himself especially to Baal-peor, and on that account the anger of Jehovah was kindled against Israel (*Num.* xxv. 1–3).

Balaam, who was from Syria, caused altars to be built, and sacrificed oxen and sheep (*Num.* xxii. 40 ; xxiii. 1, 2, 14, 29, 30).

[2] That men prophesied from the mouth of Jehovah, is evident from the prophecies of Balaam (*Num.* xxiii. 7–10, 18–24 ; xxiv. 3–9, 16–24).

He also prophesied concerning the Lord that a Star should arise out of Jacob, and a Scepter out of Israel (*Num.* xxiv. 17).

And he prophesied from the mouth of Jehovah (*Num.* xxii. 13, 18 ; xxiii. 3, 5, 8, 16, 26 ; xxiv. 1, 13).

From these facts it is evident that there existed among the nations a Divine worship similar to that instituted through Moses among the Israelitish nation. [3] That it existed even before

the time of Abram is in some measure apparent from the words
in Moses (*Deut*. xxxii. 7, 8), but more evidently from what is
said of Melchizedek king of Salem :—

That he brought forth bread and wine, and blessed Abram, and that
Abram gave him tithes of all (*Gen*. xiv. 18–20);

and that Melchizedek represented the Lord, for he is called

Priest of God Most High (*Gen*. xiv. 18);

and it is said in David concerning the Lord :—

Thou art a priest to eternity, after the manner of Melchizedek (*Ps.*
cx. 4).

Hence it was that Melchizedek brought forth bread and wine
as holy things of the church, even as they are holy things in the
sacrament of the Supper; and that Melchizedek could bless
Abram, and that Abram gave him tithes of all.

102. I have been told by angels of heaven that there was
among the ancients a Word written entirely by correspondences, but that it had been lost, and they said that it is still preserved, and is in use in that heaven where those ancient people
dwell who had possessed it in this world. The ancients who
still use that Word in heaven came partly from the land of Canaan and the neighboring countries, such as Syria, Mesopotamia, Arabia, Chaldea, Assyria, and Egypt, and also from Sidon,
Tyre, and Nineveh. The inhabitants of all these kingdoms
were in representative worship, and consequently in the knowledge of correspondences. The wisdom of that time was derived
from this knowledge, and by its means they had an interior perception, and a communication with the heavens. Those who
had an interior acquaintance with the correspondences of that
Word were called wise and intelligent, and later, diviners and
magi. But as that Word was full of correspondences which
only in a remote way signified celestial and spiritual things,
and consequently began to be falsified by many, of the Lord's
Divine providence it disappeared in course of time, and at length
was utterly lost, and another Word, written by correspondences

less remote than the other, was given by means of prophets among the sons of Israel. Yet many names of places in the land of Canaan and in the surrounding countries were retained in this Word with significations like those they had in the ancient Word. It was for this reason that Abram was commanded to go into that land, and that his descendants, from Jacob, were brought into it.

103. That there was a Word among the ancients is evident from Moses, who mentions it, and who took some things from it (*Num.* xxi. 14, 15, 27–30); the historical parts of that Word being called the *Wars of Jehovah*, and its prophetical parts the *Enunciations*. From the historical parts of that Word Moses took the following :—

Wherefore it is said in the book of the Wars of Jehovah, At Vaheb in Suphah, and the rivers of Arnon ; and the watercourse of the rivers that inclineth toward the dwelling of Ar, and betaketh itself to the border of Moab (*Num.* xxi. 14, 15).

In that Word, as in ours, the "Wars of Jehovah" meant and described the Lord's combats with hell and His victories over it at the time when He should come into the world. The same combats are meant, and are described, in many passages of the historical parts of our Word, such as the wars of Joshua with the nations of the land of Canaan, and those of the judges and kings of Israel. [2] From the prophetical parts of that Word Moses took the following :—

Wherefore the Enunciators say, Come ye to Heshbon, let the city of Sihon be built and strengthened ; for a fire is gone out of Heshbon, a flame from the city of Sihon, it hath devoured Ar of Moab, the possessors of the high places of Arnon. Woe to thee, Moab ! thou hast perished, O people of Chemosh : he hath given his sons as fugitives, and his daughters into captivity unto Sihon king of the Amorites. With darts have we destroyed them. Heshbon hath perished even unto Dibon, and we have laid waste even unto Nophah, which reacheth unto Medeba (*Num.* xxi. 27–30).

The translators say *They that speak in Proverbs*, but the rendering should be *Enunciators*, or *Prophetic Enunciations*, as is evident from the meaning of the word *m'shalim* in the Hebrew tongue, which is not merely proverbs, but also prophetic enunciations, as in *Num.* xxiii. 7, 18; xxiv. 3, 15, where it is said that Balaam uttered "his enunciation" which was prophetic, and which also was about the Lord. His enunciation is called *mashal*, in the singular. Consider also that the things taken from them by Moses are not proverbs, but prophecies. [3] That the ancient Word, like ours, was Divine or Divinely inspired, is evident from *Jeremiah*, where almost the same words occur :—

A fire is gone forth out of Heshbon, and a flame from the midst of Sihon, that hath devoured the corner of Moab, and the crown of the head of the sons of clamor. Woe unto thee, O Moab! the people of Chemosh is undone, for thy sons have been carried off into captivity, and thy daughters into captivity (xlviii. 45, 46).

Besides these books, a prophetic book of the ancient Word called the *Book of Jashar*, or the *Book of the Upright*, is mentioned by David and by Joshua. By David :—

David lamented over Saul and over Jonathan ; and wrote, To teach the sons of Judah the bow. Behold it is written in the Book of Jashar (2 *Sam.* i. 17, 18).

And by Joshua :—

Joshua said, Sun, be silent in Gibeon, and thou, Moon, in the valley of Ajalon. Is not this written in the Book of Jashar ? (*Josh.* x. 12, 13).

Furthermore : I have been told that the first seven chapters of *Genesis* appear in that ancient Word complete to the slightest expression.

XIII.

The people outside the Church who are not in possession of the Word have Light by its means.

104. There can be no conjunction with heaven unless somewhere on earth there is a church where the Word is, and where
by it the Lord is known; for the Lord is the God of heaven
and earth, and apart from Him there is no salvation. It is sufficient that there be a church where the Word is, even if it consists of comparatively few, for even in that case the Lord is
present by its means in the whole world, for by its means
heaven is conjoined with the human race. That there is conjunction by means of the Word may be seen above (n. 62–69).

105. But in what way the presence and conjunction of the
Lord and heaven exist in all lands by means of the Word shall
now be told. Before the Lord the universal heaven is like one
man, and so is the church. And that they actually appear as
a man may be seen in the work on *Heaven and Hell* (n. 59–86).
In this man, the church where the Word is read and the Lord
thereby known, is as the heart and lungs; the celestial kingdom as the heart, and the spiritual kingdom as the lungs. [2]
As all the other members and viscera subsist and live from these
two fountains of life of the human body, so also do all those in
the whole earth who have some sort of religion, worship one
God, and live aright, and who are thereby in that man and correspond to its members and viscera outside the chest which contains the heart and lungs—subsist and live from the conjunction
of the Lord and heaven with the church by means of the Word.
For the Word in the church, although existing with comparatively few, is life to all the rest, from the Lord through heaven,
just as there is life for the members and viscera of the whole
body from the heart and lungs; and there is a similar communication. [3] This is why those Christians among whom the
Word is read constitute the breast of that man. They are the

midmost of all; round about them are the Papists; around these again are those Mohammedans who acknowledge the Lord as the greatest Prophet and as the Son of God; beyond these are the Africans; while the nations and people of Asia and the Indies constitute the furthest compass. Concerning this ranking of them something may be seen in the little work on the *Last Judgment* (n. 48). Moreover all who are in that man look toward the middle region where the Christians are.

106. The greatest light is in this middle region where are the Christians who possess the Word; for light in the heavens is Divine truth that proceeds from the Lord as the sun there; and as the Word is this Divine truth, the light is greatest where dwell those who possess the Word. From this region as from its proper center, the light propagates itself from one compass to another even to the uttermost of them; and in this way comes the enlightening, by means of the Word, of all the nations and peoples that are outside the church. That the light in the heavens is Divine truth which proceeds from the Lord, and that this light confers intelligence not only on angels but also on men, may be seen in the work on *Heaven and Hell* (n. 126–140).

107. That this is the case in the universal heaven may be inferred from the similar conditions that prevail in each of the heavenly societies; for every society of heaven is a heaven in a smaller form, and is also like a man. That such is the case may be seen in the work on *Heaven and Hell* (n. 41–87). In each society of heaven also, those in the center correspond to the heart and lungs, and they possess the greatest light. This light, and the consequent perception of truth, propagates itself from that center toward the successive circuits in every direction, thus to all in the society, and it makes their spiritual life. It has been shown that when those in the center who constituted the province of the heart and lungs and possessed the greatest light, were taken away, those around them came into shadow, and into a perception of truth so scanty as to be almost none; but as soon as the others came back, the light reappeared, and they had perception of truth the same as before.

108. The same thing may be illustrated by the following experience. African spirits from Abyssinia were present with me. On a certain occasion their ears were opened so that they heard the singing of a Psalm of David in some place of worship in this world, which affected them with such delight that they too sang along with that congregation. Presently their ears were closed so that they heard nothing of the singing, but they were then affected with a delight which was still greater, because spiritual, and they were at the same time filled with intelligence, because that Psalm treated of the Lord and of redemption. The cause of this increase of delight was that there was opened to them a communication with that society in heaven which was in conjunction with those in this world who were singing that Psalm. From this and many other such experiences it has become evident to me that communication with the universal heaven is effected by means of the Word. And for this reason there exists of the Lord's Divine Providence, a universal commercial intercourse of the kingdoms of Europe —and chiefly of those where the Word is read—with the nations outside the church.

109. In this respect a comparison may be made with the heat and light from the sun of this world, which causes vegetation in trees and shrubs even when they are out of its direct rays and under a clouded sky, provided the sun has risen and shown itself in the world. It is the same with the light and heat of heaven from the Lord as the sun, this light being Divine truth, the source of all intelligence and wisdom to angels and men. It is therefore said of the Word :—

That it was with God, and was God ; that it enlightens every man that comes into the world (*John* i. 1, 9) ; and also that that light appears in the darkness (verse 5).

110. From all this it is evident that the Word which exists in the Church of the Reformed enlightens all nations and peoples by a spiritual communication ; and also that it is provided by the Lord that there shall always be a church on earth where the Word is read, and where consequently the Lord is known.

It was for this reason that when the Word had been almost completely rejected by the Papists, of the Lord's Divine Providence the Reformation was brought about, whereby the Word was again received, as also that the Word is accounted holy by a notable nation among the Papists.

111. As without the Word there is no knowledge of the Lord, and therefore no salvation, it pleased the Lord that when the Word had been wholly falsified and adulterated among the Jewish nation and thus as it were brought to nothingness, that He should descend from heaven and come into the world, and fulfill the Word, and thereby repair and restore it, and again give light to the earth's inhabitants, in accordance with His declaration :—

The people that sat in darkness have seen a great light ; and to those who sat in the region and shadow of death, light is sprung up (*Matt.* iv. 16 ; *Isa.* ix. 2).

112. As it had been foretold that darkness would arise at the end of the present church in consequence of the lack of knowledge and acknowledgment of the Lord as being the God of heaven and earth, and also in consequence of the separation of faith from charity, therefore in order that by reason of this a genuine understanding of the Word might not perish, it has pleased the Lord at this present time to reveal the spiritual sense of the Word and make it plain that the Word in this sense, and from this in the natural sense, treats of the Lord and the church, and indeed of these alone, and to discover many other things besides, by means of which the light of truth from the Word, now almost extinguished, may be restored. That the light of truth would be almost extinguished at the end of the present church is foretold in many places in the *Revelation,* and is also what is meant by the following words of the Lord in *Matthew :*—

Immediately after the affliction of those days shall the sun be darkened, and the moon shall not give her light, and the stars shall fall from heaven, and the powers of the heavens shall be shaken ; and then they shall see the Son of man coming in the clouds of heaven with glory and power (xxiv. 29, 30).

The "sun" here means the Lord in respect to love; the "moon," the Lord in respect to faith; the "stars," the Lord in respect to the knowledges of good and truth; the "Son of man," the Lord in respect to the Word; a "cloud," the sense of the letter of the Word; and "glory," its spiritual sense and the shining through of this in the sense of the letter.

113. It has been given me to know by much experience that by means of the Word man has communication with heaven. While I read the Word through from the first chapter of *Isaiah* to the last of *Malachi,* and the *Psalms* of David, I was permitted clearly to perceive that each verse communicated with some society of heaven, and thus the whole Word with the universal heaven.

XIV.

WITHOUT THE WORD NO ONE WOULD HAVE KNOWLEDGE OF A GOD, OF HEAVEN AND HELL, OF A LIFE AFTER DEATH, AND STILL LESS OF THE LORD.

114. This follows as a general conclusion from what has been already said and shown; as that the Word is Divine truth itself (n. 1–4); that it is a medium of conjunction with the angels of heaven (n. 62–69); that everywhere in it there is a marriage of the Lord and the church, and a consequent marriage of good and truth (n. 80–89); that the quality of the church is such as is its understanding of the Word (n. 76–79); that the Word exists in the heavens also, and the angels have their wisdom from it (n. 70–75); that the nations and peoples outside the church also have spiritual light by means of the Word (n. 104–113); and much more besides. From all this it can be concluded that without the Word no one would possess spiritual intelligence, which consists in having knowledge of a God, of heaven and hell, and of a life after death; nor would know anything whatever about the Lord, about faith in Him and love to Him, nor anything about redemption, by means of which nevertheless comes salvation. As the Lord also says to His disciples :—

Without Me ye can do nothing (*John* xv. 5) ;

and John :—

A man can receive nothing except it be given him from heaven (*John* iii. 27).

115. But as there are those who maintain, and have confirmed themselves in the opinion, that without a Word it is possible for a man to know of the existence of God, and of heaven and hell, and of all the other things taught by the Word, and as they thereby weaken the authority and holiness of the Word, if not with the lips, yet in the heart, therefore it is not practicable to deal with them from the Word, but only from rational light, for they do not believe in the Word, but in themselves. [To all such we would say,] Investigate the matter from rational light, and you will find that in man there are two faculties of life called the understanding and the will, and that the understanding is subject to the will, but not the will to the understanding, for the understanding merely teaches and shows the way. Make further investigation, and you will find that man's will is what is his Own (*proprium*), and that this, regarded in itself, is nothing but evil, and that from this springs what is false in the understanding. [2] Having discovered these facts you will see that from himself a man does not desire to understand anything but that which comes from the Own of his will, and also that it is not possible for him to do so unless there is some other source from which he may know it. From the Own of his will a man does not desire to understand anything except that which relates to himself and to the world; everything above this is to him in thick darkness. So that when he sees the sun, the moon, the stars, and chances to think about their origin, how is it possible for him to think otherwise than that they exist of themselves? Can he raise his thoughts higher than do many of the learned in the world who acknowledge only nature, in spite of the fact that from the Word they know of the creation of all things by God? What then would these same have thought if they had known nothing from the Word? [3] Do you believe that the wise men of old, Aristotle, Cicero, Seneca, and others, who wrote about God and the immortality of the soul, got this from themselves (*proprio*)? Not so, but from others who had it by tradition from those who first knew it from the [ancient] Word. Neither do the writers on natural theology get any such matters from themselves. They merely confirm by rational arguments what they have already become acquainted with from the church in which is the Word; and there may be some among them who confirm without believing it.

116. I have been permitted to see peoples who had been born in [remote] islands, who were rational in respect to civil matters, but had known nothing whatever about God. In the spiritual world such appear like apes, and their life is very similar to that of apes. But having been born men, and consequently being endowed with a capacity to receive spiritual life, they are instructed by angels and are made spiritually alive by means of knowledges about God as a Man. What man is, of himself, is very evident from the character of those who are in hell, among whom are to be found leading and learned men who are unwilling even to hear of God, and therefore cannot utter His name. I have seen such and have conversed with them. I have conversed also with some who burned with angry passion when they heard any one speak of God. Such being the character of some who have heard about God, who have written about God, and have preached about God (and there are many such from among the Jesuits), consider what a man would be who had never even heard of Him. It is from the will, which is evil, that these are of such a character; for, as before said, the will leads the understanding, and takes away from it the truth that is in it from the Word. If man had been able of himself to know that there is a God and a life after death, why has he not known that after death a man is still a man? Why does he believe that his soul or spirit is like a breath of air, or like the ether, and that it has no eyes with which to see, nor ears with which to hear, nor mouth with which to speak, until it shall have been conjoined and combined with its carcass and with its skeleton? Assume then the existence of a doctrine of worship that has been hatched solely from rational light, and will not that doctrine be that a man's own self is to be worshiped? For ages this is what has been done, and is done at the present day by some who know from the Word that God alone ought to be worshiped From what is man's Own, any other kind of worship, even that of the sun and moon, is impossible.

117. That from the most ancient times there has been religion, and that everywhere the inhabitants of the world have had knowledge of God, and have known something about a life after death, has not originated in themselves or their own penetration, but from the ancient Word (spoken of above, n. 101–103), and, at a later period, from the Israelitish Word. From these two Words the things of religion have spread into the Indies and their islands, and through Egypt and Ethiopia into the kingdoms of Africa, and from the maritime parts of Asia into Greece, and from thence into Italy. But as the Word could not be written in any other way than by means of representatives, which are such things in this world as correspond to heavenly things, and therefore signify them, the things of religion among many of the nations were turned into idolatry, and in Greece into fables, and the Divine attributes and predicates into so many gods, over whom they set one supreme, whom they called "Jove" [perhaps—see the *True Christian Religion*, n. 275—] from "Jehovah." It is known that they had knowledge of Paradise, of the flood, of the sacred fire, and of the four ages, from the first or golden age to the last or iron age, by which are meant the four states of the church (as in

Daniel ii. 31–35).   It is also known that the Mohammedan religion, which came later and destroyed the former religions of many nations, was taken from the Word of both Testaments.

118. Lastly, I will state of what character those become after death who ascribe all things to their own intelligence, and little or nothing to the Word.   They first become as if inebriated, then as if silly, and finally stupid, and they sit in darkness.   Of such insanity, therefore, let all beware.

THE

DOCTRINE OF LIFE

FOR THE

NEW JERUSALEM

FROM THE TEN COMMANDMENTS

BY

EMANUEL SWEDENBORG

ORIGINALLY PUBLISHED IN AMSTERDAM IN THE YEAR 1763

TRANSLATED FROM THE ORIGINAL LATIN AND EDITED
BY THE
REV. JOHN FAULKNER POTTS, B.A. LOND.

———

STANDARD EDITION

———

SWEDENBORG FOUNDATION
INCORPORATED
NEW YORK

———

Organized in 1850 as
The American Swedenborg Printing and Publishing Society

CONTENTS*

*Compiled by the Translator.

14

THE DOCTRINE OF LIFE FOR THE NEW JERUSALEM

I.

ALL RELIGION IS OF THE LIFE, AND THE LIFE OF RELIGION IS TO DO THAT WHICH IS GOOD.

1. Every man who has religion knows and acknowledges that he who leads a good life is saved, and that he who leads an evil life is damned; for he knows and acknowledges that the man who lives aright thinks aright, not only about God but also about his neighbor; but not so the man whose life is evil. The life of man is his love, and that which he loves he not only likes to be doing, but also likes to be thinking. The reason therefore why we say that the life is to do that which is good is that doing what is good acts as a one with thinking what is good, for if in a man these two things do not act as a one, they are not of his life. The demonstration of these matters shall now follow.

2. That religion is of the life and that the life of religion is to do that which is good is seen by every one who reads the Word, and is acknowledged by him while he is reading it. The Word contains the following declarations :—

Whosoever shall break the least of these commandments, and shall teach men so, shall be called the least in the kingdom of the heavens ; but whosoever shall do and teach them, the same shall be called great in the kingdom of the heavens. For I say unto you that except your righteousness shall exceed that of the Scribes and Pharisees, ye shall not enter into the kingdom of the heavens (*Matt.* v. 19, 20).

Every tree that bringeth not forth good fruit is hewn down, and cast into the fire. Therefore by their fruits ye shall know them (*Matt.* vii. 19, 20).

Not every one that saith unto Me, Lord, Lord, shall enter into the

1

kingdom of the heavens; but he that doeth the will of My Father who is in the heavens (verse 21).

Many will say to Me in that day, Lord, Lord, have we not prophesied by Thy name, and in Thy name done many mighty things? And then will I profess unto them, I never knew you, depart from Me ye that work iniquity (verses 22, 23).

Every one who heareth these words of Mine, and doeth them, shall be likened to a wise man who built his house upon the rock; and every one that heareth these words of Mine, and doeth them not, shall be likened unto a foolish man who built his house upon the sand (verses 24, 26).

Jesus said, Behold, the sower went forth to sow; some seeds fell on the hard way, others fell upon the rocky places, others fell among the thorns, and others fell into good ground; he that was sown upon the good ground, this is he that heareth the Word, and attendeth to it, who thence beareth fruit, and bringeth forth, some a hundredfold, some sixty, and some thirty. When Jesus had said these things, He cried, saying, He that hath ears to hear, let him hear (*Matt.* xiii. 3–9, 23, 43).

For the Son of man shall come in the glory of His Father, and then shall He render unto every one according to his deeds (*Matt.* xvi. 27).

The kingdom of God shall be taken away from you, and shall be given unto a nation bringing forth the fruits thereof (*Matt.* xxi. 43).

When the Son of man shall come in His glory, then shall He sit on the throne of His glory. And He shall say to the sheep on His right hand, Come ye blessed, inherit the kingdom prepared for you from the foundation of the world; for I was hungry, and ye gave Me meat; I was thirsty, and ye gave Me drink; I was a stranger, and ye took Me in; naked, and ye clothed Me; I was sick, and ye visited Me; I was in prison, and ye came unto Me. Then shall the righteous answer, When saw we Thee so? And the king shall answer and say unto them, Verily I say unto you, Inasmuch as ye did it unto one of the least of these My brethren, ye did it unto Me. And the king shall say the like things to the goats on the left, and because they have not done such things, He shall say, Depart from Me, ye cursed, into the eternal fire which is prepared for the devil and his angels (*Matt.* xxv. 31–41).

Bring forth therefore fruits worthy of repentance; even now is the axe laid unto the root of the trees; every tree therefore that bringeth not forth good fruit is hewn down and cast into the fire (*Luke* iii. 8, 9).

Jesus said, Why call ye Me Lord, Lord, and do not the things which I say? Every cne that cometh unto Me, and heareth My words, and doeth them, he is like a man building a house, and he laid a foundation upon the rock; but he that heareth, and doeth not, is like a man that built a house upon the earth without a foundation (*Luke* vi. 46–49).

Jesus said, My mother and My brethren are these who hear the Word of God, and do it (*Luke* viii. 21).

Then shall ye begin to stand, and to knock at the door, saying, Lord, open to us ; and He shall answer and say to you, I know you not whence ye are ; depart from Me, all ye workers of iniquity (*Luke* xiii. 25–27).

This is the judgment : that the light is come into the world, and men loved the darkness rather than the light, for their works were evil ; for every one that doeth evil hateth the light, lest his works should be reproved. But he that doeth the truth cometh to the light, that his works may be made manifest, that they have been wrought in God (*John* iii. 19–21).

And shall come forth ; they that have done good, unto the resurrection [of life ; and they that have done evil, unto the resurrection] of judgment (*John* v. 29).

We know that God heareth not sinners ; but if any man be a worshiper of God, and do His will, him He heareth (*John* ix. 31).

If ye know these things, blessed are ye if ye do them (*John* xiii. 17).

He that hath My commandments, and keepeth them, he it is that loveth Me ; and I will love him, and will manifest Myself unto him ; and We will come unto him, and make our abode with him. He that loveth Me not keepeth not My words (*John* xiv. 21–24).

Jesus said, I am the true vine, and My Father is the vine-dresser ; every branch in Me that beareth not fruit, He taketh away ; and every branch that beareth fruit, He cleanseth it, that it may bear more fruit (*John* xv. 1, 2).

Herein is My Father glorified, that ye bear much fruit, and ye shall be made My disciples (verse 8).

Ye are My friends if ye do the things which I command you ; I have chosen you, that ye should bear fruit, and your fruit should abide (verses 14, 16).

The Lord said to John, To the angel of the church in Ephesus write : I know thy works ; I have this against thee, that thou hast left thy first charity ; repent, and do the first works, or else I will move thy lampstand out of its place (*Rev.* ii. 1, 2, 4, 5).

To the angel of the church in Smyrna write : I know thy works (verses 8, 9).

To the angel of the church in Pergamos write : I know thy works, repent (verses 12, 16).

To the angel of the church in Thyatira write : I know thy works and charity, and thy last works are more than the first (verses 18, 19).

To the angel of the church in Sardis write : I know thy works, that thou hast a name that thou livest, but art dead ; I have not found thy works perfect before God ; repent (*Rev.* iii. 1–3).

To the angel of the church in Philadelphia write : I know thy works (verses 7, 8).

To the angel of the church of the Laodiceans write : I know thy works ; repent (verses 14, 15, 19).

I heard a voice from heaven saying, Write, Blessed are the dead who die in the Lord from henceforth ; yea, saith the Spirit, that they may rest from their labors, for their works follow with them (*Rev.* xiv. 13).

Another book was opened, which is the book of life, and the dead were judged out of the things which were written in the books, all according to their works (*Rev.* xx. 12, 13).

Behold, I come quickly, and My reward is with Me, to give to every one according to his work (*Rev.* xxii. 12).

In like manner in the Old Testament :—

Recompense them according to their work, and according to the deed of their hands (*Jer.* xxv. 14).

Jehovah, whose eyes are open upon all the ways of the sons of men, to give every one according to his ways, and according to the fruit of his works (*Jer.* xxxii. 19).

I will visit according to his ways, and will reward him his works (*Hos.* iv. 9).

Jehovah, according to our ways, according to our works doth He to us (*Zech.* i. 6).

And in many places it is said that the statutes, commandments, and laws were to be done :—

Ye shall observe My statutes, and My judgments, which if a man do, he shall live by them (*Lev.* xviii. 5).

Ye shall observe all My statutes, and My judgments, that ye may do them (*Lev.* xix. 37 ; xx. 8 ; xxii. 31).

The blessings, if they did the commandments ; and the curses if they did them not (*Lev.* xxvi. 4–46).

The sons of Israel were commanded to make for themselves a fringe on the borders of their garments, that they might remember all the commandments of Jehovah, to do them (*Num.* xv. 38, 39).

So in a thousand other places. That works are what make a man of the church, and that he is saved according to them, is also taught by the Lord in the parables, many of which imply that those who do what is good are accepted, and that those who do what is evil are rejected. As in the parable

Of the husbandmen in the vineyard (*Matt.* xxi. 33–44) :

Of the fig-tree that did not yield fruit (*Luke* xiii. 6–9) :

Of the talents, and the pounds, with which they were to trade (*Matt.* xxv. 14–31 ; *Luke* xix. 13–25) :

Of the Samaritan who bound up the wounds of him that was wounded by robbers (*Luke* x. 30–37) :

Of the rich man and Lazarus (*Luke* xvi. 19–31) :

Of the ten virgins (*Matt.* xxv. 1–12).

3. That every one who has religion knows and acknowledges that whoever leads a good life is saved, and that whoever leads an evil one is damned, is owing to the conjunction of heaven with the man who knows from the Word that there is a God, that there is a heaven and a hell, and that there is a life after death. Such is the source of this general perception. Therefore in the doctrine of the Athanasian Creed respecting the Trinity, which has been universally received in the Christian world, the following declaration, at the end of it, has also been universally received :—

Jesus Christ, who suffered for our salvation, ascended into heaven, and sitteth at the right hand of the Father Almighty, whence He will come to judge the quick and the dead ; and then they that have done good will enter into life eternal, and they that have done evil into everlasting fire.

4. In the Christian Churches, however, there are many who teach that faith alone saves, and not any good of life, or good work, and they add that evil of life or evil work does not condemn those who have been justified by faith alone, because such are in God and in grace. Wonderful to say, however, although they teach such things, they nevertheless acknowledge (in consequence of a perception from heaven common to all) that those who lead a good life are saved, and that those who live an evil one are damned. That they do acknowledge this is evident from the *Exhortation* which not only in England but also in Germany, Sweden, and Denmark is read in the places of worship before the people coming to the Holy Supper. As is well known, it is in these kingdoms that those are found who teach that faith alone.

5. The *Exhortation* read in England before the people who approach the Sacrament of the Supper, is as follows :—

The way and means to be received as worthy partakers of that Holy Table is, first, to examine your lives and conversations by the rule of God's commandments ; and whereinsoever ye shall perceive yourselves to have offended, either by will, word, or deed, there to bewail your own sinfulness, and to confess yourselves to Almighty God, with full purpose of amendment of life ; and if ye shall perceive your offenses to be such as are not only against God, but also against your neighbors, then ye shall reconcile yourselves unto them, being ready to make restitution and satisfaction, according to the uttermost of your powers, for all injuries and wrongs done by you to any other, and being likewise ready to forgive others that have offended you, as ye would have forgiveness of your offenses at God's hand ; for otherwise the receiving of the Holy Communion doth nothing else but increase your damnation. Therefore if any of you be a blasphemer of God, a hinderer or slanderer of His Word, an adulterer, or be in malice or envy, or in any other grievous crime, repent you of your sins, or else come not to that Holy Table ; lest after the taking of that Holy Sacrament the devil enter into you as he entered into Judas, and fill you full of all iniquities, and bring you to destruction both of body and soul.

6. [In this paragraph Swedenborg presents a translation into Latin of the foregoing *Exhortation.*]

7. I have been permitted to ask some of the English clergy who had professed and preached faith alone (this was done in the spiritual world), whether while they were reading in church this *Exhortation*—in which faith is not even mentioned—they believed it to be true; for example, that if people do evil things, and do not repent, the devil will enter into them as he did into Judas, and destroy them both body and soul. They said that in the state in which they were when reading the *Exhortation* they had no other knowledge or thought than that this was religion itself; but that while composing and elaborating their discourses or sermons they had a different thought about it, because they were then thinking of faith as being the sole means of salvation, and of the good of life as being a moral accessory for the public good. Nevertheless it was incontestably proved to them that with them too there was that common perception that he who leads a good life is saved, and that he who leads an evil one is damned; and that they possess this perception when they are not in what is their Own.

8. The reason why all religion is of the life, is that after death every one is his own life, for the life stays the same as it had been in this world, and undergoes no change. For an evil life cannot be converted into a good one, nor a good life into an evil one, because they are opposites, and conversion into what is opposite is extinction. And, being opposites, a good life is called Life, and an evil one Death. This is why religion is of life, and why its life is to do what is good. (That after death a man is such as had been his life in this world may be seen in the work on *Heaven and Hell*, n. 470–484.)

II.

NO ONE CAN FROM HIMSELF DO GOOD THAT IS REALLY GOOD

9. That hitherto scarcely any one knows whether the good done by him is from self or from God, is because the church has sundered faith from charity, and good is of charity. A man gives to the poor; relieves the needy; endows places of worship and hospitals; has regard for the church, his country, and his fellow-citizen; is diligent in his attendance at a place of worship, where he listens and prays devoutly; reads the Word and books of piety; and thinks about salvation; and yet is not aware whether he is doing these things from himself, or from God. He may be doing the very same things from God, or he may be doing them from self. If he does them from God they are good, if from self they are not good. In fact there are goods of this kind done from self which are eminently evil, such as hypocritical goods, the purpose of which is deception and fraud.

10. Goods from God, and goods from self, may be compared to gold. Gold that is gold from the inmost, called pure gold, is good gold. Gold alloyed with silver is also gold, but is good according to the amount of the alloy. Less good still is gold that is alloyed with copper. But a gold made by art, and resembling gold only from its color, is not good at all, for there is no substance of gold in it. There is also what is gilded, such as gilded silver, copper, iron, tin, lead, and also gilded wood and gilded stone, which on the surface may appear like gold; but not being such, they are valued either according to the workmanship, the value of the gilded material, or that of the gold which can be scraped off. In goodness these differ from real gold as a garment differs from a man. Moreover rotten wood, dross, or even ordure, may be overlaid with gold; and such is the gold to which pharisaic good may be likened.

11. From science a man knows whether gold is good in substance, is alloyed and falsified, or is merely overlaid; but he does not know from science whether the good he does is good in itself. This only does he know: that good from God is good, and that good from man is not good. Therefore, as it concerns his salvation for him to know whether the good he does is from God, or is not from God, this must be revealed. But before this is done something shall be said about goods.

12. There are civic good, moral good, and spiritual good. Civic good is that which a man does from the civic law: by means of and according to this good is the man a citizen in the natural world. Moral good is that which a man does from the law of reason: by means of and according to this good is he a man. Spiritual good is that which a man does from spiritual law: by means of and according to this good is he a citizen in the spiritual world. These goods succeed one another in the following order: spiritual good is the highest, moral good is intermediate, and civic good is last.

13. A man who possesses spiritual good is also a moral man and a civic man; but a man who does not possess spiritual good may appear to be a moral man and a civic man, yet is not so. The reason why a man who possesses spiritual good is also a moral man and a civic man, is that spiritual good has the essence of good within it, and moral and civic good have this essence from spiritual good. The essence of good can be from no other source than Him who is good itself. Think the matter over from every point of view, and try to find out from what it is that good is good, and you will see that it is so from its inmost being (*esse*), and that that is good which has within it the *esse* of good; consequently that that is good which is from good itself, thus from God; and therefore that good which is not from God, but from man, is not good.

14. From what has been said in the *Doctrine of the Holy Scripture* (n. 27, 28, 38), it may be seen that what is highest, what is intermediate, and what is last, make a one, like end, cause, and effect; and that because they make a one, the end itself is called the first end, the cause the intermediate end, and the effect the last end. From this it must be evident that in the case of a man who possesses spiritual good, what is moral in him is intermediate spiritual, and what is civic is ultimate spiritual. And for this reason it has been said that a man who possesses spiritual good is also a moral man and a civic man; and that a man who does not possess spiritual good is neither a moral man nor a civic man, although he may appear to be so both to himself and to others.

15. That a man who is not spiritual can yet think rationally and speak from that thought, like a spiritual man, is because man's understanding can be uplifted into the light of heaven, which is truth, and can see from it; but his will cannot be in the same way uplifted into the heat of heaven, which is love, so as to act from that heat. It is for this reason that truth and love do not make a one in a man unless he is spiritual. And it is for this reason also that man can speak; and it is this which makes the difference between a man and a beast. It is by means of this capacity of the understanding to be uplifted into heaven when as yet the will is not so uplifted, that it is possible for a man to be reformed and to be come spiritual; but he does not begin to be reformed and become spiritual until his will also is uplifted. It is from this superior endowment of the understanding over the will, that a man, of whatever character he may be, even if evil, is able to think and therefore to speak rationally, as if he were spiritual. That still in spite of this he is not rational, is because the understanding does not lead the will, but the will leads the understanding. The understanding merely teaches and shows the way, as has been said in the *Doctrine of the Holy Scripture* (n. 115). And so long as the will is not in heaven together with the understanding, the man is not spiritual, and consequently is not rational; for when he is left to his will or love, he throws off the rational things of his understanding respecting God, heaven, and eternal life, and adopts in their stead such things as are in agreement with his will's love, and these he calls rational. But these matters shall be elucidated in the treatises on *Angelic Wisdom*.

16. In the following pages, those who do what is good from themselves will be called natural men, because with them the moral and the civic is in its essence natural; and those who do what is good from the Lord will be called spiritual men, because with them the moral and the civic is in its essence spiritual.

17. That no one can from himself do any good that is really good, is taught by the Lord in *John*:—

A man can receive nothing except it be given him from heaven (iii. 27).
He that abideth in Me, and I in him, the same beareth much fruit; for without Me ye can do nothing (xv. 5).

"He that abideth in Me, and I in him, the same beareth much fruit," means that all good is from the Lord; "fruit" means what is good. "Without Me ye can do nothing," means that no man can from himself do anything. Those who believe in the Lord, and from Him do what is good, are called

Sons of light (*John* xii. 36; *Luke* xvi. 8);
Sons of the bridechamber (*Mark* ii. 19);
Sons of the resurrection (*Luke* xx. 36);

Sons of God (*Luke* xx. 36 ; *John* i. 12) ;

Born of God (*John* i. 13) ;

It is said that they shall see God (*Matt.* v. 8) ;

That the Lord will make His abode with them (*John* xiv. 23) ;

That they have the faith of God (*Mark* xi. 22) ;

That their works are done from God (*John* iii. 21).

These things are all summed up in the following words :—

As many as received Him, to them gave He power (*potestas*) to be sons of God, to them that believe in His name ; who were born, not of bloods, nor of the will of the flesh, nor of the will of man, but of God (*John* i. 12, 13).

To " believe in the name of the Son of God," is to believe the Word and to live according to it; "the will of the flesh," is what is proper to man's will, which in itself is evil; "the will of man," is what is proper to his understanding, which in it-self is falsity from evil; those " born of" these, are those who will and act, and also think and speak, from what is proper to themselves ; those " born of God," are those who do all this from the Lord. In short: that which is from man is not good ; but that which is good is from the Lord.

* * *

III.

IN PROPORTION AS A MAN SHUNS EVILS AS SINS, IN THE SAME PROPORTION HE DOES GOODS, NOT FROM HIMSELF BUT FROM THE LORD.

18. Who does not or may not know that evils stand in the way of the Lord's entrance to a man ? For evil is hell, and the Lord is heaven, and hell and heaven are opposites. In proportion therefore as a man is in the one, in the same pro-portion he cannot be in the other. For the one acts against the other and destroys it.

19. So long as a man is in this world, he is midway between hell and heaven; hell is below him, and heaven is above him,

and he is kept in freedom to turn himself to either the one or
the other; if he turns to hell he turns away from heaven; if
he turns to heaven he turns away from hell. Or what is the
same, so long as a man is in this world he stands midway between the Lord and the devil, and is kept in freedom to turn
himself to either the one or the other; if he turns to the devil
he turns away from the Lord; if he turns to the Lord he turns
away from the devil. Or what is again the same, so long as a
man is in this world he is midway between evil and good, and
is kept in freedom to turn himself to either the one or the other;
if he turns to evil he turns away from good; if he turns to good
he turns away from evil.

20. We have said that a man is *kept* in freedom to turn himself one way or the other. It is not from himself that every
man has this freedom, but he has it from the Lord, and this is
why he is said to be kept in it. (Concerning the equilibrium
between heaven and hell, and that man is in it and owes his
freedom to that fact, see the work on *Heaven and Hell* (n. 589–
596; 597–603). That every man is kept in freedom, and that
from no one is it taken away, will be seen in its proper place.

21. It is plainly evident from all this that in proportion as
a man shuns evils, in the same proportion is he with the Lord
and in the Lord; and that in proportion as he is in the Lord,
in the same proportion he does goods, not from self but from
Him. From this results the general law : In proportion as
any one shuns evils, in the same proportion he does
goods.

22. Two things however are requisite : first, the man must
shun evils because they are sins, that is, because they are infernal and diabolical, and therefore contrary to the Lord and
the Divine laws ; and secondly, he must do this as of himself,
while knowing and believing that it is of the Lord. But these
two requisites will be considered in subsequent chapters.—

23. From what has been said three things follow :—

i. If a man wills and does goods before he shuns evils as
sins, the goods are not good.

ii. If a man thinks and speaks pious things while not shunning evils as sins, the pious things are not pious.

iii. If a man knows and is wise in many things, and does not shun evils as sins, he is nevertheless not wise.

24. i. *If a man wills and does goods before he shuns evils as sins, the goods are not good.* This is because, as already said, he is not in the Lord before he does so. For example: if a man gives to the poor, renders aid to the needy, contributes to places of worship and to hospitals, renders good service to the church, his country, and his fellow-citizens, teaches the Gospel and makes converts, does justice in his judgments, acts with sincerity in business, and with uprightness in his works; and yet makes no account of evils as being sins, such as fraud, adultery, hatred, blasphemy, and other like evils, then he can do only such goods as are evil within, because he does them from himself and not from the Lord, and therefore self is in them and not the Lord, and the goods in which is a man's self are all defiled with his evils, and have regard to himself and the world. And yet these very deeds that have just been enumerated are inwardly good if the man shuns evils as sins (such as fraud, adultery, hatred, blasphemy, and other like evils), because in this case he does them from the Lord, and they are said to be " wrought in God" (*John* iii. 19–21).

25. ii. *If a man thinks and speaks pious things while not shunning evils as sins, the pious things are not pious.* This is because he is not in the Lord. If for example he frequents places of worship, listens devoutly to the preaching, reads the Word and books of piety, goes to the sacrament of the Supper, pours forth prayers daily, and even if he thinks much about God and salvation, and yet regards as of no moment the evils which are sins (such as fraud, adultery, hatred, blasphemy, and other like evils), he then cannot do otherwise than think and speak such pious things as inwardly are not pious, because the man himself is in them with his evils. At the time indeed he is not aware of them, yet they are present within deeply hidden out of his sight; for he is like a spring the water of which is foul from its source. His performances of piety are either mere customs of habit, or else are the outcome of self-merit or hypocrisy. They do indeed rise up toward heaven, but turn back before they get there, and settle down, like smoke in the atmosphere.

26. I have been permitted to see and hear many after death who reckoned up their good works and performances of piety, such as those mentioned above (n. 24, 25), and many others besides. Among them I have also seen some who had lamps and no oil. Inquiry was made as to whether they had shunned evils as sins, and it was found that they had not, and therefore they were told that they were evil. Afterwards also they were seen to go into caverns where evil ones like them had their abode.

27. iii. *If a man knows and is wise about many things, and does not shun evils as sins, he is nevertheless not wise.* This is so for the reason already given : that he is wise from himself and not from the Lord. If for example he has an accurate knowledge of the doctrine of his church and of all things that belong to it, if he knows how to confirm them by the Word and by reasonings, if he knows the doctrines held by all churches for ages, together with the edicts of all the councils, and even if he knows truths, and also sees and understands them ; thus if he knows the nature of faith, charity, piety, repentance and the remission of sins, regeneration, baptism, the Holy Supper, the Lord, and redemption and salvation, still he is not wise unless he shuns evils as sins, because his knowledges (*cognitiones*) are devoid of life, being of his understanding only and not at the same time of his will; and such knowledges in time perish, for the reason given above (n. 15). After death also the man himself throws them off, because they are not in accordance with his will's love. Nevertheless knowledges are in the highest degree necessary, because they teach how a man is to act; and when he acts them, then they are alive in him, and not till then.

28. All that has been said thus far is taught by the Word in many places, of which only the following shall be presented.

The Word teaches that no one can be in good and at the same time in evil, or what is the same, that no one can be (in respect to his soul) in heaven and at the same time in hell. This is taught in the following passages :—

No man can serve two masters, for either he will hate the one and love the other, or else he will hold to one and despise the other. Ye cannot serve God and mammon (*Matt.* vi. 24).

How can ye, being evil, speak good things ? for out of the abundance of the heart the mouth speaketh. The good man out of the good treasure of his heart bringeth forth good things, and the evil man out of its evil treasure bringeth forth evil things (*Matt.* xii. 34, 35).

A good tree produceth not evil fruit, nor doth an evil tree produce good fruit. Every tree is known by its own fruit ; for of thorns men do not gather figs, nor of a bramble bush gather they grapes (*Luke* vi. 43, 44).

29. The Word teaches that no one can do what is good from himself, but that he does it from the Lord :—

Jesus said, I am the true vine, and My Father is the vine-dresser. Every branch in Me that beareth not fruit He taketh away ; and every branch that beareth fruit He cleanseth it, that it may bear more fruit. Abide in Me, and I in you. As the branch cannot bear fruit of itself, except it abide in the vine, so neither can ye except ye abide in Me. I am the vine, ye are the branches ; he that abideth in Me, and I in him, the same beareth much fruit ; for without Me ye can do nothing. If a man abide not in Me, he is cast forth as a branch, and is withered ; and they gather him, and cast him into the fire, and he is burned (*John* xv. 1–6).

30. The Word teaches that in proportion as a man has not been purified from evils, his goods are not good, nor are his pious things pious, and neither is he wise : it also teaches the converse :—

Woe unto you, scribes and Pharisees, hypocrites ! for ye are like unto whited sepulchres, which outwardly indeed appear beautiful, but inwardly are full of dead men's bones, and of all uncleanness. Even so ye also outwardly indeed appear righteous unto men, but inwardly ye are full of hypocrisy and iniquity. Woe unto you, for ye cleanse the outside of the cup and of the platter, but within they are full of extortion and excess. Thou blind Pharisee, cleanse first the inside of the cup and of the platter, that the outside thereof may become clean also (*Matt.* xxiii. 25–28).

The same appears from these words in *Isaiah :*—

Hear the word of Jehovah, ye princes of Sodom ; give ear unto the law of our God, ye people of Gomorrah.   To what purpose is the multitude of your sacrifices unto Me ? bring no more a meat-offering of vanity; incense is an abomination unto Me ; new moon and sabbath, I cannot bear iniquity ; your new moons and your appointed feasts My soul hateth ; therefore when ye spread forth your hands I will hide Mine eyes from you ; yea, if ye make many prayers, I will not hear ; your hands are full of bloods.   Wash you, make you clean ; put away the evil of your doings from before Mine eyes ; cease to do evil ; though your sins have been as scarlet, they shall be as white as snow ; though they have been red, they shall be as wool (i. 10–18).

These words in brief amount to this : that unless a man shuns evils, nothing of his worship is good, and in like manner nothing of his works, for it is said, " I cannot bear iniquity, make you clean, put away the evil of your doings, cease to do evil."   In *Jeremiah :*—

Return ye every man from his evil way, and make your works good (xxxv. 15).

[**2**] That the same are not wise is declared in *Isaiah :*—

Woe unto them that are wise in their own eyes, and intelligent before their own faces (v. 21).

The wisdom of the wise shall perish, and the intelligence of the intelligent ; woe unto them that are deeply wise, and their works are done in the dark (xxix. 14, 15).

Woe to them that go down to Egypt for help, and put their stay on horses, and trust in chariots because they are many, and in horsemen because they are strong ; but they look not unto the Holy One of Israel, neither seek Jehovah.   But He will arise against the house of the evildoers, and against the help of them that work iniquity.   For Egypt is man, and not God ; and the horses thereof are flesh, and not spirit (xxxi. 1–3).

Thus is described man's self-intelligence.   " Egypt" is memory-knowledge ; a " horse," the understanding therefrom ; a " chariot," the doctrine therefrom ; a " horseman," the intelligence therefrom; of all of which it is said, " Woe to them that look not unto the Holy One of Israel, neither seek Jehovah." Their destruction through evils is meant by: " He will arise against the house of the evil-doers, and against the help of them that work iniquity." That these things are from man's Own, and that consequently there is no life in them, is meant by its being said that " Egypt is man and not God," and that " the horses thereof are flesh and not spirit." " Man," and " flesh," denote what is man's Own; " God," and " spirit," denote life from the Lord; the " horses of Egypt," denote self-intelligence. There are many such things in the Word concerning intelligence from self, and intelligence from the Lord, which can be seen only by means of the spiritual sense.

[3] That no one is saved by means of goods from self, because they are not good, is evident from the following :—

Not every one that saith unto Me, Lord, Lord, shall enter into the kingdom of the heavens, but he that doeth the will of My Father : many will say to Me in that day, Lord, Lord, have we not prophesied by Thy name, and by Thy name cast out demons, and in Thy name done many mighty things ? but then I will profess unto them, I never knew you, depart from Me, ye that work iniquity (*Matt.* vii. 21–23).

Then shall ye begin to stand without, and to knock at the door, saying, Lord, open to us ; and ye shall begin to say, We did eat and drink in Thy presence, and Thou hast taught in our streets ; but He shall say, I tell you I know ye not whence ye are, depart from Me, all ye workers of iniquity (*Luke* xiii. 25–27).

For such persons are like the Pharisee,

Who stood in the temple and prayed, saying that he was not as other men, an extortioner, unjust, an adulterer ; that he fasted twice in the week, and gave tithes of all that he possessed (*Luke* xviii. 11–14).

Such persons moreover are those who are called

Unprofitable servants (*Luke* xvii. 10).

31. That no man can from himself do what is really good, is the truth. But so to use this truth as to do away with all the good of charity that is done by a man who shuns evils as sins, is a great wickedness, for it is diametrically contrary to the Word, which commands that a man shall *do*. It is contrary to the commandments of love to God and love toward the neighbor on which the Law and the Prophets hang, and it is to flout and undermine everything of religion. For every one knows that religion is to do what is good, and that every one will be judged according to his deeds. Every man is so constituted as to be able (by the Lord's power, if he begs for it) to shun evils as of himself; and that which he afterwards does is good from the Lord.

IV.

IN PROPORTION AS ANY ONE SHUNS EVILS AS SINS, IN THE SAME PROPORTION HE LOVES TRUTHS.

32. There are two universals that proceed from the Lord: Divine good, and Divine truth. Divine good is of His Divine love, and Divine truth is of His Divine wisdom. In the Lord these two are a one,* and therefore they proceed from Him as a one, but they are not received as a one by angels in the heavens, or by men on earth. There are both angels and men who receive more from Divine truth than from Divine good; and there are others who receive more from Divine good than from Divine truth. This is why the heavens are distinguished into two distinct kingdoms, one of which is called the celestial kingdom, and the other the spiritual kingdom. The heavens that receive more from Divine good constitute the celestial kingdom, and those which receive more from Divine truth constitute the spiritual kingdom. (Concerning these two kingdoms into which the heavens are divided, see the work on *Heaven and Hell*, n. 20–28.) But still the angels of all the heavens are in wisdom and intelligence in proportion to the degree in which the good in them makes a one with truth. The

* That is, a complex whole which constitutes a unity. [TR.]

good that does not make a one with truth is to them not good; and on the other hand the truth that does not make a one with good is to them not truth. From this we see that good conjoined with truth constitutes love and wisdom in both angel and man; and as an angel is an angel, and a man a man, from the love and wisdom in him, it is evident that good conjoined with truth causes an angel to be an angel of heaven, and a man a man of the church.

33. As good and truth are a one in the Lord, and proceed as a one from Him, it follows that good loves truth and truth loves good, and they will to be a one. It is the same with their opposites: evil loves falsity, and falsity loves evil, and these will to be a one. In the following pages the conjunction of good and truth will be called the Heavenly Marriage, and that of evil and falsity the Infernal Marriage.

34. It follows from these premises that in proportion as any one shuns evils as sins, in the same proportion he loves truths (for in the same proportion he is in good, as has been shown in the preceding chapter); and also that in proportion as any one does not shun evils as sins, in the same proportion he does not love truths, because in the same proportion he is not in good.

35. It is indeed possible for a man to love truths who does not shun evils as sins; yet he does not love them because they are truths, but because they minister to his reputation, and thereby to his honors or gains, so that if they do not minister to it he loves them not.

36. Good is of the will, truth of the understanding. From the love of good in the will proceeds the love of truth in the understanding; from the love of truth proceeds the perception of truth; from the perception of truth comes thought about truth; and from all of these together comes the acknowledgment of truth which in the true sense is faith. (That this is the progression from the love of good to faith, will be shown in the treatise on *Divine Love and Divine Wisdom*.)

37. As good is not good unless it is conjoined with truth, as already said, it follows that previous thereto good does not come into manifest being. But as it continually desires to come into manifest being it longs for and procures truths in order to do so, for truths are the agency of its nourishment and formation. This is the reason why a man loves truths in the same proportion that he is in good, consequently in the same proportion that he shuns evils as sins, for it is in proportion that he does this that any one is in good.

38. In proportion as any one is in good, and from good loves truths, in the same proportion he loves the Lord, because the Lord is good itself and truth itself. The Lord is therefore with man in good and in truth. If the latter is loved from good the Lord is loved, but not otherwise. This the Lord teaches in *John :*—

He that hath My commandments, and doeth them, he it is that loveth Me ; He that loveth Me not keepeth not My words (xiv. 21, 24).

If ye keep My commandments, ye shall abide in My love (xv. 10).

The " commandments" and " words" of the Lord are truths.

39. That good loves truth may be illustrated by comparison with a priest, a soldier, a trader, and an artificer. With a *priest :*—If he is in the good of the priesthood, which is to care for the salvation of souls, to teach the way to heaven, and to lead those whom he teaches, then in proportion as he is in this good (thus from his love and its desire) he acquires the truths which he may teach, and by means of which he may lead. But a priest who is not in the good of the priesthood, but is in the delight of his office from the love of self and of the world, which to him is the only good, he too from his love and its desire acquires those truths in abundance in proportion as he is inspired by the delight which is his good. With a *soldier :*— If he is in the love of military service, and is sensible of its good, whether it be that of national defense, or that of his own fame, from this good and according to it he acquires its special knowledge, and if he is a commander, its intelligence ; these are like truths by which the delight of love which is his good is nourished and formed. With a *trader :*—If he has taken up this calling from the love of it, he learns with avidity everything that enters into and makes up that love as its means; these also are like truths, while trading is his good. With an *artificer :*—If he applies himself with earnestness to his work, and loves it as the good of his life, he purchases tools, and perfects himself by whatever pertains to a knowledge of it, and by these means he so does his work that it is a good. From these comparisons it is evident that truths are the means through which the good of love comes into manifest being, and becomes something; consequently that good loves truths in order that it may do so. Hence in the Word to "do the truth" means to cause good to come into manifest being. This is meant by

Doing the truth (*John* iii. 21) ;
Doing the Lord's sayings (*Luke* vi. 47) ;
Keeping His commandments (*John* xiv. 24) ;
Doing His words (*Matt.* vii. 24) ;
Doing the Word of God (*Luke* viii. 21) ; and by
Doing the statutes and judgments (*Lev.* xviii. 5).

And this also is to " do what is good," and to " bear fruit," for " good" and " fruit" are that which comes into manifest being (*est id quod existit*).

40. That good loves truth and wills to be conjoined with it, may also be illustrated by comparison with food and water, or with bread and wine. Both are necessary. Food or bread alone effects nothing in the body in the way of nourishment; it does so only together with water or with wine; and therefore the one has an appetite and longing for the other. Moreover in the Word " food" and " bread" mean good, in the spiritual sense; and " water" and " wine" mean truth.

41. From all that has been said it is now evident that he who shuns evils as sins, loves truths and longs for them; and that the more he shuns them, so much the more love and longing does he feel, because so much the more he is in good. The result is that he comes into the heavenly marriage, which is the marriage of good and truth, in which is heaven, and in which must be the church.

V.

In proportion as any one shuns Evils as Sins, in the same proportion he has Faith, and is Spiritual.

42. Faith and life are distinct from each other in the same way as are thinking and doing; and as thinking is of the understanding and doing is of the will, it follows that faith and life are distinct from each other in the same way as are the understanding and the will. He who knows the distinction between the two latter knows that between the two former; and he who knows the conjunction of the two latter knows that of the two former. For this reason something shall first be set forth about the understanding and the will.

43. Man possesses two faculties, one of which is called the Will, and the other the Understanding. They are distinct from each other, but are so created that they may be a one, and when they are a one they are called the Mind, so that the human mind consists of these two faculties, and the whole of man's life is in them. Just as all things in the universe that are in accordance with Divine order bear relation to good and truth, so do all things in man bear relation to the will and the understanding; for the good in a man belongs to his will and the truth in him belongs to his understanding, these two faculties being their receptacles and subjects; the will, of all things of good, and the understanding of all things of truth. The goods and truths in a man are nowhere else, and so therefore neither are the love and faith, because love is of good and good is of love, and faith is of truth and truth is of faith. It is of the utmost importance to know how the will and the understanding make one mind. They do so in the same way that good and truth make a one, for there is a like marriage between the will and the understanding to that which exists between good and truth. The nature of this latter marriage has been in some measure told in the preceding chapter, and to this we should add that just as good is the very being (*esse*) of a thing, and truth is its derivative manifestation (*existere*), so the will in man is the very being of his life, and the understanding is its derivative manifestation, for the good that is of the will shapes itself forth in the understanding, and presents itself to view within fixed and settled outlines (*certo modo*).

44. It has been shown above (n. 27, 28) that a man may know many things, may think them over, may understand them, and yet may not be wise. And as it is the province of faith to know and to think, and still more to understand, that a thing is true, a man may well believe that he has faith and yet not have it. The reason why he has it not, is that he is in evil of life, and evil of life and truth of faith cannot possibly act as a one. The evil of life destroys the truth of faith, because the evil of life is of the will and the truth of faith is of the understanding, and the will leads the understanding and makes it act as a one with itself, so that if there is anything in the understanding that is not in accord with the will, and the man is left to himself, and thinks from his own evil and the love of it, he then either casts out the truth that is in the understanding, or else by falsifying it forces it into oneness. Quite different is it with those who are in the good of life: such when left to themselves think from what is good, and love the truth that is in the understanding because it is in accord. In this way there takes place a conjunction of faith and life such as is that of truth and good, and both these conjunctions are like that of the understanding and the will.

45. From all this then it follows that just in so far as a man shuns evils as sins, just so far has he faith, because just so far is he in good, as shown above. This is confirmed also by its contrary: that he who does not shun evils as sins, has not faith because he is in evil, and evil inwardly hates truth. Outwardly indeed he may act as a friend to truth, and suffer it to be in the understanding, may even love to have it there; but when what is outward is put off, as is done after death, he first casts out truth his friend in this world, then denies that it is truth, and finally feels aversion for it.

46. The faith of an evil man is an intellectual faith, in which there is nothing of good from the will. Thus it is a dead faith, which is like the breathing of the lungs without there being any life or soul in it from the heart. Moreover the understanding corresponds to the lungs, and the will to the heart. Such faith is also like a good-looking harlot dressed up in crimson and gold, but full of disease and corruption. A harlot also corresponds to the falsification of truth, and therefore in the Word signifies it. Such faith is also like a tree luxuriant in foliage but barren of fruit, which the gardener cuts down. A tree moreover signifies a man, its leaves and blossoms signify the truths of faith, and its fruit the good of love. But very different is that faith in the understanding which has in it good from the will. This faith is living, and is like a breathing of the lungs in which there is life and soul from the heart. It is also like a lovely wife whose chastity endears her to her husband. It is also like a tree that bears fruit.

47. There are many things that appear to be mere matters of faith, such as that there is a God; that the Lord, who is God, is the Redeemer and Saviour; that there is a heaven and a hell; that there is a life after death; and many other things of which it is not said that they are to be done, but that they are to be believed. These things of faith also are dead with a man who is in evil, but are living with a man who is in good. The reason is that a man who is in good not only acts aright from the will but also thinks aright from the understanding, and this not only before the world but also before himself when he is alone. Not so a man who is in evil.

48. We have said that these things appear to be mere matters of faith. But the thought of the understanding derives its coming into manifest being (*trahit suum existere*) from the love of the will, which is the inmost being (*qui est esse*) of the thought in the understanding, as has been said above (n. 43). For whatever any one wills from love, he wills to do, he wills to think, he wills to understand, and he wills to speak; or, what is the same, whatever any one loves from the will, he loves to do, he loves to think, he loves to understand, and he loves to speak. To this is also to be added, that when a man shuns what is evil as a sin, he is in the Lord, as shown above, and the Lord then works everything. And therefore to those who asked Him what they should do that they might work the works of God, He said :—

This is the work of God, that ye believe in Him whom He hath sent (*John* vi. 28, 29).

To "believe in the Lord" is not only to think that He is, but also to do His words, as He teaches elsewhere.

49. That those who are in evils have no faith, no matter how much they may suppose themselves to have it, has been shown in the spiritual world in the case of persons of this character. They were brought into a heavenly society, which caused the spiritual sphere of faith as existing with the angels to enter into the interiors of their faith, and the result was that the angels perceived that those persons possessed only what is natural or external of faith, and not what is spiritual or internal of it, and therefore those persons themselves confessed that they had nothing whatever of faith, and that in the world they had persuaded themselves that to believe or have faith consists in thinking a thing to be true, no matter what the ground for so thinking. Very different was perceived to be the faith of those who had not been in evil.

50. From all this it may be seen what spiritual faith is; and also what is faith not spiritual. Spiritual faith exists with those who do not commit sins, for those who do not commit sins do things that are good, not from themselves but from the Lord (see above, n. 18–21), and through faith become spiritual. Faith with these is the truth This the Lord teaches in *John :—*

This is the judgment, that the light is come into the world, and men loved the darkness rather than the light, because their works were evil. For every one that doeth evil hateth the light, and cometh not to the light, lest his works should be reproved. But he that doeth the truth cometh to the light, that his works may be made manifest, that they have been wrought in God (iii. 19–21).

51. All the foregoing is confirmed by the following passages in the Word :—

A good man out of the good treasure of his heart bringeth forth that which is good ; and an evil man out of the evil treasure of his heart bringeth forth that which is evil, for out of the abundance of the heart the mouth speaketh (*Luke* vi. 45 ; *Matt.* xii. 35).

The "heart" in the Word means man's will, and as man thinks and speaks from this, it is said : "Out of the abundance of the heart the mouth speaketh."

Not that which goeth into the mouth defileth the man ; but that which goeth out of the heart, this defileth the man (*Matt.* xv. 11, 18).

The "heart" here too means the will. Jesus said of the woman who anointed His feet with ointment :—

Her sins are forgiven ; for she loved much ; thy faith hath saved thee (*Luke* vii. 47, 50) ;

from which it is evident that when sins have been remitted or forgiven, thus when they exist no longer, faith saves. That those are called "sons of God" and "born of God" who are not in the Own of their will, and consequently are not in the Own of their understanding; that is to say, who are not in evil and from this in falsity; and that these are they who believe in the Lord, He Himself teaches in *John* i. 12, 13, which passage may be seen explained above in n. 17, at the end.

52. From these premises there follows this conclusion :— That no man has in him a grain of truth more than he has of good; thus that he has not a grain of faith more than he has of life. In the understanding indeed there may exist the thought that such or such a thing is true, but not the acknowledgment which is faith, unless there is consent thereto in the will. Thus do faith and life keep step as they walk. From all this it is now evident that in proportion as any one shuns evils as sins, in the same proportion he has faith and is spiritual.

VI.

The Decalogue teaches what Evils are Sins.

53. What nation in the wide world is not aware that it is evil to steal, to commit adultery, to kill, and to bear false witness ? If men were not aware of this, and if they did not by laws guard against the commission of these evils, it would be all over with them ; for without such laws the community, the commonwealth, and the kingdom would perish. Who can imagine that the Israelitish nation was so much more senseless than other nations as not to know that these were evils ? One might therefore wonder why these laws, known as they are the world over, were promulgated from Mount Sinai by Jehovah Himself with so great a miracle. But listen : they were promulgated with so great a miracle in order that men may know that these laws are not only civic and moral laws, but are also spiritual laws ; and that to act contrary to them is not only to do evil to a fellow-citizen and to the community, but is also to sin against God. For this reason those laws, through promulgation from Mount Sinai by Jehovah, were made laws of religion ; for it is evident that whatever Jehovah God commands, He commands in order that it may be of religion, and that it is to be done for His sake, and for the sake of the man that he may be saved.

54. As these laws were the first-fruits of the Word, and therefore the first-fruits of the church that was to be again set up by the Lord with the Israelitish nation, and as they were in a brief summary a complex of all those things of religion by means of which there is conjunction of the Lord with man and of man with the Lord, they were so holy that nothing is more so.

55. That they were most holy is evident from the fact that Jehovah Himself (that is, the Lord) came down upon Mount Sinai in fire, and with angels, and promulgated them from it by a living voice, and that the people had prepared themselves for three days to see and to hear; that the mountain was fenced about lest any one should go near it and should die; that neither were the priests nor the elders to draw near, but Moses only; that those laws were written by the finger of God on two tables of stone; that when Moses brought the tables down from the mountain the second time, his face shone; that the tables were afterwards laid away in the ark, and the ark in the inmost of the tabernacle, and upon it was placed the mercy-seat, and upon this cherubs of gold; that this was the most holy thing of their church, being called the holy of holies; that outside the veil that hung before it there were placed things that represented holy things of heaven and the church, namely, the lampstand with its seven golden lamps, the golden altar of incense, and the table overlaid with gold on which were the loaves of faces, and surrounded with curtains of fine linen, bright-crimson, and scarlet. The holiness of this whole tabernacle had no other source than the Law that was in the ark. [2] On account of this holiness of the tabernacle from the Law in the ark, the whole people of Israel, by command, encamped around it in the order of their tribes, and marched in order after it, and there was then a cloud over it by day, and a fire by night. On account of the holiness of that Law, and the presence of the Lord in it, the Lord spoke with Moses above the mercy-seat between the cherubs, and the ark was called " Jehovah there." Aaron also was not allowed to enter within the veil except with sacrifices and incense. Because that Law was the very holiness of the church, the ark was brought by David into Zion; and later it was kept in the midst of the temple at Jerusalem, and constituted its shrine. [3] On account of the Lord's presence in that Law and around it, miracles were wrought by the ark in which was that Law: the waters of Jordan were cleft asunder, and so long as the ark was resting in the midst of it, the people passed over on dry ground; when the ark was carried round the walls of Jericho they fell; Dagon the god of the Philistines fell down before it, and afterwards lay on the threshold of the temple without his head; and on its account the Bethshemites were smitten to the number of many thousands; not to mention other miracles. These were all performed solely by the Lord's presence in His Ten Words, which are the commandments of the decalogue.

56. So great a power and so great a holiness existed in that Law for the further reason that it was a complex of all things of religion; for it consisted of two tables of which the one contains all things that are on the part of God, and the other in a complex all things that are on the part of man. The commandments of this Law are therefore called the "Ten Words," and are so called because "ten" signifies all. But how this Law is a complex of all things of religion will be seen in the following chapter.

57. As by means of this Law there is a conjunction of the Lord with man and of man with the Lord, it is called the "Covenant," and the "Testimony," the "Covenant" because it conjoins, and the "Testimony" because it bears witness, for a "covenant" signifies conjunction, and a "testimony" the attestation of it. For this reason there were two tables, one for the Lord and the other for man. The conjunction is effected by the Lord, but only when the man does the things that have been written in his table. For the Lord is constantly present and working, and wills to enter in, but man must open to the Lord in the freedom which he has from Him; for the Lord says :—

Behold, I stand at the door, and knock; if any man hear My voice, and open the door, I will come in to him, and will sup with him, and he with Me (*Rev.* iii. 20).

58. In the second table, which is for man, it is not said that man must do this or that good, but that he must not do this or that evil, as for example, "Thou shalt not kill, Thou shalt not commit adultery, Thou shalt not steal, Thou shalt not bear false witness, Thou shalt not covet." The reason is that man cannot do any good whatever from himself, but when he no longer does evils, then he does good, not from himself but from

the Lord. That by the power of the Lord a man is able to
shun evils as of himself if he begs for that power, will be seen
in the following pages.

59. What has been said above (n. 55) respecting the promulgation, holiness, and power of that Law, will be found in
the following places in the Word :—

That Jehovah came down on Mount Sinai in fire, and that the mountain smoked and quaked, and that there were thunderings, lightnings, a
thick cloud, and the voice of a trumpet (*Exod.* xix. 16, 18 ; *Deut.* iv. 11 ;
v. 22–26).

That before the descent of Jehovah the people prepared and sanctified
themselves for three days (*Exod.* xix. 10, 11, 15).

That bounds were set round the mountain, lest any one should come
near its base, and should die ; and that not even were the priests to come
near, but Moses only (*Exod.* xix. 12, 13, 20–23 ; xxiv. 1, 2).

That the Law was promulgated from Mount Sinai (*Exod.* xx. 2–17 ;
Deut. v. 6–21).

That that Law was written by the finger of God on two tables of stone
(*Exod.* xxxi. 18 ; xxxii. 15, 16 ; *Deut.* ix. 10).

That when Moses brought those tables down from the mountain the
second time, his face shone (*Exod.* xxxiv. 29–35).

That the tables were kept in the ark (*Exod.* xxv. 16 ; xl. 20 ; *Deut.* x.
5 ; 1 *Kings* viii. 9).

That upon the ark was placed the mercy-seat, and upon this the
golden cherubs (*Exod.* xxv. 17–21).

That the ark, together with the mercy-seat and the cherubs, constituted the inmost of the tabernacle, and that the golden lampstand, the
golden altar of incense, and the table overlaid with gold on which were
the loaves of faces, constituted the exterior of the tabernacle ; and the
ten curtains of fine linen, bright-crimson, and scarlet, its outermost
(*Exod.* xxv. 1–end ; xxvi. 1–end ; xl. 17–28).

That the place where the ark was, was called the holy of holies
(*Exod.* xxvi. 33).

That the whole people of Israel encamped around the habitation in
order according to their tribes, and marched in order after it (*Num.* ii.
1–end).

That there was then over the habitation a cloud by day and a fire by
night (*Exod.* xl. 38 ; *Num.* ix. 15–end ; xiv. 14 ; *Deut.* i. 33).

That the Lord spoke with Moses from over the ark between the
cherubs (*Exod.* xxv. 22 ; *Num.* vii. 89).

That the ark, from the Law within it, was called Jehovah-There, for when the ark set forward, Moses said, Rise up, Jehovah ; and when it rested he said, Return Jehovah (*Num.* x. 35, 36), and see further 2 *Sam.* vi. 2 ; *Ps.* cxxxii. 7, 8.

That on account of the holiness of that Law Aaron was not allowed to enter within the veil except with sacrifices and with incense (*Lev.* xvi. 2-14, etc.).

That the ark was brought into Zion by David with sacrifices and with shouting (2 *Sam.* vi. 1-19). That on that occasion, Uzzah, who touched it, died (verses 6 and 7).

That the ark was placed in the midst of the temple in Jerusalem, where it constituted the shrine (1 *Kings* vi. 19, etc. ; viii. 3-9).

That by the Lord's presence and power in the Law that was in the ark, the waters of Jordan were cleft asunder, and so long as the ark rested in the midst of it, the people passed over on dry ground (*Josh.* iii. 1-17 ; iv. 5-20).

That when the ark was carried around them, the walls of Jericho fell (*Josh.* vi. 1-20).

That Dagon the god of the Philistines fell to the earth before the ark, and afterwards lay upon the threshold of the temple headless (1 *Sam.* v. 1-4).

That on account of the ark the Bethshemites were smitten, to the number of many thousands (1 *Sam.* vi. 19).

60. That the tables of stone on which the Law was written were called "the tables of the covenant," and that from them the ark was called "the ark of the covenant," and the Law itself "the covenant," see *Num.* x. 33 ; *Deut.* iv. 13, 23 ; v. 2, 3 ; ix. 9 ; *Josh.* iii. 11 ; 1 *Kings* viii. 19, 21 ; *Rev.* xi. 19 ; and in many other places. The reason why the Law was called the "covenant," is that "covenant" signifies conjunction ; and it is therefore said of the Lord that :—

He shall be for a covenant to the people (*Isa.* xlii. 6 ; xlix. 8 ;

and He is called :—

The messenger of the covenant (*Mal.* iii. 1) ;

and His blood :—

The blood of the covenant (*Matt.* xxvi. 28 ; *Zech.* ix. 11 ; *Exod.* xxiv. 4-10).

And therefore the Word is called the "Old Covenant," and the "New Covenant." Moreover covenants are made for the sake

16

of love, friendship, association, and thus for the sake of conjunction.

61. That the commandments of this Law were called the "Ten Words," see *Exod.* xxxiv. 28; *Deut.* iv. 13; x. 4. They are so called because "ten" signifies all, and "words" signifies truths, for there were more than ten words. As "ten" signifies all,

The curtains of the tabernacle were ten (*Exod.* xxvi. 1) ;

And for the same reason the Lord said

That a certain man who was to receive a kingdom, called ten of his servants, and gave them ten pounds to trade with (*Luke* xix. 13).

And for the same reason also the Lord

Likened the kingdom of the heavens to ten virgins (*Matt.* xxv. 1).

For the same reason also,

The dragon is described as having ten horns, and upon his horns ten diadems (*Rev.* xii. 3).

In like manner the beast that came up out of the sea (*Rev.* xiii. 1).

And another beast also (*Rev.* xvii. 3, 7).

Likewise the beast in *Daniel* (vii. 7, 20, 24).

The like is signified by ten in *Leviticus* (xxvi. 26), and in *Zechariah* (viii. 23), and in other places.

This is the origin of tithes, for "tithes" (or "tenths") signify something from all.

VII.

MURDERS, ADULTERIES, THEFTS, FALSE WITNESS, TOGETHER
WITH ALL CONCUPISCENCE FOR THESE THINGS, ARE THE
EVILS WHICH MUST BE SHUNNED AS SINS.

62. It is well known that the Law of Sinai was written on two tables, and that the first table contains the things of God, and the other the things of man. That the first table contains all things that belong to God, and the second all that belong to man, does not appear in the letter, yet are they all in them, and it is for this reason that they are called the Ten Words, by which are signified all truths in the complex (as may be seen just above, n. 61). But in what way all things are in them cannot be set forth in a few words, but may be apprehended from what has been presented in the *Doctrine of the Holy Scripture* (n. 67), which see. This is why it is said "murders, adulteries, thefts, and false witness *of every kind.*"

63. A religious tenet has prevailed to the effect that no one is able to fulfill the law; the law being not to kill, not to commit adultery, not to steal, and not to bear false witness. Every civic man and moral man is able to fulfill these commandments of the law by a civic and moral life; but this tenet denies that he can do so by a spiritual life; from which it follows that his not doing these evils is only for the sake of avoiding penalties and losses in this world, and not for the sake of avoiding penalties and losses after he has left it. It is for this reason that a man with whom this tenet has prevailed, thinks these evils allowable in the sight of God, but not so in that of the world. [2] And in consequence of such thought from this his tenet, the man is in concupiscence for all these evils, and refrains from doing them merely for the world's sake; and therefore after death such a man, although he had not committed murders, adulteries, thefts, and false witness, nevertheless desires to commit them, and does commit them when the external possessed by him in this world is taken away from him. Every concupiscence he has had remains with him after death. It is owing to this that such persons act as one with hell, and cannot but have their lot among those who are there. [3] Very different is the lot of those who are unwilling to kill, to commit adultery, to steal, and to bear false witness for the reason that to do these things is contrary to God. These persons, after some battling with these evils, do not will them, thus do not desire to commit them: they say in their hearts that they are sins, and in themselves are infernal and devilish. After death, when the external which they had possessed for this world is taken away from them, they act as one with heaven, and as they are in the Lord they come into heaven.

64. It is a common principle of every religion that a man ought to examine himself, repent, and desist from sins, and that if he fails to do so he is in a state of damnation. (That this is a common principle of every religion may be seen above, n. 4–8.) Teaching the decalogue is also a common thing throughout the whole Christian world, and by it little children are commonly initiated into the Christian religion, for it is in the hands of all young children. Their parents and teachers tell them that to commit these evils is to sin against God, and in fact while speaking to the children they know nothing different. We may well wonder that these same persons, and the children too when they become adults, think that they are not under this Law, and that they are not able to do the things that belong to it. Can there be any other cause for their learning to think in this way, than that they love evils and consequently the false notions that favor them? These therefore are the people who do not make the commandments of the decalogue a matter of religion. And that these same persons live without religion will be seen in the *Doctrine of Faith*.

65. All nations in the wide world who have religion possess precepts like those in the decalogue, and all who from religion live them are saved, and all who do not live them from religion are damned. When those who live them from religion are instructed after death by the angels, they receive truths, and acknowledge the Lord; the reason of which is that they shun evils as sins, and are consequently in good, and good loves truth, and from the desire of this love, receives it (as has been shown above, n. 32–41). This is meant by the words of the Lord to the Jews :—

The kingdom of God shall be taken away from you, and shall be given to a nation bringing forth the fruits thereof (*Matt.* xxi. 43).

And also by these :—

When therefore the Lord of the vineyard shall come, He will destroy those evil men, and will let out his vineyard to other husbandmen, who shall render him the fruits in their season (*Matt.* xxi. 40, 41).

And by these :—

> I say unto you that many shall come from the east and the west, and from the north and the south, and shall sit down in the kingdom of God, but the sons of the kingdom shall be cast forth into the outer darkness (*Matt.* viii. 11, 12 ; *Luke* xiii. 29).

66. We read in *Mark* :—

> That a certain rich man came to Jesus, and asked Him what he should do to inherit eternal life, and that Jesus said to him, Thou knowest the commandments : Thou shalt not commit adultery, Thou shalt not kill, Thou shalt not steal, Thou shalt not be a false witness, Thou shalt not defraud, Honor thy father and mother. And he answering said, All these things have I kept from my youth. And Jesus looked upon him and loved him, yet said unto him, One thing thou lackest ; go, sell whatsoever thou hast, and give to the poor ; so shalt thou have treasure in the heavens ; and come, take up the cross and follow Me (x. 17–22).

It is said that Jesus "loved him." This was because the man said that he had kept those commandments from his youth. But because he lacked three things, which were that he had not removed his heart from riches, had not fought against concupiscences, and had not yet acknowledged the Lord to be God, the Lord said that he should "sell all that he had," by which is meant that he should remove his heart from riches ; that he should "take up the cross," by which is meant that he should fight against concupiscences ; and that he should "follow Him," by which is meant that he should acknowledge the Lord to be God. The Lord spoke these things as He spoke all things : by correspondences. (See the *Doctrine of the Holy Scripture*, n. 17.) For no one is able to shun evils as sins unless he acknowledges the Lord and goes to Him, and unless he fights against evils and so removes concupiscences. But more about these matters in the chapter on combats against evils.

VIII.

In proportion as any one shuns Murders of every kind as Sins, in the same proportion he has Love toward the Neighbor.

67. "Murders of every kind" include enmity, hatred, and revenge of every kind, which breathe murder, for murder lies hidden in them, like fire in wood underneath the ashes. Infernal fire is nothing else, and this is the origin of the expressions to "kindle with hatred," and to "burn with revenge." All these are "murders" in the natural sense. But in the spiritual sense "murders" mean all methods of killing and destroying the souls of men, which methods are varied and many. And in the highest sense "murder" means to hate the Lord. These three kinds of "murder" form a one, and cleave together, for he who wills the murder of a man's body in this world, after death wills the murder of his soul, and wills the murder of the Lord, for he burns with anger against Him, and desires to blot out His name.

68. These kinds of murder lie inwardly hidden in man from his birth, but from early childhood he learns to veil them over with the civic and moral behavior that he is bound to show toward men in the world, and in proportion as he loves honors or gains he guards against their appearance. This forms his external, while his internal is these kinds of murder. Such is man in himself. Now as when he dies he lays aside that external together with his body, and retains the internal, it is evident what a devil he would be unless he were reformed.

69. As the kinds of murder mentioned above lie inwardly hidden in man from his birth, as has been said, and at the same time thefts of every kind, and false witness of every kind, together with the concupiscences for them (of which we shall speak farther on), it is evident that unless the Lord provided means of reformation, a man must perish everlastingly.

The means of reformation provided by the Lord are as follows : That man is born into total ignorance; that when newly born he is kept in a state of external innocence; a little after in a state of external charity; and later in a state of external friendship; but in proportion as he comes into the exercise of thought from his own understanding, he is kept in a certain freedom of acting according to reason. This is the state that has been described above (n. 19), and the description shall be here repeated for the sake of what is to follow :—

So long as a man is in this world he is midway between hell and heaven ; hell is below him, and heaven is above him ; and he is kept in freedom to turn himself to either the one or the other ; if he turns to hell he turns away from heaven ; if he turns to heaven he turns away from hell. Or what is the same, so long as a man is in this world he stands midway between the Lord and the devil, and is kept in freedom to turn himself to either the one or the other ; if he turns to the devil he turns away from the Lord ; if he turns to the Lord he turns away from the devil. Or what is again the same, so long as a man is in this world he is midway between evil and good, and is kept in freedom to turn himself to either the one or the other ; if he turns to evil he turns away from good ; if he turns to good he turns away from evil. (See also what follows this, n. 20–22.)

70. Now as evil and good are two opposite things, precisely as are hell and heaven, or as are the devil and the Lord, it follows that if a man shuns evil as sin, he comes into the good that is opposite to the evil. The good opposite to the evil that is meant by " murder," is the good of love toward the neighbor.

71. As this good and that evil are opposites, it follows that the latter is removed by means of the former. Two opposites cannot be together, even as heaven and hell cannot; if they were together there would be lukewarmness, of which it is said in the *Revelation :*—

I know that thou art neither cold nor hot ; I would thou wert cold or hot ; but because thou art lukewarm, and neither cold nor hot, I will spew thee out of My mouth (iii. 15, 16).

72. When a man is no longer in the evil of murder, but in the good of love toward the neighbor, whatever he does is a good of this love, and therefore it is a good work. A *priest* who is in this good does a good work whenever he teaches and leads, because he acts from the love of saving souls. A *magistrate* who is in this good does a good work whenever he delivers a decision or a judgment, because he acts from the love of taking care of his country, of the community, and of his fellow-citizen. The same with a *trader:* if he is in this good, everything of his trading is a good work; there is in him the love of the neighbor; and his country, the community, his fellow-citizen, and also the members of his household, are the neighbor whose welfare he has care for in providing for his own. A *workman* also who is in this good, works faithfully from it, for others as for himself, fearing his neighbor's loss as he would his own. The reason why the doings of these men are good works, is that in proportion as any one shuns evil, in the same proportion he does good, according to the general law stated above (n. 21), and he who shuns evil as sin, does good not from himself but from the Lord (n. 18–31). The contrary is the case with him who does not regard as sins the various kinds of murder, which are enmities, hatred, revenge, and many more. Whether he be priest, magistrate, trader, or workman, whatever he does is not a good work, because every work of his partakes of the evil that is within him; for his internal is what gives it birth. The external may be good, but only as regards others, not as regards himself.

73. The Lord teaches the good of love in many places in the Word. He teaches it in *Matthew* by what He says about reconciliation with the neighbor :—

If thou art offering thy gift upon the altar, and there remember that thy brother hath aught against thee, leave there thy gift before the altar, and go thy way, first be reconciled to thy brother, and then come and offer thy gift. Be well-minded to thine adversary quickly, while thou art in the way with him ; lest the adversary deliver thee to the judge, and the judge deliver thee to the officer, and thou be cast into prison. Verily I say unto thee, thou shalt not come out thence, till thou hast paid the last farthing (v. 23–26).

To be "reconciled to one's brother," is to shun enmity, hatred, and revenge; that it is to shun them as sin is evident. The Lord also teaches in *Matthew* :—

> All things whatsoever ye would that men should do to you, do ye even so to them ; for this is the Law and the Prophets (vii. 12) ;

thus that we should not do evil. He teaches the same in many other places. The Lord also teaches that to be angry with one's brother or the neighbor rashly, and to hold him as an enemy, is also to commit murder (*Matt.* v. 21, 22).

IX.

In proportion as any one shuns Adulteries of every kind as Sins, in the same proportion he loves Chastity.

74. To "commit adultery," as mentioned in the sixth (or as it is usually called, the seventh) commandment, means, in the natural sense, not only to commit whoredom, but also to do obscene things, to speak lascivious things, and to think about filthy things. But in the spiritual sense to "commit adultery" means to adulterate the goods of the Word, and to falsify its truths. In the highest sense to "commit adultery" means to deny the divinity of the Lord, and to profane the Word. These are the "adulteries of every kind." The natural man is able to know from rational light that to "commit adultery" includes in its meaning the doing of things obscene, the speaking of things lascivious, and the thinking of things that are filthy ; but he does not know that to commit adultery means also to adulterate the goods of the Word and to falsify its truths, and still less that it means to deny the divinity of the Lord and to profane the Word. Consequently neither does he know that adultery is so great an evil that it may be called diabolism itself, for he who is in natural adultery is also in spiritual adultery, and the converse. That this is so will be shown in a separate little work entitled *De Conjugio*.* But those who from their faith and their life do not regard adulteries as sins, are in adulteries of every kind at once.

75. That in proportion as any one shuns adultery, in the same proportion he loves marriage; or what is the same, in proportion as any one shuns the lasciviousness of adultery, in the same proportion he loves the chastity of marriage, is because the lasciviousness of adultery and the chastity of marriage are two opposite things, and therefore in proportion as any one is not in the one, he is in the other. It is precisely as has been said above at n. 70.

76. No one can know the nature of the chastity of marriage except the man who shuns as a sin the lasciviousness of adultery. For a man may know that in which he is, but cannot know that in which he is not. If from description or from thinking about it a man knows something in which he is not, he nevertheless knows of it merely as of something in the dark, and there remains some doubt about it, so that no one sees anything in the light and free from doubt until he is actually in it. This last therefore is to know, whereas the other is both to know and not to know. The truth is that the lasciviousness of adultery and the chastity of marriage stand toward each other exactly as do hell and heaven, and that the lasciviousness of adultery makes hell in a man, and the chastity of marriage makes heaven. But the chastity of marriage exists solely with the man who shuns as sin the lasciviousness of adultery. (See below, n. 111.)

77. From all this we can conclude and see, in no dubious manner, whether a man is a Christian or not, and even whether a man has any religion or not. If from his faith and from his

---

* This projected little work was afterwards expanded by Swedenborg into a large one, and was published by him in Amsterdam in the year 1768, under the (translated) title : *The Delights of Wisdom concerning Conjugial Love; after which follow the Pleasures of Insanity concerning Scortatory Love.* The original MS outline for the *De Conjugio* is now preserved in the Library of the Royal Academy of Sciences in Stockholm. It was published in the original Latin at Tubingen by Dr. Jo. Fr. Im. Tafel in the year 1860. [TR.]

life a man does not regard adulteries as sins, then he is not a
Christian, and neither has he any religion.   And on the other
hand, if a man shuns adulteries as sins, and especially if on
that account he feels aversion for them, and still more especially if on that account he abhors them, then he has religion,
and if he is in the Christian Church he is a Christian.   (But
more about these matters in the little work entitled *De Conjugio*, and in the meantime see what has been said on this subject in the work on *Heaven and Hell*, n. 366–386.)

78. That to "commit adultery" means also to do obscene
things, to speak lascivious things, and to think about filthy
things, is evident from the Lord's words in *Matthew* :—

Ye have heard that it was said to them of old time, Thou shalt not
commit adultery ; but I say unto you that whosoever looketh on the
woman of another to lust after her hath committed adultery with her
already in his heart (v. 27, 28).

79. That to "commit adultery" in the spiritual sense means
to adulterate the good of the Word and to falsify its truth, is
evident from the following passages :—

Babylon hath made all the nations drink of the wine of her fornication (*Rev.* xiv. 8).

The angel said, I will show thee the judgment of the great harlot that
sitteth upon many waters, with whom the kings of the earth have committed fornication (*Rev.* xvii. 1, 2).

Babylon hath made all the nations drink of the wine of the wrath of
her fornication, and the kings of the earth have committed fornication
with her (*Rev.* xviii. 3).

God hath judged the great harlot who did corrupt the earth with her
fornication (*Rev.* xix. 2).

"Whoredom" is predicated of Babylon, because "Babylon"
means those who arrogate to themselves the Lord's Divine
sovereign power, and profane the Word by adulterating and
falsifying it; and for this reason Babylon is called :—

The mother of the whoredoms and of the abominations of the earth
(*Rev.* xvii. 5).

[2] The same is signified by "whoredom" in the Prophets, as
in *Jeremiah* :—

In the prophets of Jerusalem I have seen a horrible obstinacy in committing adultery and walking in lying (xxiii. 14).

And in *Ezekiel :—*

Two women, the daughters of one mother, committed whoredom in Egypt ; they committed whoredom in their youth ; the one committed whoredom when she was Mine, and doted on her lovers the Assyrians her neighbors ; she bestowed her whoredoms upon them, yet she forsook not her whoredoms in Egypt ; the other corrupted her love more than she, and her whoredoms were more than the whoredoms of her sister ; she added to her whoredoms, she loved the Chaldeans, the sons of Babel came to her to the bed of loves, and defiled her with their whoredom (xxiii. 2–17).

These things are said of the Israelitish and the Jewish Church, here called the "daughters of one mother." Their "whoredoms" mean adulterations and falsifications of the Word, and as in the Word "Egypt" signifies memory-knowledge, "Assyria" reasoning, "Chaldea" the profanation of truth, and "Babel" the profanation of good, it is said that they "committed whoredom" with them. [3] The same is said of "Jerusalem," by which is signified the church in respect to doctrine :—

Thou didst trust in thy beauty, and didst commit whoredom because of thy renown, so that thou pouredst out thy whoredoms on every one that passed by ; thou hast committed whoredom with the sons of Egypt thy neighbors, great of flesh, and hast multiplied thy whoredom ; thou hast committed whoredom with the sons of Asshur ; and when thou wast not satisfied with those with whom thou didst commit whoredom, thou hast multiplied thy whoredoms unto the land of traffic, to Chaldea. An adulterous woman that receiveth strangers instead of her husband ! All give hire to their harlots, but thou hast given hire to all thy lovers that they may come unto thee on every side in thy whoredoms. Wherefore, O harlot, hear the word of Jehovah (*Ezek.* xvi. 15, 26, 28, 29, 32, 33, 35).

That "Jerusalem" means the church may be seen in the *Doctrine of the Lord* (n. 62, 63).

(The like is signified by "whoredoms" in *Isa.* xxiii. 17, 18 ; lvii. 3 ; *Jer.* iii. 2, 6, 8, 9 ; v. 1, 7 ; xiii. 27 ; xxix. 23 ; *Micah* i. 7 ; *Nahum* iii. 4 ; *Hos.* iv. 10, 11 ; *Lev.* xx. 5 ; *Num.* xiv. 33 ; xv. 39 ; and elsewhere.)

For the same reason the Lord called the Jewish nation

An adulterous generation (*Matt.* xii. 39 ; xvi. 4 ; *Mark* viii. 38).

X.

IN PROPORTION AS ANY ONE SHUNS THEFTS OF EVERY KIND
AS SINS, IN THE SAME PROPORTION HE LOVES SINCERITY.

80. To "steal," in the natural sense, means not only to commit theft and robbery, but also to defraud, and under some pretext take from another his goods. But in the spiritual sense to "steal" means to deprive another of his truths of faith and his goods of charity. And in the highest sense to "steal" means to take away from the Lord that which is His, and attribute it to one's self, and thus to claim righteousness and merit for one's self. These are the "thefts of every kind." And they also make a one, as do adulteries of every kind, and murders of every kind, of which we have already treated. The reason why they make a one is that they are one within another.

81. The evil of theft enters more deeply into a man than any other evil, because it is conjoined with cunning and deceit; and cunning and deceit insinuate themselves even into the spiritual mind of man in which is his thought with understanding. That man possesses a spiritual mind and a natural mind will be seen below.

82. That in proportion as any one shuns theft as a sin, in the same proportion he loves sincerity, is because theft is also fraud, and fraud and sincerity are two opposite things, so that in proportion as any one is not in theft in the same proportion he is in sincerity.

83. Sincerity is to be understood as including integrity, justice, fidelity, and rectitude. In these no man can be from himself so as to love them from and for themselves. But *he* is in them who shuns as sins, fraud, cunning, and deceit, and is therefore in them not from himself but from the Lord (as shown above, n. 18–31). Such is the case with a priest, a magistrate, a judge, a trader, and with every one in his own office and his own work.

84. This is taught by the Word in many passages, among which are the following :—

He that walketh in righteousnesses, and speaketh uprightnesses ; he that despiseth oppressions for gain, that shaketh his hands from holding bribes, that stoppeth his ears from the hearing of bloods, and shutteth his eyes from seeing evil ; he shall dwell on high (*Isa.* xxxiii. 15, 16).

Jehovah, who shall abide in Thy tent ? who shall dwell in the mountain of Thy holiness ?   He that walketh uprightly, and doeth righteousness ; he that slandereth not with his tongue, nor doeth evil to his companion (*Ps.* xv. 1–3, etc.).

Mine eyes shall be upon the faithful of the land, that they may dwell with Me ; he that walketh in the way of the upright, he shall minister unto Me.   He that worketh deceit shall not dwell in the midst of My house ; he that speaketh lies shall not stand before Mine eyes.   In the dawning will I cut off all the wicked of the land, to cut off from the city all the workers of iniquity (*Ps.* ci. 6–8).

That unless a man is interiorly sincere, just, faithful, and upright, he is insincere, unjust, unfaithful, and base, is taught by the Lord in these words :—

Except your righteousness shall exceed that of the scribes and Pharisees, ye shall not enter into the kingdom of the heavens (*Matt.* v. 10).

The " righteousness that exceeds that of the scribes and Pharisees" means the interior righteousness in which is the man who is in the Lord.   That he is in the Lord is taught by the Lord Himself in *John :*—

The glory which Thou hast given Me I have given unto them, that they may be one even as we are one, I in them, and Thou in Me, that they may be perfected into one ; that the love wherewith Thou hast loved Me may be in them, and I in them (xvii. 22, 23, 26).

From this it is evident that they are " perfect" when the Lord is in them.   These are they who are called

The pure in heart, who shall see God ; and, Those who are perfect as is their Father in the heavens (*Matt.* v. 8, 48).

85. It has been said above (n. 81), that the evil of theft enters more deeply into a man than any other evil because it is conjoined with cunning and deceit, and that cunning and deceit insinuate themselves even into the spiritual mind of man in which is his thought with understanding. Something shall therefore now be said about the Mind of man. (That the mind of man is his understanding and will together, see above, n. 43.)

86. Man possesses a natural mind and a spiritual mind. The natural mind is below, and the spiritual mind above. The natural mind is the mind of man's world, and the spiritual mind is the mind of his heaven. The natural mind may be called the animal mind, and the spiritual mind the human mind. Man is discriminated from the animal by possessing a spiritual mind. By means of this mind he can be in heaven while still in the world; and it is by means of this mind also that man lives after death.

[2] In his understanding a man is able to be in the spiritual mind, and consequently in heaven, but unless he shuns evils as sins he cannot be in the spiritual mind and consequently in heaven, as to his will. And if he is not there as to his will, he is not in heaven, in spite of the fact that he is there in understanding, for the will drags the understanding down, and causes it to be just as natural and animal as it is itself.

[3] Man may be compared to a garden—his understanding to light, and his will to heat. In winter time a garden is in light but not in accompanying heat, but in summer time it is in light accompanied by heat. Just so a man who is in the light of the understanding alone is like a garden in winter time, whereas one who is in the light of the understanding and at the same time in the heat of the will is like a garden in summer time. Moreover the understanding is wise from spiritual light, and the will loves from spiritual heat, for spiritual light is Divine wisdom, and spiritual heat is Divine love.

[4] So long as a man does not shun evils as sins, the concupiscences of evils block up the interiors of the natural mind on the part of the will, being like a thick veil there, and like a black cloud beneath the spiritual mind, and they prevent its

being opened. But in very deed the moment a man shuns evils as sins, the Lord inflows from heaven, takes away the veil, dispels the cloud, opens the spiritual mind, and so introduces the man into heaven.

[5] So long as the concupiscences of evils block up the interiors of the natural mind (in the way we have indicated), so long is the man in hell; the moment however that these concupiscences have been dispersed by the Lord, the man is in heaven. Furthermore: so long as the concupiscences of evils block up the interiors of the natural mind, so long is the man natural; but the moment they have been dispersed by the Lord, he is spiritual. Furthermore: so long as the concupiscences of evils block up the interiors of the natural mind, so long is the man animal, differing only in his ability to think and speak, even of such things as he does not see with his eyes, which ability he derives from his capacity of uplifting his understanding into the light of heaven. The moment however that these concupiscences have been dispersed by the Lord, the man is a man, because he then thinks what is true in the understanding from what is good in the will. And furthermore: so long as the concupiscences of evils block up the interiors of the natural mind, the man is like a garden in winter time, but the moment these concupiscences have been dispersed by the Lord, he is like a garden in summer time.

[6] The conjunction in a man of the will and the understanding is meant in the Word by "heart and soul," and by "heart and spirit." For example: that we must love God

With all the heart, and with all the soul (*Matt.* xxii. 37).

And that God will give

A new heart, and a new spirit (*Ezek.* xi. 19; xxxvi. 26, 27).

The "heart" means the will and its love, and the "soul" and the " spirit," the understanding and its wisdom.

XI.

In proportion as any one shuns False Witness of every kind as Sin, in the same proportion he loves the Truth.

87. To "bear false witness," in the natural sense, means not only to play the false witness, but also to lie, and to defame. In the spiritual sense, to "bear false witness" means to declare some false thing to be true or some evil thing good, and to persuade others that it is so; and the converse. And in the highest sense, to "bear false witness" means to blaspheme the Lord and the Word. These are the three senses of "bearing false witness." That these make a one in the man who bears false witness, utters a lie, or defames, is evident from what has been shown respecting the three senses of all things of the Word, in the *Doctrine of the Holy Scripture* (n. 5–7, etc. and 57).

88. As lying and the truth are two opposite things, it follows that in proportion as any one shuns lying as sin, in the same proportion he loves the truth.

89. In proportion as any one loves the truth, in the same proportion he desires to know it, and in the same proportion is affected at heart when he finds it. No one else comes into wisdom. And in proportion as any one loves to *do* the truth, in the same proportion he is sensible of the pleasantness of the light in which the truth is. It is the same with all the other things spoken of above; with sincerity and justice in the case of one who shuns thefts of every kind; with chastity and purity in the case of one who shuns adulteries of every kind; and with love and charity in the case of one who shuns murders of every kind; and so forth. On the other hand, one who is in the opposites to these heavenly things knows nothing about them, although everything that is truly something is present in them.

17

90. It is the truth that is meant by the "seed in the field," of which the Lord said :—

A sower went forth to sow, and as he sowed some fell upon the way, and it was trodden down, and the fowls of heaven devoured it ; and some fell upon stony places, and as soon as it was sprung up, because it had no root it withered away ; and some fell among thorns, and the thorns sprung up with it and choked it ; and other fell into the good ground, and sprung up, and bare fruit manifold (*Luke* viii. 5–8 ; *Matt.* xiii. 3–8 ; *Mark* iv. 3–8).

Here the "sower" is the Lord, and the "seed" is His Word, thus the truth ; the "seed upon the way" exists with those who do not care for the truth ; the "seed upon stony places" exists with those who do care for the truth, but not for its own sake, thus not interiorly ; the "seed in the midst of thorns" exists with those who are in the concupiscences of evil ; but the "seed in good ground" exists with those who love the truths that are in the Word from the Lord, and do them from Him, thus who bear fruit. That these things are meant is evident from the explication of the parable by the Lord (*Matt.* xiii. 19–23, 37; *Mark* iv. 14–20 ; *Luke* viii. 11–15). From all this it is evident that the truth of the Word cannot take root in those who do not care for the truth, nor in those who love the truth outwardly and not inwardly, nor in those who are in the concupiscences of evil, but in those in whom the concupiscences of evil have been dispersed by the Lord. In these the "seed" —that is, the truth—takes root in their spiritual mind (concerning which above, n. 86 at the end).

91. It is a general opinion at the present day that to be saved consists in believing this thing or that which the church teaches, and that it does not consist in keeping the commandments (which are, Do not kill, Do not commit adultery, Do not steal, Do not bear false witness) in both the restricted and the extended sense. For it is maintained that works are not regarded by God, but faith, when nevertheless the truth is that in proportion as any one is in these evils, in that same proportion he has no faith. (See above n. 42–52) Take counsel of reason and observe whether, so long as he is in the concupiscence of these evils, any murderer, adulterer, thief, or false witness is able to have faith ; and also, further, whether the concupiscence of these evils can be shaken off in any other way than by refusing to will to commit them for the reason that they are sins, that is, because they are infernal and devilish. So that whoever imagines that being saved consists in believing this thing or that which is taught by the church, while himself remaining thus evil in feeling and in character, must needs be a " foolish man," in accordance with the words of the Lord in *Matthew* vii. 26. Such a church is thus described in *Jeremiah* :—

Stand in the gate of Jehovah's house, and proclaim there this word : Thus saith Jehovah of Armies the God of Israel, Amend your ways and your doings ; trust ye not in lying words, saying, The temple of Jehovah, the temple of Jehovah, the temple of Jehovah, are these. Will ye steal, murder, and commit adultery, and swear falsely, and come and stand before Me in this house, which is called by My name, and say, We are delivered, while ye do all these abominations ? Is this house become a den of robbers ? Behold, I, even I, have seen it, saith Jehovah (vii. 2–4, 9–11).

XII.

No one can shun Evils as Sins so as to be inwardly averse to them except by means of Combats against them.

92. Everybody knows from the Word and from doctrine drawn from it that the Own* of man is evil from his birth,

---

* The Latin word *proprium* is the term used in the original text that in this and other places has been rendered by the expression " Own." The dictionary meaning of *proprius*, as an adjective, is " one's own," " proper," " belonging to one's self alone," " special," " particular," " peculiar." The neuter of this which is the word *proprium*, when used as a noun means " possession," " property ;" also " a peculiarity," " characteristic mark," " distinguishing sign," " characteristic." The English adjective " own" is defined by Webster to mean " belonging to," " belonging exclusively or especially to," " peculiar ;" so that our word " own" is a very exact equivalent of *proprius*, and if we make it a noun by writing it " Own," in order to answer to the Latin *proprium*, we effect a very close translation. [Tr.]

and that this is the reason why from inborn concupiscence he loves evils and is drawn into them. This is why he desires to have revenge, and to commit fraud, defamation, and adultery. And unless he takes thought that such things are sins, and on this account resists them, he does them whenever an opportunity offers, provided that his reputation and thereby his honors and gains do not suffer. Consider also that unless he has religion the man does these things from delight.

93. As this Own of man constitutes the first root of his life, it is evident what kind of a tree a man would be unless this root were plucked up, and a new root planted in its place. He would be a rotted tree, of which it is said that it must be cut down and cast into the fire (*Matt.* iii. 10; vii. 19). And this root is not removed and a new one set in its place unless the man regards the evils that constitute the root as injurious to his soul, and on this account desires to rid himself of them. But as these evils belong to man's Own, and are therefore delightful to him, he cannot do this except against his will, with a struggle, and therefore with battling.

94. Every one does this battling who believes in the existence of hell and of heaven: that heaven is eternal happiness, and hell eternal unhappiness; and that those who do evils go to hell, and those who do goods to heaven. And one who thus fights acts from within, and against the concupiscence itself which constitutes the root of the evil, for one who fights against anything does not will it, and to desire is to will. This shows that the root of evil is not removed except by means of combat.

95. In proportion therefore as any one battles with and thus removes evil, in the same proportion good takes its place, and from this good the man in the same proportion looks evil in the face, and sees that it is infernal and horrible, and on this account he not only shuns it, but feels averse to it, and at last abhors it.

96. A man who fights against evils cannot but do so as of himself, for one who does not fight as of himself does not do so at all, but stands like an automaton that sees nothing and does nothing, and from evil he is continually thinking in favor of evil, and not against it. But be it well known that it is the Lord alone who fights in a man against his evils, and that it only appears to the man that he fights of himself, and also that the Lord wills that it should so appear to him, because without this appearance no combat takes place and therefore no reformation.

97. This combat is not severe except in the case of those who have given free rein to their concupiscences, and have indulged them of set purpose, and also in the case of those who have stubbornly cast off the holy things of the Word and of the church. With others it is not severe; let them even once in a week, or twice in a month, resist the evils they are inclined to, and they will perceive a change.

98. The Christian Church is called the church militant, and it cannot be called militant except as against the devil, and thus against the evils that are from hell. Hell is the devil. And the temptation that the man of the church undergoes is this warfare.

99. Battlings against evils, which battlings are temptations, are treated of in many places in the Word. They are meant by these words of the Lord :—

> I say unto you, Except a grain of wheat fall into the earth and die, it abideth by itself alone ; but if it die, it beareth much fruit (*John* xii. 24).

And also by these :—

> If any man would come after Me, let him deny himself, and take up his cross, and follow Me. For whosoever would save his life shall lose it ; and whosoever shall lose his life for My sake and the gospel's, the same shall save it (*Mark* viii. 34, 35).

The "cross" means temptation (as also in *Matt.* x. 38; xvi. 24; *Mark* x. 21; *Luke* xiv. 27). By his "life" is meant the life of man's Own (as also in *Matt.* x. 39; xvi. 25; *Luke* ix. 24; and especially in *John* xii. 25), which is also the "life of the flesh that profiteth nothing" (*John* vi. 63).

In regard to battlings against evils, and victories over them, the Lord speaks in the *Revelation* to all the churches :—

To the church in Ephesus : To him that overcometh, to him will I give to eat of the tree of life, which is in the midst of the paradise of God (*Rev.* ii. 7).

To the church in Smyrna : He that overcometh shall not be hurt of the second death (verse 11).

To the church in Pergamos : To him that overcometh, to him will I give to eat of the hidden manna, and I will give him a white stone, and upon the stone a new name written, which no one knoweth but he that receiveth it (verse 17).

To the church in Thyatira : He that overcometh, and that keepeth My words unto the end, to him will I give power (*potestas*) over the nations ; and the morning star (verses 26, 28).

To the church in Sardis : [He that overcometh shall be clothed in white garments, and I will not blot his name out of the book of life, and I will confess his name before My Father, and before His angels (*Rev.* iii. 5).

To the church in Philadelphia :] He that overcometh I will make a pillar in the temple of My God, and I will write upon him the name of My God, and the name of the city of My God, of the New Jerusalem, which cometh down out of heaven from My God, and My new name (verse 12).

To the church in Laodicea : He that overcometh I will give to him to sit down with Me in My throne (verse 21).

100. These battlings, which are temptations, may be seen specially treated of in the *Doctrine of the New Jerusalem*, published in London in the year 1758 (from n. 187 to n. 201) : Whence and what they are (n. 196, 197) : How and where they take place (n. 198) : What good they effect (n. 199) : That the Lord fights for man (n. 200) : Concerning the Lord's battlings or temptations (n. 201).

XIII.

A MAN OUGHT TO SHUN EVILS AS SINS AND FIGHT AGAINST THEM AS OF HIMSELF.

101. It is in accordance with Divine order that man should act in freedom according to reason, because to act in freedom according to reason is to act from himself. And yet these two faculties, Freedom and Reason, are not proper to man, but are the Lord's in him; and in so far as he is a man they must not be taken away from him, because without them he cannot be reformed, for without them he cannot perform repentance, he cannot fight against evils, and afterwards bring forth fruits worthy of repentance. Now as it is from the Lord that man possesses freedom and reason, and as man acts from them, it follows that he does not act from himself, but _as_ from himself.*

102. The Lord loves man and wills to dwell with him, yet He cannot love him and dwell with him unless He is received and loved in return. From this alone comes conjunction. For this reason the Lord has given man freedom and reason, freedom to think and will as of himself, and reason in accordance with which he may do so. To love and to be conjoined with one in whom there is nothing reciprocal is not possible, nor is it possible to enter in and abide with one in whom there is no reception. As there are in man, from the Lord, reception and reciprocation, the Lord says :—

Abide in Me, and I in you (_John_ xv. 4).

He that abideth in Me, and I in him, the same bringeth forth much fruit (verse 5).

At that day ye shall know that ye are in Me, and I in you (_John_ xiv. 20).

The Lord also teaches that He is in the truths and in the goods that a man receives, and that are in him :—

If ye abide in Me, and My words abide in you. If ye keep My commandments, ye shall abide in My love (_John_ xv. 7, 10).

He that hath My commandments, and doeth them, he it is that loveth Me ; and I will love him, and will make My abode with him (_John_ xiv. 21, 23).

So that the Lord dwells in a man in what is His own, and the man dwells in those things which are from the Lord, and thus dwells in the Lord.

103. As there is in man, from the Lord, this ability to reciprocate and return, and consequently this _mutuality_, the Lord

* That man has freedom from the Lord, see above (n. 19, 20) ; and in the work on _Heaven and Hell_ (n. 589–596, and n. 597–603). What freedom is, see the _Doctrine of the New Jerusalem_, published in London in 1758 (n. 141–149).

says that a man must do the work of repentance, which no one can do except as of himself:—

Jesus said : Except ye repent ye shall all perish (*Luke* xiii. 3, 5).

Jesus said : The kingdom of God is at hand ; repent ye, and believe the gospel (*Mark* i. 14, 15).

Jesus said : I am come to call sinners to repentance (*Luke* v. 32).

Jesus said to the churches: Repent (*Rev.* ii. 5, 16, 21, 22 ; iii. 3).

It is also said :—

They repented not of their works (*Rev.* xvi. 11).

104. As there is in man, from the Lord, this ability to reciprocate and return, and consequently this mutuality, the Lord says that a man must keep the commandments, and also that he must bring forth fruit:—

Why call ye Me Lord, Lord, and do not the things which I say ? (*Luke* vi. 46–49).

If ye know these things, blessed are ye if ye do them (*John* xiii. 17).

Ye are My friends, if ye do the things which I command you (*John* xv. 14).

Whosoever shall do and teach them shall be called great in the kingdom of the heavens (*Matt.* v. 19).

Every one therefore who heareth these words of Mine, and doeth them, I will liken to a wise man (*Matt.* vii. 24).

Bring forth therefore fruits worthy of repentance (*Matt.* iii. 8).

Make the tree good, and its fruit good (*Matt.* xii. 33).

The kingdom shall be given to a nation bringing forth the fruits thereof (*Matt.* xxi. 43).

Every tree that bringeth not forth good fruit is hewn down, and cast into the fire (*Matt.* vii. 19).

And so in many other places : from all which it is evident that a man must act of himself but from the Lord's power, which he must petition for. For this is to act *as* from himself.

105. As there is in man, from the Lord, this ability to reciprocate and return, and consequently this mutuality, a man must render an account of his works, and will be requited according to them. For the Lord says :—

The Son of man shall come, and shall render to every man according to his deeds (*Matt.* xvi. 27).

They shall come forth : they that have done good, unto the resurrection of life, and they that have done evils unto the resurrection of judgment (*John* v. 29).

Their works do follow with them (*Rev.* xiv. 13).

They were judged every man according to his works (*Rev.* xx. 13).

Behold, I come, and My reward is with Me, to give every man according to his work (*Rev.* xxii. 12).

If there were in man no reciprocality, there would be no imputation.

106. As in man there are reception and reciprocality, the church teaches that a man must examine himself, confess his sins before God, desist from them, and lead a new life. It may be seen above (n. 3–8) that every church in the Christian world teaches this.

107. Unless there were reception by man, and at the same time a taking thought as it were by him, nothing could have been said about faith, for faith is not from man. Without this reception and reciprocality, man would be like chaff in the wind, and would stand as if lifeless, with mouth open, and hands hanging down, awaiting influx, devoid of thought and action in regard to the things that concern his salvation. It is indeed true that he is by no means the agent in regard to these things, but yet he is a reagent as of himself.

But these matters will be set forth in still clearer light in the treatises on *Angelic Wisdom*.

XIV.

If any one shuns Evils for any other reason than because they are Sins, he does not shun them, but merely prevents them from appearing before the World.

108. There are moral men who keep the commandments of the second table of the decalogue, not committing fraud, blasphemy, revenge, or adultery ; and such of them as confirm themselves in the belief that such things are evils because they are injurious to the public weal, and are therefore contrary to the laws of humane conduct, practise charity, sincerity, justice, chastity. But if they do these goods and shun those evils merely because they are evils, and not at the same time because they are sins, they are still merely natural men, and with the merely natural the root of evil remains imbedded and is not dislodged; for which reason the goods they do are not goods, because they are from themselves.

109. Before men, a natural moral man may appear exactly like a spiritual moral man, but not before the angels. Before the angels in heaven, if he is in goods he appears like an image of wood, if in truths like an image of marble, lifeless, and very different from a spiritual moral man. For a natural moral man is an outwardly moral man, and a spiritual moral man is an inwardly moral man, and what is outward without what is inward is lifeless. It does indeed live, but not the life that is called life.

110. The concupiscences of evil that constitute the interiors of man from his birth can be removed by the Lord alone. For the Lord inflows from what is spiritual into what is natural; but man, of himself, from what is natural into what is spiritual; and this influx is contrary to order, and does not operate into the concupiscences and remove them, but shuts them in closer and closer in proportion as it confirms itself. And as the hereditary evil thus lurks there, shut in, after death when the man becomes a spirit it bursts the cover that had hidden it here, and breaks out like the discharge from an ulcer that has been healed only outwardly.

111. There are various and many causes that make a man moral in the outward form, but unless he is moral in the inward form also, he is nevertheless not moral. For example: if a man abstains from adulteries and whoredom from the fear of the civil law and its penalties; from the fear of losing his good name and esteem; from the fear of the consequent diseases; from the fear of his wife's tongue in his home, and the consequent inquietude of his life; from the fear of the husband's vengeance, or that of some relative; from poverty, or avarice; from disability caused either by disease, abuse, age, or impotence; nay, if he abstains from such things on account of any natural or moral law, and not at the same time on account of the spiritual law, he nevertheless is inwardly an adulterer and whoremonger, for none the less does he believe that such things are not sins. As toward God, therefore, he in his spirit makes them not unlawful, and so in spirit he commits them, although not in the body in the sight of the world; and therefore after death, when he becomes a spirit, he speaks openly in favor of them. From all this it is evident that an ungodly man is able to shun evils as injurious, but only a Christian can shun them as sins.

112. It is the same with thefts and frauds of every kind, with murders and revengeful acts of every kind, and with false witness and lies of every kind. No one can of himself be cleansed and made pure from such things, for within every concupiscence there are infinite things which the man sees only as one simple thing, whereas the Lord sees the smallest details of the whole series. In a word, a man cannot regenerate himself, that is, form in himself a new heart and a new spirit, but the Lord alone can do this, who Himself is the Reformer and the Regenerator. Therefore if a man wills to make himself new by his own sagacity and intelligence, it is merely like painting an ugly face, or smearing a skin-detergent over a part that is infected with inward corruption.

113. Therefore the Lord says in *Matthew* :—

Thou blind Pharisee, cleanse first the inside of the cup and the platter, that the outside may be clean also (xxiii. 26).

And in *Isaiah* :—

Wash you, make you clean, put away the evil of your works from before Mine eyes, cease to do evil; and then though your sins be as scarlet, they shall be as white as snow, though they have been red like crimson, they shall be as wool (i. 16, 18).

114. To what has already been said shall be added the following :—

1. Christian charity, with every one, consists in faithfully performing what belongs to his calling, for by this, if he shuns evils as sins, he every day is doing goods, and is himself his own use in the general body. In this way also the common good is cared for, and the good of each person in particular.

2. All other things that he does are not the proper works of charity, but are either its signs, its benefactions, or its obligations.

THE DOCTRINE

OF THE

NEW JERUSALEM

CONCERNING

FAITH

BY

EMANUEL SWEDENBORG

ORIGINALLY PUBLISHED IN AMSTERDAM IN THE YEAR 1763

TRANSLATED FROM THE ORIGINAL LATIN AND EDITED
BY THE
REV. JOHN FAULKNER POTTS, B.A. Lond.

STANDARD EDITION

SWEDENBORG FOUNDATION
INCORPORATED
NEW YORK

Organized in 1850 as
The American Swedenborg Printing and Publishing Society

CONTENTS*

*Compiled by the Translator.

THE DOCTRINE OF THE NEW JERUSALEM

FAITH

I.

Faith is an internal Acknowledgment of Truth.

1. At the present day the term Faith is taken to mean the mere thought that the thing is so because the church so teaches, and because it is not evident to the understanding. For we are told to believe and not to doubt, and if we say that we do not comprehend, we are told that this is just the reason for believing. So that the faith of the present day is a faith in the unknown, and may be called blind faith, and as it is something that somebody has said, *in somebody else*, it is a faith of hearsay. It will be seen presently that this is not spiritual faith.

2. Real faith is nothing else than an acknowledgment that the thing is so because it is true; for one who is in real faith thinks and says, " This is true, and therefore I believe it." For faith is of truth, and truth is of faith. If such a person does not see the truth of a thing, he says, " I do not know whether this is true, and therefore as yet I do not believe it. How can I believe what I do not intellectually comprehend? Perhaps it is false."

3. But a common remark is that no one can comprehend spiritual or theological matters because they are supernatural. Spiritual truths however can be comprehended just as well as natural ones; and even if they are not clearly comprehended, still as soon as they are heard it is possible to perceive whether

1

they are true or not.   This is especially the case with those whose affection is excited by truths.   I have been permitted to know this by much experience.   I have been permitted to speak with the uneducated, with the dull-minded, and with the utterly senseless, as also with persons who had been in falsities, and those who had been in evils, all born within the church, and who had heard somewhat about the Lord and about faith and charity ; and I have been permitted to tell them certain secrets of wisdom, and they comprehended everything and acknowledged it.   At the time however they were in that light of the understanding which every human being possesses ; and felt withal the pride of being thought intelligent.   All this happened in my intercourse with spirits.   Many others who were with me were hereby convinced that spiritual things can be comprehended just as well as natural, that is, when they are heard or read.   But comprehension by the man himself when thinking from himself is by no means so easy.   The reason spiritual things can be comprehended is that in respect to the understanding a man may be uplifted into the light of heaven, in which light none but spiritual things appear, and these are the truths of faith.   For the light of heaven is spiritual light.

4. This then is the reason why those who are in the spiritual affection of truth possess an internal acknowledgment of truth.* As the angels are in this affection, they discard the dogma that the understanding must be kept in obedience to faith, and say, " What is this ? believing when you do not see whether the thing is true ?"   And if somebody says that still it is to be believed, they reply, " Do you consider yourself the Deity that I am bound to believe you ? or do you think me mad enough to believe a statement in which I do not see the truth ?   Cause me to see it."   Thereupon the dogmatizer betakes himself elsewhere.   The wisdom of the angels consists solely in this : that they see and comprehend everything they think about.

---

* The spiritual affection of truth is the love of truth for its own sake, and because we have eternal life by means of its teaching.   See the *Apocalypse Explained* (n. 115, 444[10]). [TR.]

5. A spiritual idea (about which few know anything) inflows into those who are in the affection of truth, and inwardly tells them that what they hear or read is true, or is not true. In this idea are those who read the Word in enlightenment from the Lord. To be in enlightenment is nothing else than to be in the perception, and in the consequent internal acknowledgment, that this or that is true. These are they who are called "the taught of Jehovah" (*Isa.* liv. 13; *John* vi. 45); and of whom it is said in *Jeremiah* :—

Behold, the days come that I will make a new covenant: this shall be the covenant: I will put My law in their inward parts, and upon their heart will I write it, and they shall teach no more every man his companion, or every man his brother, saying, Know (*Cognoscite*) Jehovah; for they shall all know (*cognoscent*) Me (*Jer.* xxxi. 31, 33, 34).

6. From all this it is evident that faith and truth are a one. For this reason the ancients (who from their affection for truths thought more about them than the men of our time) instead of saying Faith, were accustomed to say Truth. For the same reason also truth and faith are one word in the Hebrew language, namely *Amuna* or *Amen*.

7. The reason the term "faith" is used by the Lord in the *Gospels* and *Revelation* is that the Jews did not believe it to be true that He was the Messiah foretold by the prophets; and where truth is not believed, there "faith" is spoken of. But still it is one thing to have faith and believe in the Lord, and another to have faith and believe in some one else. The difference will be explained below.

8. Faith separated from truth came in and took possession of the church along with the papal dominion, because the chief safeguard of that religion was ignorance of truth. For this reason also they forbade the reading of the Word, for otherwise they could not have been worshiped as deities, nor could their saints have been invoked, nor idolatry instituted to such an extent that dead bodies, bones, and sepulchres were regarded as holy, and made use of for purposes of gain. From this it is evident what enormous falsities a blind faith can bring into being.

9. Blind faith survived later with many of the Reformed, because they had separated faith from charity, for they who separate these two must needs be in ignorance of truth, and they will give the name of faith to the mere thought that the thing is so, quite apart from any internal acknowledgment. With these also, ignorance is the safeguard of dogma, for so long as ignorance bears sway, together with the persuasion that theological matters transcend comprehension, they can speak without being contradicted, and it can be believed that their tenets are true, and that they themselves understand them.

10. The Lord said to Thomas :—

Because thou hast seen Me, thou hast believed : blessed are they that do not see, and yet believe (*John* xx. 29).

This does not mean a faith separated from the internal acknowledgment of truth ; but that they are blessed who do not like Thomas, see the Lord with their eyes, and yet believe in His existence, for this is seen in the light of truth from the Word.

11. As the internal acknowledgment of truth is faith, and as faith and truth are a one (as was said above, n. 2, 4–6), it follows that an external acknowledgment without an internal one is not faith, and also that a persuasion of what is false is not faith. An external acknowledgment without an internal one is a faith in what is unknown, and a faith in what is unknown is mere memory-knowledge (*scientia*), which if confirmed becomes persuasion. They who are in such knowledge and persuasion think a thing true because somebody has said so, or they think it is true from their having confirmed it ; and yet what is false can be confirmed just as well as what is true, and sometimes better. To think a thing true from having confirmed it is to think that something another says is true, and then to confirm it without previous examination.

12. If any one should think within himself, or say to some one else, " Who is able to have the internal acknowledgment of truth which is faith? not I;" let me tell him how he may have it: Shun evils as sins, and come to the Lord, and you will have as much of it as you desire. (That he who shuns evils as sins is in the Lord, see the *Doctrine of Life for the New Jerusalem* n. 18–31; that such a one loves truth, and sees it, n. 32–41; and that he has faith, n. 42–52.)

II.

The internal Acknowledgment of Truth, which is Faith, exists with none but those who are in Charity.

13. We have already said what faith is, and will now say what charity is. In its origin or beginning, charity is the affection of good, and as good loves truth, the affection of good produces the affection of truth, and through it the acknowledgment of truth which is faith. Through this succession, the affection of good* comes forth into manifest being, and becomes charity. This is the progressive advance of charity from its origin which is the affection of good, through faith which is the acknowledgment of truth, to its final end in view, which is charity. The final end is the doing. And this shows how love, here the affection of good, produces faith—which is the same thing as the acknowledgment of truth—and through this produces charity—which is the same thing as the working of love through faith.

14. More clearly:—Good is nothing but Use, so that in its very origin charity is the affection of use; and as use loves the means, the affection of use produces the affection of the means, and from this the knowledge (*cognitio*) of them, and through this progression the affection of use comes forth into manifest being (*existit*), and becomes charity.

---

* The Latin here reads "affection of truth," which is evidently a slip of the pen or else printer's error, as the context shows. [Tr.]

15. The progression of these things is precisely like that of all things of the will through the understanding into bodily acts. The will brings forth nothing from itself apart from the understanding, nor does the understanding bring forth anything from itself apart from the will. In order that anything may come forth into manifest being, the two must act in conjunction. Or, what is the same: Affection, which belongs to the will, brings forth nothing from itself except by means of thought, which is of the understanding (the converse also being true), for in order that anything may come forth into manifest being the two must act in conjunction. For consider: If you take away from thought all affection belonging to some love, can you exercise thought? Or if from the affection you take away all thought, are you then able to be affected by anything? Or, what is much the same, if you take away affection from thought, can you speak anything? Or if you take away thought or understanding from affection, can you do anything? It is the same with charity and faith.

16. All this may be illustrated by comparison with a tree. The prime source of a tree is a seed, and in this there is an endeavor to bring forth fruit. This endeavor, roused to activity by heat, brings forth first a root, and then from that a stem or stalk with branches and leaves, and at last the fruit; and in this way the endeavor to bear fruit comes forth into manifest being. From this it is evident that the endeavor to bring forth fruit is constant through the whole progression until it attains manifest being, for if it ceased the capacity to vegetate would die at once. This is the application: The tree is man; in him the endeavor to bring forth the means is from his will in his understanding; the stem or stalk with branches and leaves, in him are the instrumental means, and are called the truths of faith; the fruits which in the tree are the ultimate effects of the endeavor to bear fruit, in man are uses; and in these his will comes forth into manifest being. From this it may be seen that the will to bring forth uses by means of the understanding is constant through the whole progression, until it comes into manifest being. (Concerning the will and the understanding, and their conjunction, see the *Doctrine of Life for the New Jerusalem*, n. 43.)

17. From what has now been said it is evident that charity, in so far as it is the affection of good or of use, brings forth faith as a means through which it may come into manifest being; and therefore that charity and faith, in working uses, act in conjunction; and also that faith does not bring forth good or use from itself, but from charity, for faith is charity in its mediate stage. It is therefore a fallacy that faith brings forth good as a tree does its fruit. The tree is not faith. The tree is the man himself.

18. Be it known that charity and faith make a one as do the will and the understanding, for charity is of the will, and faith is of the understanding. And in the same way, that charity and faith make a one as do affection and thought, because affection is of the will, and thought is of the understanding. And also that charity and faith make a one as do good and truth, because good is of affection which belongs to the will, and truth is of thought which belongs to the understanding. In a word, charity and faith make a one as do essence and form, because charity is the essence of faith, and faith is the form of charity. This shows that faith without charity is like a form without an essence, which is not anything at all; and that charity without faith is like an essence without a form, which likewise is not anything at all.

19. Charity and faith in a man are related to each other precisely as are the motion of the heart called systole and diastole, and that of the lungs called breathing. Moreover there is a full correspondence of these two with man's will and understanding, and therefore with charity and faith. For this reason the will and its affection are meant in the Word by the " heart," and the understanding and its thought by the " breath (*animam*)," and the " spirit (*spiritum*)," on which account to " give up the breath (*animam*)," or " yield up the spirit (*spiritum*)," means to cease to respire, or to expire. This shows that there cannot be faith without charity, nor charity without faith; faith without charity being like breathing with the lungs in the absence of a heart, which is impossible in any living being, but only in some artificial apparatus; and charity without faith being like a heart without any lungs, which can afford no conscious life; and therefore charity performs uses by means of faith, just as the heart does its work by means of the lungs. So great is the likeness between the heart and charity, and between the lungs and faith, that in the spiritual world every one is known in respect to the quality of his faith by his mere breathing, and in respect to that of his charity by the way his heart beats. For angels and spirits live by a heart-beat and breathing just as men do, and it is for this reason that they, equally with men in this world, feel, think, act, and speak.

20. As charity is love toward the neighbor, we will say what the neighbor is. In the natural sense, the neighbor is man both collectively and individually. Collectively, man is the church, our country, and society; individually, he is our fellow-citizen, who in the Word is called "brother" and "companion." But in the spiritual sense the neighbor is good, and as use is good, the neighbor in this sense is use. That use is the spiritual neighbor must be acknowledged by every one. For who loves a human being merely as a person? We love him for that which he has in him, and which gives him his character; thus from his quality, for this is the man. And this quality that we love is use, and is called good, so that this is the neighbor. And as, in its bosom, the Word is spiritual, therefore in its spiritual sense this is to "love the neighbor."

21. But it is one thing to love the neighbor on account of the good or use he is to us, and another to love him from the good or use we may be to him. Even an evil man can do the first, but only a good man the second, for a good man loves good from good, that is, he loves use from the affection of use. The difference between the two is described by the Lord in *Matthew* v. 42–47. Many say, "I love such a man because he loves me and does me good;" but to love any one for this only is not to love him inwardly, unless he who so loves is himself in good, and from it loves the good of the other. In this case the man is in charity, but in the other he is in a friendship which is not charity. A man who loves the neighbor from charity conjoins himself with his good, and not with his person except in so far and for so long as he is in good. Such a man is spiritual, and loves his neighbor spiritually, whereas one who loves another from mere friendship, conjoins himself with his person, and at the same time with his evil, and after death he cannot without difficulty be separated from the personality that is in evil, but the former can. Charity effects this by means of faith, which faith is the truth; and the man who is in charity by means of the truth examines thoroughly and sees what ought to be loved, and in loving and conferring benefits he regards the quality of the other's use.

22. Love to the Lord is Love properly so called, and love toward the neighbor is Charity. With man no love to the Lord is possible except in charity; it is in charity that the Lord conjoins Himself with a man. As, in its essence, faith is charity, it follows that no one can have faith in the Lord unless he is in charity. There is conjunction from charity through faith; through charity conjunction of the Lord with man, and through faith conjunction of man with the Lord. (That the conjunction is reciprocal, see the *Doctrine of Life for the New Jerusalem*, n. 102–107.)

23. In brief: In proportion as any one shuns evils as sins, and looks to the Lord, in the same proportion he is in charity, and therefore in the same proportion he is in faith. (That in proportion as any one shuns evils as sins and looks to the Lord, in the same proportion he is in charity, may be seen in the *Doctrine of Life for the New Jerusalem*, n. 67–73, and also n. 74–91; and that in the same proportion he has faith, n. 42–52. What charity properly understood is, n. 114.)

24. From all said thus far it is evident that saving faith, which is the internal acknowledgment of truth, is impossible to all except those who are in charity.

III.

The Knowledges (*cognitiones*) of Truth and of Good
are not matters of real Belief (*Fidei*) until the
Man is in Charity, but are the Storehouse of Material out of which the Faith of Charity can be
formed.

25. From his earliest childhood man has the affection of
knowing, which leads him to learn many things that will be of
use to him, and many that will be of no use. While he is growing into manhood he learns by application to some business
such things as belong to that business, and this business then
becomes his use, and he feels an affection for it. In this way
commences the affection or love of use, and this brings forth the
affection of the means which teach him the handling of the business which is his use. With everybody in the world there is
this progression, because everybody has some business to which
he advances from the use that is his end, by the means, to the
actual use which is the effect. But inasmuch as this use together with the means that belong to it is for the sake of life
in this world, the affection that is felt for it is natural affection
only.

26. But as every man not only regards uses for the sake of
life in this world, but also should regard uses for the sake of
his life in heaven (for into this life he will come after his life
here, and will live in it to eternity), therefore from childhood
every one acquires knowledges (*cognitiones*) of truth and good
from the Word, or from the doctrine of the church, or from
preaching, which knowledges are to be learned and retained for
the sake of that life; and these he stores up in his natural
memory in greater or less abundance according to such affection of knowing as may be inborn with him, and has in various
ways been incited to an increase.

27. But all these knowledges (*cognitiones*), whatever may be
their number and whatever their nature, are merely the store-

house of material from which the faith of charity can be formed,
and this faith cannot be formed except in proportion as the man
shuns evils as sins. If he shuns evils as sins, then these knowledges become those of a faith that has spiritual life within it.
But if he does not shun evils as sins, then these knowledges
are nothing but knowledges (*cognitiones*), and do not become
those of a faith that has any spiritual life within it.

28. This storehouse of material is in the highest degree
necessary, because faith cannot be formed without it, for the
knowledges (*cognitiones*) of truth and good enter into faith and
make it, so that if there are no knowledges, faith cannot come
forth into being, for an entirely void and empty faith is impossible. If the knowledges are scanty, the faith is consequently
very small and meager; if they are abundant, the faith becomes proportionately rich and full.

29. Be it known however that it is knowledges (*cognitiones*)
of genuine truth and good that constitute faith, and by no
means knowledges of what is false, for faith is truth (as before
said, n. 5–11), and as falsity is the opposite of truth, it destroys
faith. Neither can charity come forth into being where there are
nothing but falsities, for (as before said, n. 18) charity and faith
make a one just as good and truth make a one. From all this
it follows that an absence of knowledges of genuine truth and
good involves an absence of faith, that a few knowledges make
some faith, and that many knowledges make a faith which is
clear and bright in proportion to their abundance. Such as is
the quality of a man's faith from charity, such is the quality
of his intelligence.

30. There are many who possess no internal acknowledgment
of truth, and yet have the faith of charity. These are they
who have had regard to the Lord in their life, and from religion
have avoided evils, but have been prevented from thinking
about truths by worldly cares and by their businesses, as well
as by a lack of truth on the part of their teachers. But inwardly, that is, in their spirit, they still are in the acknowledgment of truth, because they are in the affection of it, and

therefore after death, when they become spirits and are instructed by angels, they acknowledge truths and receive them with joy. Very different is the case with those who have had no regard to the Lord in their life, and have not from religion avoided evils. Inwardly, that is, in their spirit, they are in no affection of truth, and consequently are in no acknowledgment of it, and therefore after death, when they become spirits and are instructed by angels, they are unwilling to acknowledge truths, and consequently do not receive them. For evil of life inwardly hates truths, whereas good of life inwardly loves them.

31. Knowledges (*cognitiones*) of good and truth that precede faith appear to some to be things of faith (or real belief), but still are not so. Their thinking and saying that they believe is no proof that they do so, and neither are such knowledges things of faith, for they are matters of mere thought that the case is so, and not of any internal recognition that they are truths; and the faith or belief that they are truths, while it is not known that they are so, is a kind of persuasion quite remote from inward recognition. But as soon as charity is being implanted, these knowledges become things of faith, but no further than as there is charity in the faith. In the first state, before charity is felt, faith appears to them as though it were in the first place, and charity in the second; but in the second state, when charity is felt, faith betakes itself to the second place, and charity to the first. The first state is called Reformation, and the second Regeneration. In this latter state a man grows in wisdom every day, and every day good multiplies truths and causes them to bear fruit. The man is then like a tree that bears fruit, and inserts seeds in the fruit, from which come new trees, and at last a garden. He then becomes truly a man, and after death an angel, in whom charity constitutes the life, and faith the form, beautiful in accordance with the quality of the faith; but his faith is then no longer called faith, but intelligence. From all this it is evident that the whole sum and substance of faith is from charity, and nothing of it from itself; and also that charity brings forth faith, and not faith charity. The knowledges of truth that go before are like the store in a granary, which does not feed a man unless he is hungry and takes out the grain.

32. We will also say how faith is formed from charity. Every man has a natural mind and a spiritual mind: a natural mind for the world, and a spiritual mind for heaven. In respect to his understanding, man is in both minds, but not in respect to his will, until he shuns and is averse to evils as sins. When he does this his spiritual mind is opened in respect to the will also; and when it has been opened there inflows from it into the natural mind spiritual heat from heaven (which heat in its essence is charity), and gives life to the knowledges of truth and good in the natural mind, and out of them it forms faith. The case here is just as it is with a tree, which does not receive any vegetative life until heat inflows from the sun, and conjoins itself with the light, as takes place in spring time. There is also a full parallelism between the quickening of man with life and the growing of a tree, in this respect, that the latter is effected by the heat of this world, and the former by the heat of heaven. It is for this reason also that man is so often likened by the Lord to a tree.

33. From these few words it may be considered settled that the knowledges of truth and good are not really things of faith until the man is in charity, but that they are the storehouse of material out of which the faith of charity can be formed. With a regenerate person the knowledges of truth become truths, and so do the knowledges of good, for the knowledge of good is in the understanding, and the affection of good in the will, and what is in the understanding is called truth, and what is in the will is called good.

IV.

THE CHRISTIAN FAITH IN ITS UNIVERSAL IDEA OR FORM.*

34. The Christian Faith in its universal idea or form is this : The Lord from eternity, who is Jehovah, came into the world to subdue the hells, and to glorify His Human ; and without this no mortal could have been saved ; and they are saved who believe in Him.

35. It is said " in the *universal* idea or form" because this is what is universal of the Faith, and what is universal of the Faith is that which must be in all things of it both in general and in particular.   It is a Universal of the Faith that God is One in Person and in Essence, in whom is the Trinity, and that the Lord is that God.   It is a Universal of the Faith that no mortal could have been saved unless the Lord had come into the world.   It is a Universal of the Faith that He came into the world in order to remove hell from man, and He removed it by combats against it and by victories over it ; thus He subdued it, and reduced it into order and under obedience to Himself.   It is also a Universal of the Faith that He came into the world in order to glorify the Human which He took upon Him in the world, that is, in order to unite it to the all-originating Divine (*Divino a Quo*) ; thus to eternity does He hold in order and under obedience to Himself hell subjugated by Himself.   And inasmuch as neither of these mighty works could have been accomplished except by means of temptations even to the uttermost of them, which was the passion of the cross, He therefore underwent this uttermost temptation.   These are the Universals of the Christian Faith concerning the Lord.

36. The Universal of the Christian Faith on the part of man is that he believe in the Lord, for through believing in Him

---

* The Latin word *idea* is evidently used here in its original Greek sense of *form*. See the *True Christian Religion* (n. 2), where Swedenborg in exactly the same connection uses the word *forma* instead of *idea*. [TR.]

there is effected conjunction with Him, by which comes salvation. To believe in Him is to have confidence that He will save, and as no one can have this confidence except one who lives aright, therefore this also is meant by believing in Him.

37. These two Universals of the Christian Faith have already been treated of specifically ; the first, which regards the Lord, in the *Doctrine of the New Jerusalem concerning the Lord ;* and the second, which regards man, in the *Doctrine of Life for the New Jerusalem.* It is therefore unnecessary to discuss them further here.

V.

The Faith of the Present Day in its Universal Idea or Form.

38. The Faith of the present day in its universal idea or form is this : God the Father sent His Son to make satisfaction for mankind, and for the sake of this merit of the Son He is moved to compassion, and saves those who believe this (or, according to others, saves those who believe this, and at the same time do good works).

39. But in order that the character of this Faith may be seen more clearly, I will adduce in their order the various things which it maintains.

The Faith of the present day maintains that :—

i. God the Father and God the Son are two; and both are from eternity.

ii. God the Son came into the world by the will of the Father to make satisfaction for mankind, who otherwise would have perished in eternal death by the Divine justice, which they also call avenging justice.

iii. The Son made satisfaction by fulfilling the law, and by the passion of the cross.

iv. The Father was moved to compassion by these deeds of the Son.

v. The Son's merit is imputed to those who believe this.

vi. This imputation takes place in an instant; and therefore it may take place, if not before, in life's last moments.

vii. There is some measure of temptation, and deliverance thereupon through this belief.

viii. Those possessing this experience, in especial have trust and confidence.

ix. In especial they have justification, the Father's full grace for the sake of the Son, the remission of all their sins, and thereby salvation.

x. The more learned maintain that in such there is an endeavor (*conatus*) toward good, which works in secret, and does not manifestly move the will. Others maintain a manifest working. Both classes hold that it is by the Holy Spirit.

xi. Of those who confirm themselves in the belief that no one can of himself do good that is really good and that is not tainted with self-merit, and that they are not under the yoke of the law, very many omit to do what is good, giving no thought to the evil and the good of life, saying to themselves that a good work does not save, and neither does an evil one condemn, because faith alone effects all things.

xii. All maintain that the understanding must be kept in subjection to faith, calling that a matter of faith which is not understood.

40. We forbear to examine and weigh these points severally in regard to their being truths, their real character being very evident from what has already been said, especially from what has been shown from the Word, and at the same time rationally confirmed, in the *Doctrine of the New Jerusalem concerning the Lord*, and in the *Doctrine of Life for the New Jerusalem*.

41. Still, in order that it may be seen what is the character of faith separated from charity, and what that of faith not separated from it, I will impart something which I heard from an angel of heaven. He said that he had conversed with many of the Reformed, and had heard what was the character of their faith, and he related his conversation with one who was in faith separated from charity, and with another who was in faith not separated, and what he had heard from them. He said that he questioned them, and they made answer. As what was said may elucidate the subject, I will here present the two conversations.

42. The angel said that with him who was in faith separated from charity he spoke as follows:—

"Friend, who are you?" "I am a Reformed Christian." "What is your doctrine and the religion you have from it?" "It is faith?" "What is your faith?" "My faith is that 'God the Father sent the Son to make satisfaction for mankind, and that they are saved who believe this.'" "What more do you know about salvation?" "Salvation is through that faith alone." "What do you know about redemption?" "It was effected by the passion of the cross, and the Son's merit is imputed through that faith." "What do you know about regeneration?" "It is effected through that faith." "What do you know about repentance and the remission of sins?" "They are effected through that faith." "Say what you know about love and charity." "They are that faith." "Say what you know about good works." "They are that faith." "Say what you think about all the things commanded in the Word." "They are in that faith." "There is nothing then that you are to do?" "What is there for me to do? I cannot of myself do good that is really good." "Can you have faith of yourself?" "I cannot." "How then is it possible for you to have faith?" "That I do not inquire into. I am to have faith."

Finally the angel said, "Surely you know something more than this about salvation." He replied, "What more is there for me to know, seeing that salvation is obtained through that faith alone?"

Then the angel said, "You answer like a fifer who sounds only one note: I hear of naught but faith. If that is all you know, you know nothing. Depart, and behold your associates."

So he departed, and came upon his associates in a desert,

where there was no grass.   He asked why that was so, and was told that it was because there was nothing of the church in them.

43. With the one who was in faith not separated from charity, the angel spoke as follows :—

" Friend, who are you ?"   " I am a Reformed Christian." " What is your doctrine and the religion you have from it ?" " Faith and charity."   " These are two things ?"   " They cannot be separated."   " What is faith ?"   " To believe what the Word teaches."   " What is charity ?"   " To do what the Word teaches."   " Have you only believed these things, or have you also done them ?"   " I have also done them."

The angel of heaven then looked at him, and said, " My friend, come with me, and dwell with us."

VI.

The Nature of Faith that is separated from Charity.

44. In order that it may be seen what the character of faith is when separated from charity, I will present it in its nakedness, in which it is as follows :—

God the Father, being angry with mankind, cast them away from Him, and out of justice resolved to take vengeance by their eternal condemnation ; and He said to the Son, " Go down, fulfill the law, and take upon Thyself the condemnation destined for them, and then perchance I shall be moved to compassion."   Wherefore He came down, and fulfilled the law, and suffered Himself to be hanged on the cross, and cruelly put to death.   When this was done, He returned to the Father, and said, " I have taken upon Myself the condemnation of mankind, therefore now be merciful ;" thus interceding for them. But He received for answer, " Toward them I cannot ; but as

I saw Thee upon the cross, and beheld then Thy blood, I have
been moved to compassion.   Nevertheless I will not pardon
them, but I will impute unto them Thy merit, but to none others
than those who acknowledge this.   This shall be the faith by
which they can be saved."

45. Such is that faith in its nakedness. Who that possesses
any enlightened reason does not see in it absurdities that are
contrary to the Divine essence itself ?   As for instance that
God, who is love itself, and mercy itself, could out of anger and
its consequent revengefulness condemn men and accurse them
to hell.   Or again, that He wills to be moved to mercy by His
Son's taking upon Him their condemnation, and by the sight
of His suffering upon the cross, and of His blood.   Who that
possesses any enlightened reason does not see that the Deity
could not say to another coequal Deity, " I do not pardon them,
but I impute to them Thy merit ?"   Or, " Now let them live
as they please ; only let them believe this and they shall be
saved."   Besides many other absurdities.

46. The reason why these absurdities have not been seen is
that they have induced a blind faith, and have thereby shut
men's eyes, and stopped up their ears.   Shut men's eyes and
stop up their ears, that is, contrive that they do not exercise
thought from any understanding, and then say whatever you
please to persons on whom some idea of eternal life has been
imprinted, and they will believe it ; even if you should say that
God is capable of being angry and of breathing vengeance ;
that God is capable of inflicting eternal condemnation on any
one ; that God wills to be moved to mercy through the blood of
His Son ; that He will impute and attribute this to man as
merit and as man's ; and that He will save him by his merely
thinking so.   Or again, that one God could bargain such things
with another God of the one essence, and impose them upon
Him ; and other things of the same kind.   But open your eyes
and unstop your ears, that is, think about these things from
understanding, and you will see their incongruity with the real
truth.

47. Shut men's eyes and stop up their ears, and contrive that they do not think from any understanding, and can you not then lead them to believe that God has given all His authority to a man, to be as God upon earth? Can you not lead them to believe that the dead are to be addressed in prayer? that men are to bare the head and bend the knee before images of the dead? and that their lifeless bodies, their bones, and their graves, are holy and are to be venerated? But if you open your eyes and unstop your ears, that is, think about these things from some understanding, will you not behold preposterous absurdities that human reason must abhor?

48. When these things and others like them are received by a man whose understanding has been closed up by his religion, may not the temple in which he performs his worship be compared to a den or cavern under-ground, where he does not know what the objects are of which he catches sight? And may not his religion be compared to dwelling in a house that has no windows? and the voice of his worship to sound, and not to speech? With such a man an angel of heaven can hold no converse, because the one does not understand the language of the other.

VII.

In the Word they who are in Faith separated from Charity are represented by the Philistines.

49. In the Word all the names of nations and peoples, and also those of persons and places, signify the things of the church. The church itself is signified by "Israel" and "Judah," because it was instituted among them; and various religious principles are signified by the nations and peoples around them, those accordant with the church by the good nations, and those discordant with it by the evil nations. There are two evil religious principles into which every church in course of time degenerates, one that adulterates its goods, and the other that falsifies its truths. That which adulterates the goods of the church springs from the love of rule, and that which falsifies the truths of the church springs from the conceit of self-intelligence. The religious principle that springs from the love of rule is meant in the Word by " Babylon," and that which springs from the conceit of self-intelligence is meant in the Word by "Philistia." Who at the present day belong to Babylon is known, but not who belong to Philistia. To Philistia belong those who are in faith and not in charity.

50. That they belong to Philistia who are in faith and not in charity, is evident from various things said in the Word about the Philistines, when understood in the spiritual sense, as well from their strife with the servants of Abraham and of Isaac (recorded in *Gen.* xxi. and xxvi.), as from their wars with the sons of Israel (recorded in the book of *Judges*, and in the books of *Samuel* and of *Kings*) ; for in the spiritual sense all the wars described in the Word involve and signify spiritual wars. And as this religion, namely, faith separated from charity, is continually desiring to get into the church, the Philistines remained in the land of Canaan, and often harried the sons of Israel.

51. As the Philistines represented those who are in faith separated from charity, they were called " the uncircumcised," by whom are meant those who are devoid of spiritual love, and consequently are in natural love only : spiritual love is charity. The reason such were called the uncircumcised is that by the circumcised are meant those who are in spiritual love. (That the Philistines are called the " uncircumcised," see 1 *Sam.* xvii. 26, 36 ; 2 *Sam.* i. 20 ; and elsewhere.)

52. That those who are in faith separated from charity were represented by the Philistines, is evident not only from their wars with the sons of Israel, but also from many other things recorded about them in the Word, such as that about Dagon their idol, and about the hemorrhoids and mice with which they were smitten and infested for placing the ark in the temple of their idol, and from other things occurring at the same time, as recorded in 1 *Sam.* v. and vi.; and likewise from what is said about Goliath, who was a Philistine, and was slain by David, as related in 1 *Sam.* xvii.   For Dagon from the navel upward was like a man, and below was like a fish, and thus represented their religion, in that from faith it was as it were spiritual, but was merely natural from having no charity.   The "hemorrhoids" with which they were smitten, signified their filthy loves.   The "mice" by which they were infested, signified the devastation of the church through falsifications of truth.   And "Goliath" whom David slew, represented their conceit of self-intelligence.

53. That those who are in faith separated from charity were represented by the Philistines, is evident also from the prophetic parts of the Word where they are treated of, as from the following :—

Against the Philistines : Behold, waters rise up out of the north, and shall become an overflowing stream, and shall overflow the land and the fullness thereof, the city and them that dwell therein, so that men shall cry, and that every inhabitant of the land shall howl.   Jehovah shall lay waste the Philistines (*Jer.* xlvii. 1, 2, 4).

The "waters that rise up out of the north," are falsities from hell; their "becoming an overflowing stream, and overflowing the land and the fullness thereof," signifies the laying waste of all things of the church through these falsities; the "city and them that dwell therein," signifies the laying waste of all things of its doctrine; that "men shall cry, and that every inhabitant of the land shall howl," signifies a lack of all truth and good in the church; "Jehovah shall lay waste the Philistines," signifies the destruction of such.   In *Isaiah :—*

Rejoice not thou, all Philistia, because the rod that smote thee is broken ; for out of the serpent's root shall come forth a basilisk, whose fruit shall be a flying fire-serpent (xiv. 29).

"Rejoice not thou, all Philistia," signifies let not those who are in faith separated from charity rejoice that they still remain;

" for out of the serpent's root shall go forth a basilisk," signifies the destruction of all truth in them by the conceit of self-
intelligence ; " whose fruit shall be a flying fire-serpent," signifies reasonings from falsities of evil against the truths and
goods of the church.

54. That circumcision represented purification from evils
belonging to love merely natural, is evident from these passages :—

> Circumcise your heart, and take away the foreskins of your heart, lest
> Mine anger go forth because of the evil of your doings (*Jer.* iv. 4).
> Circumcise therefore the foreskin of your heart, and be no more stiff-
> necked (*Deut.* x. 16).

To " circumcise the heart" or " the foreskin of the heart," is to
purify one's self from evils.   On the contrary therefore, one
who is " uncircumcised" or " foreskinned" means one not purified from the evils of love merely natural, thus one who is not
in charity.   And as one who is unclean in heart is meant by
" one uncircumcised," it is said :—

> No [son of a stranger] uncircumcised in heart, and uncircumcised in
> flesh, shall enter into My sanctuary (*Ezek.* xliv. 9).
> No uncircumcised person shall eat the passover (*Exod.* xii. 48).
> And that such a one is condemned (*Ezek.* xxviii. 10 ; xxxi. 18 ; xxxii.
> 19).

VIII.

THOSE WHO ARE IN FAITH SEPARATED FROM CHARITY ARE MEANT BY THE DRAGON IN THE *REVELATION*.

55. It has been said above that in course of time every
church falls away into two general religious principles that are
evil, one springing from the love of rule, and the other from
the conceit of self-intelligence, and that in the Word the former
is meant and described by " Babylon," and the latter by " Philistia." Now as the *Revelation* treats of the state of the Christian Church, especially such as it is at its end, it therefore

treats both generally and specifically of these two evil religious principles. The religious principle meant by " Babylon" is de- scribed in chapters xvii. xviii. xix., and is there the "harlot sitting upon the scarlet beast;" and that meant by "Philistia" is described in chapters xii. xiii., and is there the "dragon," also the "beast that came up out of the sea," and the "beast that came up out of the earth." That this religious principle is meant by the dragon and his two beasts could not heretofore be known, because the spiritual sense of the Word was not opened, and therefore the *Revelation* has not been understood, and especially because the religious principle of faith sepa- rated from charity has so prevailed in the Christian world that no one was able to see it, for every evil religious principle blinds the eyes.

56. That the religious principle of faith separated from charity is meant and described in the *Revelation* by the dragon and his two beasts has not only been told me from heaven, but has also been shown me in the World of Spirits, which lies be- neath heaven. Those in this separated faith, when assembled together, I have seen appearing like a great dragon with a tail outstretched toward the sky; and others of the same descrip- tion I have seen singly appearing like dragons. For there are appearances of this nature in the world of spirits on ac- count of the correspondence of spiritual things with natural. For this reason the angels of heaven call such persons dragon- ists. There is however more than one kind of them; some con- stitute the head of the dragon, some its body, and some its tail. They who constitute its tail are they who have falsified all the truths of the Word, and it is therefore said of the dragon in the *Revelation* that with its tail it drew down the third part of the stars of heaven. The "stars of heaven" signify knowledges of truth, and a "third part" signifies all.

57. Inasmuch as the dragon in the *Revelation* means those who are in faith separated from charity, and as hitherto this has not been known, being indeed actually hidden through a lack of knowledge of the spiritual sense of the Word, a general exposition shall here be given of what is said in the twelfth chapter about the dragon.

58. In *Rev.* xii. it is said :—

A great sign was seen in heaven, a woman encompassed with the sun, and the moon under her feet, and upon her head a crown of twelve stars ; and she being with child, cried, travailing in birth, and in pain to be delivered. And another sign was seen in heaven ; and behold a great red dragon, having seven heads and ten horns, and upon his heads seven diadems. And his tail drew the third part of the stars of heaven, and did cast them into the earth. And the dragon stood before the woman who was ready to be delivered, that when she was delivered, he might devour her child. And she brought forth a man child, who was to pasture all the nations with a rod of iron ; and her child was caught up unto God, and unto his throne. And the woman fled into the wilderness, where she hath a place prepared of God, that they may nourish her there a thousand two hundred and sixty days. And there was war in heaven ; Michael and his angels fought with the dragon, and the dragon fought and his angels ; and they prevailed not, neither was their place found any more in heaven. And when the dragon saw that he was cast into the earth, he persecuted the woman who brought forth the man child. And unto the woman were given two wings of the great eagle, that she might fly into the wilderness into her place, where she would be nourished for a time, and times, and half a time, from the face of the serpent. And the serpent cast out of his mouth water as a flood after the woman, that he might cause her to be carried away by the flood. And the earth helped the woman, and the earth opened her mouth, and swallowed up the flood that the dragon cast out of his mouth. And the dragon was wroth with the woman, and went away to make war with the remnant of her seed, who keep the commandments of God, and hold the testimony of Jesus Christ (*Rev.* xii. 1–8, 13–17).

59. The exposition of these words is as follows : " A great sign was seen in heaven," signifies a revelation by the Lord concerning the church to come, and concerning the reception of its doctrine, and those by whom it will be assailed. The " woman encompassed with the sun, and the moon under her feet," signifies a church that is in love and in faith from the Lord ; " and upon her head a crown of twelve stars," signifies wisdom and intelligence from Divine truths in the men of that church ; " and she being with child," signifies its nascent doctrine ; " cried, travailing in birth, and in pain to be delivered," signifies resistance by those who are in faith separated from charity. "And another sign was seen in heaven," signifies further revelation; "and behold, a great red dragon," signifies faith separated from charity; he is said to be "red" from love that is merely natural; "having seven heads," signifies a false understanding of the Word; "and ten horns," signifies power in consequence of its reception by many; "and upon his heads seven diadems," signifies falsified truths of the Word; "and his tail drew the third part of the stars of heaven, and did cast them into the earth," signifies the destruction of all knowledges of truth. "And the dragon stood before the woman that was ready to be delivered, that when she was delivered, he might devour her child," signifies their hatred, and their intention to destroy the doctrine of the church at its birth. "And she brought forth a man child," signifies the doctrine; "who was to pasture all the nations with a rod of iron," signifies that this doctrine will convince by the power of truth natural from spiritual; "and her child was caught up unto God and unto His throne," signifies the protection of the doctrine by the Lord, from heaven. "And the woman fled into the wilderness," signifies the church among a few; "where she hath a place prepared of God," signifies the state of it such that provision may meanwhile be made for its existing with many; "that they may nourish her there a thousand two hundred and sixty days," signifies until it grows to its appointed state. "And there was war in heaven; Michael and his angels fought with the dragon; and the dragon fought and his angels," signifies dissent and battling by those who are in faith separated from charity against those who are in the doctrine of the church respecting the Lord and the life of charity; "and they prevailed not," signifies that they were overcome; "neither was their place found any more in heaven," signifies that they were cast down thence. "And when the dragon saw that he was cast into the earth, he persecuted the woman who brought forth the man child," signifies the infestation of the church by those in faith separated from charity, on account of its doctrine. "And unto the woman were given two wings of the great eagle, that she might fly into the wilderness into her place," signifies cautious care and foresight while the church is as yet among few ; " where she would be nourished for a time, and times, and half a time, from the face of the serpent," signifies while the church is growing to its appointed state. " And the serpent cast out of his mouth water as a flood after the woman, that he might cause her to be carried away by the flood," signifies their abundant reasonings from falsities whereby to destroy the church. " And the earth helped the woman, and the earth opened her mouth, and swallowed up the flood that the dragon cast out of his mouth," signifies that their reasonings, being from falsities, fell of themselves to the ground. " And the dragon was wroth with the woman, and went away to make war with the remnant of her seed," signifies their persistent hatred ; " who keep the commandments of God, and hold the testimony of Jesus Christ," signifies against those who live the life of charity, and believe in the Lord.

60. The next chapter (*Rev.* xiii.) treats of the dragon's two beasts, the first seen coming up out of the sea, in verses 1–10, and the other one out of the earth, in verses 11–18. That these are the dragon's beasts is evident from verses 2, 4, and 11. The first beast signifies faith separated from charity in respect to confirmations of it from the natural man. The other beast signifies faith separated from charity in respect to confirmations of it from the Word, which also are falsifications of truth. As the exposition of these passages contains the argumentations of those who are in such faith, and would be too tedious if set forth in detail, I pass it by, and merely give the exposition of the concluding words :—

He that hath understanding, let him count the number of the beast ; for it is the number of a man ; and his number is six hundred and sixty-six (verse 18).

" He that hath understanding, let him count the number of the beast," signifies let those who are in enlightenment examine the nature of the confirmations of that faith manufactured from the Word; "for it is the number of a man," signifies that the nature of these confirmations is one of self-intelligence; "and his number is six hundred and sixty-six," signifies all the truth of the Word in a falsified condition.

IX.

THOSE WHO ARE IN FAITH SEPARATED FROM CHARITY ARE MEANT BY THE "GOATS" IN *DANIEL* AND IN *MATTHEW*.

61. That the "he-goat" in *Dan.* viii., and the "goats" in *Matt.* xxv. mean those in faith separated from charity, is evident from the fact that they stand contrasted with the "ram" and the "sheep," by which are meant those who are in charity. For in the Word the Lord is called the "Shepherd," the church the "fold," and the men of the church taken collectively the "flock," and individually, "sheep." And as the "sheep" are those in charity, the "goats" are those who are not in charity.

62. That those in faith separated from charity are meant by the "goats" shall now be shown.

i. From experience in the spiritual world.

ii. From the Last Judgment, and the character of those upon whom it was executed.

iii. From the description in *Daniel* of the combat between the ram and the he-goat.

iv. Lastly, from the neglect of charity by those of whom mention is made in *Matthew*.

63. i. *That those who are in faith separated from charity are meant in the Word by "goats," shown from experience in the spiritual world.* In the spiritual world there appear all things that are in the natural world. There appear houses and palaces. There appear paradises and gardens, and in them trees of every kind. There appear fields and meadow-land, plains and grassy swards, flocks and herds, all precisely like those on

our earth, there being no difference except that the latter are
from a natural origin, while the former are from a spiritual
origin. And therefore angels, being spiritual, behold the things
which are of spiritual origin, just as men do those of natural
origin. [2] All things that appear in the spiritual world are
correspondences, for they correspond to the affections of the
angels and spirits. For this reason they who are in the love
of what is good and true, and consequently in wisdom and intelligence, dwell in magnificent palaces that are surrounded by
paradises full of correspondent trees, around which again are
fields and plains with flocks lying there, and these are appearances. With those however who are in evil affections there are
correspondences of an opposite character; such are either in
hells confined in workhouses that are windowless, and yet have
light in them like that of a will-o'-the-wisp, or else they are
in deserts and dwell in hovels surrounded by an unbroken
barrenness where there are serpents, dragons, screech-owls, and
many other creatures that correspond to their evils. [3] Between heaven and hell there is an intermediate place called the
World of Spirits, into which every human being comes immediately after death, and where one person has intercourse with
another just as among men on earth. Here too all things that
appear are correspondences. Here too appear gardens, groves,
forests of trees and shrubs, and flowery and grassy plains, together with beasts of various kinds, both gentle and savage,
all in correspondence with the affections of those who dwell
there. [4] There have I often seen sheep and goats, and combats between them like that described in *Dan.* viii. I have
seen goats with horns bent forward and bent backward, and
I have seen them attack the sheep with fury. I have seen
goats with two great horns with which they violently struck
the sheep. And when I looked to see what these things meant,
I saw some who were disputing about charity and faith; and
from this it was evident that faith separated from charity was
what appeared as a goat, and that charity from which is faith
was what appeared as a sheep. And as I have seen such things

often I have come to know with certainty that those who are in faith separated from charity are meant in the Word by "goats."

64. ii. *That those in faith separated from charity are meant in the Word by " goats," shown from the Last Judgment and the character of those upon whom it was executed.* The Last Judgment was executed upon no others than those who in externals had been moral, but in internals had not been spiritual, or but little spiritual. As to those who had been evil in both externals and internals, they had been cast into hell long before the Last Judgment, while those who had been spiritual in externals and at the same time in internals had also long before that event been uplifted into heaven ; and the Last Judgment was not executed upon those in heaven, nor upon those in hell, but upon those who were midway between the two, where they had made for themselves imaginary heavens. That the Last Judgment was executed upon these exclusively, may be seen in the short work on the *Last Judgment* (n. 59 and 70) ; and still further in the *Continuation of the Last Judgment* (n. 16–19), where it treats of the Judgment upon the Reformed, of whom those who had been in faith separated from charity in their life as well as in their doctrine, were cast into hell, while those who had been in that same faith as to their doctrine only, and in their life had been in charity, were uplifted into heaven ; from which it was evident that none but these were meant by the "goats" and the "sheep" in *Matt.* xxv. where the Lord is speaking of the Last Judgment.

65. iii. *That those in faith separated from charity are meant in the Word by "goats," shown from the description in* Daniel *of the combat between the ram and the he-goat.* In the book of *Daniel* all things treat, in the spiritual sense, of the things of heaven and the church, as do all things in the universal Holy Scripture (as is shown in the *Doctrine of the New Jerusalem concerning the Holy Scripture,* n. 5 – 26). So therefore does what is said in *Daniel* about the combat of the ram and the he-goat, which in substance is as follows :—

In vision I saw a ram that had two high horns, and the higher one came up last, and I saw that with the horn he pushed westward, and northward, and southward, and magnified himself. Afterwards I saw a he-goat coming from the west over the faces of the whole earth, that had a horn between his eyes, and he ran at the ram with the fury of his strength, and broke his two horns, cast him to the earth, and trampled upon him. But the great horn of the he-goat was broken, and instead of it there came up four horns, and out of one of them came forth a little horn, that grew exceedingly toward the south, and toward the sunrise, and toward the beauteous land, and even to the army of the heavens, and he cast down some of the army, and of the stars, to the earth, and trampled upon them. Yea, he exalted himself even to the prince of the army, and from him the continual sacrifice was taken away, and the dwelling-place of his sanctuary was cast down, because he cast down the truth to the earth. And I heard a holy one saying, How long shall be this vision, the continual sacrifice, and the wasting transgression, that the holy place and the army shall be given to be trampled upon? And he said, Until evening morning; then shall the holy place be made righteous (*Dan.* viii. 2–14).

66. It is very evident that this vision foretells future states of the church, for it is said that the continual sacrifice was taken away from the prince of the army, that the dwelling-place of his sanctuary was cast down, and that the he-goat cast down the truth to the earth, besides that a holy one said, "How long shall be this vision, the continual sacrifice, and the wasting transgression, that the holy place and the army shall be given to be trampled upon?" and that the answer was, "Until evening morning; then shall the holy place be made righteous;" for "evening" means the end of the church when there will be a new church. The "kings of Media and Persia," spoken of in the same chapter, mean the same as the "ram;" and the "king of Greece" means the same as the "he-goat." For the names of the kings, nations, and peoples, and also those of persons and places, mentioned in the Word, signify the things of heaven and of the church.

67. The exposition of the foregoing prophetic utterances is as follows:—The "ram that had two high horns, the higher of which came up last," signifies those who are in faith from charity; his "pushing with it westward, northward, and southward," signifies the dispersing of what is evil and false; his "magnifying himself," signifies growth; the "he-goat coming from the west over the faces of the whole earth," signifies those who are in faith separated from charity, and the invasion of the church by them; the "west" being the evil of the natural man; that "had a horn between his eyes," signifies self-intelligence; that he "ran at the ram with the fury of his strength," signifies impetuously attacking charity and the faith of charity; that he "broke the ram's two horns, cast him down to the earth, and trampled upon him," signifies scattering to the winds both charity and faith, for whoever does this to charity does it to faith also, because these make a one; that the "great horn of the he-goat was broken," signifies the non-appearing of self-intelligence; that "instead of it there came up four horns," signifies applications of the sense of the letter of the Word by way of confirmation; and that "out of one of them there came forth a little horn," signifies an argumentation that no one is able of himself to fulfill the law, and do what is good; that "this horn grew toward the south, toward the sunrise, and toward the beauteous land," signifies a rising up thereby against all things of the church; "and unto the army of the heavens, and he cast down some of the army, and of the stars, and trampled upon them," signifies the destruction in this manner of all the knowledges of good and truth pertaining to charity and faith; that he "exalted himself to the prince of the army, and from him was taken away the continual sacrifice, and the dwelling-place of his sanctuary," signifies that in this way this principle ravaged all things that pertain to the worship of the Lord and to His church; that he "cast down the truth to the earth," signifies that it falsified the truths of the Word; "evening morning, when the holy place shall be made righteous," signifies the end of that church, and the beginning of a new one.

68. iv. *That those in faith separated from charity are meant by "goats," shown from the neglect of charity by those of whom mention is made in* Matthew. That the "goats" and "sheep" in *Matt.* xxv. 31–46 mean the very same persons as those meant by the "he-goat" and "ram" in *Dan.* viii. is evident from the fact that works of charity are recounted to the sheep, and it is said that they had done them; and that the same works of charity are recounted to the goats, and it is said that they had done them not, and that the latter are condemned on that account. For works are neglected by those who are in faith separated from charity, in consequence of their denying that there is anything of salvation or of the church therein; and when charity, which consists in works, is set aside in this way, faith also falls to the ground, because faith is from charity; and when there are no charity and faith there is condemnation. If *all* the evil had been meant there by the goats, there would not have been recounted the works of charity they had not done, but the evils they had done. The same persons are meant by the "he-goats" also in *Zechariah :—*

Mine anger was kindled against the shepherds, and I will visit upon the he-goats (x. 3).

And in *Ezekiel :—*

Behold, I judge between cattle and cattle, between the rams and the he-goats. Is it a small thing to you that ye have eaten up the good pasture, but ye must also tread down with your feet the residue of the pastures? ye have pushed all the feeble sheep with your horns, till ye have scattered them abroad ; therefore will I save My flock, that it may no more be for a prey (xxxiv. 17, 18, 21, 22, etc.).

X.

FAITH SEPARATED FROM CHARITY DESTROYS THE CHURCH AND ALL THINGS THAT BELONG TO IT.

69. Faith separated from charity is no faith, because charity is the life of faith : its soul, and its essence. And where there is no faith because no charity, precisely *there* there is no church. And therefore the Lord says :—

20

When the Son of man cometh shall He find faith on the earth ? (*Luke* **x**viii. 8).

70. At times I have heard the goats and the sheep holding a colloquy as to whether those who have confirmed themselves in faith separated from charity possess any truth ; and as they said that they possessed a great deal, the matter in dispute was submitted to an examination. They were then questioned as to whether they knew what love is, what charity is, and what good is ; and as these were the things that they had set aside, the only reply they could make was that they did not know. They were questioned as to what sin is, as to what repentance is, and what the remission of sins ; and as they replied that those who have been justified through faith have their sins remitted so that they no longer ·appear, it was avouched to them, " This is not the truth." They were questioned as to what regeneration is, and they replied either that it is baptism, or that it is the remission of sins through faith. It was avouched to them that " this is not the truth." They were questioned as to what the spiritual man is, and they replied that it is one who has been justified through the confession of their faith. But it was avouched to them that " this is not the truth." They were questioned concerning redemption, concerning the union of the Father and the Lord, and concerning the unity of God, and they gave answers that were not truths. Not to mention other points concerning which they were questioned. After these interrogatories and the replies, the matter in dispute came to judgment, and the judgment was that those who have confirmed themselves in faith separated from charity do not possess any truth.

71. That such is the case cannot be credited by them while they are in the natural world, because those who are in falsities see no otherwise than that falsities are truths, and that it is not a matter of much consequence to know more than what belongs to their faith. And as their faith is divorced from the understanding (for it is a blind faith) they make no investigation into this matter, which is one that can be investigated solely from the Word by the means of an enlightening of the understanding. The truths therefore that are in the Word they turn into falsities by thinking of faith when they see mention made of "love," "repentance," the "remission of sins," and many other things that must belong to action.

72. But I wish to say emphatically that it is those who have confirmed themselves by both doctrine and life in faith alone who are of this character, and by no means those who, although they have heard and have believed that faith alone saves, have nevertheless shunned evils as sins.

INDEX OF SCRIPTURE PASSAGES *

Note.—In this Index,

Full-faced figures.......... **1, 3,** designate verses fully quoted;

preceded by points .... **..1,** show that beginning of verse is not given;

with points above...... **ï,** that the middle part is not given;

with points following.. **1..,** that the end of the verse is not given.

The omission of one word is indicated by one dot; of two or three words, by two dots; of four or more words, by three dots.

Italic figures .... *1, 3,* designate verses given in substance.

Figures in parentheses.... (1, 3), indicate verses merely referred to.

* Arranged and edited by the Rev. C. G. Hubbell. Originally compiled by the Rev. Samuel H. Worcester for each of the Four Doctrines separately. Here his four indexes are combined in one, and the titles are abbreviated as follows:

L. for the *Doctrine of the Lord;*

S. for the *Doctrine of the Holy Scripture;*

Life for the *Doctrine of Life;*

F. for the *Doctrine of Faith.*

1

INDEX OF WORDS

FOR

THE FOUR DOCTRINES*

In the following Index, "L" indicates the *Doctrine of the New Jerusalem concerning the Lord;* "S," the *Doctrine of the Holy Scripture;* "Life," the *Doctrine of Life;* "F," the *Doctrine of Faith,* and "Q," the *Nine Questions, relating to the Lord, the Trinity, and the Holy Spirit.*

The numbers following each reference designate the paragraphs of the given book as numbered by Swedenborg, and the numbers in parenthesis refer to the subdivisions as given in the *Swedenborg Concordance;* the Roman numerals following "Q" refer to the number of the Question.

A.

S. The sound of *A* (probably " a" as in "father") is used by the angels of the third heaven—90 (2).

AARON.

S. Where the name *Aaron* occurs in the Word, in the Word that exists in heaven there is found "the priestly office"—71.

ABADDON.

S. Spiritual signification of *Abaddon* —13 (3).

ABHORS.

Life. Man has religion as he *abhors* adultery—77; one learns to *abhor* evil by shunning it as a sin—95.

ABILITY.

Life. Man has *ability* from the Lord to reciprocate His life; hence there is mutuality between God and man—103, 104.

ABODES.

S. Truths of the sense of the letter of the Word are the *abodes* of genuine truths —40.

ABRAHAM.

S. Where the name *Abraham* occurs in the Word, in the Word that exists in heaven there is found "the Lord as to His Divinity"—71.

ABSURDITIES.

F. Any one of enlightened reason must see the *absurdities* in the doctrine of faith separate from charity—45; why not seen before this—46, 47.

ABUSE.

S. Spirits beneath the heavens *abuse* communication with them by means of the internal sense—64.

ABYSSINIA.

S. Account of spirits from *Abyssinia* affected by the singing of a psalm—108.

ACCOMMODATED.

S. How truths of the sense of the letter of the Word are *accommodated* to the simple and to little children—40; see **51.**

ACKNOWLEDGE.

S. Man caused to *acknowledge* truth from an interior perception—58.

* Compiled by the Rev. Charles H. Mann.

ACKNOWLEDGMENT.

F. Faith is an internal *acknowledgment* of truth—1; faith is nothing else than an *acknowledgment* that a thing is so because it is true—2; those who are in the spiritual affection of truth possess an internal *acknowledgment* of truth—4; to be in enlightenment is nothing else than to be in the perception and in the consequent internal *acknowledgment* that this or that is true—5; the Reformed give the name of faith to the mere internal *acknowledgment*—9; "Blessed are they who do not see and yet believe" does not mean faith separate from the internal *acknowledgment* of truth —10; an external *acknowledgment* is not faith . . . such an *acknowledgment* is a faith in what is unknown, which is a mere memory faith—11; how one may have the internal *acknowledgment* of truth which is faith—12; the internal *acknowledgment* of truth which is faith exists with none but those who are in charity —13; those who are in no inward *acknowledgment* of truth in this world, if they are in a state of charity from religion, will come into such an *acknowledgment* from instruction in the spiritual world—30.

ADAM.

Q. (As to whether regarding *Adam* as a church does not contradict his being the "son of God," as stated in *Luke* iii.) *Adam* is there said to be "of God," that is, created by Him, and is not called His "son"—VIII.

ADMITTED.

L. No one can be *admitted* into heaven who thinks of three Gods—55 (3); see 61.

S. Those *admitted* into heaven who are devoid of truths, are cast down—61 (3).

ADULTERY.

S. The three ways of understanding the command against *adultery;* first, by a man; secondly, by a spiritual angel; and thirdly, by a celestial angel—67 (3). See WHOREDOM.

Life. Various kinds and degrees of *adultery* described—74; "In proportion as any one shuns *adulteries* of every kind

as sins, in the same proportion he loves chastity" (chap. ix.) set forth and explained—74-79; *adultery* is so great an evil it may be called diabolism itself—74; those who do not regard *adulteries* as sins are in *adulteries* of every kind at once—ib.; in proportion as one shuns *adulteries* as sins he loves marriage—75; no one can know the chastity of marriage but the man who shuns the lasciviousness of *adultery* as a sin—76; whether one be a Christian or not is shown by his shunning or his not shunning *adulteries* as sins—77; if one shuns *adulteries* for reasons other than because they are sins (examples enumerated) he is still inwardly an adulterer—111.

ADVENT.

L. Why the Lord made His *advent* into the world as set forth in the Scripture—3; the Lord's *advent* meant by the expressions "that day" or "that time" used in the Word (passages adduced)— 4; various kinds of *advent* meant by various kinds of "day" and "time" mentioned—5; see also 14 (9); passages adduced which refer more openly to the Lord's *advent*—6; the Lord came into the world to subjugate the hells and glorify His human—12; without the Lord's *advent* no mortal could have been saved— 17-18; when His *advent* is spoken of the Lord is called the "Son of man"—26; the height to which the hells had grown before the Lord's *advent* described, and the reason stated—33 (3); the Lord's *advent* called the "Gospel of the kingdom" —42.

S. The "day of Jehovah" means the Lord's *advent*—14 (3); the state of the church before and after the Lord's *advent* set forth—99.

F. Universals of faith giving reasons why the Lord came into the world—35.

Q. The representative Human before Jehovah's *advent* could not spiritually enlighten men—VI.

AFFECTION.

L. By spirit is meant the varying *affection* of life in man—48.

S. As often as man is in the *affection* of truth for the sake of truth, he acknowl-

edges it from an internal perception . . .
for perception comes from *affection*—58 ;
those who have studied the Word from
the *affection* of knowing truth raised into
heaven—61 (3); in the celestial kingdom,
vowel marks in the (Hebrew) Word denote *affections*—74.

F. Those in the spiritual *affection* of
truth possess an internal acknowledgment of it—4 ; a spiritual idea inflows
into those who are in the *affection* of
truth, and inwardly tells them whether
what they hear or read is true or not—5 ;
in its origin charity is the *affection* of
good . . . the *affection* of good produces
the *affection* of truth—13 ; *affection* brings
forth nothing from itself except by
means of thought—15.

AFRICA.

S. Things of religion spread into *Africa*
from the two Words of the Lord—117.

AFRICANS.

S. Before the Lord the universal
heaven is as one man—the position of
the *Africans* in that man—105 (3) ; concerning certain *African* spirits who were
deeply affected by hearing a Psalm read
—108.

AGE.

L. The consummation of the *age*
means the last time of the church—26.

AGENCY.

Life. Truths are the *agency* for the
nourishment and formation of good—37.

AID.

L. Every man ascends into heaven by
means of the Lord's *aid*, but the Lord
ascended into heaven of Himself—35
(11).

AIR.

S. Signification of "sun and *air* darkened"—13 (2) ; doctrine not confirmed
from the Word like house in the *air*—54e.

ALLOY.

Life. Good compared with gold, and
inferior good to gold with an *alloy*—10 ;
science can tell of the degree of gold in
an *alloy*, but not the degree of good

which springs partly from self and partly
from the Lord—11.

ALLOWABLE.

Life. The man who holds the religious
tenet that no one is able to fulfill the law,
thinks moral evils *allowable* before God.
but not *allowable* before the world—63.

ALPHA.

L. Why the Lord is called the *Alpha*
and the Omega—36.

AMMON, THE SONS OF.

S. *The sons of Ammon* signify the
adulterations of good and truth—18 (3).

ANCIENT CHURCHES.

S. All the *ancient churches* were
churches representative of heavenly
things—20 (2).

ANCIENTS.

S. That there was among the *ancients*
a Word written entirely by correspondences, which has been lost—102 ; where
it prevailed and other things concerning
it—ib.

F. The *ancients* instead of saying faith
were accustomed to say truth—the reason
—6.

ANGEL.

L. *Angels* have all their wisdom from
the Word which is Divine Truth itself—
2 ; before the Lord's advent the *angels* of
heaven were infested by the hells, to so
great a height had these grown—33 (3) ;
all *angels* are in the spiritual sense of
the Word—37 (2) ; spirits and *angels* are
constantly with man—ib. ; trine in the
Lord illustrated by trine in *angels*—46
(3) ; *angels* teach every man after death
what the Holy Spirit is—46 (4) ; *angels*
have breathing and the beating of the
heart as well as men—51 (3).

S. The *angels* of the Lord's celestial
kingdom (the third heaven) are in the
Divine proceeding called Celestial, that
is, are in the good of love from the Lord ;
the *angels* of the Lord's spiritual kingdom are in the Divine proceeding called
Spiritual, that is, in truths of wisdom
from the Lord—6 ; men of the Most An-

cient Church able to speak with *angels* by means of correspondences—21 ; they thus thought conjointly with *angels*—Ib. ; the Lord's *angels* in heaven are in the spiritual sense of the Word—26 ; the heaven where *angels* are would fall to pieces without the world as a foundation —34 ; man has association with *angels* by means of the letter of the Word—62 ; why this is—63 ; spiritual *angels* in spiritual sense, and celestial *angels* in celestial sense of Word—64 ; a spiritual *angel* calls forth what is spiritual and a celestial what is celestial from the Word when man reads it—65 ; how the spiritual and celestial *angels* draw their respective senses from the Word, illustrated by examples—67 ; an additional reason given why association with *angels* exists by means of the Word—68 ; *angels* get all their wisdom from the Word—70 ; this is acknowledged by the *angels*—73 ; there is a copy of the Word in every heaven written by *angels*—72 ; the wisdom of the celestial *angels* surpasses that of the spiritual *angels* almost as much as theirs does the wisdom of man—74 ; after death every man is instructed by *angels*—93 ; *angels* reject the external of the Word when used by man to confirm the loves of the world—96 ; *angels* are men because the good and truth that proceed from the Lord are a man—100.

Life. An *angel* is an *angel* from the love and wisdom in him—32.

F. An *angel* is beautiful according to tne quality of his faith—31 ; conversation between an *angel* and one who was in faith separate from charity, and between an angel and one who was in faith united to charity—41 to 43 ; an *angel* of heaven could hold no converse with a man whose understanding had been closed up by his religion—48.

Q. Before the assumption of the Human the Lord manifested Himself by means of an *angel*—II. ; see also VI.

ANGELIC HEAVEN.

Q. The Lord had a Divine Rational before the assumption of the Human by means of the *angelic heaven*—II. ; Divine love and wisdom proceed from the Lord as the sun of the *angelic heaven* as do heat and light from the sun of the natural world—V.

ANGER.

L. "Day of *anger*" signifies the advent of the Lord to Judgment—5.

S. *Anger* is predicated of good, and in the opposite senses of evil, while wrath is predicated of truth and in the opposite sense of falsity—84 ; why *anger* is attributed to the Lord—94.

ANIMAL.

Life. The natural mind may be called the *animal* mind—86 ; man is discriminated from the *animal* by having a spiritual mind—ib. ; so long as the concupiscences of evils block up the interiors of the natural mind, so long is man an *animal*—ib. (5).

ANIMAL SPIRIT.

S. The substances which are the origins of the fibres of the animal kingdom extract and call forth their *animal spirit* from the chyle—66.

ANOINTED.

L. Why the Lord is called the "*Anointed*"—42 ; see also 19 (8).

ANSWERS.

S. *Answers* from heaven given only through the ultimate sense of the Word —44 (3).

APES.

S. Peoples who have known nothing of God, because without revelation concerning Him, appear in the spiritual world like *apes*—116.

APPAREL.

L. Meaning of the Lord's *apparel* as referred to in the Word—14 (2).

APPARENT TRUTHS.

S. Not hurtful to accept *apparent truths* in letter of Word if not confirmed—95 ; illustrated by *apparent truths* of nature—ib. (3) ; why hurtful to confirm them—96.

APPEARANCES.

S. Truths of the sense of the letter of the Word are in part *appearances* of truth

—40; in some places in the sense of the letter of the Word truths are not naked, but clothed, and are then called *appearances* of truth ; the reason—51 ; genuine truth in the sense of the letter of the Word appears only to those who are in enlightenment from the Lord—57 ; *appearances* of truth in the Word if confirmed become falsities—91 ; illustrated by the heresies in Christendom—92 ; illustrated from nature—95 ; the reason set forth—96.

F. Correspondential *appearances* in the spiritual world described—63.

Life. That man fights of himself against evils only an *appearance*, why the Lord so wills—96.

APPEARING.

Life. Shunning evils for any other reason than because they are sins only prevents them from *appearing*—108.

ARABIA.

S. Why the science of correspondences was known and cultivated in *Arabia*—21 ; see 102.

ARGUMENTATIONS.

S. *Argumentations* from fallacies signified by the "breastplates" of the locusts in *Rev.* ix.—13 (3).

ARISTOTLE.

S. Where *Aristotle* got his knowledge of God and the immortality of the soul—115 (3).

ARK.

Life. Reverence accorded the *ark* and miracles accomplished by the *ark* on account of the holiness of the law contained in it—55 (2 and 3).

ARTIFICER.

Life. How charity is shown in the life of an *artificer*—39.

AS.

Life. Every man is able *as* of himself to shun evils by the Lord's power if he begs for it—31 ; necessity that a man should fight against evils *as* of himself—96 ; a man ought to shun evils as sins and fight against them *as* of himself (general article)—101.

ASCEND.

L. Signification of the statement that the Lord *ascended* into heaven—35 (11).

ASIA.

S. Before the Lord the universal heaven is as one man ; the position of the people of *Asia* in that man—105.

ASSHUR.

S. *Asshur* signifies reason—18.

ASSOCIATION.

S. *Association* with the angels is brought about by means of the sense of the letter of the Word (chap. vi.)—62 ; the reason of this—63 ; another reason—68.

ASSYRIA.

S. The science of correspondence was known and cultivated in *Assyria*—21 ; *Assyria* signifies the reasoning derived from the memory-knowledge in the natural man—79 (4) ; those who used the Ancient Word came partly from *Assyria*—102. See ASSHUR.

ATHANASIAN CREED.

L. The doctrine of the *Athanasian Creed* that the Divine and Human in the Lord are not two but one—29 ; doctrine of, agrees with the truth provided that by a Trinity of Persons is understood a Trinity of Person (seriatim passages, chap. xi.)—55-61 ; quoted in full—56 ; inconsistency of, in allowing a man to think three gods, but obliging him to say one—57 ; re-transcribed with Trinity of Person substituted for Trinity of Persons—58 ; the *Creed's* treatment of the Lord's incarnation true, provided we distinguish between the human from the mother, and the Human from the Father—59.

Life. The doctrine of the *Athanasian Creed* concerning the necessity of a good life, quoted—3.

ATONEMENT.

L. Popular belief in the church concerning the *atonement*—18.

ATTRIBUTES.

L. The Divine *attributes* are justice, love, mercy, and good (reasoning thence against the possibility of there being anything of vengeance in Him)—18; redemption and salvation are an *attribute* proper to the Lord's Divine Human—34 (3).

AUTOMATON.

Life. Unless man acts as of himself he becomes like an *automaton*—96.

AWAKE.

S. To *awake* signifies the life after death which is spiritual—17 (2).

BABEL; BABYLON.

L. Not long after its setting up anew the church was turned into *Babylon*—65.

Life. *Babel* signifies the profanation of good—79 (2).

F. The religious principle that springs from the love of rule is meant in the Word by *Babylon*—49.

BALANCES.

S. The "pair of *balances*" (in *Rev.* vi.) signifies the estimation of truth so small that there is scarcely any—12.

BALDNESS.

S. *Baldness* signifies the Word without its ultimate sense—35; *baldness* was considered a great disgrace in Israel, and why—ib. (4).

BAPTIZE, BAPTISM.

L. By *baptism* is meant spiritual washing—18 (4); that it was the Lord's Human that was *baptized*—19 (9); what is meant by *baptizing* into the name of the Father, the Son, and the Holy Spirit—46 (2); what is meant by *baptizing* with the Holy Spirit and with fire—51 (4).

BAPTIST, JOHN THE.

L. Why *John the Baptist* had his raiment of camel's hair—15 (8).

BARE.

S. The Word is like a man with face and hands *bare*, for all things therein which concern man's salvation are *bare*—55.

BASILISK.

F. "Out of the serpent's tooth shall go forth a *basilisk*" signifies the destruc-

tion of all truth by the conceit of self-intelligence—53e.

BASIS.

S. The sense of the letter of the Word the *basis* of its spiritual and celestial senses (title of chap. iii.)—27; see 30, 31, 32, and 36; how this is—38 (2); the human race is the *basis* of the heavens—34.

BATTLING. See COMBAT.

Life. He does *battling* against evils as sins who believes in a hell and a heaven (etc.)—94; treated of in the Word (passages given)—99; see 100.

BEARD.

S. The *beard* signifies the ultimate of truth—35 (2).

BEARING.

L. What is meant by *bearing* iniquities—15 (2); see also 16; a prophet's *bearing* the iniquities of Israel did not take them away, but represented and showed them—16 (3).

BEAST.

S. Who are meant by the *beast* in *Rev.* xix.—25.

Life. What makes the difference between a man and a *beast*—15.

F. Signification of the two *beasts* described in *Rev.* xiii.—60.

BEATING.

L. Angels have *beating* of the heart; what it signifies—51 (3).

F. Angels and spirits live by the heartbeat as men do; the reason—19.

BEGINNING.

L. From the *beginning* God was in first principles but not in ultimates—36.

S. That the Lord had been only in first principles is meant by "In the beginning was the Word" (*John* i.)—98.

BEING.

Life. That good to be good must be good from its inmost *being*, that is, from God—13e.

BELIEVE, BELIEF.

L. Who are meant by "those who believe in His name" (*John* i.)—18 (5).

Life. What is meant by " to *believe* in the name of the Son of God" (*John* i.)—17; what is meant by " to *believe* in the Lord"—48e ; one may *believe* that he has faith, and yet not have it (the reason)—44; general opinion that salvation consists in *believing* what the church teaches (the fallacy of this)—91 ; the *belief* that will lead one to shun evils—94.

F. Angels refuse to *believe* what they do not understand—4 ; meaning of the Lord's words to Thomas " because thou hast seen me thou hast *believed*"—(*John* xx.)—10 ; to *believe* in the Lord the universal of Christian faith, what it is to *believe*—36.

BENEFACTIONS.

Life. Other works than the duties of one's calling the *benefactions* of life—114.

BETRAYAL.

L. Signification of the Lord's *betrayal* by Judas—16 (6).

BLACK.

S. What is meant by the *black* horse (*Rev.* vi.)—12 (2).

BLASPHEMY.

L. What *blasphemy* against the Holy Spirit means—50 (2).

BLIND.

S. The signification of the *blind* receiving their sight—17 (4) ; what it is that *blinds* a man as to his reception of spiritual truth—60.

F. Faith of the present day declared to be *blind*—1 ; why this *blind* faith continued among the Reformed—9 ; why this *blind* faith has not been sooner enlightened—46.

BLIND FAITH.

F. What enormous falsities a *blind faith* can bring into being, seen in the doctrines of the Papists—8.

BLOOD.

L. What is meant by *bloods* in *John* i. —18 (5) ; *blood* or wine signifies the good of faith from the Lord—27.

S. What it means to "drink the *blood* of the sacrifice" (*Ezek.* xxxix.)—15 (3).

BLOTTED OUT.

S. The knowledge of correspondences *blotted out* among the Israelites and Jews (why)—22.

BLUE.

S. *Blue* (in the tabernacle) signifies truth from a celestial origin—46e.

BODY OF THE LORD.

L. That even the *body of the Lord* became Divine—29 (2) ; why the Lord rose as to His whole *body*—35 (9) ; that after resurrection the *body of the Lord* was no longer material but Divine substantial—35 (10).

Q. Before the incarnation was the Divine Human a Person subsisting as the *Body* of God?—VI.

BORN.

L. That the Divine Human should have been *born* of a virgin essential to the Lord's coming into the world—20; Jesus *born* of the Virgin Mary was the Son of God—21 ; see 29 (2), 30 ; from His *birth* the Lord had a human from the mother which was successively put off—35 (3) ; the Lord's human in time was *born* of the Virgin Mary—59.

Life. Man's being *born* into total ignorance a means for his reformation—69.

BOW.

S. The *bow* signifies doctrine from the Word fighting against falsities—79 (2).

BRANCH.

F. The *branches* of a tree signify the truths of faith with man—16.

BREAD.

L. Meaning of " the *bread* which came down from heaven"—27.

Life. The relation of good to truth compared with that of *bread* to wine—40.

BREAST.

S. Those Christians among whom the Word is constitute the *breast* (of the one Man whom the church on earth is like)—105 (3).

BREASTPLATE.

S. What the *breastplates* of the locusts of *Rev.* ix. mean—13 (3).

BREATHING, BREATH.

L. Why the Lord *breathed* on His disciples—51 (3) ; angels have *breath*—ib.

F. In the spiritual world every one is known in respect to the quality of his faith from his *breathing*—19.

Q. The *breath* of Jehovah's mouth is wisdom—IV.

BRIDE.

L. When the church is a *Bride* (distinguished from " Wife")—63.

BRIDEGROOM.

S. The *bridegroom* (*Matt.* **xxv.**)—signifies the Lord—17 (2).

BROTHER.

S. *Brother* is predicated of good, companion of truth—84.

BURIAL.

L. Signification of the Lord's *burial*—16 (6).

BUSINESS.

F. Man acquires an affection for use through an affection for his *business*—25.

BUY.

S. What to *buy* signifies—17 (2).

CALF.

S. A *calf* signifies the natural affection—18 (3) ; *calves* and oxen signify the affections and powers of the natural man —23.

CALVIN.

Q. *Calvin* denied that in Christ Man is God and God is Man ; he merely affirmed that Christ is God and Man—II.

CANAAN.

S. The science of correspondences was known and cultivated in the land of *Canaan*—21 ; where our Word has *Canaan* the Word of the angels has " the church" —71.

CARE.

F. Concerning those who have been prevented from thinking about truths by worldly *cares*—30.

CAUSE.

S. Of the trine in every Divine work the middle term may be called *cause*—28.

CAVERNS.

Life. Certain ones who had reckoned on their good works and piety but who had not shunned evils as sins, seen to go into *caverns*—26.

F. The temple of a man whose understanding has been closed up by his religion compared to a *cavern*—48.

CEDAR.

S. *Cedar* signifies the rational good and truth of the church—18 (3). See also ib. (5) ; and 23 (2).

CELESTIAL.

S. The *celestial* proceeds from the Divine love, and is the inmost—6 ; the Word is *celestial* by correspondence—8 ; the *celestial* a more interior sense of the Word than the spiritual—19 ; depends for its integrity upon the sense of the letter of the Word—27 ; the *celestial* is one of the kingdoms of the heavens—34 ; the *celestial* is the inmost of successive order from the Lord—38 (2) ; the *celestial* angels are in the *celestial* sense of the Word—64 ; a *celestial* angel calls forth what is *celestial* in the Word when a man is reading it—65 ; there is a *celestial* degree of life with man, his relation to it by means of the Word—68 ; the wisdom of *celestial* angels surpasses that of spiritual angels —74.

Q. The Lord from eternity had a Divine *Celestial*—II.; He has now united it to the Divine Natural—V. See CELESTIAL SENSE.

CELESTIAL SENSE.

S. There is a more interior sense (than the spiritual) called *celestial*—19 ; can with difficulty be made plain—ib.; why there is such a sense—ib.; from it the Word gives life to those who devoutly read—ib. ; the *celestial sense* is the life of the Word—39 ; the naked goods of the Word are in its *celestial sense*—40 ; from this sense our Word is like a flame—42 ; the Word shines and is translucent because of its spiritual and *celestial senses*—

58; man is brought into association with celestial angels through the *celestial sense* —63; see 64; illustration of the *celestial sense* of the Word as shown in the interpretation of the commandments—67; the *celestial sense* of the Word refers specially to the Lord—80.

CHALDEA.

S. The science of correspondences was known and much cultivated in *Chaldea* —21; the ancients with whom the ancient Word is still in use in heaven were partly from *Chaldea*—102.

Life. *Chaldea* signifies the profanation of truth—79 (2).

CHARACTERS.

Q. May the Trinity be properly said to be one and the same Lord in three *characters?*—VII.

CHARIOTS.

S. Signification of the sound of the wings of the locusts (*Rev.* ix.) as *chariots* —13 (3).

Life. A *chariot* signifies doctrine—30 (2).

CHARITY.

Life. Christian *charity* defined—114.

F. The internal acknowledgment of truth, which is faith, exists only with those who are in *charity*—13; (chap. ii. with this title, 13-24); *charity* has its origin from the affection of use—14; more fully set forth—17; makes a one with faith—18; related to faith as the heart is related to the lungs—19; until one is in *charity* the knowledges of truth and good are not matters of real belief (chap. iii.)—25-33; cannot come into being where there is nothing but falsities—29; but those having the faith of *charity* by a good life can come into truths after death—30; according to one's *charity* such is his faith (the progression of *charity* traced)—31; how faith is formed from *charity*—32; conversation with an angel concerning *charity* and faith—41-43; *charity* is the life of faith, its soul and its essence—69.

CHASTITY.

Life. One loves *chastity* in proportion as he shuns adulteries (chap. ix.)—74-79;

the *chastity* of marriage makes heaven with a man which he can possess only in proportion as he shuns the lasciviousness of adultery—76.

CHERUBS, CHERUBIM.

S. *Cherubs* and *cherubim* represent the guard which protects the spiritual sense of the Word from profanation— 97 (2), *et seq.* See also 46e; why these guards have been set—26 (2).

CHILD, CHILDREN.

S. *Children* signify innocence and charity—23; the letter of the Word adapted to the simple and *children*—40.

Life. *Children* initiated into the Christian religion by learning the decalogue—64.

F. The signification of the woman (*Rev.* xii.) being with *child*—59; the *child* that she was to bear signifies the doctrine of the church—ib.

CHRIST.

L. The Jewish Church understood by "the Son of God" the Messiah (that is, the *Christ*) whom they expected, and who should be born at Bethlehem— 19 (8).

CHRISTIANS, CHRISTIAN.

S. *Christians* constitute the breast of the universal man which is constituted of all the heavens before the Lord (the reason)—105 (3).

Life. A man who does not regard adulteries as sins is not a *Christian*—77; an ungodly man is able to shun evils as injurious, but only a *Christian* can shun evils as sins—111; teaching the decalogue is general throughout the whole *Christian* world. By it children are initiated into the *Christian* religion—64.

F. The *Christian* faith in its universal idea or form (general article)—34.

CHRISTIAN CHURCHES.

Life. In the *Christian churches* many teach that faith alone saves—4.

CHURCH, CHURCHES.

L. The states of the *church* were represented by the prophets (illustrated by examples taken from the Word)—15; the *church* itself signified by the Lord as the Grand Prophet—ib. (8); *church* in respect to the Word, represented by the Lord—16 (5); to set up a new *church* one of the purposes for which the Lord was sent into the world—20; a *church* is a *church* from the Lord—55 (5); when a *church* is a Bride, and when a Wife (distinguished)—63; the *church* not set up anew at the Lord's coming among those at Jerusalem, but among those outside the city—64 (3) (8).

S. The men of the *church* on earth are in the Divine Natural—6; by the opening of the seals, etc. (*Rev.* vi.), are described the successive states of the *church* —12; the state of the *church* is treated of in *Rev.* ix.—13; the things of the *church* among the sons of Jacob were correspondences—20 (2); the doctrine of the *church* is to be drawn from the sense of the letter of the Word and to be confirmed thereby (chap. v.)—50-61; the *church* is from the Word and is such as is its understanding of the Word (chap. viii.)—76-79; the *church* is within man—78; there is a marriage of the Lord and the *church* with each and everything of the Word (chap. ix.)—80-90; in the spiritual sense the hidden things in the Word refer especially to the *church*—80; for a man to be a man of the *church*, his will and his understanding must make a one—83; the *church* is also said to be the Lord, and why—89; the state of the *church* was completely changed by the Lord's becoming the Word in ultimates (shown in what respect changed)—99; all the *churches* before the Lord's advent were representative *churches*—ib.; see also 20 (2); the people outside of the *church* have light by means of the Word (see title to chap. xiii.)—104-113; there must be somewhere on earth a *church* in order to have conjunction with heaven—104; the *church* before the Lord is as one man—105; the *church* is where the Word is read and the Lord thereby known—ib.; is as the heart and lungs—ib.; it is provided by the Lord that there shall always be a *church* on earth where the Word is read —110. See also MOST ANCIENT CHURCH, and NEW JERUSALEM CHURCH.

F. In the Word the *church* was represented by Israel and Judah, and its principles by the various nations about them—49; the states of the *church* are represented by the vision of Daniel (viii. 1-14)—66; Faith separated from charity destroys the *church* and all things that belong to it (chap. x.)—69-72.

Q. Before the incarnation all things of the *church* were representative and like shadows—VI.; does the regarding Adam as a *church* contradict his being a son of God as given in *Luke* iii.?— VIII.; Noah and his three sons when mentioned in *Ezek.* xiv. are significative of a *church*—IX.

CICERO.

S. Where *Cicero* got his knowledge of God and immortality—115 (3).

CIRCUMCISED.

F. By the *circumcised* are meant those who are in spiritual love—51; *circumcision* represents purification from evils belonging to love merely natural (passages adduced)—54.

CITIZEN.

Life. Man is a *citizen* of the spiritual world according to his spiritual good—12.

CITY.

L. City signifies doctrine from the Word, and Holy *City* the doctrine of Divine truth from the Lord—64.

S. Where in our Word we have the *cities* on this side and beyond Jordan, the Word of the angels has various things of the church and of its doctrine —71.

CIVIC.

Life. Civic good defined—12; to be really a *civic* man one must possess spiritual good—14; the laws of the decalogue known among all nations as laws of *civic* order—53.

CLEANSE.

S. What it means to "*cleanse* the inside of the cup and platter"—40 (2).

CLERGY. See ENGLISH CLERGY.

CLOTHED.

S. The portions of the Word that are not actually necessary for man's spiritual life and consequent salvation are *clothed* —55; appearances of truth that are *clothed* may be caught at as naked truths (the injury thence)—91, 92.

CLOUD.

S. The *cloud* that overshadowed the disciples at the transfiguration signified the Word in the sense of the letter—48.

COLUMN.

S. Successive order compared to a *column*—38.

COMBAT, COMBATS.

L. *Combats* against the hells are meant by temptations—12; (see 33); the passion of the cross the last *combat* whereby the Lord fully conquered the hells and fully glorified His Human—3, 12; by means of *combats* the Lord conquered hell—12; His *combats* described in the Word—14; Last Judgment effected by means of His *combats*—ib. (10); the same are much treated of in the Psalms and Prophets— 34 (4); by means of them He became our Saviour—ib. (5).

S. The wars of Jehovah mean the Lord's *combats* with hell—103.

Life. No one can shun evils as sins except by *combats* against them (chap. xii.)—92-100; those who believe in heaven and hell are brought into this *combat*—94; the *combat* is not severe except with those who have given free rein to their concupiscences—97.

F. It is a universal of the Christian faith that the Lord removed hell from man by *combats* against it—35; *combat* between the ram and the he-goat described in Daniel (viii. 2-14) explained as to its spiritual meaning—65.

COMFORTER.

L. What is meant by the *Comforter*— 51 (2).

COMMANDMENTS.

S. The natural, spiritual, and celestial senses of five of the *commandments* given —67.

Life. Difference in spiritual effect between shunning the *commandments* as evils and shunning them as sins—108; the *commandments* of the Lord are truths —38; the *commandments* must also be kept by fighting against the concupiscences forbidden by them—66; man has the ability from the Lord to keep the *commandments* (confirmatory passages)— 104. See DECALOGUE.

COMMINGLED.

L. Human nature from the mother cannot be *commingled* with the Divine essence in the Lord—35.

COMMONWEALTH.

Life. The *commonwealth* would perish without laws enjoining the commandments—53.

COMMUNICATION.

S. How *communication* is effected with the various heavens by means of the Word—64; the law of *communication* abused by evil spirits—ib.

COMPANION.

S. *Companion* is predicated of truth— 84.

COMPLEX.

S. The Natural which flows from the Lord is the *complex* of the Celestial and the Spiritual—6.

Life. The decalogue a *complex* of all things of religion—54; (see also 62).

COMPREHEND.

F. One must *comprehend* a truth in order really to believe it—2; spiritual can be *comprehended* just as well as natural ones—3.

CONCEIVED.

L. The Lord could not have set up a church except from a Human *conceived* from Jehovah—20; the Son of God is Jesus *conceived* of Jehovah—21; see 29, 30, and 59.

CONCEPTION. See also CONCEIVED.

L. The Lord came into the world to unite the Human to the Divine which was in Him from *conception*—3 iii.; the Father wherever mentioned means the

Divine which was in the Lord from *conception*—32 (7).

CONCUPISCENCE.

Life. All *concupiscence* for evils should be shunned as sin—62; every *concupiscence* which a man has not shunned remains with him after death—63 (2); to "take up the cross" (*Mark* x. 21) signifies to shun *concupiscences*—66; one removes *concupiscences* by fighting against his evils as sins—ib.; the state of man so long as *concupiscences* block up the interiors of the natural mind, described, and the effect upon him of their being dispersed by the Lord set forth—86 (5); the truth of the Word cannot take root in those who are in the *concupiscences* of evil, but in those in whom these *concupiscences* have been dispersed by the Lord—90; no one can have faith who is in the *concupiscences* of evil, nor can the *concupiscence* for evils be shaken off in any other way than by refusing to will or commit them for the reason that they are sins—91; from inborn *concupiscence* man loves evils and is drawn into them —92; any one who thus fights (against evils as sins) acts from within, and against the *concupiscence* itself which constitutes the root of the evil—94; this combat is not severe except with those who have given free rein to their *concupiscences*—97; the *concupiscences* of evil can be removed by the Lord alone—110; within every *concupiscence* there are infinite things—112.

CONDEMNATION, CONDEMN. See also DAMNED.

L. What was meant by the Lord's *condemnation* by the chief priests and elders—16 (5).

S. "Death" (*Rev.* vi.) signifies eternal *condemnation*—12; heresies do not *condemn* man, but an evil life does—92.

CONFESSION.

L. The life of the whole heaven and the wisdom of all the angels are founded upon the acknowledgment and consequent *confession* of one God—55 (3).

CONFIRM, CONFIRMED.

S. The doctrine of the church to be *confirmed* by the letter of the Word (chap.

v.)—50-61; note especially 54; the effect of *confirming* from the Word the doctrine of a false religion—60; experience in the spiritual world with those who have done this from evil loves—61; (see 94); hurtful to *confirm* heresies from the Word (chap. x.)—91-97; wisdom consists in seeing what is true and not in *confirming* whatever one pleases—91; the hurtfulness of *confirming* falsities—92; this hurtfulness illustrated from nature —95 (2) (3); the reason set forth—96; instances cited of those in ancient time who remain in their false religions because they *confirmed* themselves in them, and of those in the same religion who were able to renounce their falsities because not *confirmed* in them—93.

F. To think a thing true because *confirmed* is to think from authority; what is false can be *confirmed* just as well as what is true—11.

CONJUNCTION, CONJOINED.

S. The Lord is *conjoined* with man through the Word—78; by means of the sense of the letter of the Word there is *conjunction* with the Lord and association with the angels (chap. vi.)—62-69; the reason—62; *conjunction* with the angels shown by experience—64; see also 104.

Life. The *conjunction* of the will and understanding in a man is meant by "heart and soul" in the Word (passages) —86 (6); *conjunction* comes only from loving and being loved in return—102; it is truth *conjoined* with good that causes an angel to be an angel—32.

CONQUERED.

L. The Lord fully *conquered* the hells by the combat that is signified by the passion of the cross—12.

CONQUERS.

L. Why man is drawn out of hell when from the Lord he *conquers* in temptation—33 (2).

CONSONANTS.

S. The angels of the third heaven do not pronounce any *consonants*—90 (2).

CONSUMMATION OF THE AGE.

L. The *consummation of the age* means the last time of the church—26.

CONTAINANT.

S. The sense of the letter of the Word is the *containant* of the spiritual and celestial senses (chap. iii.)—27-36; the human race a *containant* of the heavens—34.

Q. Wisdom is the *containant* of truths —IV.

CONTEMPT.

S. The worshiper of nature, who thence thinks from self, easily falls into *contempt* for the Word—1.

CONTRADICTIONS.

S. There are things in the Word which appear like *contradictions*, though viewed in its own light it contains no *contradiction*—51; illustrations of this given from the Word—ib. (2) (9).

CORRESPONDENCE, CORRESPONDENCES.

S. Degrees cannot be known unless *correspondence* is known, for degrees make one by *correspondences*—7; the Word written exclusively by *correspondences*—8; the Lord spoke exclusively by *correspondences* because He spoke from the Divine that was in Him—17; ib. (3); it has not been hitherto known what *correspondence* is— 20; the *Book of Job* full of *correspondences*—ib. (2); Divine things present themselves in the world by *correspondences*—ib. (3); men of the Most Ancient Church spoke with angels by means of *correspondences*—21; *correspondences* were gathered from that church and transmitted to posterity—ib.; the idolatries of the nations originated from a knowledge of *correspondences* (the reason)—23; see ib. (2) and 26; the knowledge of *correspondences* blotted out among the Israelites and Jews—22; the knowledge of them survived among the Orientals until the Lord's coming—23 (3); why this knowledge was not disclosed in times after those—24; the things of the letter of the Word being *correspondences* are receptacles and abodes of genuine truth —40; no one comes into a knowledge of the spiritual sense of the Word through *correspondences* unless he be first in genuine truths from doctrine—56; see also 91; there was an ancient Word written entirely by *correspondences*—102; hence a knowledge of them existed among the people who used that Word—ib.; but this Word having been falsified and lost, another was written by *correspondences* less remote—ib.

F. All things that appear in the spiritual world are *correspondences* (illustrations given)—63 (2) (3) (4).

COVENANT.

L. The Lord as to the Human called "a *covenant* to the people"—30 (3).

Life. Why the Law (of the Decalogue) was called a *covenant*—57; passages from the Word given—60.

COVERING.

S. Why precious stones were called his "*covering*" (*Ezek.* xxviii.)—45e.

CREATED.

L. All things have been *created* from the Divine love by means of the Divine wisdom—1e.

Q. Adam said to be *created* by God, and is not called the son of God, in *Luke* iii.—VIII.

CREATION.

Q. *Creation* is an attribute of the Divine Esse—VII.

CREED. See ATHANASIAN CREED.

CROSS.

L. The passion of the *cross* was the last combat by which the Lord fully conquered the hells and fully glorified His Human (chap. iii.)—12-14; by the passion of the *cross* He did not take away sins but He bore them—15; by its means the full unition of the Divine and Human in the Lord was effected—34; referred to in 65.

Life. That he should take up his *cross* signified that he should fight against concupiscences—66e; the *cross* means temptation—99.

F. The passion of the *cross* was the uttermost temptation of the Lord—35; the faith of the present day teaches that by the passion of the *cross* the Son made satisfaction for the sins of the world—39.

CROWN.

L. The signification of putting a *crown* of thorns on the Lord—16 (6).

S. A *crown* (*Rev.* vi. 2) signified eternal life, the prize of victory—12; the locusts having *crowns* (*Rev.* ix. 7) signifies that they appeared to themselves as conquerors—13 (2).

F. The signification of the *crown* of twelve stars on the woman described in *Rev.* xii.—59.

CRUCIFIXION.

L. The signification of *crucifying* the Lord—16 (6).

CRUEL.

L. A day *cruel* means the advent of the Lord to judgment—5.

CUNNING.

Life. The evil of theft enters more deeply into a man than other sins because it is conjoined with *cunning*—81; see also 83 and 85.

CURTAINS.

S. The letter of the Word is signified by the *curtains* of the tabernacle—46; 42e.

DAGON.

F. The religion represented by *Dagon*—52.

DAMNATION.

Life. That a man who does not repent and desist from sin is in a state of *damnation* is a common principle in every religion—64.

DAMNED.

Life. All who do not from religion live precepts are *damned*—65.

DARKNESS.

L. A day of *darkness* signifies the advent of the Lord when He was no longer known—5.

DAVID.

L. Why the Lord did not admit that He was the son of *David*—35 (5) (6); why the Lord was meant by *David*—42; evidence that the Lord was called *David* (passages)—43; *David* wrote of the Lord when writing of himself—44.

S. Where in our Word we have *David*, in the Word of the angels there is the kingly office of the Lord—71.

DAY.

L. Passages from the Word adduced in which the expression " that *day*" is used, meaning " the Lord's advent"—4; what is meant by various kinds of *day* mentioned in the Word—5; see also 14 (9).

S. The *day* of Jehovah means the Lord's advent—14 (3).

DAY-SPRING.

L. The *day-spring* from on high signifies the Lord from eternity—30.

DEAD.

Life. The faith of an evil man is a *dead* faith—46.

DEAF.

S. Signification of the *deaf* receiving their hearing—17 (4).

DEATH, DEAD.

L. That the Lord conquered *death*, what it means—12.

S. *Death* (*Rev.* vi. 8) signifies eternal damnation—12 (2); when the *dead* were raised by the Lord it signified that they who otherwise would spiritually perish would become living—17 (4).

Life. After *death* man himself throws off those things which do not accord with his life—27; when what is outward is put off, as is done after *death*, the man who has not shunned evils as sins first casts out truth—45; every concupiscence man has had remains with him after *death*—63 (2); they who live according to the precepts of their religion, are instructed by the angels after *death*, receive truths, and acknowledge the Lord—65; the man who does not shun adulteries as sins, after *death* speaks openly in favor of them—111.

DECALOGUE.

Life. The *decalogue* teaches what evils are sins (chap. vi.)—53–61; why so solemnly proclaimed from Mount Sinai—53; reason of the holiness of these laws—54, 56; evidence of their holiness

—55; why called Covenant and Testimony—57; why they do not command man to do good, but instead command him not to do this or that evil—58; passages confirmatory of these teachings—59-61; why these commandments were called "ten"—61; teaching the *decalogue* to children initiates them into the church—64; all nations which have religion have precepts like those in the *decalogue*—65.

DECEIT.

Life. The evil of theft enters more deeply into a man than any other evil because it is joined with *deceit*—81; see also 83 and 85.

DEFAME.

Life. To *defame* is a form of false witness—87.

DEFRAUD.

Life. To steal also signifies to *defraud*—80.

DEGREES.

S. The Divine in proceeding from the Lord to its ultimates descends through three *degrees*—6; the distinction between these *degrees* can be known only through correspondence—7; with every man there are three *degrees* of life—68; so long as he is in this world man is in the Natural degree—ib.

DEITIES.

S. How the ancients began to worship images as *deities*—23.

DELIGHT.

S. The *delight* of African spirits on hearing a Psalm sung, and its increase as they were introduced into what was spiritual—108.

DESISTING FROM SINS.

Life. A common principle in every religion is that a man should *desist from his sins*—64.

DESTRUCTION.

L. A day of *destruction* means the advent of the Lord when He is no longer known—5.

S To confirm falsities even to the *destruction* of genuine truths is what condemns—92; the reason—96.

DEVIL.

L. The *devil* means hell—13; the Lord could take away sins only after He had deprived the *devil*, that is, hell, of all his power—17; otherwise the *devil* would have plucked the truth out of man's heart—ib.; the *devil*, which is hell—61 (2).

DIABOLISM.

Life. Adultery is so great an evil that it may be called *diabolism* itself—74.

DIADEMS.

S. Precious stones and *diadems* signify Divine truths in their ultimates—44 (4).

DIAMOND.

S. The Word from its spiritual light is like a *diamond*—42.

DISCIPLES.

S. The twelve *disciples* mean the church as to all its goods and truths—51 (7).

DISPERSED.

Life. As soon as concupiscences are *dispersed* by the Lord, what spiritual effects follow—86 (5).

DISTRESS.

L. A day of *distress* means the advent of the Lord to Judgment—5.

DIVIDING THE LORD'S GARMENTS.

L. What is meant by the *dividing of the Lord's garments*—16 (6).

DIVINE.

L. By the Lord from eternity is meant His *Divine* a quo—30e; the Word is *Divine* because written about the Lord—14 (11); the *Divine* and the Human of the Lord cannot be separated—21; see 29 (2); that the Lord made *Divine* the Human from the *Divine* in Himself—29; that in Him the Human and the *Divine* are not two but one—ib.; that the *Divine* in Him operated through the Human as the soul through the body—32 (2); the *Divine* and

Human in Him operated unanimously—ib. (3); the Divine was united to the Human and the Human to the Divine—ib. (4); the whole *Divine* which proceeds from Jehovah God from its first beginnings in heaven to its ultimates in the world has a tendency to the human form—32 (8); the full unition of the *Divine* with the Human in the Lord, how effected—34; the Lord is Jehovah and God both as to the *Divine* and the Human—ib.; that the *Divine* and Human in the Lord are one Person—ib. (3); that the *Divine* could not be tempted—35 (3); the unition between *the Divine* and the Human in Him reciprocal and plenary—ib. (8); the *Divine* called the Father and the *Divine* called the Son are one in the Lord—46; the three *Divines* in the Lord (Father, Son, and Holy Spirit) defined—ib. (2); usual in the Word to name two or three *Divines* which yet are one—(5); that the Lord's *Divine* is the Father in the Trinity of Person—57.

S. No one has known heretofore wherein is the *Divine* of the Word—1; the *Divine* descending from the Lord in the Word comes through three degrees and contains them within it—6; the Word conceals within it *Divine* and all angelic wisdom—8; it was because the Lord spoke from the *Divine* that was within Him that He spoke by correspondences—17 (3).

DIVINE GOOD.

S. Divine good proceeds from the Lord's Divine love, hence the celestial sense of the Word—19; in the celestial sense the things in the Word refer to the *Divine good*—80; the Lord is *Divine good* and Divine truth itself and hence is the Man from whom every man is a man; and all *Divine good* and Divine truth is in its form a man—100.

DIVINE HUMAN.

L. The *Divine Human* is meant in the Word by the Son of God—19; see especially—ib. (9); that the *Divine Human* should have been born of a virgin was essential to the Lord's coming into the world—20; the "Son of God" means the Human which the Lord assumed in the world which was the *Divine Human*—20; the *Divine* and the *Human* in the Lord cannot be separated—21, 29; the Lord made His Human Divine from the Divine in Himself (chap. vii.)—29-36; by the term "the Son," when used alone, is meant the *Divine Human*—30 (4); the *Divine Human* is to be approached (the reason)—32 (5); the *Divine Human* is meant by the Holy One of Israel—40; the *Divine Human* is called the Son—46 (2); that in the Trinity the Lord's *Divine Human* is called the Son—57; the Divine put on from the Father in the place of the human from Mary put off, is the *Divine Human*—59.

S. The power to save man the Lord took upon Himself even to His *Divine Human*—49.

Q. (Answering the Question as to whether the *Divine Human* was a Person before the incarnation, and if so whether it was not then different from what it was afterwards)—There was no *Divine Human* before the incarnation except a representative one—VI; the *Divine Human* is one of the essentials of the Divine Trinity—VII.

DIVINE NATURAL.

S. The men of the church on earth are in the *Divine Natural*—6; since His coming into the world the Lord is immediately present in His *Divine Natural* which He put on in the world—99.

DIVINE PROCEEDING.

L. The Lord's *Divine Proceeding* is the Holy Spirit—46; is the Holy Spirit in the Trinity—57.

DIVINE TRUTH.

L. The Word is the *Divine truth* itself—2; the *Divine truth* from the Lord is the Holy Spirit—51 (4).

S. The Holy Scripture, or Word, is the *Divine Truth* itself—1; *Divine truth* is in its fullness in the sense of the letter of the Word (chap. iv.)—37-49; those who are in *Divine truths* see *Divine truths* in natural light while reading the Word—41; the *Divine truth* which must be of doctrine appears to none but those who are in enlightenment from the Lord—50,

57; the Lord is His own *Divine truth*, and when this is loved, the Lord is in it with the man—57; conjunction of the Lord and man through the letter of the Word is in the man's love for and faith in *Divine truth*—62; the Lord is the *Divine truth* itself—78; the spiritual sense of the Word refers to *Divine truth*—80; the Lord came into the world to become *Divine truth* in ultimates (chap. xi.)—98-100; before the Lord's advent *Divine truth* was seen in shade, after it in light —99; as the Lord is Divine good and *Divine truth* itself and hence is a Man, all Divine good and *Divine truth* is in form a man—100; the *Divine truth* which proceeds from the Lord as a sun is the light in the heavens—106.

DIVINE WISDOM.

S. That is called spiritual which proceeds from His *Divine wisdom*—6; the light of heaven is *Divine wisdom* which to the eyes of the angels is light—73.

DIVINITY.

L. When the Lord's *Divinity* is treated of He calls Himself "the Son" and "the Son of God"—22; the early Christians discriminated the Lord into three Persons (why this was permitted)—55 (2).

S. The internal sense of the Word bears witness to its *Divinity* so that even the natural man will be convinced if he is willing—4; by committing adultery a celestial angel understands denying the Lord's *Divinity*—67 (3); the *Divinity* of the Word comes from the marriage of good and truth in it—81.

Q. The Lord was manifested before His incarnation by an angel whom He filled with His *Divinity*—II.

DOCTRINE.

L. Why Jerusalem means the church as to *doctrine*—64; in the church now to be set up by the Lord the *doctrine* will be new—65; by the "Holy City Jerusalem" is meant the New Church as to *doctrine*—63.

S. The wall of the Holy Jerusalem and its foundations signify *doctrine* from the literal sense of the Word—10e; see also 43; the spiritual sense of the Word has been at this day disclosed because the *doctrine* of genuine truth has now been revealed—25; the *doctrine* of the church is to be drawn from the sense of the letter of the Word (chap. v.)—50-61; the Word cannot be understood without *doctrine*—51; illustrated from examples taken from the Word—ib. (2) to (8); those who read the Word without *doctrine* are in obscurity—52; it must be drawn from the sense of the letter of the Word—53; by means of *doctrine* the Word shines with light—54; why *doctrine* can be drawn in full from this source—55; cannot be procured by means of the spiritual sense furnished through a knowledge of correspondences—56; the genuine truth of *doctrine* appears in the sense of the letter to those only who are in enlightenment —57; the first duty of those in enlightenment is to get for themselves *doctrine* from the sense of the letter of the Word —59; truth is in the shade of night with those who read the Word from the *doctrine* of a false religion—60; any *doctrine* of worship which is hatched solely from rational light will be that man's self is to be worshiped—116.

DOGMA.

F. The angels discard the *dogma* that the understanding must be kept in obedience to faith—4; with the Reformed also, ignorance is the safeguard of *dogma* —9.

DOOR.

S. A *door* (*Matt.* xxv.) signifies entrance into heaven—17 (3).

DOVE.

L. What a *dove* represents—51 (4).

DRAGON, DRAGONISTS.

F. The *dragon* in the Revelation means those who are in faith separate from charity (chap. viii.)—55-60; illustrations from experiences in the spiritual world—56; exposition of the references to the *dragon* in *Rev.* xii.—57-59.

DRAWN.

S. The doctrine of the church is to be *drawn* from the sense of the letter of the Word—50; how the spiritual angels *draw* out their sense, and the celestial angels theirs, from the sense of the letter of the Word—67.

DRINK.

S. To "*drink* the blood of the sacrifice" signifies to appropriate to one's self Divine truth from the Word—15e.

E.

S. In the third heaven they cannot utter the vowel "*e*" (pronounced like "a" in baby), but instead of it they utter "eu"—90 (2).

EARTH.

L. What is meant in the Word by a new *earth*—62, 65. See also NEW EARTH.

EDEN.

S. The precious stones in *Eden* (mentioned in *Ezekiel* xxvii.) mean the truths of the sense of the letter of the Word—45.

EDOM

S. *Edom* signifies the natural—18 (3).

EFFECT.

S. The last of the three essentials in every Divine work may be called the *effect*—28.

EFFICACY.

Q. The representative Human before the incarnation was not of such *efficacy* as to be able spiritually to enlighten men—VI.

EGYPT.

S. *Egypt* signifies memory-knowledge—18 (3).

Life. *Egypt* signifies memory-knowledge—79 (2).

ELECT.

S. What is meant by gathering together the *elect* from the four winds (*Matt.* xxiv.)—14 (2).

ELIJAH.

S. Where in our Word we have *Elijah*, in the Word of the angels there is "the prophetical Word"—71.

EMPTYING OUT. See HUMILIATION.

END.

S. The first of the three essentials in every Divine work may be called the *end*—28.

ENEMIES.

L. The Lord's *enemies* when mentioned in the Word, mean the hells—14 (8).

ENGLISH CLERGY.

Life. The state of the *English clergy* when reading the Exhortation before the Holy Supper—7.

ENLIGHTENMENT, ENLIGHTEN.

S. Genuine truth appears in the sense of the letter of the Word to those only who are in *enlightenment* from the Lord—57; if those who search the Word love truths because they are truths, and make use of them for life, they are in *enlightenment* from the Lord—59.

F. What *enlightenment* is—5.

Q. The representative Human made use of before the incarnation could not *enlighten* men—VI.

ENMITY.

Life. Murder lies deeply hidden in *enmity*—67.

ENOCH.

S. That *Enoch* collected correspondences and transmitted the knowledge of them—21.

ENUNCIATIONS.

S. The prophetical part of an ancient Word called *Enunciations* (entire number)—103.

EPHRAIM.

S. The understanding of the Word both true and false is described by *Ephraim*—79 (2) (3) (6) (7) and (with confirmatory references) (8).

ERROR.

S. A man who worships nature and thinks from himself may easily fall into *error* in respect to the Word—1.

ESSE.

Q. By "*Esse*" is meant the inmost of the Divine Trinity; its functions set forth—VII.

ESSENCE.

L. The Lord's human *essence* is just as is His Divine *essence*—35 (11) ; God is one in *essence*—54, 55 (2) (6), and 65.

S. In its *essence* the Word is both Divine love and Divine wisdom—3 ; in its *essence* the internal sense of the Word is spiritual—4.

Life. Spiritual good has the *essence* of good within it, and it is from spiritual good that moral and civic good, when really good, have this *essence*—13.

F. In its *essence* faith is charity—22.

Q. The Divine *essence* transcends both the angelic and the human rational—II. ; soul, body, and proceeding in the Divine Trinity constitute one *essence*—III. ; Divine wisdom together with Divine love constitute one *essence*—IV. ; in its *essence* the heat of the sun of the angelic heaven is love and its light wisdom—V. See also SUBSTANCE.

ETERNITY.

L. That the Lord is God from *eternity* —1 ; there was no Son born from *eternity* —19.

Q. The Lord was Divine love from *eternity*—II.

EU.

S. The sound of " *eu*" is pronounced by the celestial angels instead of the sound of " e"—90 (2).

EVANGELISTS.

L. The *Evangelists* treat but little of the Lord's combats—33 (4) ; why in the Word of the *Evangelists* the Lord is called Lord, God, Messiah, or Christ, and the Son of God—35 (2).

EVENING.

F. *Evening* means the end of the church when there will be a new one —66.

EVIL, EVILS.

S. The "pale horse" (*Rev.* vi.) signifies the understanding of the Word annihilated by *evils* of life—12 (2) ; the power of Divine truth is directed especially against falsities and *evils*, thus against hell—49.

Life. In proportion as a man shuns *evils* as sins he does goods (chap. iii.)— 18-31 ; it is in this proportion only that he loves truths (chap. iv.)—32-41 ; in this proportion only does he have faith and is spiritual (chap. iv.)—42-52 ; a man cannot be in both *evils* and goods at the same time—28 ; confirmatory passages from the Word—30 ; see also 41 ; the decalogue teaches what *evils* are sins—53 ; why *evils* are forbidden and goods are not commanded—58 ; murders, adulteries, thefts, and false witness, together with all concupiscence for these things, are the *evils* which must be shunned as sins (chap. vii.)—62-66 ; as *evil* and good are two opposite things . . . it follows that if a man shuns *evil* as sin, he comes into the good that is opposite to the *evil*—70 ; *evil* removed by means of good—71 ; the *evil* of theft enters more deeply into a man than any other *evil* because it is joined with cunning and deceit—81 ; no one can shun *evils* as sins so as to be inwardly averse to them except by combats against them (chap. xii.)—92-100 ; a man ought to shun *evils* as sins and to fight against them as of himself (chap. xiii.)—101-107 ; if any one shuns *evils* for any other reason than because they are sins, he does not shun them, but merely prevents them from appearing before the world (chap. xiv.)—108-113 ; the concupiscences for *evil* can be removed by the Lord alone—110 ; see also 112, 113 ; an ungodly man can shun *evils* as injurious, but only a Christian can shun them as sins— 111 ; unless a man shuns *evils* as sins he cannot be in the spiritual mind, and consequently as to his will—86 (2) ; so long as a man does not shun *evils* as sins, the concupiscences of *evil* block up the interiors of the natural mind . . . but the moment a man shuns *evils* as sins, the Lord inflows from heaven—ib. (5).

F. Shun *evils* as sins, and come to the Lord, and you will have as much faith as you desire—12 ; in proportion as any one shuns *evils* as sins, and looks to the Lord, he is in charity—23 ; the faith of charity cannot be formed except in proportion as a man shuns *evils* as sins—27 · *evil* of life inwardly hates truths—30.

EXALTED.

L. The day in which Jehovah shall be *exalted* means the advent of the Lord to establish a new church—5.

EXAMINE.

Life. That a man ought to *examine* himself—64.

EXHORTATION.

Life. The *Exhortation* read in England before the people who approach the Sacrament of the Supper (given in full)—5; the same in Latin—6; discussion with the English clergy in the spiritual world concerning their ideas when reading this *Exhortation*—7.

EXTERNAL SENSE. See Senses of the Word.

S. The *external sense* of the Word is as a body to its internal sense—4.

EXTINCTION.

Life. An evil life cannot be converted into a good life (nor the opposite) because conversion into what is opposite is *extinction*—8.

EZEKIEL.

L. Various things *Ezekiel* was commanded to do in order to represent the church—15 (5) (7); see also 16 and ib. (2); passages in the Word referred to in which *Ezekiel* is called the son of man—28.

S. Various things *Ezekiel* was commanded to do in order to represent the state of the church—16; things done by *Ezekiel* to represent the violence done by the Jews to the letter of the Word—35.

FABULOUS STORIES.

S. The *fabulous stories* of the highest antiquity were nothing but correspondences—20 (2)'; the science of correspondences, cultivated in many kingdoms of Asia, when carried to the sea-coast was there turned into *fabulous stories*—21.

FACE.

S. His "*face* that did shine as the sun" (at the transfiguration) signified the Lord's Divine good—48; the Word is like a man clothed whose *face* and hands are bare—55.

FACULTIES.

S. With every man there are two *faculties* of life, understanding and will—83.

Life. With every man there are two *faculties*, the will and the understanding (description of their relationships)—43; these two *faculties*, Freedom and Reason, are not proper to man, but are the Lord's in him—101.

FAITH.

L. There is a *faith* of God, and there is a *faith* of man (their differences)—18 (3); we must put our *faith* in the Lord who is both Father and Son—32 (6).

S. They who are in the *faith* that the Word in its bosom is divine holiness see Divine truths in natural light while reading the Word—41; the acknowledgment which is called *faith*, how produced—58.

Life. Christian churches teach that *faith* alone saves—their inconsistency—4; man has *faith* in proportion to his shunning evils as sins (chap. v.)—42-52; a dead *faith* and a living *faith* described and distinguished—46, 47; those in evils have no *faith* (shown by experiences in the spiritual world)—49; what spiritual *faith* is and what is *faith* not spiritual—50; passages from the Word confirming these doctrines concerning *faith*—51; no one has a grain of *faith* more than he has of life—52.

F. *Faith* is an internal acknowledgment of truth (chap. i.)—1-2; what the term *faith* means in present-day thought—1; real *faith* is an acknowledgment that a thing is so because it is true—2; this internal acknowledgment of truth is from a spiritual affection—4; *faith* and truth are the same—6; why the term *faith* was used by the Lord in the Gospels and *Revelation*—7; how *faith* and truth came to be separated in the church—8; why a blind *faith* survived later with the Reformed—9; shun evils as sins and come to the Lord and you will have as much of *faith* as you desire—12; *faith* exists only with those who are in charity (chap. ii.)—13-24; brought forth from charity as a means through which charity may come into manifest being—17; charity and *faith* related to each other like affection and thought—18; compared to the relation of the heart and the lungs—19; in its essence *faith* is charity—22; hence *faith* is impossible except to those in charity—24; knowledges of truth a storehouse out of which *faith* may be formed (chap. iii.)—25-33; the necessity of this storehouse of material—28; but these knowledges must be genuine, not knowledges of what is false—29; many who have regard to the Lord in their life, may have the *faith* of charity though they have no inward acknowledgment of truth—30; the formation of *faith* from charity described—32; the Christian *faith* in its universal idea or form (chap. iv.)—34-37; the *Faith* of the present day in its universal idea or form (chap. v.)—38-43; the various things which the present-day *faith* maintains, adduced—39; conversation between an angel and many of the Reformed; with one who was in *faith* separate from charity, and then with one who was in a *faith* united to charity—showing the difference between a *faith* from charity and *faith* separated from charity—41-43; the nature of a *faith* that is separated from charity, shown in its nakedness (chap. vi.)—44-48; those in *faith* separated from charity represented by the Philistines (chap. vii.)—49-54; by the dragon in *Revelation* (chap. viii.)—55-60; by the goats in *Daniel* and in *Matthew* (chap. ix.)—61-68; *faith* separated from charity destroys the church and all things that belong to it (chap. x.)—69-72.

FAITH ALONE. See also FAITH.

Life. Many in the Christian church teach that *faith alone* saves—error of this teaching—4.

F. It is those who have confirmed themselves by both doctrine and life in *faith alone* that are meant, and not those who, although believing that *faith alone* saves, have shunned evils as sins—72.

FALSE.

Life. To declare some *false* thing true, or some evil thing good, is spiritual *false* witness—87.

F. Knowledges of what is *false* do not constitute faith, but its opposite—29.

FALSE WITNESS.

S. The command against *false witness* as interpreted, first by a man; secondly by a spiritual angel, and thirdly by a celestial angel—67 (5).

Life. In proportion as any one shuns *false witness* of every kind as sin, in the same proportion he loves the truth (chap. xi.)—87-91; the various degrees and kinds of *false witness* described—87.

FALSIFICATION.

S. The harlot with the dead horse (in a memorable relation) signified the *falsification* of the Word—26 (5).

FALSITY.

S. Concerning those who are in *falsities* from ignorance—15 (2); those who are not enlightened by the Lord but by themselves see *falsities* by the light of *falsities*—91; appearances of truth in the Word when confirmed become *falsities*—92; those who have confirmed themselves in the *falsities* of their religion remain steadfast in them in the spiritual world—93; especially if self-love, or the pride of their own understanding have led to the confirmation—92.

Life. Evil loves *falsity* and *falsity* loves evil—33.

F. Charity cannot come forth into being where there are nothing but *falsities*—29; as *falsity* is the opposite of truth, it destroys faith—29; those who are in *falsities* see no otherwise than that *falsities* are truths—71.

FATHER.

L. By the Lord's being sent by the *Father* into the world is meant that He was conceived from Jehovah the *Father* —20; in the state of glorification the Lord was in the Human from the *Father* —35 (3); in the state of humiliation He prayed to the *Father*—ib.; the Divine itself is called the *Father;* why it cannot be approached directly—32 (5); the Lord is both *Father* and Son—ib. (6); where the word *Father* is mentioned in the Word, the Divine of the Lord from conception is meant—ib. (7) ; the Lord's Divine is called the *Father*—34 (3) ; see also 46 (2).

S. The command that we shall honor *father* and mother, how interpreted, first by a man, secondly by a spiritual angel, and thirdly by a celestial angel—67.

F. The relation of God the *Father* to the Son, as held at the present day, set forth—39.

FIDELITY.

Life. See SINCERITY—83.

FIGURES.

Q. The enlightenment of men before the incarnation was effected solely by means of types and *figures*—VI.

FILTHY.

Life. To "commit adultery" means in the natural sense, not only to commit whoredom, but to think about *filthy* things—74.

FINITE.

Q. In man the trinity is *finite*—III.

FIRE.

L. What it means to be baptized with *fire*—51 (4).

S. The sun is an ocean of *fire*—95 (2) ; *fire* signifies good, and flame truth—84 (2).

Life. What infernal *fire* is—67.

FIRST.

L. In the beginning God was a Man in *first* principles but not in ultimates—36 ; why called "the *First* and the Last" —ib.

S. In every Divine work there is a *first*, a middle, and a last—27. See DE-GREES.

FIRST-FRUITS.

Life. The laws of the decalogue were the *first-fruits* of the Word—54 ; their holiness thence—ib.

FISH.

S. A *fish* signifies knowledge—23 (2).

FIVE.

S. *Five* signifies some—17 (3).

FLAME.

S. From its celestial sense our Word is like a *flame* that enkindles—42 ; fire signifies good, and *flame* truth—84 (2).

FLESH.

S. To become *flesh* is to become the Word in ultimates—98.

Q. It is asked whether the Lord's human sonship had regard solely to the human *flesh*—I.

FOLLOW.

Life. To "*follow* the Lord" means to acknowledge Him as God—66.

FOOD.

Life. The relation of *food* to water used to illustrate the relation of goodness to truth—40.

FOOTSTOOL.

L. Signification of making His enemies His *footstool*—14 (8).

FOREST.

S. A *forest* means knowledge—18 (3).

FORM.

Q. The question is asked whether the Divine Human of Jehovah was before the incarnation a Person subsisting as the *Form* of God—VI.

FOUNDATION.

S. The *foundations* of the wall of the New Jerusalem mean the truths of the sense of the letter of the Word—43.

FRANKINCENSE.

S. The *frankincense* offered the Lord by the wise men signified spiritual good —23 (3).

FRAUD.

Life. Theft is also *fraud*, and *fraud* and sincerity are two opposites—82.

FREEDOM.

Life. How man is kept in *freedom* by the Lord—19-20 ; *freedom* and reason are the Lord's in man, man must act from *freedom* according to reason—101 ; why these are given by the Lord—102.

FRIENDSHIP.

Life. The part of external *friendship* in the regeneration of man—69.

F. Should be distinguished from charity—21.

FRUIT.

Life. *Fruit* means what is good (spiritually)—17; *fruit* (in a tree compared to a man) signifies the good of love—46.

F. Faith does not bring forth good, or use, as a tree does its *fruit*, from itself, but from charity—17.

FULFILL.

L. Meaning of the saying that the Lord *fulfilled* all things of the Law—8.

S. That the Lord came into the world to *fulfill* all things of the Word (chap. xi.)—98–100.

FULLNESS.

S. Everything Divine is in its *fullness* when it is in its ultimate degree—6; divine truth in the sense of the letter of the Word is in its *fullness* (chap. iv.)—37–49; see 53; 97 (3).

GARDEN.

S. A *garden* means wisdom—18 (3); *Gardens* and groves signify wisdom and intelligence 23 (2); the Word is like a *garden*—96a.

Life. Man compared to a *garden*—86 (3).

GARMENTS.

L. Dividing the Lord's *garments* at the crucifixion—its meaning—16 (5).

S. The *garments* of the priesthood or of holiness represented Divine truth from Divine good—44; the Lord's *garments* at the transfiguration represented the Divine truth—48; stripping persons of their *garments* (in the spiritual world) is a sign that they are devoid of truths—52; for in that world *garments* are truths—ib.

GATES.

S. The word in its ultimate or natural sense is signified by the *gates* (of the New Jerusalem)—36.

GENESIS.

S. The first seven chapters of *Genesis* appear in the Ancient Word—103 (3).

GENTILES.

S. Why the *Gentiles* are meant by Lazarus—40 (4).

GENUINE.

F. The knowledges of only *genuine* truth and good constitute faith—29.

GENUINE TRUTH.

S. The doctrine of *genuine truth* has now been revealed—25; the *genuine truth* appears in the sense of the letter to none but those who are in enlightenment from the Lord—57.

GENUINE TRUTHS.

S. Apparent truths of the sense of the letter have *genuine truths* concealed within them—95; illustrated by the appearance that the sun moves when in reality it stands still—ib. (3).

GETHSEMANE.

L. What the Lord suffered in *Gethsemane*, and on the cross, the last of His temptations—12.

GLADNESS.

S. *Gladness* mentioned in connection with joy (the reason; passages adduced) —87; *gladness* is predicated of truth—84.

GLOOM.

L. Day of *gloom* means the advent of the Lord when He was no longer known —5.

GLORIFICATION, GLORIFY.

L. The Lord came into the world to *glorify* His human—3, 12; what is meant by the Lord's *glorification*—13; His state of *glorification* in its relation to His humiliation described—35 (3); the *glorification* of His Human shown by passages from the Evangelists—ib. (7); that the Lord rose on the third day signified His *glorification*—16 (6); after His *glorification* the Lord was Divine wisdom and Divine truth itself—51 (3).

S. The *glorification* of the Lord is the *glorification* of His Human that He assumed in the world—99.

F. The Lord came into the world to *glorify* His human, without which no mortal could have been saved—34; see also 35.

GLORY.

L. Why the Lord is called King of *Glory*—14 (9); to "give *glory*" means to glorify, or to unite to Himself—30 (3).

S. The Word in its *glory* represented by the Lord at the transfiguration—48.

GOATS.

F. Those who are in faith separate from charity are meant by the *goats* in *Daniel*, and in *Matthew* (chap. ix.)—61-68. See also HE-GOAT.

GOD

L. *God* was the Word—1; who are meant by the sons of *God*—18 (5); the Lord is *God* and Man—21; by incarnation *God* became Man, as in first principles so also in ultimates—36; that the Lord is called *God* of Israel and *God* of Jacob (passages quoted)—39; the Lord is called *God*—41; *God* is one, and the Lord is that *God* (passages) (chap. ix.)—45; *God* is one in Person and in Essence, and the Lord is that *God*—54; that this is clear from many things said by the Lord Himself—60; see also 65; the first thing taught every man after death who looks to *God*—46 (4); the reason Christians have acknowledged three Divine Persons and thus three *Gods*—55; those who in simplicity believe in three Persons in *God* are taught that *God* is one, for no one is admitted into heaven who thinks three *Gods*—ib. (3); if there is one *God* He must be one in Person and in Essence—ib. (6).

S. When men began to worship *God* in three Persons heavenly truths were hid from them—24; why Jehovah and *God* are mentioned in the Word as two when they are only one—88; the knowledge of *God* could come to man only through the Word—114, 115; certain peoples in the other world who in this have known nothing about *God* (described)—116; man's spiritual life is by means of a knowledge of *God* as a Man—ib.; the knowledge of *God* in most ancient times came from an ancient Word—117.

Life. Good that is really good can be done only from *God*—9; what is meant by its being said. "Egypt is man and not *God*" (*Isa.* xxxi. 3)—30 (2).

F. That *God* is One is a universal of faith—35.

Q. (In answer to the question as to whether the Spirit of *God* in the Old Testament were not the same as the Holy Spirit of the New)—The Spirit of *God* and the Holy Spirit are two distinct things—V.; the Spirit of *God* neither did nor could operate on man except imperceptibly—ib.; Adam not said in *Luke* to be a "son of *God*," but simply "of *God*," that is, created by Him—VIII.

GODS.

Q. Regarding the Trinity as three Persons would of necessity make three *Gods*—VII.

GO FORTH.

L. To *go forth* when applied to God signifies nothing other than to enlighten and teach by His presence—46 (4).

GOG.

S. *Gog* means external worship without the internal—18 (3).

GOLD.

S. The gift of *gold* offered by the wise men means celestial good—23 (3); the Israelites unwilling to learn that the arcana of the Word refer to the Lord, but quite willing to learn their reference to *gold*—23 (4).

Life. Goods from God and goods from self compared to *gold* that is pure and that which appears like *gold* but is not—10.

GOOD, GOODS.

S. Some of the words and names of the Word are predicated of *good* and some of truth, and some include both—80; in the Word there frequently occur two expressions, one of which refers to *good* and the other to truth—81; truths admit of what is hard, but not *good*—90; every man is his own *good* from which he is a man, for *good* and truth that proceeds from the Lord is in its form a man

—100; when the man of the church is in truths, the Lord inflows into his truths with *good*—82; expressions in the Word referring to *good* in contrast with those referring to truth—84.

Life. The life of religion is to do that which is *good*—1; no one from himself can do *good* that is really *good* (chap. ii.) —9-17; degrees of *good* illustrated by various alloys of gold, graded down into a composition of metal which has no gold in it—10; how to know whether the *good* one does is from God or not from God, must be revealed—11; various kinds of *good*, civil, moral, and spiritual, described and illustrated—12, 13; the interrelations of these kinds of *good*—14; why a man can think truth before he can will *good*—15; that man cannot from himself do *good*, taught in the Word (passages cited)—17; in proportion as a man shuns evils as sins in the same proportion he does *goods*, not from himself but from the Lord (chap. iii.)—18-31; if a man wills and does *goods* before he shuns evils as sins, the *goods* are not *good*—24; demonstrated from passages from the Word—28-30; the doctrine that no one can from himself do *good* which is really *good* must not be abused—31; the relation between *good* and truth—33-36; *good* exists only in truth, hence its love for truth—37; *good* comes into existence by means of truth, illustrated by various professions in this world—39; *good* lives in man's will as its receptacle, and is the being (*esse*) of truth—43; no man has a grain of truth more than he has of *good*—52; why man is not commanded in the decalogue to do *good*—58; when a man is in the *good* of love, all that he does is *good* —72; shown from the Word (passages adduced)—73; to deprive one of his *goods* of charity is spiritually to steal—80; with men who shun evils merely because they are evils and not at the same time because they are sins, the *goods* they do are not real *goods*—108; as evil and *good* are two opposites, it follows that if a man shuns evil as a sin he comes into the *good* that is opposite—70.

F. *Good* is nothing but Use—14; *Good* of life inwardly loves truths—30.

GOOD OF LOVE.

S. Wherever there is the *good of love* there resides also wisdom—74; when a man forms his understanding by genuine truths and also has his will infilled with the *good of love* from the Lord, he has therefrom a life of truth and a life of good—83.

GOSPEL OF THE KINGDOM.

L. The Lord's advent called the *Gospel of the kingdom*, passages adduced showing why—42.

GOSPELS.

S. That the Lord, who is the same as Jehovah, spoke the Word which is in the *Gospels*—2.

GRAIN.

Life. No man has a *grain* more of truth than he has of good, nor a *grain* of faith more than he has of life—52.

GREECE.

S. The science of correspondences was carried over from places on the sea-coast of Asia into *Greece*—21; the things of religion spread from the maritime parts of Asia into *Greece*—117.

F. The king of *Greece* (*Dan.* viii.) means the same as the he-goat—66.

GROVE.

S. A *grove* means intelligence—18 (3).

GUARD, GUARDS.

S. *Guards* have been set by the Lord to prevent anybody from entering into the spiritual sense of the Word who will pervert its genuine truths—26 (2); a vision illustrating how *guards* are placed over the spiritual sense—ib. (3); the explanation of this vision—ib. (4); the literal sense of the Word is a *guard* to its genuine truths; how it operates— 97.

GUARD.

S. How the spiritual sense is *guarded* by the Lord—56e; the literal sense of the Word is a *guard* to the genuine truths which lie hidden within (the reason, and how it is accomplished)—97.

H.

S. Why the letter "*h*" was added to the names of Abram and Sarai—90.

HAIR.

L. The prophets represented the Word in its ultimate sense by a garment of *hair* —15 (8).

S. Hair signifies the ultimate of truth —35 (2) ; why the Nazirites let their *hair* grow—ib. (3) ; illustrated from effects of despising the Word in the spiritual world —ib. (4) ; *hair* of the head signifies heavenly wisdom and Divine truth in ultimate things—49 (3) ; why the Son of man (*Rev.* i.), and the Ancient of days (*Dan.* vii.) are described as to their *hair* —ib. (5).

HARLOT.

S. The *harlot* with a dead horse (in a memorable relation) signified the falsification of the Word—26 (5).

Life. The faith of an evil man compared to a good-looking *harlot* dressed up in crimson and gold—46.

F. Meaning of the *harlot* described in the *Revelation* as sitting on the scarlet beast—55.

HATES, HATRED.

Life. Evil inwardly *hates* truth, however an evil man may seem to love it— 45 ; murder lies hidden in *hatred*—67 ; "to be reconciled to one's brother" is to shun enmity, *hatred*, and revenge as sins —73.

HEAD.

S. The *head* (of the prophet Ezekiel ; *Ezek.* v. 1) signifies wisdom from the Word—35 (2) ; the *head* signifies the heavenly wisdom which angels and men have from the Lord—49 (3).

HEART.

L. The *heart* is one of man's two fountains of life—47 ; the life from the *heart's* motion acts as one with his will's love —ib.

S. In each society of heaven those in the center correspond to the *heart* and lungs, and are in the greatest light—107 ; the *heart* and lungs of the universal

heaven (which before the Lord is as one man) is the church, where the Word is read and the Lord is known—105.

Life. A dead faith is like the breathing of the lungs without there being any life or soul in it from the *heart*—46 ; the will corresponds to the *heart*—ib. ; the *heart* in the Word means man's will—51 ; the conjunction of a man's will and understanding is meant in the Word by the coupling of the two words "*heart*" and "soul," also of the words "*heart*" and "spirit"—86 (6).

F. Charity and faith compared to the *heart* and lungs—19 ; in the spiritual world the beating of one's *heart* shows the state of his charity—ib.

HEAT.

S. Heat from the sun of this world compared to the *heat* from the sun of heaven, which is the Lord—109.

Life. The will of man cannot be elevated into the *heat* of heaven which is love, and act from it as the understanding can into the light of heaven—15 ; man compared to a garden and his will to *heat*—86 (3) ; spiritual *heat* is Divine love—ib.

F. Spiritual *heat* from heaven flows into man as he shuns evils as sins—32.

Q. Heat proceeds from the sun of the angelic heaven as does *heat* from the sun of the natural world—V. ; in its essence the *heat* of the sun of the angelic heaven is love—ib.

HEAVEN.

L. At the Lord's coming He reduced *heaven* into order so that it made a one with the church—3 ; why a man is elevated into *heaven* when he conquers in temptations—33 (2) ; no one is admitted into *heaven* who thinks of three Gods— 55 (3) ; no one admitted into *heaven* who does not acknowledge the Lord alone— 61 ; what is meant by the new *heaven* in *Rev.* xxi.—62, 65.

S. Communication with the *heavens* given by means of the spiritual sense of the Word—5 ; the *heavens* dependent upon the human race as their basis, containant, and support—34 ; light from *heaven* flows into the intellectual of those who are in Divine truths and causes them to recognize Divine truths in the Word—41; the Word is in all the *heavens* (chap. vii.)—70-75; light in the *heavens* from the Divine truth from the Word—106, 107; every verse of the Word communicates with a particular society in *heaven*—113; a knowledge of the existence of *heaven* given only by means of the Word—114, 115; the spiritual sense of the Word is guarded by the Lord as *heaven* is guarded, for *heaven* is in it—56; concerning the writing of the Word in the *heavens*—90; it is hurtful to confirm the apparent truth of the Word to the destruction of its genuine truth, because each and all things of the sense of the letter of the Word communicate with *heaven*—96; the ancient Word is used in the *heaven* where the people who used that Word dwell—102; there can be no conjunction with *heaven* unless there be somewhere on earth a church where the Word is—104.

Life. Man's relation to *heaven* while he dwells on earth, set forth—19; no one can be in both *heaven* and hell at the same time—18, 28; the spiritual mind is the mind of man's *heaven*—86; as soon as a man's concupiscences of evils are dispersed by the Lord, the man is in *heaven* —ib. (5).

Q. By means of influx into the angelic *heaven* the Lord had a Divine Rational before the assumption of the Human— II.

HEBREW.

S. The letters of the Word with the angels of the celestial kingdom resemble the ancient *Hebrew* letters—71; a piece of paper marked with *Hebrew* letters sent down from heaven—90; why certain *Hebrew* letters have a dot in the center—ib. (2).

HE-GOAT.

F. Signification of the combat between the ram and the *he-goat* in *Daniel* —65.

HELL, HELLS.

L. Unless the *hells* had been subjugated no man could have been saved— 3; the Lord judges no one to *hell*—25;

man is unaware that evil spirits from *hell* induce spiritual temptations—33; the man is elevated into heaven when he conquers—ib.(2); the Lord fought against and conquered *hell*—ib. (2); to what a height the *hells* had grown up before the Lord's advent—ib. (3); before the Last Judgment the power of *hell* prevailed over the power of heaven . . . but this power was broken by the Last Judgment —61 (2).

S. No one could have known of the existence of *hell* unless there had been a Word—114; what man is of himself, evident from the character of those who are in *hell*—116.

Life. Evil is the same as *hell*—18; in this world man is kept midway between heaven and *hell* (the reason)—19; man cannot at the same time be in both heaven and *hell*—28; so long as concupiscences of evils block up the interiors of the natural mind, the man is in *hell*—86 (5).

F. The Lord came into the world to subdue the *hells*—34; the Lord came into the world to remove *hell* from man, which He accomplished by combats against it —35.

HEMORRHOIDS.

F. The *hemorrhoids* of the Philistines mean filthy loves—52.

HERESIES.

S. It is possible for *heresies* to be drawn from the sense of the letter of the Word, but it is hurtful to confirm them (chap. x.)—91-97; *heresies* do not condemn, but an evil life does—92; those who read the Word without doctrine are pliant to *heresies*—52; why it is hurtful to confirm any *heretical* doctrine—96.

HERO.

L. Why the Lord is called *Hero*—14 (9).

HIDDEN.

S. The nature of the wisdom that lies *hidden* in the Word—75.

Life. When a man thinks and speaks pious things without shunning evils as sins, the evils are within deeply *hidden* out of his sight—25.

HIEROGLYPHICS.

S. The *hieroglyphics* of the Egyptians were nothing but correspondences—20 (2).

HILLS.

S. *Hills* mean the lower, mountains the higher, and valleys the lowest things of the church—18 (3); a *hill* signifies a heaven under the highest—23 (2).

HIMSELF.

Life. Man must fight against evils as of *himself*, or he does not fight at all—96; a man ought to shun evils and to fight against them as of *himself* (chap. xiii.)—101-107.

HINDS.

S. The *hinds* which the voice of Jehovah causeth to be in travail, mean the nations who are in natural good—18 (5).

HOLINESS.

L. The one only source of *holiness* in the Word is that it was written about the Lord—17.

S. There is *holiness* in every sentence and in every word, and in some places in even the very letters of the Word—3; the *holiness* of the Word witnessed by the internal sense—4; in order that it may be known wherein the *holiness* of the Word consists, the spiritual sense has now been revealed—18; illustrations of how the spiritual sense makes the inspiration and *holiness* of the Word—ib. (2) (3); Divine truth is in its *holiness* in the sense of the letter of the Word—37; how this is shown—38 (2); they who are in the faith that the Word is Divine *holiness* within, may see Divine truths in the letter of the Word when reading it—41; *holiness* of the Word from the marriage of each and every thing of it—81; *holiness* of the Word illustrated by the memorable relation about a piece of paper with Hebrew characters on it sent down from heaven—90.

HOLY.

L. What is meant by "the *Holy* One of Israel"—40.

S. What was signified by "the *Holy* of Holies"—46; the Word is *holy* in every word from its spiritual sense—18.

Life. Evidences brought forward to show that the laws promulgated from Sinai were most *holy*—55; why so *holy*—56; passages from the Word to show how *holy* was the law deposited in the ark—59.

HOLY JERUSALEM.

S. The spiritual meaning of the description of the *Holy Jerusalem*, as given in *Rev.* xxi., set forth—10; the letter of the Word meant by the city's walls—36.

HOLY OF HOLIES.

S. Signified what is inmost of heaven and the church—46.

HOLY ONE OF ISRAEL.

L. *Holy One of Israel*, one of the Lord's names, referring to Him as to His Divine Human—40; Jehovah and *Holy One of Israel* are one and the same—ib.

S. In the universal marriage in everything in the Word, *Holy One of Israel* signifies the Lord as to the Divine truth, while Jehovah means the Lord as to the Divine good—88.

HOLY SCRIPTURE. See SCRIPTURE.

HOLY SPIRIT.

L. The *Holy Spirit* is the Divine Proceeding from the Lord, and this is the Lord Himself (chap. x.)—46-54; why the Lord told the disciples to baptize into the name of the *Holy Spirit*—46 (2); the *Holy Spirit* is none other than the Lord—ib. (4); what is meant by going forth and proceeding—ib.; see 51 (2) (3); what is blasphemy against it—50 (2); it is Divine truth from the Lord—51 (4) (5); what is meant by being baptized with it—51 (4); that it is not said in the Prophets that they spoke the Word from the *Holy Spirit*—53.

S. The Lord spoke the Word (of the Gospels) partly from the spirit of His mouth, which is the *Holy Spirit*—2.

Q. The *Holy Spirit* (to be distinguished from the Spirit of God in the Old Testament) proceeds solely from the Lord, operates on man perceptibly, and enables him to comprehend spiritual truths in a natural way—V.; the *Holy Spirit* is the same as the Divine sphere if by this is meant the Divine Love and Wisdom which proceed from Jehovah the Lord from the sun of the angelic heaven —ib.; regeneration is an attribute of the *Holy Spirit*—VII.; the *Holy Spirit* is the primary power (*virtus*), or operation, of the Divine Human from the Divine Esse —ib.

HONOR.

S. What is meant by *honor* (in the command, "honor thy father and thy mother") in the natural, the spiritual, and the celestial sense—67.

HORNS.

S. That some of the Hebrew letters in ancient time had little *horns* that turned upward—90.

F. Meaning of the *horns* (*Dan.* viii.) with which the he-goat pushed—67.

HORSE.

S. What was signified by the locusts appearing like *horses*—13 (2); signification of dead *horse* (in memorable relation)—26 (5); the spiritual sense of John's vision of the *horses* of various colors (*Rev.* vi.) set forth as signifying various states of the understanding of the Word—12. See also WHITE HORSE.

Life. Signification of *horses* (*Isa.* xxxi. 1-3)—30 (2).

HOSEA.

L. Things that *Hosea* was commanded to do that he might represent the states of the church—15 (6).

S. Without the spiritual sense no one could know why *Hosea* was commanded to do certain things—16; the Prophet *Hosea* from the first chapter to the last treats of the falsification of the Word, and of the destruction of the church thereby—79 (7).

HOWL.

F. Meaning of *howl* (in *Jer.* xlvii. 4) —53.

HUMAN.

L. That the Lord was buried signified the rejection of the residue of the mater-

nal *human*—16 (6); the salvation of man became possible after the Lord had deprived hell of all its power and had glorified His *Human*—17; the Lord's *Human* was conceived of Jehovah and born of the virgin Mary (passages given showing this)—19 (2); by the Son of God prophesied in the Old Testament to come into the world, nothing else is meant than the *Human* which the Lord assumed in the world—19 (9); it was His *Human* that was meant when Jesus at His baptism was called His Son—ib.; the Lord's conquering the hells, teaching the Word, and setting up a new church could not have been done except by a *Human*—20; cannot be separated from the Divine—21; see also 29 (3); the Divine and the *Human* in the Lord are not two but one— 29; the Lord made Divine His *Human* from the Divine that was in Himself, and thus became one with the Father (chap. vii.)—29-36; as the Lord's soul was the very Divine of the Father, it follows that His body, or *Human*, must also have become Divine—29 (2); the Son is His *Human*—30; the Divine operated through the *Human* as a soul through its body—32 (2); the Divine and *Human* operated unanimously—ib. (3); the Divine was united to the *Human* and the *Human* to the Divine—ib. (4); the *Human* is to be approached and is the Son of God—ib. (6); see also ib. (7); many can form no idea of the fact that the *Human* in the Lord was made Divine (the reason)—ib. (8); the Lord's *Human* was made Divine by means of temptations—33; the full unition of the Divine and the *Human* in the Lord was effected by the passion of the cross—34; the Lord is Jehovah and God both as to the Divine and as to the *Human*—ib.; passages adduced—ib. (2); the Divine and the *Human* are one Person, and that the *Human* also is Divine—ib. (3); redemption and salvation an attribute proper to the *Human* because it endured temptations—ib.; relation between the *human* which was assumed from Mary, and afterwards put off, and the *Human* from the Divine within the Lord, which was put on—35; the quality of the glorified *Human*—ib. (6); the relation between the Divine and the *Human* was reciprocal and plenary—ib. (8); the Lord ascended into heaven with the Divine and *Human* united into one—ib. (11); after He assumed the *Human* God became Man as in first principles so also in ultimates— 36; if we make proper distinction between the *human* from the mother and the *Human* from the Father, what the Athanasian Creed says of the incarnation is true (illustrated)—59; the Lord came into the world to glorify His *Human* (how He accomplished it)—65.

S. The glorification of the Lord is the glorification of His *Human* which He assumed in the world—99.

Life. The spiritual mind is called the *human* mind (in distinction from the natural or animal mind)—86.

Q. The Lord was the Word or Divine truth even as to the *Human*—I.; as to the *Human* He was called the Son of man—ib.; by the assumption of the *Human* Jehovah put on the Divine Rational —II.; the Lord is Life itself even in respect to His *Human*—III. See also DIVINE HUMAN.

HUMAN FORM.

L. That the whole Divine has a tendency to the *human form*—32 (8).

HUMAN RACE.

S. The *human race* is the basis, containant, and support of the heavens—34.

HUMILIATION.

L. The Lord's state of *humiliation* described—35 (3); one of the meanings of "spirit" is spiritual life to those in *humiliation*—49 (2).

I.

S. The angels of the third heaven cannot utter the vowel "*i*" ("*i*" as in machine)—90 (2).

IDEA.

F. The Christian faith in its most universal *idea* (set forth)—34; the faith of the present day in its most universal *idea* (set forth)—38.

IDOLATROUS, IDOLATRY.

S. The representative things of the church being converted into things *idolatrous*—22; the reason the Israelites were *idolaters*—23 (4).

IGNORANCE.

S. Falsities from *ignorance* do no harm to those who do not suffer themselves to be led astray by evils—15 (2).

Life. That man is born into total *ignorance* is a means of reformation provided by the Lord—69.

F. *Ignorance* of truth was the chief safeguard of the Papal religion—8; they who separate faith from charity must needs be in *ignorance* of truth—9; *ignorance* is the safeguard of the dogma of the Reformed—ib.

IMAGE.

Life. Before the angels in heaven a natural moral man appears, if in goods, like an *image* of wood, and if in truths like an *image* of marble—109.

IMMORTALITY.

S. The wise men of old got the doctrine of *immortality* from others who had it from tradition from those who first knew it from the ancient Word—115 (3).

IMPERCEPTIBLY.

Q. The Spirit of God (in the Old Testament) could operate on man only *imperceptibly*, whereas the Holy Spirit (of the New Testament) can operate perceptibly—V.

IMPUTATION, IMPUTED.

L. The *imputation* of the Lord's merit is nothing but the remission of sins after repentance (chap. v.)—18; the Lord's merit and righteousness can never be *imputed* to man—ib. (3).

Life. If there were in man no reciprocality, there would be no *imputation*— 105.

F. The doctrine of *imputation* as held in the faith of the present day—39; see also 42.

INCARNATION.

L. With what understanding of the subject of *incarnation* the words of the Athanasian Creed are true—59.

Q. Before the *incarnation* there was no Divine Human, except a representative one—VI.; after the *incarnation* representatives ceased—ib.

INDIES.

S. The peoples of the *Indies* are farthest from the Lord in the order of the spiritual world—105 (3); from the two Words (the ancient and the present Word) the things of religion spread into the *Indies*—117.

INDIGNATION.

L. A day of *indignation* of Jehovah signifies His advent—14 (9).

INFERNAL.

Life. The conjunction of evil and falsity is called the *infernal* marriage—33.

INFESTING, INFEST.

L. At the time of the Lord's coming the hells were *infesting* every man that came into the world and that went out of the world—14; before the Lord's advent the hells were beginning to *infest* the very angels of heaven—33 (3).

INFINITE.

Life. There are *infinite* things within every concupiscence—112.
Q. The Trinity in the Lord, unlike the trinity in each man, is *infinite*—III.

INFLUX.

S. When men read the Word while themselves and the world are the ends in view, they cannot receive through heaven any *influx* from the Lord—61 (2).
Life. *Influx* from what is natural into what is spiritual is contrary to order, and does not operate into man's concupiscences so as to remove them—110.

INIQUITY, INIQUITIES.

L. What is meant by the Lord's bearing *iniquities*, and what by taking them away—15; also ib. (2); also see 16.
S. The word *iniquity* is predicated of falsity (as sin is of evil)—84.

INMOST.

S. In its *inmost* sense the Word is celestial—6.

INNOCENCE.

Life. That when newly born a man is kept in a state of external *innocence* is a means of reformation provided by the Lord—69.

INSPIRED.

S. The Word is *inspired* from its spiritual sense—18; in the sanctuary of every larger society of heaven there is kept a copy of the Word written by angels and *inspired* by the Lord—72.

INSTANT.

F. According to the faith of the present day the imputation of the Son's merit takes place in an *instant*—39 (vi).

INSTANTANEOUS.

S. The evolution (of the spiritual and celestial senses of the Word from its natural sense) is *instantaneous*—63.

INSTRUCTED.

S. After death every man is *instructed* by angels—93.

INTEGRITY.

Life. See SINCERITY—83.

INTELLECTUAL.

Life. The faith of an evil man is an *intellectual* faith in which there is nothing of good from the will—46.

INTELLIGENCE.

L. All the spiritual *intelligence* of the angels is from the Word—2.
S. Of what character those become after death who ascribe all things to their own *intelligence*—118.
Life. Man's self *intelligence* described —30 (2); the angels of all the heavens are in *intelligence* in proportion to the degree in which good with them makes one with truth—32.
F. In the state of regeneration man's faith is not called faith but *intelligence*— 31; such as is the quality of a man's faith from charity, such is the quality of his *intelligence*—29.

INTERCOURSE.

F. In the World of Spirits one person has *intercourse* with another just as among men on earth—63 (2).

INTERIOR SENSE.

S. In its *interior sense* the Word is spiritual—6.

INTERIORS.

Life. The *interiors* of the natural man are blocked up by concupiscences of evils so long as man does not shun evils as sins—86 (4) ; and so long he is in hell—ib. (5).

INTERMEDIATE PLACE. See WORLD OF SPIRITS.

INTERNAL SENSE.

S. The *internal sense* has been revealed to Swedenborg—4.

IRON.

S. Their having breastplates as "breastplates of *iron*" (*Rev. ix.*) signified argumentations from fallacies by which they prevail—13 (3).

ISAAC.

S. Where in our Word we have *Isaac*, in the Word of the angels they have the Lord as to His Divine Human—71.

ISAIAH.

L. Why *Isaiah* was commanded to do certain things to represent the church—15 (4).

S. Without the spiritual sense no one could know why *Isaiah* was commanded to do certain things—16 ; how *Isaiah* suffered represented the violence done by the Jews to the sense of the letter of the Word—35.

ISLANDS.

S. The spiritual state of peoples who have been born on *islands* and had known nothing whatever about God—116.

ISRAELITISH.

S. The knowledge of correspondences was altogether lost and annihilated among the *Israelitish* people—22 ; the *Israelitish* people were at heart idolaters (their state described)—23 (4).

JACOB.

L. The Lord is called The Mighty One of *Jacob* because He conquered the hells—14 (9).

S. Where in our Word we have *Jacob*, in the Word of the angels they have the Lord as to His Divine Human—71.

JASHAR, BOOK OF.

S. The *Book of Jashar* mentioned by David and by Joshua—103 (3).

JEHOVAH.

L. The Lord from eternity is *Jehovah*—30 ; is called "day-spring from on high"—ib. (4) ; by *Jehovah*, after His Human was glorified, is meant the Divine and Human together—ib. ; assumed the Human to save men—31 ; the Lord's Divine is called *Jehovah*—34 (3) ; the Lord called *Jehovah* (passages adduced)—38 ; *Jehovah* called Redeemer and Saviour—ib. ; *Jehovah* and "the Holy One of Israel" the same—40 ; see also 45 ; Spirit used for *Jehovah*—50 (2) ; spoke the Word through the prophets—52-54 ; was the Lord from eternity—54 ; called by various names in the Word (the reason)—55.

S. *Jehovah* spoke the Word—2 ; day of *Jehovah* means the Lord's advent—14 (3) ; *Jehovah* when mentioned with God and Holy One of Israel, means the Lord as to Divine good, and the other names, as to Divine truth—88 ; the Greeks named their supreme God Jove from *Jehovah* [perhaps, see *T. C. R.* 275]—117.

F. That *Jehovah* came into the world to subdue the hells and glorify His Human—34.

Q. (In answer to the question as to whether before the incarnation the Divine Human of *Jehovah* was a Person)—*Jehovah* filled an angel with His Spirit—VI. ; before His actual advent *Jehovah* presented Himself in a representative Human—ib.

JEREMIAH.

L. Why *Jeremiah* was commanded to do certain things to represent the church—15 (4) ; references given in *Jeremiah* where occur the four expressions "the word of Jehovah came unto me," "Jehovah said unto me," "Jehovah said," and "the word of Jehovah"—53.

S. Without the spiritual sense no one could know why *Jeremiah* was commanded to do certain things—16.

JERUSALEM.

L. The Holy City *Jerusalem* means the New Church as to doctrine—63; the reason *Jerusalem* means the Church as to doctrine—64 (passages adduced, read the whole number). See also HOLY JERUSALEM and NEW JERUSALEM.

S. The inconsistency of what is said concerning *Jerusalem* if considered without doctrine—51 (8); where in our Word we have *Jerusalem*, in the Word of the angels they have the church as to doctrine—71.

Life. By *Jerusalem* is signified the church in respect to doctrine—79 (3).

JESUITS.

S. Many of those who hate God (in hell) are from the *Jesuits*—116.

JESUS.

L. The Human was meant when *Jesus* at His baptism was called by Jehovah His Son—19 (9); the Son of God is *Jesus*—21; *Jesus* is the Son of God conceived of Jehovah and born of the virgin Mary—29 (2).

JEWISH NATION.

L. That the Lord was betrayed by Judas signified that He was betrayed by the *Jewish nation*—16 (6).

S. The inconsistency of the prophecies made concerning the *Jewish nation* if not interpreted according to doctrine—51 (8); after the Word had been falsified and adulterated by the *Jewish nation*, it pleased the Lord to come and fulfill the Word, and thereby repair and restore it—111.

JEWS.

L. The meaning of *Matthew* viii. 20, *Luke* ix. 58, that the Word would have no place among the *Jews*—27 (2).

JOB.

S. The book of *Job* is an ancient book full of correspondences—20 (2).

JOHN THE BAPTIST. See BAPTIST.

JOY.

S. *Joy* is predicated of good (in distinction from which gladness is predicated of truth)—84; often in the Word *joy* is associated with gladness because *joy* is of love and gladness is of wisdom (passages adduced)—87.

JUDGMENT.

L. The Lord is called "the Son of Man" when the *judgment* is treated of—25; the reason given—ib.

S. The commandment against the exercise of *judgment* (*Matt.* vii. 1, 2) explained—51 (5); *judgment* is predicated of truth, and in the opposite sense of falsity—84; *judgment* is associated in the Word with righteousness (or justice) because *judgment* is of truth, and righteousness is of good (illustrative passages from the Word given)—85. See LAST JUDGMENT.

JUSTICE. See also RIGHTEOUSNESS.

L. The necessity that the Lord should make an atonement for man supposed to be on account of *justice* which by some is called "vengeful *justice*"—18.

S. *Justice* is predicated of good and in the opposite sense of evil—84; *justice* is associated in the Word with judgment because judgment is predicated of truth and *justice* of good (illustrative passages from the Word given)—85.

Life. Sincerity is to be understood as including integrity, *justice*, fidelity, and rectitude—83.

KILL.

S. The interpretation given to the command against murder as made, first, by a man; secondly, by a spiritual angel; and, thirdly, by a celestial angel—67 (4).

KING, KINGS.

L. *Kings* in *Ps.* cx. 5, means those who are in falsities from evils—14 (8); the Lord called *King* of Glory because He conquered the hells without the aid of any angel—ib. (9); the reason the Lord is called *King* explained in full—42.

S. By the *kings* of the earth (*Rev.* xix. 19) are meant the Reformed who are in false things of doctrine—25; a *king* signifies the truth of the church—45.

KINGDOM.

L. From the Lord's being called King, heaven and the Church are called His *kingdom*—42.

S. Heaven discriminated into two *kingdoms,* celestial and spiritual—34; angels of the spiritual *kingdom* draw out the spiritual sense of the Word, and those in the celestial *kingdom* the celestial sense—65; "the *kingdom* of God" (*Matt.* xxv.) means heaven and the church — 17 (2); the "*kingdom* of heaven" (*Matt.* xxv.) means the church —ib. (3); the "*kingdom* of God" (*Luke* xvii. 21) means the Lord, and from Him the church—78.

Life. Why the heavens are distinguished into two distinct *kingdoms*—32.

KNOW.

S. "Not to *know* them" when spoken by the Lord signifies not to be in His love (*Matt.* xxv.)—17 (3).

KNOWLEDGES.   See also MEMORY-
KNOWLEDGES.

Life. One's *knowledges* (of heavenly things) are devoid of life unless he shuns evils as sins—27; nevertheless *knowledges* are in the highest degree necessary—ib.

F. Spiritual heat from heaven (which heat in its essence is charity) gives life to the *knowledges* of good and truth in the natural mind, and out of them it forms faith—32; the *knowledges* of truth and good are not matters of real belief until the man is in charity, but are the storehouse of material out of which the faith of charity can be formed (chap. iii.)—25-33; why every one should acquire *knowledges* of truth and good in childhood—26; yet they are merely the storehouse of material from which the faith of charity can be formed in proportion as the man shuns evils as sins—27; this storehouse of *knowledges* necessary in the highest degree (the reason)—28; but they must be *knowledges* of genuine good and truth, not *knowledges* of what is false—29; these *knowledges* may appear o be the things of faith even when not yet applied to life, but they are not—31;

the general doctrine of *knowledges* in their relation to faith—33.

LAMB.

L. Instead of God it is sometimes said "the *Lamb*," and instead of the *Lamb* God (the reason)—46 (5).

S. *Lamb* signifies innocence—18 (3).

LAMPS.

S. The *lamps* (*Matt.* xxv.) signify the truths of faith—17 (2).

Life. What is meant by having *lamps* with no oil—26.

LAND.

S. The *land* of Jehovah is the church —79 (4).

LASCIVIOUS, LASCIVIOUSNESS.

Life. To speak *lascivious* things is a violation of the sixth (usually called the seventh) commandment—74; see also 78; the *lasciviousness* of adultery is directly opposite to the chastity of marriage—75; see 76.

LAST.

L. Why the Lord is called "the First and the *Last*"—36.

S. In every Divine work there is a first, a middle, and a *last*—27.

LAST JUDGMENT.

L. The Lord came into the world to execute a *Last Judgment*—3; it was effected by means of combats with the hells—14 (10); the Lord called Son of man where the *Judgment* is treated of, the reason—25; effected by Divine truth —ib.; before the *Last Judgment* the power of hell prevailed, but since then every one who craves to be enlightened, can be so—61; the doctrines of the New Church could not be revealed before the *Last Judgment*, the reason—65.

F. Upon whom the *Last Judgment* was executed, and their character—64.

LAW, LAWS.

L. What is meant by the *Law* in the universal Holy Scripture, in a restricted sense and in a wider, and in the widest sense—8-10; what is meant by the Lord's fulfilling all things of the *Law*— 11; see also 65; it is believed in the church that the Lord effected the atonement by making satisfaction for men's sins through His fulfilling all things of the *Law*—18.

S. The *Law* written on the two tables of stone signifies the Lord as to the Word —46.

Life. Why these *laws* (the Ten Commandments) were promulgated from Mount Sinai with so great a miracle, known as they were the world over— 53; these *laws* were the first-fruits of the Word—54; the prevalence of a religious tenet that no one is able to fulfill the *law* (the spiritual effect of holding or not holding it, on the state of those entering the spiritual world)—63; the religious tenet that no one can fulfill the *law* by a spiritual life an error—63; the effect of such a belief upon those who having been under its control in this world enter the other life—ib. (2); that they love evils and the false notions that accompany them the reason—64.

F. The effect of believing that one cannot keep the *law* set forth—39 xi.; the little horn (of the he-goat) signifies the argument that no one of himself is able to fulfill the *law*—67.

LAZARUS.

S. The reason the Gentiles are meant by *Lazarus*—40 (3) (4).

LEADS.

Life. The will *leads* the understanding and makes it act as one with itself— 44.

LEAVES.

Life. The *leaves* and blossoms of a tree signify the truths of faith—46.

LETTER.

L. In the *letter* of the Word things which form a one are distinguished as if they did not form a one—55.

S. The *letter* of the Word appears like common writing—1; the *letter* receives its life from the spirit—4; the spiritual sense does not appear in the sense of the *letter*—5; the sense of the *letter* of the Word is the basis, the containant, and the support of its spiritual and celestial senses (chap. iii.)—27-36; the *letter* of

the Word if not understood is dead—77. See also SENSE OF THE LETTER.

LETTERS.

S. The spiritual style of the Word consists solely of *letters*, each of which contains a meaning—71; a paper marked with Hebrew *letters* sent down from heaven—90; angels discern complete meanings in the very *letters*—ib.; writing in the third heaven consists of curved *letters*, each possessing a complete meaning—ib. (2).

LIE.

S. To multiply *lying* (*Hosea* xii. 1) is to falsify truths and thus destroy the church—79 (5).

Life. To *lie* is one way of bearing false witness in the natural sense—87; as far as one shuns *lying* as a sin so far he loves the truth—88.

LIFE.

L. "*Life*" is Divine love—1; by "spirit" is meant man's *life* (shown from illustrations, and from the Word)—47; by "spirit" is also meant the varying affection of *life* in man,—*e.g.*, as the *life* of wisdom, the excitation of *life*, etc.—48; the *life* of the whole heaven is founded upon the acknowledgment and consequent confession of one God, and that this one God is also Man, and that He is the Lord—55 (3).

S. The reason there is *life* in the Lord's words—2; see ib. (3); how man has *life* by means of the Word—3; the spiritual sense gives *life* to the letter—4; how the Lord pours *life* into man's intelligence— 82; no one would have knowledge of a *life* after death unless there were a Word —114; from the most ancient times something has been known of a *life* after death —117.

Life. All religion is of the *life* and the *life* of religion is to do that which is good (chap. i.)—1-8; confirmations of this doctrine from the Word—2; the reason this has been acknowledged in all religions— 3; every one remains in his own *life* unchanged after death—8; the distinction between faith and *life* set forth—42; no man has a grain of faith more than he has of *life*—52.

F. Evil of *life* inwardly hates truths, and good of *life* inwardly loves them—30; it is only those who have confirmed themselves in faith alone both in doctrine and also in *life* that are not saved—72.

LIGHT.

L. The reason the Lord is called the *Light*—1; "*light*" is Divine wisdom—ib.; a day or time of no *light* signifies the advent of the Lord when He was no longer known—5; a "*light* of the nations" (*Isa.* xlii. 6-8) is the Lord as to the Human—30 (3).

S. How the *light* of heaven (in which is the spiritual sense of the Word) flows into a man's natural *light*—41; spiritual sense of Word like a *light* that enlightens—42; angels are in *light* in proportion to their understanding of the Word—73; the *light* of heaven is Divine wisdom—ib.; is Divine truth there—106; those in lands outside the church who are not in possession of the Word have *light* by its means (chap. xiii.)—104-113; the greatest *light* is in the center of heaven where are the Christians who possess the Word—106; the same is true of each society of heaven—107; illustrations from the *light* of the sun of this world of the penetration of the *light* of the Word to the remotest quarters—109.

Life. No one sees anything in the *light* and free from doubt until he is actually in it—76.

Q. Wisdom proceeds from the sun of heaven as does *light* from the sun of the world—V.; in its essence the *light* of heaven is wisdom—ib.; the *light* of the sun of this world therefore corresponds to wisdom—ib.

LIKENESSES.

S. The truths of the sense of the letter of the Word are as it were *likenesses* and comparisons taken from things such as exist in nature—40.

LITERAL SENSE.

S. The *literal sense* of the Word is a guard to the genuine truths that lie hidden within—97. See also EXTERNAL SENSE, SENSE OF THE LETTER, and ULTIMATE SENSE.

LOCUSTS.

S. The "*locusts* that came out of the smoke of the pit" signify falsities in the outermost things such as exist with those who have become sensuous—13 (2).

LORD.

L. Universal Holy Scripture treats of the *Lord*: the *Lord* is the Word (chap. i.)—1-7; why the *Lord* is called the Word—1; subjects concerning the *Lord* treated of in all the Prophets of the Old Testament, enumerated—3; the *Lord's* advent meant by the expressions "that day" and "that time" used in the Word (passages adduced)—4; various purposes or effects of the advent of the *Lord* meant by the various kinds of day or time mentioned—5; passages adduced concerning the *Lord's* advent—6; that the *Lord* fulfilled all things of the Law means that He fulfilled all things of the Word (chap. ii.)—8-11; came into the world to subjugate the hells and glorify His Human; and the passion of the cross was the final combat, whereby He fully conquered the hells, and fully glorified His Human (chap. iii.)—12-14; He came into the world to reduce into order all things in heaven and derivatively on earth; passages adduced—14; everything in the Word is written about the *Lord*—ib. (11); by the passion of the cross the *Lord* did not take away sins, but bore them (chap. iv.)—15-17; spiritual meaning of the treatment the *Lord* received at the time of the crucifixion—16 (5) (7); the imputation of His merit means nothing but the remission of sins after repentance (chap. v.)—18; in respect to the Divine Human is called Son of God, and in respect to the Word called Son of man (chap. vi.)—19-28; see also 22-23; seriatim passages where called the Son of man with quotations—24-27; what is meant by the *Lord's* being sent into the world—20; the *Lord* is God and Man in one Person—21; designated by various names in the Old Testament according to the subject treated of (examples given)—22; judges no one to hell, nor casts any one into hell, but an evil spirit does the latter for himself—25; the *Lord* made Divine His Human from the

Divine that was in Himself, and thus became one with the Father (chap. vii.)—29-36; from eternity He is Jehovah—30; by the *Lord* is meant His Divine and His Human together as a one—ib. (4) ; assumed the Human to save men—31; made His Human Divine from the Divine in Himself—32; hence we must put faith in the *Lord* since He is both the Father and the Son—32 (6) ; made His Human Divine by means of temptations—33 ; of the combats of the *Lord* the *Psalms* and Prophets treat much—ib. (4) ; He thus became our Saviour—ib. (5) ; full unition of the Divine and Human in the *Lord*, by what means it was effected—34 ; is Jehovah and God as to both the Divine and the Human—ib. (4) ; the *Lord* put off the human from the mother and put on the Human from the Father, by successive steps—35; hence He is both God and Man—ib. ; His state of humiliation and His state of glorification described—ib. (3) ; He did not admit that He was the son of David (the reason)—ib. (5) ; the unition of the Divine and Human was reciprocal; reciprocal also must be the uniting of the *Lord* with man and of man with the *Lord*—ib. (8) ; why unlike every man He rose as to His whole body—ib. (9) ; the *Lord's* Human substance or essence is like to His Divine—ib. (11) ; in Him God thus became Man, as in first principles so also in ultimates—36; the *Lord* is God Himself, from Whom and concerning Whom is the Word (chap. viii.)—37-44; the universal Holy Scripture is concerning the *Lord*, therefore the *Lord* is the Word—37; the *Lord* existed before His advent into the world (passages adduced)—ib. (3) ; in the Word is called Jehovah (passages cited)—38; is called God of Israel and God of Jacob (passages)—39; is also called Holy One of Israel, which means the *Lord* as to the Divine Human (passages)—40; is called *Lord* and God (passages)—41; why called King and Anointed (passages)—42; His advent called Gospel of the kingdom—ib. ; He is called David (passages)—43; why David so frequently wrote of the *Lord* in the *Psalms*—44; God is One, and the *Lord* is that God (chap. ix.)—45; the

Holy Spirit is the Divine proceeding from the *Lord*, and this is the *Lord* Himself (chap. x.)—46-54; trine in the *Lord* illustrated by trine in an angel—ib. 46 (3) ; that the *Lord* only is meant by the Father, Son, and Holy Spirit in *Matt.* xxviii. 19, shown—ib. (6) ; that the *Lord* is meant by the Comforter, the Spirit of Truth, and the Holy Spirit—51 (2) ; hence before the Lord was glorified, it was said that the Holy Spirit was not yet—ib. (3) ; that the *Lord* spoke the Word through the prophets—52-54 ; by what interpretation the Athanasian Creed is true concerning the *Lord*—55-61; from Divine permission Christians at first received the doctrine of three Persons in order to receive the idea that the *Lord* is God, Infinite, Almighty, and Jehovah—55 (4) ; that the *Lord* is God and Man in one Person, shown from things said by Him—60; why the truths concerning the *Lord* are now for the first time made publicly known—61; no one can come into the New Church, nor be admitted into heaven, who does not acknowledge the *Lord* as God of heaven and earth—ib. ; the universal heaven acknowledges Him alone—ib. ; final summary of doctrines concerning the *Lord*—65.

S. The *Lord* has revealed (to Swedenborg) the internal sense—4; from the *Lord* proceed the Celestial, the Spiritual, and the Natural, one after another—6 ; the *Lord's* advent meant by day of Jehovah—14 (3) ; the *Lord* spoke by correspondences (the reason) — 20 (3) ; the reason the Israelitish and Jewish nation did not acknowledge the *Lord*—23 (4) ; only to him who from the *Lord* is in genuine truths will the spiritual sense of the Word henceforth be imparted—26; heaven closed against him who purposes to open that sense from himself and not from the *Lord*—ib. ; the *Lord* is the Word—47; the *Lord* at His transfiguration represented the Word in its glory—48; to those only who are in enlightenment from the *Lord* does the genuine truth of the Word appear in the sense of the letter—57; the reason the *Lord* flows into the natural sense of the Word with such—58; there is conjunction with the *Lord* by means of the sense of the letter

of the Word—62; the effects resultant in
heaven from the *Lord* being in the Word
—73; the *Lord* is present with man and
conjoined to him through the Word—78;
there is a marriage of the *Lord* and the
church in the Word (chap. ix.)—80-90;
the church is the *Lord* forasmuch as
the man of the church is in the *Lord*
and the *Lord* in him—89; anger, wrath,
and vengeance attributed to the *Lord* in
the Word, how explained—94; the *Lord*
came into the world to fulfill all things
of the Word, and thereby to become Divine truth or the Word even in ultimates
(chap. xi.)—98-100; the *Lord's* becoming
the Word in ultimates completely
changed the state of the church (the
changes described)—99; how the *Lord*
is the Word—100; the *Lord* must be
known in order to have conjunction
with heaven—104; how He is known
in lands where they have not the Word
—105; why it pleased the *Lord* to come
into the world and fulfill the Word—
111; the reason it has pleased the *Lord*
now to reveal the spiritual sense—112;
no one could have a knowledge of the
Lord unless there were a Word (chap.
xiv.)—114-118.

Life. In proportion as a man shuns
evils as sins, in the same proportion he
does goods, not from himself but from
the *Lord* (chap. iii.)—18-31; in this
world man is midway between the *Lord*
and the devil—19; the *Lord* keeps man
in freedom so that he can turn toward
Him, or away from Him—20; man loves
the *Lord* in proportion as he is in good,
and from good loves truths (the reason)
—38; no one is able to shun evils as sins
unless he acknowledges the Lord—66;
to deny the Divinity of the *Lord* is, in
the highest sense of the Word, spiritual adultery—74; to attribute to one's
self the attributes of the *Lord* is, in the
highest sense of the Word, to steal—80;
to blaspheme the *Lord* is in the highest
or celestial sense to bear false witness—
87; it is the *Lord* alone who fights in a
man against his evils—96; freedom and
reason in man are the *Lord's* in him—
101; the *Lord* loves man, and desires to
be conjoined to him, but cannot without
reciprocality on man's part—102; from

the *Lord* man has this ability to reciprocate, thus this mutuality (what follows)—102-107.

F. Love to the *Lord* is love properly
so called—22; those who have had regard to the *Lord* in their lives, are inwardly in the acknowledgment of truth,
however much outwardly they may lack
it from lack of instruction—30; the *Lord*
from eternity came into the world to
subdue the hells and to glorify His
Human (a universal of Christian faith)
—34; God is one in Person and in Essence, in whom is the Trinity, and that
the *Lord* is that God (a universal of
Christian faith)—35; the *Lord's* redemp-
tive works in other respects enumerated
—ib.; the universal of the Christian faith
on the part of man as to what he should
believe in respect to the *Lord*—36.

Q. (In answer to the question as to in
what sense the *Lord* called himself the
Son of man)—He called Himself the Son
of man because He was the Word, or
Divine truth even as to the Human—I.;
(to the question as to whether the *Lord*
had a rational soul from the Father)—the
Lord did put on the Divine Rational by
the assumption of the Human—II.; in
the *Lord* the Trinity is infinite, in this
respect is unlike the trinity in man—III.;
that the *Lord* was the Divine wisdom
which together with the Divine love
constitutes the Divine Essence, and thus
one and the same God—IV.; the *Lord*
has united the Divine Natural to the
Divine Celestial—V.; He is Divine truth
—ib.; is alone holy—ib.; from Him proceed Divine love and Divine wisdom—
ib.; may not the Holy Trinity be said
to be one and the same *Lord* in three
characters, etc.?—Question VII.

LOST.

S. Knowledge of correspondences
among the Israelitish and Jewish people
was *lost* (the reason)—22; concerning
the Word which has been *lost*—101; see
also 102.

LOT.

L. The meaning of casting *lots* for the
Lord's under-vesture—16 (6).

Life. The *lot* of those who are unwilling to do evils for the reason that to do these things is contrary to God—63 (3).

LOVE, TO LOVE.

L. Divine wisdom and Divine *love* make a one—1 ; Divine *love* is "life"—ib. ; wisdom is in *love* and *love* in wisdom—ib. ; all things created from Divine *love* by means of Divine wisdom—ib.

S. From the Lord proceeds Divine *love*—3 ; what proceeds from *love* is called celestial—6.

Life. Good *loves* truth, and truth good ; evil *loves* falsity, and falsity evil —33 ; a man who does not shun evils as sins may *love* truths, but only for worldly advantages and not because they are truths—35 ; from the *love* of good proceeds the *love* of truth—36 ; in proportion as any one from good *loves* truths, he *loves* the Lord—38 ; that good *loves* truth, illustrated by the case with a priest, a soldier, a trader, and an artificer—39 ; illustrated also by foods being taken with water, and bread with wine —40 ; the *love* of the will is the very being (*esse*) of the thought in the understanding—48 ; the good of *love* taught by the Lord in *Matthew*—73 ; truth and *love* do not make a one in a man unless he is spiritual—15 ; an angel is an angel, and a man a man, from the *love* and wisdom in him—32 ; a man *loves* the neighbor in proportion as he shuns murders as sins— (chap. viii.)—67-73 ; to *love* and to be conjoined with one in whom there is nothing reciprocal is not possible—102.

F. How *love* produces faith—13 ; that we *love* a person from his quality—20 ; *love* toward the neighbor is charity—22 ; *love* to the Lord is *love* properly so called —22.

Q. The Lord from eternity was *love*— II. ; the Divine wisdom together with Divine *love* constitutes the Divine Essence—IV.

LUKEWARMNESS.

Life. The meaning of the *lukewarmness* mentioned in *Rev.* iii.—71.

LUNGS.

F. Faith compared to the *lungs*, in relation to which charity is as the heart—19.

LUTHER.

Q. *Luther*, as distinguished from Calvin, teaches that in Christ Man is God and God is Man—II.

MAGIC.

S. When correspondences were converted into *magic*, the knowledge of them was blotted out—22.

MAGISTRATE.

Life. A *magistrate* in executing the law from the love of the neighbor, used as an illustration of doing a good work —72 ; see also 83.

MAN, MEN.

L. By *Man* (*Hominem*) is signified the church—16 (7) ; the Lord's work on earth could not have been done unless He had been made *Man*—20 ; the Lord is God and *Man*, and God and *Man* in the Lord are not two but one Person—21 ; what "*man* of thy right hand" means— 27 (2) ; why the prophets were called sons of *man*—28 ; the uniting of the Lord with *man* and of *man* with the Lord must be reciprocal—35 (8) ; by assuming the Human, God became *Man*, as in first principles so also in ultimates—36 ; the life of the whole heaven and the wisdom of the angels are founded upon the acknowledgment and consequent confession of one God, and upon the faith that this one God is also *Man*, and that He is the Lord, who is at once both God and *Man*—55 (3) ; that God and *Man* are one in the Lord, shown by things said by Him—60 ; the Lord's words to His disciples in order to evince still further that He was not a spirit but a *Man*—35 (10).

S. "Their faces were as the faces of *men*" signified that they appeared to themselves as conquerors and as wise— 13 (2) ; the upper part (of Dagon) was like a *man* because a *man* signifies intelligence—23 (2) ; a "*man*" (*Rev.* xxi.) signifies intelligence—43 ; the external Divine sphere of the Word is represented as a *man* (*Ezek.* i. 5)—97 (5) ; every *man* is his own love, and consequently his own good and his own truth (set forth further)— 100 ; meaning of the Commandments as understood by a *man* contrasted with their meaning as understood by a spiritual and by a celestial angel—67; a reason why the association of *man* with angels exists by means of the natural sense of the Word—68; as the wisdom of spiritual angels surpasses that of *men*, so does the wisdom of celestial angels surpass that of the spiritual—74; when the *man* of the church is in truths, how the Lord inflows and vivifies them—82; every *man* is his own love, and thence his own good and his own truth, from this is *man* a *man*—100; since the Lord is Divine good and Divine truth itself, He is the *Man* from whom every *man* is a *man*—ib.; before the Lord the universal heaven is like one *man*, and so is the church—105; all those in the whole earth who have some sort of religion, worship one God, and live aright, are in that *man*—ib. (2); the Christians among whom the Word is read constitute the breast of that *man*—ib. (3); how people who know nothing of God are made spiritually alive by means of knowledges about God as a *Man*—116.

Life. Those who do good from themselves called natural *men*, and those who do good from the Lord called spiritual *men*—16; a *man* is a *man* from the love and wisdom in him—32; *man* is discriminated from the animal by his possessing a spiritual mind—86; *man* is in hell so long as concupiscences of evils block up the interiors of his natural mind, but in heaven as soon as these lusts have been dispersed by the Lord—ib. (5); what is meant by its being said that "Egypt is *man* and not God"—30 (2); what *man* is in himself set forth—68; these two faculties, Freedom and Reason, are the Lord's in *man*—101.

F. What *man* is collectively, and what individually (distinguished)—20; what is signified by the expression "for it is the number of a *man*" (*Rev.* xiii. 18) —60; when charity succeeds faith as the first thing in a *man's* life, then first is he truly a *man*—31; the universal of the Christian faith on the part of *man* is that he believe in the Lord—36; meaning of the *man*-child brought forth by the woman described in *Rev.* xii.—59.

MAN OF WARS.

L. Why the Lord is called a *Man of wars*—14 (9).

MANGER.

S. The *manger* in a stable (in a memorable relation) signified spiritual instruction for the understanding—26 (3) (4); why this signification—ib.

MARBLE.

Life. Before the angels of heaven a natural moral man, if in truths, appears like an image of *marble*—109.

MARRIAGE.

S. There is a *marriage* of the Lord and the church, and a derivative *marriage* of good and truth, in each and every thing of the Word (chap. ix.)—80-90; from this comes a *marriage* in the sense of the letter of the Word—80; it is shown there in the frequency of two expressions which appear like repetitions of the same thing—81; *marriage* of good and truth in a man described—83; examples of such expressions (see PAIRS) —84-87; it is on account of the *marriage* of the Lord with the church, that Jehovah and God, and also Jehovah and the Holy One of Israel, are mentioned as if they are two although they are one—88; from this *marriage* it is evident that all things of the Word treat of the Lord —89.

Life. The conjunction of good and truth the heavenly *marriage*, that of evil and falsity the infernal one—33; the more man shuns evils as sins the more he comes into the heavenly *marriage*—41; in proportion as any one shuns adultery, in the same proportion he loves *marriage*—75; no one can know the nature of the chastity of *marriage* except the man who shuns as a sin the lasciviousness of adultery—76.

MARY.

L. *Mary* is called the Lord's mother, but not from His own mouth—35 (4); in respect to the glorified Human the Lord was not the son of *Mary*—ib. (5).

MASORITES.

S. Everything in the Old Testament was counted, even to the letters, by the *Masorites*—13 (4).

MASTER.

S. In the natural sense it is lawful to call a person *master*, but not in the spiritual—51 (6).

MATERIAL.

L. The Lord put off the human from the mother which was *material*—35 (2) ; His body (after the resurrection) was no longer *material*, but Divine substantial —ib. (10).

MATERNAL.

L. When the things first said in the Athanasian Creed about the incarnation are understood of the *maternal* human, and the things which follow them, of the Divine Human—all things there are in agreement with the truth—59.

MEDIA.

F. The kings of *Media* mean the same as the ram—66.

MEDIATELY.

S. Before His coming into the world the Lord was present with the men of the church *mediately*, whereas since His coming into the world He is present with them immediately—99.

MEDIUM.

S. Without a *medium* the Lord does not pour new truths into a man—26 (2).

MELANCHTHON.

Q. *Melanchthon* teaches that in Christ Man is God and God Man—II.

MELCHIZEDEK.

S. That there was a Divine Worship antedating that established through Moses, evidenced by what is said of *Melchizedek*, who represented the Lord—101 (3).

MEMORY-KNOWLEDGES.

S. That the whole church has been devastated by *memory-knowledges* (*scien-*

tifica) perverting all truth and confirming falsity—15.

F. An external acknowledgement without an internal one is a faith in what is unknown, and a faith in what is unknown is mere *memory-knowledge*—11.

MERIT.

L. The imputation of the Lord's *merit* is nothing but the remission of sins after repentance—18 ; *merit* can never be imputed to man—ib. (3).

Life. To claim *merit* for one's self is, in the highest sense of the command against theft, to steal from the Lord—80.

F. According to the faith of the present day, the Son's *merit* is imputed to those who believe—39 v.

MESOPOTAMIA.

S. The ancients who still use the ancient Word in heaven were partly from *Mesopotamia*—102.

MESSIAH.

L. The *Messiah* whom they had expected, was understood in the Jewish Church by the Son of God—19 (8) ; the Lord was called King and Anointed because He was the *Messiah*, and " *Messiah*" means king and anointed—42.

S. The Israelitish and Jewish nation wanted a *Messiah* who would exalt them above every other nation, hence they rejected the Lord—23 (4).

MICE.

F. The *mice* by which the Philistines were infested signify falsifications of truth—52.

MICHAELS.

S. Certain ones who believed that they would be *Michaels* because of their devotion to the Word, but who had studied it from the love of self (their state in the other world)—61.

MIDDLE.

S. In every Divine work there is a first, a *middle*, and a last—27 ; the spiritual sense is the *middle* sense of the Word —31 ; the greatest light (in the World of Spirits) is in the *middle* region—106.

MIDWAY.

Life. So long as a man is in this world he is kept *midway* between heaven and hell, or the Lord and the devil, and is kept in freedom to turn either way—19; see 69.

MILITANT.

Life. Why the Christian church is called *militant*—98.

MIND.

Life. The human *mind* consists of two faculties—the will and the understanding—43; it is of the utmost importance that man should know this—ib.; man possesses a natural *mind* and a spiritual *mind*—86; a man can be in his spiritual *mind* in his understanding, but unless he shuns evils as sins, he cannot be in his spiritual *mind* as to his will—ib. (2) ; man's *mind* compared to a garden—ib. (3) ; unless he shuns evils as sins, his spiritual *mind* cannot be opened on account of the concupiscences of evils blocking up the interiors of his natural *mind*—ib. (4) ; so long as the interiors of his *mind* are thus blocked up, the man is natural, and is in hell—ib. (5) ; cunning and deceit insinuate themselves even into the spiritual *mind* of man—81.

F. Every man has a natural *mind* and a spiritual *mind*, a natural *mind* for the world and a spiritual *mind* for heaven—32; in respect to his understanding man is in both *minds*, but not in respect to his will until he shuns evils as sins and is averse to them—ib.

MINERAL KINGDOM.

S. Illustrations from the *mineral kingdom* to show how each kind of angel draws from the Word things homogeneous to his nature—66.

MIRACLES.

S. The Lord's *miracles* were Divine because they signified the various states among those with whom the church was to be set up anew by the Lord—17 (4) ; all *miracles* related in the Word contain things relating to the Lord, heaven, and the church, and this makes them Divine —ib.

MOAB.

S. *Moab* signifies the adulteration of good—18 (3).

MOHAMMEDANS.

S. The *Mohammedans* are next to the Papists in their distance from the center in the spiritual world, and farther in than the Africans—105 (3) ; the *Mohammedan* religion was taken from the Word of both Testaments—117.

MONTH.

Life. Let them for once in a week or twice in a *month* resist the evils they are inclined to, and they will perceive a change—97.

MOON.

S. The "*moon* which shall not give her light" (*Matt.* xxiv.) means the Lord as to faith—14 (2).

MORAL.

Life. *Moral* good is that which a man does from the law of reason, according to which good he is a man—12 ; the laws of the decalogue known as *moral* laws before their promulgation from Mount Sinai—53 ; in what way a *moral* man shuns evils—108 ; being *moral* in outward form and not in inward is still not being *moral* (illustrated) —111 ; a man who possesses spiritual good is also a *moral* man, but a man who does not possess spiritual good is not a *moral* man, though he appears to be one—13 ; in the case of a man who possesses spiritual good, what is *moral* in him is intermediate spiritual—14 ; the *moral* with those who do what is good from themselves is in its essence natural, and the *moral* with those who do what is good from the Lord is in its essence spiritual—16 ; comparison between the appearance of a natural *moral* man and a spiritual *moral* man, before the angels—109.

F. The Last Judgment was executed solely upon those who in externals had been *moral*, but not in internals—64.

MORNING.

S. The state of the church after the Lord's advent is called "*morning*"—99.

MOSES.

L. *"Moses"* means all the books that have been written by *Moses*—9.

S. Where in our Word we have *Moses,* in the Word of the angels they have the historical Word—71; by *Moses* and Elias seen at the transfiguration is meant the Word—98; *"Moses* and Elias" (in the transfiguration) represented the historical and the prophetical Word—48.

MOST ANCIENT CHURCH.

S. Men of the *Most Ancient Church* were of a genius so heavenly that they spoke with angels—21.

MOTHER.

L. The Lord did not call His *mother, Mother,* but Woman, the reason—35 (4).

S. The differences in the interpretations given to the command to honor father and *mother,* first, by a man, secondly, by a spiritual angel, and, thirdly, by a celestial angel—67.

MOUNTAINS.

S. *Mountains* signify the higher things of the church—18 (3); a *mountain* signified the highest heaven, and a hill the heaven under it—23 (2).

MOURNING.

S. *Mourning* is predicated of good, and in the opposite sense of evil—84.

MURDER.

Life. *Murders,* etc., together with all concupiscence for these things, are the evils which should be shunned as sins (chap. vii.)—62-66; the good opposite to the evil meant by *"murder"* is the good of love toward the neighbor—70; in proportion as any one shuns *murders* of every kind as sins, in the same proportion he has love toward the neighbor (chap. viii.)—67-73; the various kinds and degrees of *murders*—67; *murder* lies inwardly hidden in man from his birth, and unless the Lord provided the means of reformation he would perish everlastingly—68-69; when a man is no longer in the evil of *murder,* but in the good of love toward the neighbor, whatever he does is a good of that love, and therefore is a good work—72.

MUTUALITY.

Life. On account of the *mutuality* preserved between the Lord and man, the Lord says that a man must do the work of repentance, which no one can do except as of himself—103; because of this also the Lord says that he must keep the commandments and must bring forth fruit—104; because of the *mutuality* which man has from the Lord, he must render an account of his works—105. See RECIPROCALITY.

MYRRH.

S. The *myrrh* offered by the wise men as a gift to the Lord at the nativity, means natural good—23 (3).

NAKED, NAKEDNESS.

S. The truths of the sense of the letter of the Word are not *naked* truths but appearances of truth—40; *naked* truth is in the spiritual sense and *naked* good in the celestial sense—ib.; see also 91; why the truths in some places in the sense of the letter are not *naked,* but clothed—51.

F. The nature of faith separate from charity presented in its *nakedness*—44.

NAME, NAMES.

L. As applied to the Lord *"name"* means truth—25; various *names* that are given to the Lord in the Word (the reason, and passages adduced)—34; see also 55; in the spiritual sense the *names* of persons and places signify something of the Lord, and derivatively, something of heaven and the church from Him, or else something opposite to them—2.

S. In the spiritual sense all the *names* in the Word signify things of heaven and the church—15; in the Word's spiritual and celestial senses some of the *names* are predicated of good, and some of truth, and some include both—80; many *names* of places in the land of Canaan and in the surrounding countries were retained in this Word with significations like those they had in the ancient Word—102; no *names* of persons or places occur in the Word in heaven, but in place thereof the things which the *names* signify—71.

Life. To "believe in the *name* of the Son of God," is to believe in the Word and to live according to it—17.

F. In the Word all the *names* of nations and peoples, and also those of persons and places, signify the things of the church—49.

NATION.

S. *Nation* is predicated of good and in the opposite sense of evil—84; the reason the word "*nations*" is associated with the word "peoples" in the Word (passages given)—86; *nations* and peoples outside the church receive spiritual light from those that have the Word—104-108; it is for this reason that in the Lord's Divine Providence there exists a universal commercial intercourse of the kingdoms of Europe with the *nations* outside the church—108.

Life. All *nations* which have religion possess precepts like those of the decalogue—65.

NATURAL.

S. From the Lord proceed the Celestial, the Spiritual, and the *Natural*, one after another—6; the *natural* is from the celestial and the spiritual, being their complex—ib.; the two kingdoms of the heavens founded upon the *natural* kingdom in which are men—34; the spiritual style of the Word differs entirely from a *natural* style—71. See DIVINE NATURAL.

Life. Those who do what is good from themselves are to be called in this book *natural* men—16; man possesses a *natural* mind and a spiritual mind, the *natural* mind is below, and the spiritual above—86; so long as a man does not shun evils as sins, the concupiscences of evil block up the interiors of the *natural* mind—ib. (4); so long as concupiscences of evils block up the interiors of the *natural* mind, so long the man is in hell —ib. (5); before men a *natural* moral man may appear exactly like a spiritual moral man, but not before angels—109.

F. The affection of use which a man has for his business for the sake of life in this world, is a *natural* affection only— 25; that those who have confirmed themselves in faith separate from charity do not possess any truth, is not credited by themselves while they live in the *natural* world—71.

Q. The Lord did not possess a Divine *Natural* before He assumed the Human —II.; the Holy Spirit enables man to understand spiritual truths in a *natural* way —V.; for the Lord has united the Divine *Natural* to the Divine Celestial and the Divine Spiritual—ib.; the Lord is Divine truth in the *natural* sense—ib.

NATURAL SENSE.

S. The *natural sense* of the Word is the basis, the containant, and the support of its spiritual sense and of its celestial sense—30; the *natural sense* is the ultimate sense of the Word—31; see also 32; is signified by the wall of the Holy Jerusalem—36; the celestial and spiritual senses of the Word are simultaneous in its *natural sense*—38 (2); from its *natural sense* the Word is like a ruby and a diamond—42; through the spiritual and celestial senses the Lord flows into the *natural sense*—58; the celestial and spiritual senses of the Word are evolved from its *natural sense* while a true man is in it—63; how from the *natural sense* the spiritual angels draw forth their own sense, and the celestial angels theirs (illustrated)—67; the spiritual sense of the Word revealed at this time in order to make it plain that the Word, from that sense, treats of the Lord and the church in the *natural sense*— 112. See also EXTERNAL SENSE, LITERAL SENSE, SENSE OF THE LETTER, and ULTIMATE SENSE.

NATURAL WORLD.

L. By the *natural world* is meant the world where men dwell—62.

NATURE.

S. A man who worships *nature* may easily fall into error in respect to the Word, and into a contempt for it—1; that which is from the Divine descending into *nature* is turned into such things as correspond to Divine things— 20 (3).

NAZIRITE.

S. The *Nazirites* represented the Lord in respect to the Word in its ultimates—35 (3); the Lord's power from the ultimate things of truth was represented by the *Nazirites* in the Jewish Church—49 (2); why the *Nazirites* were forbidden to shave their hair—ib. (4).

NEEDY.

S. Needy is an expression that is predicated of truth and in the opposite sense of falsity—84.

NEIGHBOR.

Life. In proportion as any one shuns murders of every kind as sins, in the same proportion he has love toward the *neighbor* (chap. viii.)—67-73.

F. What the *neighbor* is, described collectively, individually, and spiritually—20; difference between the two kinds of love to the *neighbor*, the natural and the spiritual—21.

NEW.

L. The meaning of "Behold, I make all things *new*"—65; the *new* things contained in "the present little work" (*The Doctrine of the Lord*) enumerated—65. See NEW EARTH, NEW HEAVENS, NEW JERUSALEM.

NEW CHURCH.

L. That the Lord came into the world (as treated of in all the Prophets of the Old Testament) in order to establish a *New Church*—3; a *New Church* is meant by the Holy City Jerusalem—63; it has been told in the *Revelation* (chaps. xxi. and xxii.) that a *New Church* in which true doctrine relative to the Lord will hold the chief place, is to be instituted by the Lord at the end of the former church—61; by the New Jerusalem (spoken of in the *Revelation*) is meant a *New Church* (chap. xii.)—62-65.

NEW EARTH.

L. By the *new earth* (described in *Rev.* xxi.) is meant a newness of the church in the natural world—62; see also 65.

NEW HEAVEN.

L. By the *new heaven* (described in *Rev.* xxi.) is meant a newness of the church in the spiritual world—62; see also 65.

NEW JERUSALEM.

L. By the *New Jerusalem* in the *Revelation* a New Church is meant (chap. xii.) —62-65; the Holy City *New Jerusalem* means a New Church as to doctrine—63.

S. By the foundation of the walls of the *New Jerusalem* is meant the truth of the sense of the letter of the Word—43.

NINEVEH.

S. The science of correspondences was known and cultivated in *Nineveh*—21; the ancients who still use the ancient Word in heaven were partly from *Nineveh*—102.

NOAH.

Q. (Replying to the question as to how it is, if there be no individual named *Noah*, that he is mentioned in *Ezekiel* with Daniel and Job)—*Noah* is mentioned in *Ezekiel* because mentioned in *Genesis*, and with a like meaning—IX.

NOBLE.

S. A church is a *noble* church if in genuine truths, an ignoble church if not —77.

NORTH.

F. The "waters that rise up out of the *north*" (*Jer.* xlvii. 2) are falsities from hell—53.

NOT.

Life. Why it is said in the second table (of the decalogue) that man must *not* do this or that evil, instead of saying that he must do this or that good—58.

NOURISHMENT.

Life. Truths are the agency for the *nourishment* of good—37.

NUMBER, NUMBERS.

S. What is signified by the *number* 144; and by the *number* 12—43 (2); *numbers* do not appear in the Word in heaven, but instead there appear the things to which the *numbers* correspond—71.

F. What is meant by the *number* of the beast, and the *number* of a man, and by his "*number* is 666" (*Rev.* xiii. 18)—60.

O.

S. In the third heaven they make use of the vowel "*o*" (probably "*o*" as in note) because it gives a full sound—90 (2).

OAK.

S. The *oak* means the sensuous good and truth of the church—18 (3).

OBEDIENCE.

F. That the Lord reduced hell under His *obedience*—35.

OBSCENE.

Life. To do *obscene* things is contrary to the sixth (commonly called the seventh) commandment—74; see also 78.

OBSCURITY.

S. They who read the Word without doctrine are in *obscurity* as to every truth —52.

OCEAN.

S. The sun is an *ocean* of fire—95 (2).

OIL.

S. *Oil* (in the parable of the ten virgins, *Matt.* xxv.) signifies the good of love —17 (2).

OLD TESTAMENT.

L. The subjects concerning the Lord that are treated of in the *Old Testament* enumerated—3; the whole Word of the *Old Testament* is about the Lord—19 (9).

S. In order that everything in the *Old Testament* should be preserved, even the letters, of the Lord's Divine Providence, were counted by the Masorites— 13 (4); examples from prophetical parts of the *Old Testament* of passages which would not be intelligible without a spiritual sense—15.

OLIVE.

S. The *olive* means the celestial good and truth of the church—18 (3); the *olive* signified the good of love—23 (2).

OMEGA.

L. Why the Lord is called the Alpha and the *Omega*—36.

OMNIPOTENCE.

L. To sit at the right hand of God signifies *omnipotence*—14 (8); see also 35 (10) (11).

ONE.

L. The Divine love and the Divine wisdom in the Lord make a *one*—1; the Divine and the Human in the Lord are not two, but *one*—29; by the term "Lord," and also by "Jehovah," after His Human was glorified, is meant the Divine and the Human together as a *one*—30 (4); the Lord's Divine called the Father, and the Divine Human called the Son, are not two, but *one* (passages in evidence)—34 (3); see also 46; God is *one* and the Lord is that God (chap. ix.)—45; see also 54; the sense of the letter of the Word of such a nature that things which form a *one* are distinguished as if they did not —55; they who believe in simplicity in three Persons, but of the three make a *one*, after death are instructed—ib. (3); God is *one* in Person and Essence—55 (6); according to Athanasian Creed allowable to think three Gods, not allowable to say, or name more than *one*—57; it is usual in the Word to name two Divines, and sometimes three which yet are *one*—46 (5); God is *one* in both Person and Essence —54.

S. The three degrees make *one* by correspondences—7; for a man to be a man of the church his will and his understanding must make a *one*—83; before the Lord the universal heaven is like *one* man—105.

Life. What is highest, what is intermediate, and what is last make a *one*— 14; in the Lord His Divine good and His Divine truth are a *one*, and therefore proceed from Him as a *one*, but they are not received as a *one* by angels in the heavens or by men on earth—32; angels of the heavens in wisdom and intelligence in proportion to the degree in which good in them makes a *one* with the truth—ib.; man's will and understanding were so created that they may be a one—43; of the utmost importance to know how the will and the understanding make *one* mind—ib.; evil of life and truth of faith cannot possibly act as a *one*—44.

F. Faith and truth are a *one*—6; see also 11; charity and faith make a *one* as do will and understanding, as do affection and thought, good and truth, essence and form—18; it is a Universal of Faith that God is *one*—35.

OPEN.

Life. So long as a man does not shun evils as sins, they prevent the spiritual mind from being *opened*—86 (4).

OPPOSITES.

Life. As good and evil are *opposites*, it follows that the latter is removed by means of the former. Two *opposites* cannot be together—71; an evil life cannot be converted into a good one, nor a good life into an evil one, because they are *opposites*, and conversion into what is *opposite* is extinction—8; being *opposites*, a good life is called life, and an evil one death—ib.; heaven and hell are *opposites*—18; evil and good are two *opposite* things—70; the lasciviousness of adultery and the chastity of marriage are two *opposites*—75; he who is in the *opposites* to heavenly things knows nothing about them—89.

ORDER.

L. That the Lord reduced heaven into *order*, so that it made a one with the church—3.

S. Two kinds of *order*, successive and simultaneous, defined—38; how simultaneous *order* is derived from that which is successive—ib. (2). See SIMULTANEOUS ORDER, and SUCCESSIVE ORDER.

ORGAN.

Q. Man is only an *organ* of life—III.

ORIENTALS.

S. The knowledge of correspondences survived among a number of the *orientals*, even until the Lord's advent—23 (3).

OWN.

S. Nothing blinds a man but his *Own*, and the confirmation of what is false—60; man's *Own* is the love of self, and the derivative conceit of self-intelligence—ib.; when men read the Word while themselves and the world are their ends in view, they think constantly from their *Own*, which is thick darkness—61 (2); in this state man cannot be withdrawn by the Lord from his *Own*—ib.; man's will is his very *Own* which is nothing but evil, and man is unwilling to understand anything which does not come from the *Own* of his will, and from this *Own* he does not wish to understand anything except that which relates to himself and the world—115, ib. (2).

Life. The *Own* of man is evil from his birth—92; as this *Own* of man constitutes the first root of his life, it is evident what kind of a tree he would make unless, etc.—93.

OX.

S. *Oxen* signify affections and powers of the natural mind—23; the *ox* signifies natural affection—18 (3).

PAIRS.

S. In the Word there are *pairs* of expressions that appear like repetitions (examples and explanation)—84; the existence of such *pairs* shown by extensive citations—85-87.

PALACES.

F. Houses and *palaces* appear in the Spiritual World—63; those in wisdom and intelligence dwell in magnificent *palaces*—ib. (2).

PALE.

S. The *pale* horse (*Rev.* vi.) signifies the understanding of the Word annihilated by evils of life, etc.—12.

PAPISTS.

S. The *Papists* are meant by the beast (*Rev.* xvii. 3)—25; Christians among whom the Word is read are in the center of the spiritual world, the *Papists* are round about them—105 (2); the Reformation was brought about because the Word had been almost completely rejected by the *Papists*—110.

F. The chief safeguard of the rule of the *Papists* is ignorance of truth—8.

PARALLELISM.

F. There is a full *parallelism* between the quickening of man and the growing of a tree—32.

PARTAKES.

Life. Every work (of the man who does not regard evils as sins) *partakes* of the evil that is within him ; for his internal is what gives it birth—72.

PASSION.

L. The Lord is called the Son of man when His *passion* is treated of (the reason and passages adduced)—24. For *passion* of the cross, see CROSS.

PEOPLE, PEOPLES.

S. People is predicated of truth and in the opposite sense of falsity—84 ; *peoples* are coupled with nations in the Word, because *peoples* mean those in truths, and in the opposite sense those in falsities, and nations mean those in good and in the opposite sense those in evils (passages given)—86 ; the *people* outside the church who are not in possession of the Word have light by its means (chap. xiii.)—104-113 ; *peoples* who have in this world known nothing of God appear like apes in the spiritual world—116.

PERCEPTIONS.

S. Marks in the Word of the spiritual kingdom denote *perceptions*—74 ; man acknowledges the truth of the Word from an interior *perception*—58 ; *perception* comes from affection, and thought from *perception*, and thus is produced the acknowledgment which is called faith—ib.

Life. The source of the general *perception* that whoever leads a good life is saved, and that whoever leads an evil one is damned—3 ; this *perception* from heaven is common to all (its effect on the reception of the doctrine that faith alone saves)—4 ; the existence of this *perception* among the English clergy—7 ; from the love of truth proceeds the *perception* of truth, from the *perception* of truth comes thought about truth, and from all these together comes the acknowledgment of truth—36.

PERCEPTIBLE.

Q. That the Holy Spirit (unlike the Spirit of God mentioned in the Old Testament) operates on man *perceptibly*—V·

PERFECT.

Life. Those who are *perfect* when the Lord is in them—84.

PERISH.

L. Unless the Lord had come into the world and revealed Himself, mankind would have *perished*—3.

PERSON, PERSONS.

L. In the spiritual sense the names of *persons* signify something of the Lord—2 ; the Divine and the Human in the Lord are one *Person*—21 ; see also 34 (3), 35 (2) ; God is one in both *Person* and Essence—54 ; the doctrine of the Athanasian Creed agrees with the truth, provided that by a Trinity of *Persons* is understood a Trinity of *Person* (chap. xi.) —55-61 ; it was of Divine permission that Christians at first received the doctrine of three *Persons* (the reason given)—55 (4) ; every one sees in himself that if God is one, He is one in both *Person* and Essence—ib. (6) ; a Trinity of *Person* stated—57 ; see also 65 ; in the Lord, God and Man are one *Person*—60.

S. There are no names of *persons* in the Word of the angels—71.

F. A man who loves the neighbor from charity conjoins himself with his good and not with his *person*, whereas one who conjoins another from mere friendship, conjoins himself with his *person*—21.

Q. The Divine Trinity in one *Person* is to be understood as soul, body, and proceeding operation—III. ; there is a like trinity in man which together constitute one *person*—ib. ; was the Divine Human of Jehovah before the incarnation a *Person?*—VI.; the Most Holy Trinity is to be apprehended in one *Person*—VII.

PERSUASION.

F. A *persuasion* that a thing is so is not faith—11.

PHARISAIC.

Life. *Pharisaic* good may be compared to rotten wood, dross, or even ordure overlaid with gold—10.

PHILISTINES.

F. They who are in faith separate from charity are represented by the *Philistines* (chap. vii.)—49-54; evident from various things said in the Word about the *Philistines*—50; hence called "the uncircumcised"—51; evident from many other things besides their wars with Israel—52; evident also from the prophecies concerning them—53.

PIERCING.

L. Signification of *piercing* the Lord's side at the crucifixion—16 (6).

PIETY, PIOUS.

Life. A person is not *pious* who does not shun evils, as sins—25; illustrated by the state of many after death—26; in proportion as a man has not been purified from evils, his *pious* things are not *pious*, taught in Word (passages cited) —30.

PLACES.

L. In the spiritual sense the names of *places* signify something of the Lord, and derivately, something of heaven and the church—2.

S. There are no names of *places* in the Word of the angels, but instead thereof, the things which the *places* signify—71.

POOR.

S. *Poor* is predicated of good, and in the opposite sense of evil—84.

POPLAR.

S. The *poplar* signifies the natural good and truth of the church—18 (3).

POWER.

S. The Divine truth is in its *power* in the sense of the letter of the Word—37; the reason—38 (2); how great and of what nature is the *power* of the Divine truth in the heavens and on earth, set forth—49.

Life. Every one is so constituted as to be able (by the Lord's *power*, if he begs for it) to shun evils as of himself—31.

Q. *Power* (*virtus*) mentioned as the third of the trinity in man—VII.

PRAY.

L. In His state of humiliation the Lord *prayed* to the Father as to one who was other than Himself—35 (3).

PRECIOUS STONES.

S. *Precious stones* signify Divine truths in their ultimates—44 (4); the truths of the sense of the letter of the Word, signified by the *precious stones* in the garden of Eden (mentioned in *Ezekiel* xxvii.)—45.

PRESENCE.

L. To "go forth" and to "proceed" (as the Holy Spirit) is nothing else than to enlighten and teach by the *presence* of the Lord—46 (4).

S. In the sense of the letter of the Word, and not elsewhere, the Lord is *present* with man—53; the Lord is *present* with a man through the reading of the Word, but is conjoined with him through his understanding of its truth—78; before His coming into the world the Lord was *present* with the men of the church mediately, through heaven, but since His coming He is *present* immediately—99.

PRESENT DAY.

F. The faith of the *present day* in its universal idea or form, set forth—38, 39.

PRIEST, PRIESTS.

L. That the Lord was condemned by the chief *priests* and elders, signified that He was so treated by the whole Jewish Church—16 (6).

Life. How good loves truth, illustrated in the life of a *priest*—39; see also 72; and 83; a *priest* when he is in the good of love toward the neighbor, does a good work whenever he teaches and leads—72.

PRIESTHOOD.

S. Aaron's *priesthood* represented the Lord as to Divine good, and as to the work of salvation—44.

PRINCE OF THIS WORLD.

L. The *prince of this world* means hell —13.

PRIOR.

S. The three degrees are distinguished from each other like *prior*, posterior, and postreme—7.

PROCEED.

L. To "go forth" and to "*proceed*" (applied to the Holy Spirit) is nothing else than to enlighten and teach—46 (4).

S. From the Lord *proceed* two things, Divine love and Divine wisdom—3; from the Lord *proceed* the Celestial, the Spiritual, and the Natural, one after another (each defined and described)—6.

Life. Divine good and Divine truth are two universals which *proceed* from the Lord—32; they *proceed* as a one, but are not received as a one by angels and men—ib.; (differences of reception described)—ib.

PROCEEDING.

L. The Word is the Divine *proceeding* —2.

S. The Word is the Divine *proceeding* —19; in the ultimate sense of the Word the Divine *proceeding* is in its fullness— 44 (3).

Q. The Divine *proceeding* is mentioned as the third essential of the Trinity—VII.

PROFANE.

S. By committing adultery a celestial angel understands to deny the Lord's divinity and *profane* the Word—67 (3).

PROMULGATION.

Life. By their *promulgation* from Mount Sinai the laws of the decalogue were, from being merely civil laws, made also laws of religion—53.

PROPHET, PROPHETS.

L. In the Gospels in many places, *Prophets* mean all the things that have been written in the books of the *Prophets*—9; what is meant by the *prophet* bearing the sins of the house of Israel, and what by the Lord's being called "the *Prophet*," and "the Great *Prophet*" —15 (2) (8), 16 (5); how the *prophets* represented the Word in its ultimate sense (illustrated)—15 (8); why called sons of man—28; the *Prophets* (that is, these books of the Word) treat much of the Lord's combats—33 (4); *Prophets* and Psalms all treat of the Lord—special phases enumerated—37; Word spoken through the *prophets*—52; what is meant by their being in vision—ib.; what by Jehovah's speaking to them—ib.

S. By means of the various things the *prophets* suffered and endured they represented the violence done by the Jews to the sense of the letter of the Word (illustrated)—35; the *prophets* represented the Word; what was meant by Ezekiel shaving off the hair of his head and of his beard—ib. (2).

Q. *Prophet* signifies the truth of the church from the Word—I.; the Lord is called in a pre-eminent degree, the *Prophet*—ib.; why the *prophets* called themselves sons of man—ib.

PROPORTION.

Life. In *proportion* as a man shuns evils as sins, in the same *proportion* he does goods, not from himself but from the Lord (chap. iii.)—18-31; set forth more fully in 21; in *proportion* as one shuns evils as sins in the same *proportion* he loves truths—32; angels of all the heavens are in wisdom and intelligence in *proportion* to the degree in which the good in them makes a one with truth—ib.; see 34; in *proportion* as any one is in good, and from good loves truths, in the same *proportion* he loves the Lord—38; in *proportion* as any one shuns evils as sins, in the same *proportion* he has faith and is spiritual (chap. v.)—42-52; in *proportion* as any one shuns murders of every kind as sins, in the same *proportion* he has love toward the neighbor (chap. viii.)—67-73; in *proportion* as any one shuns adulteries of every kind as sins, in the same *proportion* he loves chastity (chap. ix.)—74-79; see especially, 75; in *proportion* as any one shuns thefts of every kind as sins, in the same *proportion* he loves sincerity (chap. x.)—80-86; in *proportion* as any one shuns false witness of every kind as sin, in the same *proportion* he loves the truth (chap. xi.)—87-91; in *proportion* as any one battles with and thus removes evils, in the same *proportion* good takes its place—95.

F. In *proportion* as any one shuns evils as sins and looks to the Lord, in the same *proportion* he is in charity, and thence in faith—23.

PSALMS.

L. *Psalms* and Prophets treat much of the Lord's combats—33 (4); they all treat of the Lord by treating of His works—37; why David so often wrote of the Lord in his *Psalms* when writing about himself—44.

S. An account of certain African spirits hearing a *Psalm* of David and being greatly affected thereby—108.

PURPOSE.

Life. The combat (against evils) is not severe except in the case of those who have indulged them of set *purpose* —97.

PURSES.

S. An account of large *purses* full of silver, representing knowledges of truth in great abundance—26 (3) (4).

QUALITY.

F. We love a human being for his *quality*—20; the *quality* we love is his use —ib.; see also 21.

RACE. See HUMAN RACE.

RAM.

F. The *ram* and the sheep (*Dan.* viii.) mean those in charity—61; spiritual sense of the combat between the *ram* and he-goat as related in *Daniel* viii.— 65; the *ram* signifies those in faith from charity—67.

RAPHAELS.

S. Concerning certain ones who expected to be *Raphaels* because they had confirmed from the Word the tenets of their faith—61.

RATIONAL.

S. How the light of heaven illumines man's intellectual called the *rational*— 41; those who do not believe in the Word, it is practicable to deal with only from *rational* light—115; a doctrine hatched from *rational* light will be that a man's self is to be worshiped—116.

Life. Man is not *rational* so long as the will is not in heaven together with the understanding—15 (2).

Q. In what sense did the Lord call Himself the Son of man if He took not a *rational* soul from the mother?—I.; had the Lord a *rational* soul from the Father? —the Lord put on the Divine *Rational* when He assumed the Human—II.; the Divine Essence transcends both the angelic and the human *rational*—ib.; the Divine *Rational* existed by means of influx—ib.

READ.

S. The man who *reads* the Word from the Lord, and not from himself alone, is filled by it with the good of love and the truths of wisdom—3; why the Word gives life to those who devoutly *read* it —19; they who are in Divine truths, and in the faith that the Word is Divine, see Divine truths in natural light when *reading* the Word in enlightenment from the Lord—41; those who *read* the Word without doctrine are in obscurity as to every truth—52; see also 57; how when he (Swedenborg) *read* the Word communication was effected with the various heavens—64; how the two senses are evolved from the natural sense when a man *reads* the Word—65; the Lord is present with man as he *reads* the Word, and is conjoined to him according to his understanding of it—78.

REAGENT.

Life. Man is a *reagent* in his relation to the Lord—107.

REASON.

Life. Freedom and *reason* are the Lord's in man, without them he cannot be reformed or regenerated—101; why they were given by the Lord—102.

REASONINGS.

S. That the locusts appeared "like horses prepared for war" signified their *reasonings*—13 (2); see also the meaning of "the sound of their wings was as the sound of chariots running to war"—ib. (3).

F. "Whose fruit shall be a flying fire-serpent" (*Isa.* xiv. 29) signifies *reasonings* from falsities of evil—53.

RECEPTACLES.

S. The truths of the sense of the letter of the Word are *receptacles* of genuine truths—40.

Life. Man's will and understanding are the *receptacles* of good and truth—43.

RECIPROCAL.

L. The unition of the Divine and the Human in the Lord was *reciprocal*—35 (8); it is the same with all unition, unless it is *reciprocal* it is not full—ib.

Life. *Reciprocality* is essential to man's conjunction with God—102; man has this ability of *reciprocal* action from the Lord —103; as in man there is *reciprocality* the church teaches that he should examine himself, confess his sins, desist from them, and lead a new life—106.

RECOMPENSE.

L. By a day of *recompense* is meant the advent of the Lord to judgment—5.

RECONCILIATION.

Life. The Lord teaches the good of love in what He says about *reconciliation* with the neighbor—73.

RECTITUDE.

Life. See SINCERITY—83.

RED.

L. The "apparel" which was "*red*" (*Isa.* lxiii.) means the Word to which violence had been done—14 (2).

F. The dragon was said to be "*red*" from love that is merely natural—59.

REDEEMER.

L. On account of the Lord's combats He is called *Redeemer*—33 (4); because He glorified His Human, he thereby became *Redeemer*—ib.; the *Redeemer* and Saviour of the world is no other than the Lord in respect to the Divine Human —34 (3); Jehovah is called *Redeemer* (passages given) and is therefore the same as the Lord—38; see also 45; that the Lord became man's *Redeemer*—65.

Q. The question is asked whether the Most Holy Trinity may not be one and the same Lord in three characters, distinctions of offices, or relations toward men, as Creator, *Redeemer*, and Sanctifier—VII.

REDEMPTION.

L. The Lord is called Son of man when *Redemption*, Salvation, Reformation, and Regeneration are treated of— 27; *Redemption* is an attribute proper to the Human—34 (3).

S. Without the Word man would not know anything about *Redemption*—114.

Q. *Redemption* is an attribute of the Divine Human from the Divine *Esse*— VII.

REDUCE.

F. That the Lord *reduced* hell into order—35.

REFORMATION.

L. The Lord is called the Son of man when *Reformation* is treated of (passages) —27.

S. It was because the Word was almost completely rejected by the Papists that the *Reformation* was brought about of the Lord's Divine Providence—110.

Life. Unless means were provided for man's *reformation*, man would perish everlastingly (the means enumerated)— 69.

F. *Reformation* is the first state of faith—31.

REGENERATION.

L. The Lord is called Son of man when *Regeneration* is treated of—27.

F. *Regeneration* is the second state of man's spiritual progress, and exists when charity is in the first place—31.

Q. Regeneration is an attribute of the Holy Spirit—VII.

RELIGION.

S. In what way a man remaining in a false *religion* into which he was born will yet receive truths in the other life and be saved—92; illustrated by certain ones in a false *religion* who remained in its falsities, and others of the same *religion* who withdrew from them—93; that from the most ancient times there has been a *religion* has not been due to the penetration of men—117.

Life. All *religion* is of the life, and the life of *religion* is to do that which is good—1; this statement confirmed by passages from the Word—2; the reason of this—8; the laws of the decalogue made laws of *religion* through promulgation from Mount Sinai by Jehovah—53; it is a common principle of every *religion* that a man ought to examine himself, repent, and desist from sins—64; all nations in the wide world which have *religion* possess precepts like those of the decalogue—65; if from his faith and his life a man does not regard adulteries as sins, he has no *religion* (the contrary also stated)—77; unless a man has *religion* he does evils from delight—92.

F. The temple of a man whose understanding has been closed up by his *religion* compared to a den under ground—48.

RELIGIOUS PRINCIPLES.

F. In the Word *religious principles* are represented by the names of nations and peoples, and by those of persons and places—49.

REMISSION.

L. The imputation of the Lord's merit is nothing but the *remission* of sins after repentance (chap. v.)—18; described by the Lord in *John*—ib. (5).

REPENT, REPENTANCE.

L. Sins cannot be taken away from a man except by actual *repentance*—17 (3); *repentance* described—ib.; that the Lord and His disciples preached *repentance*—18 (4).

Life. It is a common principle of every religion that a man should *repent* —64; man cannot perform *repentance* without freedom and reason—101; man must do the work of *repentance* because he has ability from the Lord—103.

REPETITIONS.

S. The frequent occurrence in the Word of two expressions which appear like *repetitions*, but which are from the marriage of goodness and truth—81; see also 82 and 85.

REPRESENT.

L. A prophet's bearing the iniquities of the house of Israel did not take them away, but *represented* them—16 (3).

REPRESENTATIVES.

S. The *representatives* of the church and their conversion into things of idolatry and magic—22; the Word could not be written in any other way than by *representatives*—117.

Q. Before the incarnation all things of the church were *representatives*—VI.; these ceased after the incarnation like the shades of evening or night at the rising of the sun—ib.

REPRESENTATIVE CHURCHES.

S. All the churches that had existed before the Lord's advent were *representative churches*—99.

REQUISITES.

Life. There are two *requisites* of salvation, first, that a man should shun evils as sins, and, secondly, that he should do this as of himself—22.

RESIST.

Life. Let men even once in a week or twice in a month *resist* the evils they are inclined to, and they will perceive a change—97.

RESURRECTION.

L. The Lord's *resurrection* signifies His glorification—16 (6); differently from any man the Lord *rose* as to His whole body—35 (9).

REVEALED.

Life. What good is in itself must be *revealed*—11.

REVELATION, BOOK OF.

F. The *Book of Revelation* treats generally and specifically of the two great evil religious principles, the love of ruling and the conceit of self-intelligence—55.

REVENGE.

Life. Murder lies hidden in *revenge* —67.

RIGHTEOUSNESS. See also JUSTICE.

L. By combats against the hells the Lord became *Righteousness*—14; the Lord's *righteousness* can never be imputed to man—18 (3).
Life. In the highest sense to claim *righteousness* is to steal—80.

RIGHT HAND.

L. To sit on the *right hand* of God signifies omnipotence—14 (8); see also 35 (10) (11); applied to the Lord—60; "the man of thy *right hand*" means the Lord in respect to the Word (the reason)—27 (2).

RITES.

S. The *rites* of the ancient churches consisted exclusively of correspondences —20 (2).

RITUALS.

L. Many arcana of the Lord's glorification are contained in the *rituals* of the Israelitish church—14 (11).

ROOT.

Life. Those in whom the truth of the Word cannot take *root* (enumerated)— 90; as man's Own constitutes the first *root* of his life, how needful that it be plucked up set forth—93; that the *root* of evil is not removed except by combat —94; with the merely natural *root* of evil remains embedded—108.

RUBY.

S. In its natural sense the Word is like a *ruby*—42.

SACKS.

S. The meaning of the great purses having the appearance of *sacks* told in a memorable relation—26 (3) (4).

SACRIFICE.

L. By a day of *sacrifice* in the Word is meant the advent of the Lord to judgment—5.

SACRIFICES.

S. Worship by means of *sacrifices* was known before the Word was given to the Israelitish nation—101.

SALVATION, SAVED.

L. *Salvation* can be awarded only after a man has performed repentance— 18 (2); no man could have been *saved* unless the Lord had come into the world (the reason)—17; see also 33 (3); *salvation* is an attribute proper to the Human—34 (3); the Lord is called the Son of man when *salvation* is treated of —27; every man who is *saved* ascends into heaven—35 (11).
S. All things in the Word that concern man's *salvation* are bare—55.
Life. The general opinion of the present day concerning the nature of *salvation* stated—91; every one who has religion knows that whoever leads a good life is *saved*—3.
F. It is a universal of faith that no mortal could have been *saved* unless the Lord had come into the world—35; the idea of how man is *saved* as held in the faith of the present day—39 xi.

SAMSON.

S. The Lord's power from the ultimate things of truth, represented by *Samson*—49 (2).

SANCTIFIER.

Q. The question is asked whether the Most Holy Trinity may not be one and the same Lord in three characters, distinctions of offices, or relations towards men, as Creator, Redeemer, and *Sanctifier*—VII. See REDEEMER and CREATOR.

SANCTUARY.

S. The Word is called the *Sanctuary* in which the Lord dwells with man—2 (4); in every larger society of heaven a copy of the Word is kept in its *sanctuary* —72; in the *sanctuary* where the copy of the Word is kept there is a flaming and bright light—73.

SANDY.

S. He who is confirmed in the doctrine of a false religion is in a *sandy* plain where there is not even grass—96a.

SATAN.

L. *Satan* means hell—13.

SATISFACTION.

F. The teaching of the present day concerning how God the Son made *satisfaction* to the Father—39 ii.

SAVIOUR.

L. How the Lord became the *Saviour* —33 (4) (5); the *Saviour* is none other than the Lord in respect to the Divine Human—34 (3); Jehovah is called *Saviour* and is therefore the Lord (passages adduced)—38; see also 45; read in this connection 65.

SAY.

L. Allowable in the Athanasian Creed to think three Gods, but not allowable to *say* more than one—57.

SCARLET.

S. " *Scarlet* double-dyed" (*Exod.* xxvi. 1) signifies spiritual good—46.

SCIENCE.

Life. From *science* one may know of the quality of gold, but the quality of good can be known only from revelation—11.

SCORPION.

S. " *Scorpion*" (*Rev.* ix.) signifies their persuasiveness—13 (2).

SCRIPTURE.

L. Universal Holy *Scripture* treats of the Lord (chap. i.)—1-7; see especially 7.

S. The Holy *Scripture* or Word is Divine Truth itself (chap. i.)—1-4.

SEALED.

S. The 144,000 who were *sealed* (*Rev.* vii.), explanation of the account—11.

SEE.

t. A doctrine of the angels that we must *see* a thing in order really to believe it (set forth)—4; the meaning of the Lord's words to Thomas (blessed are they who do not *see*, and yet believe —*John* xx. 29) explained—10.

SEED.

Life. It is truth that is meant by the *seed* in the field as related in the parable of the sower (exposition of the parable) —90.

SELF, HIMSELF.

Life. The goods one does from *self* are not good—9; in proportion as one shuns evils as sins, in the same proportion he does goods not from *himself* (chap. iii.) —18; every one is so constituted as to be able (by the Lord's power, if he begs for it) to shun evils as of *himself*—31; a man who fights against evils cannot but do so as of *himself*—96; to act in freedom according to reason is to act from *himself* —101.

SELL.

Life. To " *sell* all that he had" means to remove his heart from riches—66.

SENSE OF THE LETTER.

S. The *sense of the letter* of the Word was represented by purses full of silver —26 (4); the prophets of the Old Testament by means of the various things they suffered and endured, represented the violence done by the Jews to the *sense of the letter* of the Word—35; the spiritual, celestial, and thence Divine nature of the Word does not appear in the *sense of the letter*—6; the *sense of the letter* of the Word is the basis, the containant, and the support of its spiritual and celestial senses (chap. iii.)— 27-36; without the *sense of the letter* the Word would be like a palace without a foundation (other similes)—33; *sense of the letter* signified by the wall of the holy Jerusalem—36; Divine truth in the *sense of the letter* of the Word is in its fullness, in its holiness, and in its power (chap. iv.)—37–49; in the *sense of the letter* is the very Word itself—39; the spiritual sense without the *sense of the letter* is not the Word—ib.; the truths of the *sense of the letter* are appearances of truth —40; the truths of the Word's *sense of the letter* are meant by the foundations of the wall of the New Jerusalem—43; also by the Urim and Thummim—44; by the precious stones in the garden of Eden (described in *Ezekiel* xxviii.)—45; by the curtains and veils of the Tabernacle—46; by the external things of the Temple at Jerusalem—47; the power of the *sense of the letter*, how shown—49; the doctrine of the church is to be drawn from the *sense of the letter* of the Word, and is to be confirmed thereby (chap. v.)—50–61; in the *sense of the letter* the Word is like a man clothed (an illustration)—55; genuine truth appears in this sense to none but those who are in enlightenment from the Lord—57; by means of the *sense of the letter* of the Word there is conjunction with the Lord and association with the angels (chap. vi.)—62–69; how association with angels is effected by the *sense of the letter*—63; how this kind of communication may be abused by spirits beneath the heavens—64; the celestial and spiritual senses lie hidden within the *sense of the letter*—80; it is possible for heresies to be drawn from the *sense of the letter* of the Word, but it is hurtful to confirm them (chap. x.)— 91–97; the effect of a man's applying the *sense of the letter* to confirm the loves of the world—96; the *sense of the letter* acts as a guard against perverting the Divine truths that lie within—97.

SENSES OF THE WORD.

S. The way in which the evolution of the *senses of the Word* is effected—65; for the three *senses of the Word* consult the following references: first, EXTERNAL SENSE, LITERAL SENSE, NATURAL SENSE, SENSE OF THE LETTER, and ULTIMATE SENSE; secondly, INTERNAL SENSE and SPIRITUAL SENSE; and thirdly, CELES-

TIAL SENSE. (This last is sometimes called " *Highest Sense*.")

SENSUOUS.

S. The state of the church when man, having become *sensuous*, persuades himself that falsities are truths, is treated of in *Rev.* ix.—13; the locusts (*Rev.* ix.) having " teeth as the teeth of lions" signifies that *sensuous* things appeared to them as having power over all things— ib. (2).

SENT.

L. The Lord's being *sent* by the Father into the world means that He was conceived from Jehovah the Father—20.

SERPENT.

S. In ancient times they made images of *serpents* because *serpents* signified the sagacity of the sensuous man—23.

F. " For out of the *serpent's* root shall go forth a basilisk" (*Isa.* xiv. 29) signifies the destruction of all truth by the conceit of self-intelligence—53.

SHADE.

S. With those who read the Word from the doctrine of a false religion, and still more if they confirm it from the Word, the truth of the Word is as it were in the *shade* of night—60.

SHADOWS.

Q. Before the incarnation all things of the church were like *shadows*—VI.

SHAVE.

S. The prophet (*Ezek.* v.) *shaved* off the hair of his head and of his beard that he might represent the state of the Jewish Church in respect to the Word —35 (2).

SHEEP.

S. *Sheep* signify charity—18 (3).

F. In the Word the Lord is called the " Shepherd," the church the " fold," and the men of the church taken collectively the " flock," and individually " *sheep* "—61.

SHUN.

Life. As evil and good are two opposite things, it follows that if a man *shuns* evil as sin, he comes into the good that is opposite to the evil—70; see also 83; the reason given in 58. See also EVIL, PROPORTION, and SINS.

SIDE.

L. That they pierced the *side* of the Lord signified that they had completely extinguished all the truth of the Word and all its good—16 (6).

SIDON.

S. *Sidon* signifies the knowledge of good—18 (3).

SIGN.

F. A great *sign* in heaven, a woman encompassed by the sun (*Rev.* xii.) explained as to its spiritual sense—58, 59.

SILVER.

S. *Silver* in great purses represented (in a memorable relation) the great abundance of truths in the Word—26 (3) (4).

SIMPLE, SIMPLICITY.

L. On account of their *simplicity* the first Christians were permitted to discriminate the Divinity into three Persons —55 (2) ; they who believe this in *simplicity*, and do not confirm themselves in the idea of three Gods, after death receive instruction as to the truth from the angels—ib. (3).

S. The science of correspondences was not disclosed to the Christians of the primitive church because they were so very *simple*—24 ; the appearances of the letter of the Word are accommodated and adapted to the comprehension of the *simple*—40; the Word in the heavens is so written that the *simple* understand it in *simplicity* and the wise in wisdom— 72; they who believe in the Divine anger, wrath, and vengeance, in *simplicity*, are not condemned for that simple faith—94; the principle of belief in *simplicity*, and that it does not injure, illustrated from nature—95.

SIMULTANEOUS.

S. The spiritual and celestial senses are *simultaneous* in the natural sense— 37; *simultaneous* order described—38;

formed from successive order—ib. (2) ; see also 65.

SINCERITY.

Life. In proportion as any one shuns thefts of every kind as sins, in the same proportion he loves *sincerity* (chap. x.)— 80–86 ; what similar virtues are included in *sincerity*—83; confirmatory passages from the Word—84.

SINS.

L. By the passion of the cross the Lord did not take away *sins*, but bore them (chap. iv.)—15–17 ; what is meant by bearing the *sins* of the people—16; what by taking them away—17 ; the imputation of the Lord's merit is nothing but the remission of *sins* after repentance (chap. v.)—18; the Lord and His disciples preached the remission of *sins*— ib. (4).

Life. In proportion as a man shuns evils as *sins*, in the same proportion he does goods, not from himself, but from the Lord (chap. iii.)—18–31 ; in the same proportion also he loves truths (chap. iv.)—32–41; has faith and is spiritual (chap. v.)—42–52; the decalogue teaches what evils are *sins* (chap. vi.)—53–61; the evils to be shunned as *sins* enumerated—62; applied to murders of every kind—67; to adulteries of every kind— 74; to thefts of every kind—80; to false witness of every kind—87; no one can shun evils as *sins* so as to be inwardly averse to them except by combats against them (chap. xii.)—92–100; man ought to shun evils as *sins* and fight against them as of himself (chap. xiii.) —101–107; if any one shuns evils for any other reason than because they are *sins*, he does not shun them, but merely prevents them from appearing before the world (chap. xiv.)—108–114.

SLEEP.

S. To "*sleep*" and to "*awake*" signify the life of man in this world which is natural life, and his life after death which is spiritual—17 (2).

SNARES.

L. The "*snares* of death" (*Ps.* xviii. 5) signify temptations—14 (6).

SOCIETY.

S. Communications with the heavens is with various *societies* according to the variations of the internal sense—64; this is abused by evil spirits—ib.; in every larger *society* a copy of the Word is kept in its sanctuary—72; every *society* of heaven is a heaven in a smaller form, and is like a man—107; in each *society* of heaven those in the center correspond to the heart and lungs—ib.; an account of a communication being opened to certain African spirits with a *society* in heaven which was in conjunction with those in the world who were singing a Psalm—108; each verse in the Word communicates with some *society* in heaven—113.

SOLDIER.

Life. That good loves truth, illustrated by comparison with a *soldier*—39.

SOLITUDE.

S. "*Solitude*" is predicated of truth or falsity—84.

SON.

L. There is no such thing as a *Son* born from eternity—19; that the Lord from eternity does not mean the *Son* which was born of Mary in time—30; by the *Son*, alone, is meant the Divine Human—ib. (4); see also 34 (3) and 46 (2); the Lord is both Father and *Son*—32 (6); not harmful for the first Christians to believe in a Trinity of three Persons so long as they believed the *Son* to be Infinite, Uncreate, Almighty, God, and Lord—55 (2).

F. The doctrine of Father and *Son* as held in the present-day faith of the church, set forth—38, 39.

Q. The question is asked whether the *Son* signifies the same as the Divine wisdom—IV.

SON OF GOD.

L. The Lord's Human conceived of Jehovah and born of the virgin Mary is the *Son of God*—19 (2); see also 32 (7); the *Son of God* meant Messiah in the Jewish Church—19 (8); the *Son of God* is Jesus—21; the Human itself which was in the Divine from conception, is the *Son of God*—32 (7); the Human from the Divine within Him is the Divine Human, and is the *Son of God*—35. See SON OF GOD AND SON OF MAN, and SON OF MAN.

Life. To "believe in the name of the *Son of God*" is to believe the Word and to live according to it—17; those are called "*sons of God*" (*John* i. 12, 13) who are not in what is of self in their will—51.

SON OF GOD AND SON OF MAN.

L. In respect to the Divine Human the Lord is called *Son of God*, and in respect to the Word, the *Son of man* (chap. vi.)—19-28; the Lord is called *Son of God* when His Divinity, His oneness with the Father, His Divine Power, faith in Him and life from Him are being treated of, and *Son of man* when His passion, Judgment, His advent, and, in general, redemption, salvation, reformation, and regeneration are treated of—22. These last are elaborated in 23-27. See SON OF MAN.

SON OF MAN.

L. When the Lord is called *Son of man*—23; He is called *Son of man* when His passion is treated of—24; when Judgment—25; when His advent is treated of—26; and when redemption is treated of—27; the "*Son of man*" signifies the Lord in respect to the Word—16 (7); see 50 (2); a word "against the *Son of man*" is something said against the Word by wrongly interpreting its meaning—50 (2). See also SON OF GOD AND SON OF MAN.

Q. Replying to the question "In what sense did the Lord call Himself the *Son of man?*"—He was so called because He was the Word, or Divine truth as to the Human; in the spiritual sense *Son of man* signifies the truth of the church from the Word; the Lord therefore called Himself *Son of man* as to the Human—I.

SONS OF GOD.

L. Who are meant by "*sons of God*" in *John* i. 13—18 (5).

SONS OF MAN.

L. Why the prophets were called "*sons of man*"—28.

Q. Why the prophets called themselves "*sons of man*"—I.

SOUL.

L. The Divine in the Lord was His *soul*—29 (2); as the Lord's *soul* was the very Divine of the Father, His body, or Human, must also have become Divine —ib.; the Divine operated through the Human as the *soul* does through the body—32 (2); see also 35 (2); the life from the respiration of the lungs is what is properly meant by spirit, and also by *soul*—47.

S. Heart is predicated of the good of love, and *soul* of the truth from that good —84; the spiritual sense of the Word is related to its external sense as *soul* is to body—4; see also 5.

Life. Conjunction of man's will and understanding meant in the Word by man's heart and *soul*—86 (6).

SPEAK.

L. What is meant by God's *speaking* to the prophets—52.

S. In what way the men of the Most Ancient Church could *speak* with the angels—21; the Lord does not *speak* to man except in what is full—97 (3).

Life. Why a man who is not spiritual can *speak* like a spiritual man—15.

SPHERE.

S. The external Divine *sphere* of the Word is described (*Ezek.* i. 4)—97 (5); see further on in same reference.

SPIRIT.

L. By "*spirit*" when said of the Lord is specifically meant the life of His wisdom—51; what is meant by "*spirit*"—46 (7)-53; by *spirit* is meant man's life (passages)—47; also the varying affections of life in man (illustrations and passages quoted)—48; also the life of one who is regenerate, which is called spiritual life —49; also spiritual life in those who are in humiliation—ib. (2); when said of the Lord, *spirit* means His Divine life, thus the Lord Himself (passages re-

ferred to)—50; *spirit* is used for Jehovah, thus the Lord—ib. (2); blasphemy against—ib.; when said of the Lord, *spirit* means specifically His wisdom (passages)—51; when mentioned in the writings of the prophets, *spirit* means the Divine truth from the Lord—51 (5). See also HOLY SPIRIT.

S. The internal sense of the Word is the *spirit* which gives life to the letter —4; in the Word alone there is *spirit* and there is life—69.

Life. The conjunction of man's will and understanding is meant in the Word by "heart and *spirit*"—86 (6).

SPIRITS.

L. *Spirits* are constantly with man, but understand spiritually all that man understands naturally—37 (2); see also 48 (7).

S. *Spirits* and angels are like men in this world—70; *spirits* are men—100; an experience concerning certain African *spirits*—108.

SPIRITUAL.

S. From the Lord proceed the Celestial, the *Spiritual*, and the Natural, one after another—6; see also 38 (2); the Word is interiorly *spiritual* and celestial —8; they who have confirmed themselves in the falsities of the papal dominion neither can nor will apprehend anything *spiritual*—24; the wisdom of the celestial angels surpasses that of the *spiritual*—74. See also HEAVEN, SPIRITUAL SENSE, and STYLE.

Life. There is *spiritual* good—defined —12; a man who possesses *spiritual* good is also a moral man, and a civic man— 13; those who do good from the Lord are called *spiritual*—16; in proportion as any one shuns evils as sins he is *spiritual* (chap. v.)—42-52; what *spiritual* faith is —50; what *spiritual* adultery is—74; man possesses a *spiritual* mind (see MIND)— 86; a *spiritual* moral man and a natural moral man, their similarities and differences—109; why a man who is not *spiritual* can yet speak rationally, like a *spiritual* man, set forth—15; cunning and deceit insinuate themselves even into the *spiritual* mind—81.

F. The faith of the present day is not *spiritual*—1; *spiritual* things may be comprehended as well as natural—3.

Q. The Lord from eternity had a Divine *Spiritual* but not a Divine Natural —II.; *spiritual* truths may be comprehended in a natural way—by what means—V.

SPIRITUAL INTELLIGENCE.

L. All men have their *spiritual intelligence* from the Word—2.

SPIRITUAL SENSE.

S. In the Word there is a *spiritual sense* hitherto unknown (chap. ii.)—4-26; what the *spiritual sense* is—5; in the *spiritual sense* all things hang together in a continuous connection—13 (4); without the *spiritual sense* the prophetical parts of the Old Testament are in many passages not intelligible—15; without the *spiritual sense* no one could know why the prophets were commanded to do certain things (illustrations)—16; from the *spiritual sense* it is that the Word is divinely inspired and holy in every word—18; the *spiritual sense* is now revealed in order that it may be known where in the Word its holiness lies hid—ib.; see also 25; illustrations of this—18 (2) (3); hitherto the *spiritual sense* of the Word has been unknown— 20; for a long time the *spiritual sense* will not be recognized (the reason)—25; henceforth the *spiritual sense* will be imparted solely to him who from the Lord is in genuine truths—26; for this sense treats solely of the Lord and His kingdom—ib.; a man can do violence to this sense if he wishes from a knowledge of correspondences and from self-intelligence to investigate it—ib.; guards have been set in order to prevent any one from entering into the *spiritual sense* of the Word improperly—ib. (2); the *spiritual sense* has its continant, its basis, and its support in the sense of the letter of the Word (chap. iii.)—27-36; the spiritual and celestial senses without the natural sense are not the Word—39; naked truths are in the *spiritual sense*— 40; from its *spiritual sense* the Word is like a light that enlightens—42; the doc-

trine of genuine truth cannot be procured by means of the *spiritual sense* (the reason)—56; the Word shines because of this sense—58; angels of the spiritual kingdom associated with men by means of the *spiritual sense*—63; spiritual angels are in the *spiritual sense*—64; how the *spiritual sense* is evolved from the natural when a man reads the Word—65; illustrated by examples—67; in the *spiritual sense* the things in the Word refer especially to the church—80; why the *spiritual sense* is revealed at the present time—112. See SENSES OF THE WORD.

Illustrative expositions of the *spiritual sense* are to be found as follows:

L. Isa. lix. 16, 17, 20—14 (3); *Isa.* lxiii. 1-9—14 (2); *Jer.* xlvi. 5, 10—14 (4); the *spiritual* meaning of the events accompanying the Lord's passion (text not quoted)—16 (5) (6).

S. Gen. iii. 24—97 (2); *Exod.* xxviii. 6, 15-21, 29, 30—44 (2) (3); *Ps.* xxix. 3-9 —18 (4) (5); *Isa.* x. 26-32, 34 (brief)—15; *Isa.* xi. 13-16—15 (2); *Ezek.* i. (whole chap., brief)—97 (5); *Ezek.* xxviii. 12-13— 45; *Ezek.* xxviii. 12-14, 16—97 (4); *Ezek.* xxxix. 17-21—15 (3); *Hos.* v. 3, vi. 10— 79 (6); *Hos.* ix. 3—79 (4); *Hos.* xii. 1—79 (5); *Matt.* xvii. 1-5—48; *Matt.* xxiii. 25, 26—40 (2); *Matt.* xxiv. 29-31—14; see also 112; *Matt.* xxv. 1-12—17 (2) (3); *Matt.* xxvi. 64—49 (2); *Mark* xiv. 62—49 (2); *Matt.* xix. 28—51 (7); *Luke* xvi. 19, 20— 40 (3); *Rev.* vi.—12; *Rev.* vii.—11; *Rev.* ix.—13; *Rev.* xix. 11-18—9; *Rev.* xxi.— 10; *Rev.* xxi. 17-20—43.

Life. Isa. xxxi. 1-3—30 (2); *Ezek.* xxiii. 2-17—79; *Matt.* xiii. 3-8—90; *Mark* iv. 3-8—90; *Mark* x. 17-22—66; *Luke* viii. 5-8—90.

F. Isa. xiv. 29—53; *Dan.* viii. 2-14— 65-67; *John* xx. 29—10; *Rev.* xii. 1-8, 13- 17—58, 59.

SPIRITUAL WORLD.

L. What is meant by the term "*spiritual world*"—62.

F. Experiences in the *spiritual world* showing who are meant by the "goats" —63; in the *spiritual world* all things that appear are correspondences—ib. (2).

STAR.

S. The "*star* fallen from heaven" (*Rev.* ix.) signifies the knowledges of truth destroyed—13 (2); the "*star* that went before them" (*Matt.* ii.) signifies knowledge from heaven—23 (3); concerning those who had believed that they would shine in heaven like the *stars* —61; the *stars* (which shall fall from heaven—*Matt.* xxiv.) mean the Lord in respect to the knowledges of good and truth—112.

F. "The *stars* of heaven" (which the dragon dragged down with his tail) signify knowledges of truth—56.

STATE.

L. The Lord's two *states* while He was in the world, of humiliation and glorification, described and explained—35 (3); as man's life varies according to his *state* (enumerated)—48.

S. The successive *states* of the church in respect to its understanding of the Word, described (in *Rev.* vi.)—12.

F. Man's two *states* (of reformation and regeneration) described—31.

STEAL. See also THEFTS.

S. Interpretation of the Commandment "Thou shalt not *steal*" by a man, by a spiritual angel, and by a celestial angel—67 (2).

Life. Meaning of "to *steal*" in the natural, the spiritual, and the highest senses—80.

STEPS.

L. The Lord made His Human Divine by successive *steps*—32; see also 35 and ib. (7).

STONES. See PRECIOUS STONES.

STOREHOUSE.

F. The knowledges of truth and of good are the *storehouse* of material out of which the faith of charity can be formed (chap. iii.)—25-33; see also 27; this *storehouse* essential to the formation of a true faith—28.

STORIES.

S. The fabulous *stories* of highest antiquity were nothing but correspondences—20 (2).

STRONG.

L. "Their *strong* ones" (*Jer.* xlvi. 5) are the hells—14 (4).

STRUGGLE.

Life. Man cannot remove his evils except with a *struggle*—93.

STUPID.

S. Those who ascribe all things to their own intelligence finally become *stupid*—118.

STYLE.

S. Letter of the Word appears in a *style* that is strange, neither so sublime nor brilliant as apparently are the writings of the day—1; the natural man judges the Word by its *style* in which the Divine wisdom and life do not appear —3; the Word in heaven is written in a spiritual *style* which differs entirely from a natural *style* (description of differences)—71.

SUBJECTS.

Life. The will and the understanding are the *subjects* of good and truth—43.

SUBJUGATE, SUBJUGATION.

L. Unless the hells had been *subjugated* no man could have been saved—3; the Last Judgment executed by the Lord when He was in the world by the *subjugation* of the hells—14 (10); the Lord came into the world to *subjugate* the hells (chap. iii.)—12-14; the Lord completely *subjugated* the hells by His own power— 33 (2).

SUBSTANCE, SUBSTANTIAL.

L. The Lord's body after His resurrection was Divine *substantial*—35 (10); the Lord's human *substance*, or essence, is just the same as is His Divine *substance* or essence—ib. (11).

SUCCESSIVE ORDER.

S. In heaven and the world there are both *successive* and simultaneous order— 38; simultaneous order derived from the *successive*—ib. (2); see also 65. Consult ORDER and SIMULTANEOUS.

SUMMARY.

Life. The Decalogue in a brief *summary* is a complex of all those things of religion by which man has conjunction with the Lord—54.

SUN.

S. The "*sun* and air darkened" signifies the light of truth become thick darkness—13 (2) ; in the Word the *sun* is said to rise and set, when yet the *sun* stands motionless, for it is an ocean of fire (used to illustrate the statements of the Word according to appearances)—95.

Q. Divine love and Divine wisdom proceed from the *sun* of the angelic heaven as do light and heat from the *sun* of the natural world—V. ; the light and heat of the *sun* of the natural world correspond to the Divine love and the Divine wisdom—ib.

SUPPER.

S. That at the end of the church the spiritual sense of the Word is to be opened, is signified by the great *supper* to which the angel standing in the sun invited all to come (*Rev.* xix.)—9.

SUPPORT.

S. The human race is the basis, continant, and *support* of the heavens—34 ; the sense of the letter of the Word is the *support* of its spiritual and celestial senses (chap. iii.)—27-36; see also 38. Consult NATURAL SENSE, CONTAINANT, and BASIS.

SWEDEN.

Life. An Exhortation read in the churches in *Sweden* demonstrates that they believe that those who lead a good life are saved—4.

SWORD.

S. "A great *sword*" (*Rev.* vi.) signifies falsity fighting against truth—12.

SYRIA.

S. How the science of correspondences came to be known and cultivated in *Syria*—21 ; those who still use the ancient Word came partly from *Syria*—102.

TABERNACLE.

S. The Word is called the "*Tabernacle*" in which the Lord dwells with man—2 (4) ; sense of the letter of the Word was signified by the curtains and veils of the *Tabernacle*—46 ; the holy things of the Word were signified by all the things of the *Tabernacle*—ib.

Life. How the holiness of the *tabernacle* from the Law in the ark was recognized by the children of Israel in the wilderness—55 (2).

TABLE.

Life. Why the Law was written on two *tables*—56 ; that the first *table* (of the decalogue) contains the things of God, and the second the things of man—62.

TAIL (of Dragon).

F. What is meant by the *tail* of the Dragon in the *Revelation*—56-59.

TAKING AWAY.

L. What is meant by *taking away* iniquities—15 (2) ; by bearing the iniquities of the house of Israel the prophet did not *take* them *away*, but only represented and showed them—16 (3) ; the Lord did not *take away* sins by the passion of the cross, but He *takes* them *away* from those who believe in Him and live according to the Commandments—17 (2) ; sins cannot be *taken away* from a man except by actual repentance—ib. (3) ; stated also in 65.

TEACH.

S. The Lord *teaches* every one by means of the Word, and He *teaches* from those truths which the man already has —26 (2) ; from the sense of the letter of the Word the Lord *teaches* and enlightens man—50.

F. Who they are that are called "the *taught* of Jehovah" (*Isa.* liv. 13 ; *John* vi. 45)—5.

TEMPLE.

S. The *Temple* at Jerusalem represented heaven and the church, and hence the Word—47 ; its external parts represented the letter of the Word—ib ; "in His *temple* every one saith Glory," means that there are Divine truths in each and everything in the Word; for the *temple* signifies the Lord, and therefore the Word—18 (5).

TEMPTATIONS.

L. The Passion of the cross the Lord's last *temptation*—3; the Lord conquered hell and glorified His Human by means of *temptations*—12; His *temptations* in the wilderness and what He suffered at Gethsemane explained—ib.; to bear iniquities means to endure grievous *temptations*—15 (2); the Lord made His Human Divine by means of *temptations*—33; *temptations* are combats against evils and falsities—ib.; are induced by evil spirits—ib.; by means of them the Lord became our Saviour—ib. (4); man is drawn out of hell and elevated into heaven when from the Lord he conquers in them—ib. (2); see statement—65.

Life. Man's *temptation* is the Christian's warfare—98; see 99, 100 (passages adduced).

F. The Lord subdued the hells and glorified His Human by means of *temptations*—35.

TEN.

Life. Why the decalogue is called *ten* words—61; passages from Scripture showing meaning of *ten*—ib.; the origin of tithes (or tenths)—ib.; see also 62.

TEN COMMANDMENTS.

L. The *ten commandments* of the decalogue in a restricted sense meant by the Law—8.

TERRIBLE.

L. By "*terrible* day" is meant the advent of the Lord to Judgment—5; the *terrible* day of Jehovah refers to His advent—14 (9).

TESTAMENT. See OLD TESTAMENT and NEW TESTAMENT.

TESTIMONY.

Life. Why the decalogue is called a *testimony*—57.

THEFTS.

Life. In proportion as any one shuns *thefts* of every kind as sins, in the same proportion he loves sincerity (chap. x.)—80-86; this evil enters more deeply than any other into man because conjoined with cunning—81; and 85.

THEOLOGY.

S. The writers on natural *theology* do not get such things as the doctrine of the immortality of the soul from themselves, but they confirm them by rational argument from the Word—115 (3).

THINK.

L. According to the Athanasian Creed it is allowable to *think* three Gods, but not to say three—57.

Life. Why a man who is not spiritual may yet *think* rationally—15.

THOMAS.

F. The Lord's words to *Thomas* (*John* xx. 29) explained—10.

THORNS. See CROWN OF THORNS.

THIRD HEAVEN. See CELESTIAL HEAVEN.

THREE.

S. *Three* signifies what is perfect (the reason)—29; see also TRINE; there are *three* things in every Divine work—what they may be called and how they are related—28.

F. A "*third* part" signifies all—56.

THUMMIM.

S. The truths and goods of the sense of the letter of the Word signified by the *Thummim*—44.

THUNDER.

S. The "voice of Jehovah," here (*Ps.* xxix.) called "*thunder*," means the Divine truth or Word in its power—18 (5).

TIME.

L. That *time* in the Word means the Lord's advent (passages adduced)—4; what is meant by various kinds of *time* mentioned—5.

TRADER.

Life. The work of a *trader* is good when he is in the good of love toward the neighbor (illustrated)—72; see also 83.

TRANSCENDS.

Q. The purely Divine Essence *transcends* both the angelic and the human rational—II.

TRANSFIGURATION.

L. The quality of the Lord's glorified Human was shown to Peter, James, and John at the *transfiguration*—35 (6).

S. The Word in its glory was represented by the Lord at the *transfiguration* —48; what the Lord was as the Word in ultimates He showed His disciples at the *transfiguration*—98.

TRANSLUCENT.

S. Why the Word shines and is *translucent* with the "pure in heart"—58.

TRANSMUTED.

L. The human nature from the mother was not *transmuted* into the Divine Essence—35.

TRAVAILING.

F. The *travailing* of the woman, described in *Rev.* xii., signifies the resistance to the nascent doctrine of the church by those who are in faith separate from charity—59.

TREE.

S. A *tree* used to illustrate the evolution of the spiritual and celestial senses from the Word—66 ; the Word compared to a garden containing various kinds of *trees*—96a ; signification of the "way of the *tree*" of life" (*Gen.* iii. 24)—97 (2).

Life. A *tree* signifies a man—46.

F. The growth of a *tree* used to illustrate the progress of a man in his regenerative unfolding—16 ; see also 31 and 32 ; a *tree* is not faith, but man—17.

TRIBE.

S. Each *tribe* mentioned in *Rev.* vii. signifies some specific thing of the church —11.

TRIBES.

S. Where in our Word we have *tribes* of Israel, in the Word of the angels they have "various things of heaven and the church"—71.

TRINE.

L. That there is a *trine* in the Lord, what it is—46 (2) ; illustrated by the *trine* in an angel—ib. (3) ; referred to in the Word under distinct names—55 ; those who receive this in simplicity without confirming themselves in the idea of three Gods are afterwards instructed that the Lord is that *trine*—ib. (3).

S. In every complete thing there is a *trine*—28.

TRINITY.

L. The Lord commanded baptism into the name of the Father, the Son, and the Holy Spirit because there is in Him a *Trinity* (explanations)—46 (2) ; the doctrine of the Athanasian Creed agrees with the truth, provided that by a *Trinity* of Persons is understood a *Trinity* of Person, and that the *Trinity* is in the Lord (chap. xi.)—55-61 ; whence has arisen the recognition by Christians of three Divine Persons—55 ; why it was permitted at first that Christians should receive the doctrine of three Divine Persons—ib. (4) ; what a *Trinity* of Person is—57 ; that God is one and that the *Trinity* is in Him—60.

F. It is a universal of the Christian faith that God is One, in whom is the *Trinity*, and that the Lord is that God— 35.

Q. How the *Trinity* in one Person is to be understood—III. ; there is a like *trinity* in man, illustrated and compared —ib. ; a further elucidation of the *Trinity* —VII.

TRIUNE GOD.

L. When it is known what the Lord is and what the Son, it will be possible to think with understanding of the *Triune God*—19. See Trinity.

TRUTH. See Truths.

L. The Word is the Divine *truth* itself —2 ; the Divine *truth* is what judges every one—25 ; the Spirit of *truth* is the Lord— 51 (2) ; the Divine *truth* from the Lord is the Holy Spirit—ib. (4).

S. The Holy Scripture, or Word, is Divine *truth* itself (chap. i.)—1-4 ; it is this because Jehovah spoke it—2 ; expressions in the Word referring to *truth*, in contrast to others referring to good (examples given)—84; they who read the Word without doctrine are in obscurity as to every *truth*—52; with those who read the Word from the doctrine of a false religion, still more if they confirm it, the *truth* of the Word is as it were in the shade of night—60.

Life. Evil of life and *truth* of faith cannot possibly act as a one—44; *truth* and love do not make a one in a man unless he is spiritual—15; evil inwardly hates *truth* —45; in proportion as any one shuns false witness of every kind as sin, in the same proportion he loves the *truth* (chap. v.)— 87-91; in proportion as any one loves the *truth*, in the same proportion he desires to know it—89; in proportion as any one loves to do the *truth*, in the same proportion he is sensible of the pleasantness of its light—ib.; *truth* is what is meant by the seed in the parable of the sower (*Matt.* xiii.; *Mark* iv.; *Luke* viii.)—90.

F. Faith is an internal acknowledgment of *truth* (chap. i.)—1-12; those who are in spiritual affection of *truth* possess an internal acknowledgment of *truth*—4; faith and *truth* are a one—6; how one may be able to have an internal acknowledgment of truth—12; the internal acknowledgment of *truth* exists with none but those who are in charity (chap. ii.)— 13-24; there are many who possess no internal acknowledgment of *truth*, and yet have the faith of charity—30; with a regenerate person the knowledges of *truth* become truths—33; that the he-goat (*Dan.* viii.) "cast down the *truth* to the earth" signifies that it falsified the truths of the Word—67.

Q. The Divine wisdom is the Divine *truth*—IV.; the Lord is the Divine *truth* —ib.

TRUTHS. See TRUTH.

S. Heavenly *truths* were hidden from the men of the Reformation (the reason) —24; to him who is in genuine *truths* will the spiritual sense of the Word be henceforth imparted by the Lord—26; the reason set forth—ib. (2); the *truths* of the sense of the letter of the Word not naked *truths* but appearances of truth—

40; they who are in Divine *truths* see Divine *truths* in natural light while reading the Word—41; *truths* in ultimates represented by precious stones and diadems— 44 (4); the fight against evils and falsities must be waged by means of *truths* from the sense of the letter of the Word —49; by *truths* is a man saved—ib.; with those who love *truths* because they are *truths*, there exists enlightenment from the Lord—57; where there are *truths* there resides no more of wisdom than there is good of love together with it— 74; the power to see *truths* given after death—who avail themselves of it—93.

Life. In proportion as any one shuns evils as sins, in the same proportion he loves *truths* (chap. iv.)—32-41; it is possible for one to love *truths* who does not shun evils as sins, but he does not love them because they are *truths*—35; why a man loves *truths* in the same proportion that he is in good—37; *truths* the means through which the good of love comes into existence—39; no man has a grain of *truth* more than he has of good—52; to deprive another of his *truths* of faith is to steal in the spiritual sense—80.

F. Spiritual *truths* can be comprehended just as well as natural ones—3; a spiritual idea inflows into those who are in the affection of truth and inwardly tells them what things are *truths*—5; those represented by the goats have no *truths*, shown by a colloquy between the sheep and the goats—70.

Q. All things of wisdom are *truths*— IV.; the comprehension of spiritual *truths* in a natural way—V. See also APPARENT TRUTHS and GENUINE TRUTHS.

TUMULT.

L. A day of *tumult* means the advent of the Lord to Judgment—5.

TWO.

S. In the Word *two* senses, the spiritual and the celestial, lie hidden within the sense of the letter—80; the frequent occurrence of *two* expressions because of the marriage of each and everything in the Word—81; with every man there are *two* faculties of life—83.

Life. Man possesses *two* faculties;

what they are—43; why there are *two* tables in the decalogue—57; see also 62.

F. The faith of the present day teaches that God the Father and God the Son are *two*—39 i.

TYPES.

Q. Before the incarnation enlightenment was effected by means of *types*—VI.

TYRE.

S. How the science of correspondences came to be known and cultivated in *Tyre*—21; " *Tyre*" signifies the church in respect to the knowledges of truth and good—97 (4); the ancients who still use the ancient Word in heaven were partly from *Tyre*—102.

U.

S. In the third heaven they use the vowel " *u*" (probably like the " *u*" in rule—oo) because it gives a full sound—90 (2).

ULCERS.

Life. Concupiscences of evil not removed by the Lord compared to *ulcers*—110.

ULTIMATE, ULTIMATES.

L. God became Man in *ultimates*—36.

S. Everything Divine is in its fullness in its *ultimate* degree—6; every Divine work perfect and complete in its *ultimate*—28; the whole is in the *ultimate*—ib.; *ultimate* of truth signified by hair and beard—35 (2); how successive order becomes simultaneous order in the *ultimate*—38; illustrated from the Word—ib. (2); truths in *ultimates* signified by precious stones and diadems—44 (4); the Lord came into the world to fulfill all things of the Word, and thereby to become Divine truth or the Word even in *ultimates* (chap. xi.)—98–100.

ULTIMATE SENSE.

S. In its *ultimate sense* the Word is natural—6; see also 31; the *ultimate sense* of the Word is the Basis, the Containant, and the Support of the two interior senses—32; in its *ultimate sense* the Word

is signified by the wall of the holy Jerusalem—36. See also EXTERNAL SENSE, LITERAL SENSE, NATURAL SENSE, and SENSE OF THE LETTER.

UNCIRCUMCISED.

F. Why the Philistines were called *uncircumcised*—51. See also CIRCUMCISED.

UNDERSTANDING.

S. By the opening of the seals, etc. (*Rev.* vi.), are described the successive states of the church in respect to its *understanding* of the Word—12; the church is from the Word and is such as is its *understanding* of the Word (chap. viii.)—76–79; the Word is with a man according to his *understanding* of it—77; the Lord is present with a man and conjoined to him according to his *understanding* of the Word—78; *understanding* of the Word treated of in many of the Prophets—79; described by Ephraim—ib. (2) (3) and (6); *understanding* one of the faculties of man—the receptacle of truth and the derivative wisdom—83; various kinds of *understanding* of the Word compared to a garden with a variety of delicacies and delights—96a; that a genuine *understanding* of the Word might not perish the spiritual sense is revealed—112; man's *understanding* subject to his will—115; merely teaches and shows the way—ib.; falsities in the *understanding* from evils in the will—ib.; man from himself does not wish to *understand* anything but that which comes from his Own—ib. (2).

Life. Man's *understanding* can be uplifted into the light of heaven before his will is uplifted into its heat—15; it is because of this that it is possible for a man to be reformed and to become spiritual—ib.; from the love of good in the will proceeds the love of truth in the *understanding*, from this the perception of truth, from this thought about truth, and from all these its acknowledgment which is faith—36; how the will and *understanding* make one mind—43; as to his *understanding* man is able to be in his spiritual mind and thus in heaven, but not as to his will unless he shuns evils as sins—86 (2).

F. In reference to the *understanding* a man may be uplifted into the light of heaven (illustrated)—3; the dogma that the *understanding* must be made obedient to faith discarded by the angels—4; the progression of the things of the will through the *understanding*—15; what men may be made to believe if their *understanding* is closed—47; the temple of such a one compared to a den or cavern under ground—48.

UNDER-VESTURE.

L. The signification of casting lots upon the Lord's *under-vesture*—16 (6).

UNITION.

L. The *unition* of the Divine and the Human was the glorification of the Lord —13; how the *unition* was effected—29 (3); serially treated—30-36; full *unition* of Divine and Human effected by the cross—34; His *unition* with the Divine was His state of glorification in this world —35 (3); the *unition* between the Divine and the Human was reciprocal and plenary—ib. (8).

UNIVERSALS.

Life. Divine good and Divine truth are the two *universals* which proceed from the Lord—32.

F. The Christian faith in its *universal* idea, or form, stated—34; why the word "*universal*" is used in this connection— 35; what the *universal* of the Christian faith on the part of man is—36; the faith of the present day in its *universal* idea or form, stated—38, 39.

UNKNOWN.

S. In the Word there is a spiritual sense hitherto *unknown* (chap. ii.)—4-26; especially considered—20.

F. The faith of the present day is a faith in the *unknown*—1.

URIM.

S. The truths and goods of the sense of the letter of the Word are meant by *Urim* and Thummim—44.

USE.

S. Enlightenment exists with those who make truths of *use* for life—57.

F. The will to bring forth *uses* by means of the understanding (illustrated by comparison with the growth of a tree) is constant through the whole progression of man's life—16; *use* is one's spiritual neighbor—20; *use* defined, and how the affection of it progresses into manifest charity, described—14; man's business is his *use*, and his affection for it develops into a love of *use*—25; that man should regard *uses* for the sake of his life in heaven the reason for his instruction in the things of religion—26.

VALLEYS.

S. Valleys signify the lowest things of the church—18 (3).

VEGETABLE KINGDOM.

S. As the subjects of the *vegetable kingdom* draw each its proper nourishment from nature, so does each class of angels and men draw from the Word according to its nature—66.

VEIL, VEILS.

S. The *veils* of the Tabernacle represented the sense of the letter of the Word—46; also external things of heaven and the church—ib.

Life. From childhood man learns to *veil* over the kinds of murder hid in him from birth—68; like a thick *veil* man's affections for evils block up the interiors of the natural mind unless he shun evils as sins—86 (4).

VENGEANCE.

L. The day of *vengeance* signifies the advent of Jehovah—14 (9); there is no *vengeance* in the presence of the Divine attributes—18.

VERSE.

S. Each *verse* of the Word communicates with some society of heaven—113.

VESTURE. See UNDER-VESTURE.

VICTORIES.

L. The Lord made His Human Divine by means of continual *victories* in temptations—33.

F. It is a universal of faith that the Lord removed hell from man by *victorie.* over it—35.

VINE.

S. The *vine* signifies truth from the good of love—23 (2); the *vine* signifies the spiritual good and truth of the church—18 (3).

VINEGAR.

L. What is meant by offering the Lord *vinegar* to drink—16 (6).

VIOLENCE.

S. In what way a man, if he has a knowledge of correspondence, can do *violence* to the spiritual sense of the Word—26; to pervert the Divine truths that lie hidden in the Word inflicts *violence* upon it—97.

VIRGIN.

L. The church could not have been set up unless a Human had been born of a *virgin*—20; the Son of God is Jesus born of the *virgin*—21; see also 29 (2), 30, and 59.

S. *Virgins* signify those who are of the church—17 (3).

VISION.

L. What is meant by the prophets being in *vision* (passages adduced)—52.

VISITATION.

L. A day of *visitation* means the advent of the Lord to Judgment—5.

VOICE.

S. "The *voice* of Jehovah" (*Ps.* xxix.) means the Divine truth, or Word, in its power—18 (5).

VOWELS.

S. In the third heaven, the *vowels* indicate a sound that corresponds to the affection—90 (2); see A, E, I, O, U, Eu, and Y.

WALL.

S. The *wall* of the New Jerusalem (*Rev.* xxi.) signifies doctrine from the literal sense of the Word—10; *wall* signifies the Word in its ultimate or natural sense—36.

WAR, WARFARE.

L. A day of *war* represented the advent of the Lord to Judgment—5; *wars*

of the Israelites represented the Lord's combat with the hells—14 (11).

S. The "*Wars* of Jehovah" (the name of the historical parts of the ancient Word) meant and described the Lord's combats with the hells—103.

Life. *Warfare* signifies the temptation which the man of the church undergoes from the devil and hell—98.

F. *War* in heaven between Michael and his angels, and the dragon (*Rev.* xii.) signifies battling between those in faith separate from charity, and those who are in the faith of charity—59; all the *wars* described in the Word involve and signify spiritual *wars*—50.

WARS OF JEHOVAH.

S. *Wars of Jehovah* was the name of the historical parts of an ancient Word —103.

WASTE.

S. *Waste* is predicated of good, and in the opposite sense of evil—84.

F. That Jehovah "shall lay *waste* the Philistines" (*Jer.* xlvii.) signifies the destruction of such—53.

WATER, WATERS.

S. The *waters* (*Ps.* xxix.) mean the truths of the Word—18 (5).

Life. The need which good has of truth, compared to the relation of food and *water*—40.

F. The "*waters* that rise up out of the north" (*Jer.* xlvii. 1) are falsities from hell—53.

WEDDING.

S. The "*wedding*" (*Matt.* xxv.) means the marriage of the Lord with heaven and the church by means of the good of love and faith—17 (2).

WEST.

F. The "*west*" (*Dan.* viii. 4) signifies the evil of the natural man—67.

WHITE HORSE.

S. The spiritual meaning of John's vision of the *White Horse* (*Rev.* xix. 11-18) set forth—9.

WHOREDOM. See also ADULTERY.

S. *Whoredom* signifies the falsification of the understanding of the Word—79 (6); also (7).

Life. If a man abstains from *whoredom* from outer reasons (enumerated) only, he is still an adulterer—111.

WIFE.

L. The church is a bride when she desires to receive the Lord, and a *wife* when she does receive Him—63.

S. A chaste *wife* (in a memorable relation) signified the conjunction of good and truth—26 (5).

Life. Faith in the understanding which has in it good from the will, is like a lovely *wife*—46.

WILDERNESS.

L. The Lord's temptations from childhood summarily described by His temptations in the *wilderness*—12.

S. The "*wilderness*" and the "*wilderness* of Kadesh*" (*Ps.* xxix.) mean the church in which there is not anything true and good—18 (5).

F. The woman fled into the *wilderness* signifies the church among a few—59.

WILL.

S. Two faculties in man, *will* and understanding; *will* the receptacle of good and the derivative love—83; the understanding is subject to the *will* and not the *will* to the understanding—115; see also 116.

Life. The *will* of a man not spiritual cannot be uplifted into the heat of heaven as his understanding can into its light—15; from good which is of the *will* comes faith which is of the understanding (the progression)—36; *will* and understanding the two faculties of the mind—everything in the universe has reference to these two—43; utmost importance to know how the *will* and the understanding make one mind—ib.; the *will* leads the understanding and makes it act as a one with itself—44; man is not in heaven unless he is there as to his *will*, in spite of the fact that he is there in understanding—86 (2).

F. The *will* brings forth nothing from itself apart from the understanding—15; the endeavor in man to bring forth the means, is from his *will* in his understanding—16.

WINE.

L. "Blood" or "*wine*" (*John* vi. 53) is the good of faith from the Word, and thus from the Lord—27.

Life. The relation of good and truth compared to that of bread and *wine*—40.

WISDOM.

L. The Lord is Divine *wisdom* itself—1; all things created from Divine love by means of Divine *wisdom*—ib.; Divine *wisdom* is "light"—ib.; spirit in the Word signifies the Divine *wisdom* from the Lord—51; the *wisdom* and life of all the angels are founded on the acknowledgment and confession of one God and that He is a Man—55 (3); angels have all their *wisdom* from the Word—2; by "spirit" is meant the life of *wisdom*—48.

S. From the Lord proceed two things, Divine love and Divine *wisdom*—3; angelic *wisdom* in the heavens is derived from the Word (chap. vii.)—70-75; the wise understand the Word in the heavens in *wisdom*, and the simple in simplicity—72; angels acknowledge that their *wisdom* is through the Word—73; Divine *wisdom* the light of heaven—ib.; the *wisdom* of celestial angels surpasses that of the spiritual as does that of the spiritual the *wisdom* of men—74; the nature of the *wisdom* that lies hidden in the Word—75.

Life. The angels of all the heavens are in *wisdom* in proportion to the degree in which the good in them makes a one with truth—32; no one comes into *wisdom* excepting the one who loves truth—89.

F. In the second state of regeneration, man grows in *wisdom* every day—31; the *wisdom* of the angels consists solely in this, that they see and comprehend everything they think about—4.

Q. The Lord from eternity is Divine love and *wisdom*—II.; all things were made through the Divine *wisdom*—IV.

WISE.

S. Being *wise* consists in seeing whether a thing is true before it is confirmed, and not in confirming whatever one pleases—91.

Life. A man is not *wise* who does not shun evils as sins—23; see 27; for confirmatory passages from the Word, see 30.

WITNESS.

S. The internal sense of the Word can bear *witness* to its Divinity and Holiness —4; the commandment against false *witness* as understood by a spiritual and a celestial angel—67 (5).

WOMAN.

L. Why the Lord did not call His mother, Mother, but *Woman*—35 (4).

S. That the locusts (*Rev.* ix.) "had hair as the hair of *women*" signified that they appeared to themselves as if they were in the affection of truth— 13 (2).

F. Spiritual signification of the *woman* described in *Rev.* xii.—59.

WOOD.

Life. A natural moral man, if he is in goods, appears before the angels in heaven like an image of *wood*—109.

WORD.

L. The *Word* is Divine truth itself from which angels have all their wisdom—2; is among the angels in the heavens—ib.; is also the Divine proceeding—ib.; all things of the *Word* written concerning the Lord—ib.; contains not only a natural but a spiritual sense—ib.; why it is said that the *Word* was made flesh—ib.; what it means when it is said that the Lord fulfilled all things of the *Word*—11; that the *Word* has been written solely about the Lord is its only source of holiness—7; see also 14 (11); Jews were suffered to treat the Lord as they had treated the *Word*—15 (2); was represented by the prophets— ib. (8); all the *Word* is from the Lord and is concerning Him (chap. viii.)—37- 44; was spoken by the Lord through the

prophets—52; usual in *Word* to name two Divines and sometimes three, when yet there is only one (explanation)—46 (5); it is not said in the Prophets that the *Word* was spoken from the Holy Spirit, but from Jehovah (the reason, references given in *Jeremiah*)—53, 54; is of such a nature in its letter that things which form a one are distinguished from each other as if they did not form a one —hence doctrine of a Trinity of Persons (illustrated)—55; that the Lord fulfilled all things of the Law means that He fulfilled all things of the *Word*—8; the Lord in respect to the *Word* is called the Son of man—22-28; see 50; as the *Word* He suffered, judges, came into the world, redeems, saves, reforms, and regenerates—ib.; "a word against the Son of man" is something said against the *Word* by wrongly interpreting its meaning—50e.

S. In the spiritual world all who despise the *Word*, and falsify its sense of the letter, appear bald—35 (4); why the *Word* in the celestial kingdom is written differently from that in the spiritual kingdom—74; the Holy Scripture or *Word* is Divine truth itself (chap. i.)— 1-4; spoken through Moses and the prophets by Jehovah Himself—2; and in the Gospels by the Lord (who is Jehovah)—ib.; hence called a "fountain," a "river," the "Sanctuary," and the "Tabernacle"—ib. (4); its style such that there is holiness in every sentence —3; why the *Word* conjoins man with the Lord and opens heaven—ib.; its internal sense revealed (to Swedenborg) by the Lord—4; in the *Word* there is a spiritual sense hitherto unknown (chap. ii.)—4-26; it is the spiritual sense which renders the *Word* spiritual—5; the nature of the *Word* does not appear in the sense of the letter—6; because it is spiritual and celestial it is written exclusively by correspondences—8; see 20 (3); the spiritual sense is in all things of the *Word* and in every single particular of it—9; the successive states of the church in respect to its understanding of the *Word*, signified by the vision of horses in *Rev.* vi.—12; the *Word* divinely inspired and holy from its spiritual sense

—18; there is a still more interior sense of the *Word* called celestial—19; why the spiritual sense of the *Word* now disclosed—25; to whom the spiritual sense of the *Word* will be henceforth imparted —26; the sense of the letter of the *Word* is the Basis, the Containant, and the Support of its spiritual and celestial senses (chap. iii.)—27-36; what the *Word* would be without the sense of the letter (various comparisons)—33; in the sense of the letter of the *Word* Divine truth is in its fullness, in its holiness, and in its power (chap. iv.)—37-49; the very *Word* itself is in the sense of its letter—39; the letter of the *Word* represented by foundations of the wall of the New Jerusalem—43; by the Urim and Thummim—44; by the precious stones in the garden of Eden described by *Ezekiel* (xxviii.)—45; by the curtain and veils of the Tabernacle— 46; by the external things of the Temple at Jerusalem—47; the *Word* in its glory was represented by the Lord when He was transfigured—48; from the sense of the letter of the *Word* is to be drawn the doctrine of the church (chap. v.)—50-61; the *Word* cannot be understood without doctrine—51; illustrated by examples—ib. (2) to (9); those who read the *Word* without doctrine are in obscurity—52; doctrine must be drawn from the sense of the letter of the *Word* —53; by means of doctrine the *Word* becomes intelligible and shines with light—54; doctrine cannot be procured by means of the spiritual sense of the *Word*—56; no enlightenment in the *Word* for those who do not love truths because they are truths, and make use of them for life—57; why the *Word* shines and is translucent with such as love truths because they are truths—58; the state of those who have studied the *Word* to confirm the tenets of their faith, but not for life—61, and ib. (2); conjunction with the Lord and association with the angels by means of the sense of the letter of the *Word* (chap. vi.)— 62-69; the reason of this conjunction— 62, 63; the spiritual angels are in the spiritual sense of the *Word*, and the celestial in the celestial—64; spiritual and celestial senses of the *Word* simul-

taneously in the natural—65; how they are evolved from the natural—ib.; illustrations of this—66, 67; the *Word* is in all the heavens and is the source of angelic wisdom (chap. vii.)—70-75; the *Word* in heaven written in a spiritual style— 71; so written (in the heavens) that the simple understand it in simplicity and the wise in wisdom—72; the angels acknowledge that all their understanding is through the *Word*—73; flaming and bright light in the sanctuary where the *Word* is kept—ib.; in the *Word* that is in this world, all angelic wisdom, which is unutterable, lies hidden—75; the church is from the *Word*, and is such as is its understanding of the *Word* (chap. viii.)—76-79; the *Word* is the *Word* according to the understanding of it in a man—77; through the *Word* the Lord is present with a man and conjoined with him—78; there is no church except where the *Word* is rightly understood—79; falsification of the understanding of the *Word* meant by whoredom— ib. (6); the Prophet Hosea from first to last treats of the falsification of the *Word* —ib. (7); such as is the understanding of the *Word* in the church such is the church—ib. (8); in each and everything of the *Word* there is a marriage (chap. ix.)—80-90; hence the frequent appearance in it of two expressions that appear like repetitions of the same thing—81; illustration of such apparent repetitions —84-88; the Divinity and holiness of the *Word* illustrated by a story of a piece of paper sent down from heaven—90; why it is hurtful to confirm the apparent truths or the *Word*—96; the *Word* compared to a garden—96*a*; the literal sense of the *Word* a guard to its genuine truths —97; the Lord came into the world to fulfill all things of the *Word* (chap. xi.) —98-100; how the Lord is the *Word*— 100; before the *Word* which is now in the world there was a *Word* which is lost (chap. xii.)—101-103; the *Word* among the ancients written entirely by correspondences, described; and why it was lost and another given in its place stated—102: reference to this ancient *Word* in Moses—103: and in other parts of the *Word*—ib. (3), the people outside of the church who are not in possession of the *Word* have light by its means (chap. xiii.)—104-113; the greatest light in the spiritual world is among the Christians who possess the *Word*—106; communication with the universal heaven effected by means of the *Word*—108; the *Word* in the church of the Reformed enlightens all nations—110; provided by the Lord that there should always be a church on earth where the *Word* is read—ib.; why the Lord came when the *Word* had been fully falsified and adulterated—111; why the Lord reveals the spiritual sense of the *Word* at the present time—112; experimental evidence that by means of the *Word* man has communication with heaven—113; unless there were a *Word* no one would have knowledge of a God, of heaven and hell, of a life after death, and still less of the Lord (chap. xiv.)—114-118; the religion of the most ancient times came from an ancient *Word*—117; the Mohammedan religion was taken from the *Word* of both Testaments—ib.; the insanity to which those come who ascribe all things to their own intelligence and little or nothing to the *Word*—118.

Life. To profane the *Word* is spiritual adultery in the highest sense—74; to blaspheme the *Word* is to bear false witness in the highest sense—87; the laws of the decalogue were the first-fruits of the *Word*—54.

Q. The Lord is the *Word*—I.; the *Word* mentioned in *John* i. is the Divine love and the Divine wisdom together—IV.; "Holy" in the *Word* is predicated solely of Divine truth—V.

WORK, WORKS.

S. In every Divine *work* there is a first, a middle, and a last (or ultimate)—27; every Divine *work* is complete in its ultimate—28; in every Divine *work*, good is conjoined with truth, and truth with good—81.

Life. Unless a man shuns evils nothing of his *works* is good—30; every *work* of a man partakes of the evil or the good that is within him—72; man must render an account of his *works* because he has ability to do good *works* from the Lord—

105; *works* are what make a man of the church, taught by the Lord in parables —2.

WORKHOUSE.

F. Those who are in evils are either in hells confined in *workhouses* that are windowless, or else in deserts—63 (2).

WORKMAN.

Life. How a *workman* practises charity —72.

WORLD.

L. Why the Lord came into the *world* —3; also chap. iii. 12-14; the *world* in *John* xii. 31, xvi. 11, 33, means hell—13; what is meant by the term "spiritual *world*," and what by "natural *world*"—62. See also SPIRITUAL WORLD and NATURAL WORLD.

S. The natural *world* an essential basis for the heavens—34; a successive and a simultaneous order in this *world*—38; in the natural *world* and in the spiritual *world* simultaneous order is formed from successive—ib. (2); in the Word in this *world* all angelic wisdom lies hidden —75; why the Lord came into the *world* (chap. xi.)—98-100.

Life. So long as a man is in this *world* he is midway between hell and heaven—19; referred to in 69; the natural mind is the mind of man's *world*—86; a man described who thinks that evils are allowable before God but not before the *world* —63; hence such a man refrains from doing them merely for the *world's* sake —ib. (2); if any one shuns evils for any other reason than because they are sins, he merely prevents them from appearing before the *world* (chap. xiv.)—108-114.

WORLD OF SPIRITS.

F. An intermediate place between heaven and hell called *world of spirits*—63 (3).

WORSHIP.

L. Why Jerusalem signifies the church in respect to *worship*—64.

S. *Worship* by means of sacrifices known before the time of Moses—101;

a doctrine of *worship* hatched solely from rational light will be that self is to be worshiped—116; the gifts of gold, and frankincense, and myrrh (*Matt.* ii.) signified celestial, spiritual, and natural good, from which three is all *worship*—23 (3).

Life. Unless a man shuns evils, nothing of his *worship* is good—30.

WRATH.

L. A day or time of *wrath* means the advent of the Lord to Judgment—5.

Y.

S. In the third heaven they utter the vowel "*y*" instead of "i" (see footnote to reference)—90 (2).

ZEBAOTH.

L. Jehovah *Zebaoth* means Jehovah of the armies of war—14 (9).

ZION.

S. Where in our Word we have *Zion*, in the Word of the angels they have the church in respect to the Word—71.

THE END